Culture, Cognition and Behaviour

About the Editor

Aradhana Shukla is Professor and Head of the Department of Psychology, Kumaun University Campus, Almora. Her areas of interest are cognitive psychology, developmental psychology and cross-cultural psychology. She has published five books, namely, *Development of Representational Competence in Children, The Indian Girl, Vyaktitva ka Manovigyan, Indian Tribes and Paryavaran Manovigyan and Psyche of Indian Women* and *Glossary of Psychology* are in progress. She has published many research papers in edited volumes and journals of national and international repute. In addition, she has completed three major projects on child development from UGC and NCERT and violence against women from UNICEF.

Culture, Cognition and Behaviour

Edited by
Aradhana Shukla
Prof; and Head, Department of Psychology, Kumaun University Campus, Almora

CONCEPT PUBLISHING COMPANY, NEW DELHI-110059

ISBN 13: 978-81-8069-639-8 ISBN 10: 81-8069-639-1

First Published 2009

Published and Printed by

Concept Since 1974

Concept Publishing Company
Regd. Office:
A/15-16, Commercial Block, Mohan Garden
New Delhi-110059 (India)
Phones : 25351460, 25351794, *Fax* : 091-11-25357109
Email : publishing@conceptpub.com,
website: www.conceptpub.com

Editorial Office:
H-13, Bali Nagar, New Delhi-110 015, India.

Cataloging in Publication Data--*Courtesy:* D.K. Agencies (P) Ltd. <docinfo@dkagencies.com>

Culture, cognition and behaviour / edited by Aradhana Shukla.

p. cm.
Contributed articles.
Includes bibliographical references.
Includes index.
ISBN 13: 9788180696398 ISBN 10: 8180696391

1. Cognition and culture--India. 2. Cognition and culture. 3. Personality and culture-India. 4. Personality and culture. 5. Clinical health psychology--India. 6. Clinical health psychology. 7. Health. I. Shukla, Aradhana.

DDC 153.0954 22

Preface

It is fashion today in mainstream psychology in both the theoretical as well as empirical perspective as in other social scientific disciplines to talk about culture. Cultural loss has quickly become one of the most important and pressing issue faced by psychologists today. In most common parlance the word 'culture' is used in six categories which are given below:

1. *Descriptive use* shows light on the different types of activities and behaviour associated with culture.
2. *Historical definiton* refers the heritage and traditions associated with the groups of people.
3. *Normative use* describes the rules and norms that are associated with culture.
4. *Psychological description* emphasizes learning, problem solving and other behavioural processes associated with culture.
5. *Structural definition* emphasizes the societal or organizational element of the culture.
6. *Genetic description* refers the origin of culture.

In this way culture may be defined as the dynamic system of rules explicit and implicit established by group in order to ensure their survival involving attitudes, values, beliefs, norms and behaviour shared by a group communicated across generation, relatively stable but with the potential change across time.

It has been commonly observed that some psychological processes like memory, learning categorization, concept formation, thinking, decision-making and creativity serve as the psychological construct and they are determined differently in people living in various cultural backgrounds. This relationship is revealed in many areas which shows a tie between culture and cognition but sometimes cognitive characteristics, trades or disposition that people take with them in different situations, contexts and interactions with others are generally considered by their personality. Culture and personality are most productively analyzed by together as the dynamic and mutual consultation. The relation of the culture and psychology is revealed by two approaches, namely, cultural psychology and indigenous psychology.

Culture exerts considerable influence in the social arena. How we interact with others, perceive others, and work with others—all are influenced by the culture in which we live. We have all learned in particular ways of behaving, perceiving and working based on our own culture, upbringing and milieu. We may believe that our way is the way people of all culture should take in their own behaviour and interaction, but what is true for us is often not true for people of other culture and/or group.

Keeping these view in consideration this volume is planned and materialized in five subsequent sub-sections. In section one "Concept of Culture" a relationship among culture, cognition and behaviour is elucidated by Aradhana Shukla. Second section named as "Culture and Cognition" is comprised by seven empirical papers. Sunita Singh and R.C. Mishra have shed light on development and acculturative influences on categorization behaviour of Kharwar children. In this very context Shanta Niraula with R.C. Mishra have studied spatial cognition of children in Nepal. Linguistic Profile of Kumaun is presented by Aradhana Shukla and Aneeta Joshi in an integrated study (Hindu, Muslim, Sikh and Christian) sketched the pattern of school related outcomes in children. Shobhna Joshi studied the dynamics of educational development. In tribal children and eye-witness memory, accuracy in contextual factor is mentioned by Yogesh Arya. Last but not the least the paper is presented by Rekha Singhal in which she has made a bond between culture and knowledge system.

Section three named as "Culture and Personality" deals with the relationship between culture and personality and it consists of five papers. In first paper namely family and socialization by Aradhana Shukla has made an attempt to bring out the familial and social factors that determine the character of Kumaunies and identity style preference is presented by Rakesh Kumar Srivastava with its context and consequences. Shabana Bano and R.C. Mishra have focused on social identity awareness in Hindu and Muslim children. A relationship between mind and languages has been established by

Minati Panda and A.K. Mohanty. On socio-cultural platform, Vidya Singh and Aradhana Shukla have narrated the Development Impact of Type of Race and Experiential Deprivation on Achievement Motivation. Section four, i.e. "Culture and Health" deals with the relationship between culture and psycho-physical wellness. There are six empirical papers in this section. In first paper Poornima Awasthi and R.C. Mishra present "illness beliefs and coping strategies of Cancer and Diabetic women and psycho-social mediators of health is shared by Anubhuti Dubey. Health cognition and practices of Kharwar women is presented by R.C. Mishra's paper and learning of disabled children is studied by Nishi Tripathi and Bhoomika R. Kar with special reference to their language related impairment. Shikha Dixit has provided some intervention strategies to understand and promote community health. In the last paper of this section Shraddha Joshi and Aradhana Shukla have explored the Developmental Impact of Physical Condition and Family Type of Familial Relations.

Last section of "Conclusion" deals with the concluding comments by Aradhana Shukla in which she has tried to provide some strategies to improve the quality of life prevailing in impoverished segment.

A closed perusal of the articles reveals that attempt has been made to relate culture, cognition and behaviour in wider perspective. As the editor feels this volume will give fresh breeze to the readers to think over the issues which have been presented here. They may be helpful to carve out some trends and directions for future vision in the interesting field of human inquiry.

Aradhana Shukla

Acknowledgements

While preparing this volume the editor received help and encouragement from many sources for which she is thankful to them. The editor is extremely grateful to the contributors who made this volume easy by their valuable thoughts. Deepest indebtedness is due to Prof. R.C. Mishra, Prof., Department of Psychology, Banaras Hindu University, Varanasi for thought provoking suggestions wherever and whenever required. Assistance given by Ms. Shraddha Joshi cannot be denied. In spite of thanking I wish bright and prosperous future for her. The editor is thankful to Mr. Abhishek Yadav for the organization of the manuscript through computer. The publication has been undertaken by Concept Publishing Company, New Delhi, with active interest and supervision of Shri Ashok Kumar Mittal to whom she is thankful.

Aradhana Shukla

Contents

SECTION-IV

CULTURE AND HEALTH

SECTION-V

CONCLUSION

List of the Contributors

Ajit K. Mohanty, Professor and Head, Department of Psychology, Zakir Husain Centre for Educational Studies, JNU, New Delhi.

Aneeta Joshi, Lecturer, Department of Psychology, Government Degree College, Narayannagar.

Anubhuti Dubey, Lecturer, Department of Psychology, Deen Dayal Upadhayaya University, Gorakhpur.

Aradhana Shukla, Professor and Head, Department of Psychology, Kumaun University Campus, Almora.

Bhoomika R. Kar, Department of Psychology, Centre for Behavioural and Cognitive Sciences, University of Allahabad, Allahabad.

Minati Panda, Associate Professor, Department of Psychology, Zakir Husain Centre for Educational Studies, JNU, New Delhi.

Nishi Tripathi, Coordinator of the Counselling Centre, Department of Psychology, University of Allahabad, Allahabad.

Poornima Awasthi, Lecturer, Department of Psychology, Banaras Hindu University, Varanasi.

Rakesh Kumar Srivastava, Reader and Head, Department of Psychology, Degree College Malikpura, Gazipur.

Ramesh Chandra Mishra, Professor, Department of Psychology, Banaras Hindu University, Varanasi.

Rekha Singhal, Professor, Personnel Management and Organizational Behaviour, Indian Institute of Forest Management, Nehru Nagar, Bhopal.

Shanta Niraula, Professor, Department of Psychology, Padmakayan Multiple Campus, Kathmandu University, Nepal.

Shabana Bano, Lecturer, Department of Psychology, Government P.G. College, Gyanpur.

Shikha Dixit, Associate Professor, Department of Humanities and Social Science, Indian Institute of Technology, Kanpur.

Shobhna Joshi, Lecturer, Department of Psychology, Banaras Hindu University, Varanasi.

Shraddha Joshi, Research Scholar, Department of Psychology, Kumaun University Campus, Almora.

Sunita Singh, Research Scholar, Department of Psychology, Banaras Hindu University, Varanasi.

Vidya Singh, Research Scholar, Department of Psychology, Kumaun University Campus, Almora.

Yogesh Kumar Arya, Lecturer, Department of Psychology, Banaras Hindu University, Varanasi.

SECTION-I

CONCEPT OF CULTURE

1

Culture and Our Understanding

Aradhana Shukla

In recent years considerable attention has been paid to the cultural perspectives in Psychology. It has been found that multidimensional variations of behaviour are prompted by cultural differences because culture is the experience of our nature which is revealed in our modes of living and thinking, literature, religion, customs and all other possible roots of life which could be inculcated by a person. Cultures, in the form of shared organizations of human creations like symbols and ideas, are often revealed to us as narratives and to understand them, we construct them by reading, interpreting and communicating them for that we employ various strategies such as translation, representation and elaboration. Both psychologists and anthropologists, as it granted that an individual human entity is part of the whole, the same business is implied for the culture.

Over the past 100 years or so, many scholars have made explicit attempt to define the concept of culture. Although these definitions share many similarities, they sometimes exhibit important differences as well. Well over 100 years ago, for example, Tylor (1865) defined culture as all capabilities and habits learned by the members of a society. Linton (1936) referred culture as a social heredity. Kroeber and Kluckholn (1952) defined culture as a 'pattern of' and 'for behaviour acquired and transmitted by symbols, constituting the distinct achievements of human groups' including their embodiments in artifacts. Rohner (1984) defined culture as the totality of equivalent and complementary learned meanings maintained by a human population, or by identifiable segments of a population, and transmitted from one generation to the next. Triandis (1972) contrasted objective aspects of culture, such as tools, with subjective aspects, such as words, shared beliefs, attitudes, norms, roles and values. This distinction is also related to Kroeber and Kluckholn's (1952) concept of explicit and implicit culture. Jahoda (1984) argued that culture is a descriptive term that captures not only rules and meanings, but also behaviours. Some theorists have defined culture in terms of personality (Pelto and Pelto, 1975; Schwartz, 1978) and others as shared symbol systems transcending individuals (Geertz, 1973). Berry, Poortinga, Segall and Dasen (1992) define culture simply as the shared way of life of a group of people.

A few years ago, Poortinga (1990) offered an interesting and different definition of culture. Noting the tremendous range of possible behaviours a person might exhibit in any situation, and the fact that the actual behaviours practiced are typically limited, Poortinga attempted to distinguish between the various sources of constraints on people's behaviours: external or internal, distal and proximal. Mechanisms leading to internal constraints arise from distal sources that involve genetic transmission mechanisms which lead to internal constraints and arising from the behaviour repertoire available to members of a certain socio-cultural group, in a way differs from individuals belonging to some other group.

As the brief review indicates, many different attempts have been made to define and describe culture, perhaps as many as there are theorists and serious students of culture. A few years ago, Soudijn, Hutschemaekers and Cande Vijver (1990) analysed 128 definitions of culture in order to identify common dimensions in them. Their analysis revealed five semantic dimensions within which the definitions could be placed.

A moment's reflection on the contents of culture suggests that it is inescapably psychological in its composition. Perhaps, the two are intertwined in such a manner that it is not possible to think of human nature independent from culture. The difference between the two is only on the levels of analysis and abstraction; one focuses on individual level processes and their modifications, while the other made further attempts to unravel the pattern of structure on a global level. In this dialogue, biology and ecology also play an important role. Human beings are biological organisms too and have many genetically programmed dispositions which are expressed in behaviour in a specific ecological-environmental context. As Cole (1996) argued, "culture is the unique medium of human existence, a medium that acts both as constraint and tool of human action. This medium has co-evolved with the biological constitution of our species". In this way, culture and behaviour, thus are reciprocally related and the dichotomy is false (D'Andrade, 1990), created only for analytical convenience and disciplinary priorities. Against this background the cultural constitution of psychology will be examined. This would help us to understand why culture is conceived in psychological discourse in the way that it is. We can quote Shrivastava and Mishra (1999) here:

> "Every culture has its own values, traditions, rituals, sanctions and norms. There has been increasing realization that imperative change due to dynamism of environment can be facilitated by understanding and recognition of cultural dimensions of the society. Cultural norms and values are deeply rooted and no fundamental change can be brought and stabilized by ignoring culture. Procedure and mechanism for introducing, accepting and assimilating changes are present in every culture. It will be inappropriate to perceive all current Indian values as wrong and making effort to change them. Rather there are certain values, which need to be reserved and nurtured. They can give us a cultural edge. Such, differentiation requires vision, analysis of the cultural dimensions. This need is the identification of functional and dysfunctional aspects of our culture."

This particular notion is also presented by Bidney (1953). He states that culture is the product of agro facts, multifacts, artifacts and sociofacts. In his own words, "In culture comes the behaviour, made or acquired by men, within society along with social, artistic and social virtues and organizations which act". In accordance with Pedington (1952), "Culture is the gross total of that materialistic and intellectual means and materials by which a person adapts the environmental demands and gratifies his/her biological and social demands."

Some other definitions of culture are as follows:

(i) "Culture is that complex whole which includes knowledge, belief, art, morals, law, custom and any other capabilities acquire by man as a member of society."—*Tylor*

(ii) "Culture is the handiwork of man and the medium through which he achieves his ends."—*Malinowski*

(iii) "Culture is an organized body of convention understanding manifest in art and artifact, which, persisting through tradition, characterizes a human group."—*Redfield*

(iv) "Culture is the quintessence of all nature goods of the world and of those gifts and qualities which, while belonging man, lie beyond the immediate sphere of his needs and wants."
—*Joseph Piepe*

(v) "Culture is the body of thought and knowledge, both theoretical and practical, which only man can possess."
—*E.V. de-Roberty*

(vi) "Culture is the super organic environment and distinguished from the organic of physical, the world of plants and animals."—*Spencer*

(vii) "Culture is an accumulation of thoughts, values and objects, it is the social heritage acquired by us from preceding generations through learning, and distinguished from the biological heritage which is passed on to us automatically through the genes."—*Graham Wallas*

(viii) "Culture is the socially transmitted system of idealized ways in knowledge, practice and belief, along with the artifacts that knowledge and practice produce and maintain as they change in time."—*Arnold W. Green*

(ix) "Culture is the embodiment in custom, tradition, etc., of the learning of a social group over the generation."—*Lapiere*

(x) "Culture is the expression of our nature in our modes of living and our thinking, intercourse, in our literature, in religion, in recreation and enjoyment."—*MacIver*

(xi) "Culture is the sum total of man's efforts to adjust himself to his environment and to improve his modes of living."
—*Koenig*

(xii) "Culture refers to the social mechanisms of behaviour and to the physical and symbolic products of these behaviours."
—*Lundberg*

(xiii) "Culture is the sum total of integrated learned behaviour patterns, which are characteristics of the members of a society and which are, therefore, not the result of biological inheritance."—*E.A. Hoebel*

(xiv) "Culture is the totality of group ways of thought and action duly accepted and followed by a group of people."

—*A.F. Walter Paul*

(xv) "The culture of a people may be defined as the sum total of the marital and intellectual equipment whereby they satisfy their biological and social needs and adapt themselves to their environment."—*Ralph Piddington*

(xvi) "Culture is the total content of the physico-social, bio-social and psycho-social products man has produced and the socially created mechanisms through which these social products."—*Anderson* and *Parker*

(xvii) "Culture is the complex whole that consists of everything we think and do and have as members of society."—*Bierstedt*

(xviii) "Culture includes those general attitudes, views of life and specific manifestations of civilization that give a particular people its distinctive place in the world."—*Sapir*

(xix) "Culture is the entire accumulation of artificial objects, conditions, tools, techniques, ideas, symbols and behaviour-patterns peculiar to a group of people possessing a certain consistency of its own, and capable of transmission from one generation to another."—*Cooley*, *Argell* and *Corr*

According to Matsumoto (2000), culture as a dynamic system of rules, explicit and implicit, established by group in order to ensure their survival, involves attitudes, values, beliefs, norms and behaviours, shared by a group but harboured differently by each specific unit within the group communicated across generations, relatively stable but with the potential to change across time.

Coverage of Culture

The coverage of culture may be described in terms of the following dimensions:

Dynamic

Culture as an abstract concept, describes average, mainstream tendencies; it cannot describe the behaviours of all people in any culture. Thus, there will always be some degree of discrepancy, however small, between behaviours and culture. This discrepancy creates a dynamic tension. In this sense, culture is not static. It is always dynamic and changing, exist in a tensive relationship with the actual behaviours it is supposed to explain and predict. It fact, this degree of tension may be an important aspect of culture itself. Some cultures may be characterized by a high degree of tension whereas others may be characterized by relatively less.

System of Rules

Culture does not refer to any single behaviour, rule, attitude or value. It refers, instead to the entire system of these constructions. In this sense, culture is like a syndrome, as referred by Triandis (1994), involves a constellation of separate but interrelated psychological components. We can prefer the metaphor system rather than syndrome; however, syndrome implies a core element with manifestations emanating from it not unlike a disease pathogen with symptomatology, whereas system focuses on the functional, working relationship among the various components.

Groups and Units

Culture exists on multiple levels—across individuals within groups and across groups within a larger group (such as a business corporation). This definition of culture, therefore, makes it applicable for analysis at multiple levels. For example, a large corporation often comprises multiple departments or sections.

System of Rules

Both official company policy (explicit) and the unofficial way things are done (implicit)—which constitutes that company's organizational culture. In this context, the group may be the company as a whole and the units the various sections or departments within it.

To Ensure their Survival

The system of Rules which comprise cultural existance is essential to ensure the survival of the Group. These rules also allow units within the group to coexist with one another, provides a framework for social order instead of the potential chaos of a free-to-all. They also allow groups and units to balance the needs of the group's survival with the desires, wishes and needs of the unit, taking into account the larger social context and resources at hand. This concept is related to Poortinga's (1990) definition discussed earlier involve constraints on behaviour.

Attitudes, Values, Beliefs, Norms and Behaviours

This definition of culture does not refer to tools, homes, utensils, or other physical objects, although these too are important, artifacts of culture. It does not refer to physical or necessarily observable attributes, such as skin colour, facial morphology, and the like. It does not refer to citizenship or living space within a particular area or region. Rather, it focuses on ideas, attitudes, values, beliefs—the contents of the mind of each and every individual who lives in that particular culture. Not only do these aspects of culture exist in people's minds, but they also exist as a social consciousness above and beyond individual. The behaviour that are shared are indeed observable and are often seen in rituals or common, automatic behaviour patterns that arise because of shared cultural values and behavioural norms. These elements collectively constitute the subjective aspects of culture (Triandis, 1972) as opposed to the objective aspects. Without seeking to diminish the importance of the objective elements in culture, we deem the subjective element more important for our understanding of cultural influences on behaviour.

Shared by a Group

Sharing refers to the degree to which individuals within a particular group have or hold the same value, attitude, belief, norm, or behaviour. It does not necessarily refer to sharing in the physical sense; rather, this sharing refers to a psychological sharing of an attribute in members of the culture.

Harbored differently by each Specific Unit

As pointed out earlier, culture, describes average, mainstream tendencies of a group of units; it does not describe accurately all aspects of behaviour for all units in the group. Individual units will harbour that culture's values, belief, behaviour, and the like, in differenting degress; that is, they will exhibit individual differences in their adherence or conformity of culture. The recognition of individual difference in culture forms one of the bases for understanding the limitations of stereotypes, and is also related to Pelto's (1968) classification of stern *versus* liberal societies.

Communicated to Generations, Relatively Stable

Fads that come and go, even though they have a life of their own and are shared by many people one time, are not necessarily considered culture in the sense used here. Instead, culture is that system of rules that is durable, relatively stable over time, and hence especially important in helping units within the group. Core aspects of the system of rules are transmitted from generations to generations.

But with the Potential to Change Across Time

Despite the relative stability of culture, however, it is never static. As described earlier, culture is a dynamic entity, always in a tense relationship with the behaviours, attitudes, values, beliefs, and norms it is supposed to describe. Units change our time, and because culture exists in a reciprocal relationship with its components, the tension allows for that culture itself may change over time. Change is inveilable when the system described by culture no longer accurately describes the mainstream average tendency of the group. We have witnessed drastic cultural changes over the past 30 years in the American culture, as well as in other cultures (such as Japan's). We witness today the changes taking place in many of the former Soviet bloc cultures Eastern Europe.

Pedington has classified culture in two ways. They are as follows:

(i) *Materialistic Culture*: Man made things for civilization like television, computer, home etc.

(ii) *Immaterialistic Culture*: Knowledge, belief, values, systems, laws, institution etc. Both aspects of culture are coincidental.

Herskovitz (1957) believes culture as the man-made part of the environment. He follows Pedington and states aspects of culture, e.g. natural or God gifted and materialistic or man-made culture. Linton defines culture as 'the sum total of knowledge, attitudes and natural behaviour patterns showed and transmitted by the members of a particular society'.

Thus, it is apparent that it is very difficult job to provide a universally accepted definition of culture. Therefore, "Culture in total can be defined as a particular life cycle style, adjustment pattern and behavioural norms of a particular society. Culture is comprised with all sorts of ideas and behaviour which are acquired by a person through structural interaction. A person gets them by vocals, postures examples not by heredity" (Gupta and Shah, 2002).

Nature of Culture

There are many characteristics of culture and they are as follows:

(i) *Culture is Man Made*: Culture can only be seen in human society. There are some psycho-physical characteristics in human beings which discriminate them from other species.

(ii) *Culture is Learned*: Culture is the sum of behavioural standard that are learned by the human being in the society prevailing around him. This process is called socialization. Although a person learns so many things for his personal use as well as for social welfare but it cannot be considered as culture. Behaviours that are meant for many groups majority or society, culture is formed by them. Group behaviour generates customs, traditions or stereotypes and can only be seen in human society.

(iii) *Culture is Transmitted*: Since culture can be learned hence, it is transmitted from older to younger generation. The young generations take knowledge from the older group and adds his own experiences and language which plays a major role in this context.

(iv) *Every Society has its Own Culture*: A society is found different from the other because of its geographical and social circumstances. Society inverts many new ideas for the fulfilment of its demands and these inventions give a new culture to the society. Needs of one society are entirely different from the other and they cause cultural variation. But it is not the end. In spite of these cultural variations there is a general similarity that can be seen in all societies. Thus, it is opined that culture is accompanied by the similarities as well as differences in the societies.

(v) *Culture has Social Quality*: Culture is entirely a contribution of society and it is emerged by group habits, behaviours and experiences. The components of culture, e.g. customs, language, art, tradition, religion, science, philosophy represent not only the life style of a person but also reveal the life style of whole society.

(vi) *Culture is Idea for the Group*: The people of a given culture follow the specific culture and shape themselves accordingly. When two cultures are compared it is very difficult for the psychologist to make the distinction.

(vii) *Culture Satisfies Human Needs*: It is the primitive quality of a culture to satisfy the needs of the persons living in that particular culture. There are many psychological and social needs of a person and he has formed culture in order to meet the demands of his life.

(viii) *Culture has Adaptability*: Culture has a quality on the basis of which a person adjusts himself according to his society and other circumstances.

(ix) *Culture has the Integrative Quality*: Culture is comprised of many units for instance social unites like culture trait and culture complex are embedded interpretation of units from a culture and maintain its systems.

(x) *Culture is Fundamental in Forming Human Personality*: The relative significance of cultured environment or ecology cannot be denied after birth the person makes a close perusal of his environment and soaks its properties into himself. The major influences on culture are rituals, custom, religion, philosophy, art and science they lay their print on the person's behaviour.

(xi) *Culture is both Super Individual and Super Organic*: The meaning of super individual denotes that culture is not formed by any particular and consumes not only one part of the culture but culture is formed by total segment.

On the ground of this discussion its can be said that culture has its own consistency and it is comprised with many features. Thus, it is surely fair to say that human behaviour is a gross product of consequences of person × environment interaction. Also, it is governed by the internal difference that a person may have. Thus, it can be said that it impacts and structures the behavioural pattern in a particular spectrum.

REFERENCES

Berry, J.W., Poortinga, Y.H., Segall, M.H. and Dasen, P.R. (1992), *Cross-Cultural Psychology: Research and Applications.* New York Cambridge University Press.

Cole, M. (1996), *Cultural Psychology, A Once and Future Discipline.* Cambridge. Harvard University Press.

D'Andrade, R.G. (1990), Culture and Personality. A False Dichotomy in D.K. Jardon and M.J. Swartz (Eds.), *Personality and the Cultural Construction of Social Thought,* London.

Geertz, C. (1973), *The Interpretation of Cultures.* New York: Basic Books.

Jahoda, G. (1984), Do we need a Cocept of Culture? *Journal of Cross-Cultural Psychology,* 15 (2), 139-151.

Kroeber, A.L. and Kluckholn, C. (1952), *Culture: A Critical Review of Concepts and Definitions* (Vol. 47, No. 1), Cambridge, M.A.: Peabody, Museum.

Linton, R. (1936), *The Study of Man: An Introduction,* New York: Appleton.

Matsumoto, D. (2000), *Culture and Psychology.* Wadsworth, Canada.

Pelto, P.J. and Pelto, G.H. (1975), Intra cultural diversity: Some Theoretical Issues. *American Ethnologist,* 2, 1-18.

Poortinga, H.Y. (1990), Presidential Address. IACCP towards a Conceptualization of Culture for Psychology. *Unpublished Paper,* Tilburg University, The Netherlands.

Rohner, R.P. (1984), Toward a Conception of Culture for Cross-Cultural Psychology. *Journal of Cross-Cultural Psychology,* 15, 111-138.

Schwartz, S.H. (1978), Temporal Instability as a Moderator of the Attitude Behaviour Relationship. *Journal of Personality and Social Psychology,* 36 (7), 716-724.

Shrivastava, M. and Mishra, P.C. (1999), Culture as a Vehicle for Change. *Paper Presented in NAOP-X* held at Department of Psychology, Lucknow University, Lucknow.

Soudijn, K.A., Hutschemaekers, G.J.M. and Van deVijver, F.J.R. (1990), Culture Conceptualizations. In F.J.R. Van deVijver, and G.J.M. Hutschemaekers. (eds.). *The Investigation of Culture: Current Issues in Cultural Psychology.* Tilburg, Tilburg University Press.

Triandis, H.C. (1972), *The Analysis of Subjective Culture.* New York: Wiley.

Triandis, H.C. (1994), *Culture and Social Behaviour.* New York: Weley.

Tylor, E.B. (1965), *Researches into the Early History of Mankind and Development of Civilization.* London: John Murray.

SECTION-II

CULTURE AND COGNITION

2

Developmental and Acculturative Influences on Categorization

Sunita Singh and *Ramesh Chandra Mishra*

The study of human cognition is the study of how people learn and think (Pick, 1980). A number of processes are involved in cognition. Eysenck, Arnold and Meili (1975) consider cognition as "an expression for every process by which a living creature obtains knowledge of some objects, or becomes aware of its environment". Psychologists have long been interested in individual and group differences in cognitive functioning. The assessment of cognitive skills as far as being present or absent, high or low, has been of a prominent concern in large number of studies. It has also raised serious debates concerning the origin, development and expression of these skills among people (Mishra, 2001).

In the last two decades, several studies have been conducted to examine the similarities and differences in the cognition of people from different cultural background. How people acquire, organize, retain and retrieve information, and how do they use them to solve their problems in life have been the main theme in these studies (Berry, Segall, Poortinga and Dasen, 2002; Mishra, 1997, 1998). A number of tasks have been used to assess the cognitive functioning in members of different cultures. Comprehensive reviews by Pick (1980), Barbara (1981), Sinha (1982), and Mishra (1997, 2001, 2002) reveal that the cross-cultural differences in cognitive functioning are almost inevitable.

Asking people to classify a small collection of pictures, shapes or objects in groups in context of "likeness" or "similarity" of objects has been one strategy to understand people's cognitive functioning. A number of dimensions of similarity involved in the grouping of objects have been examined in various studies. In previous studies, developmental and cross-cultural differences used form and colour as the base for grouping shapes have been frequently outlined (Jahoda, Deregowski and Sinha, 1974; Serpell, 1969; Suchman, 1966; Suchman and Trabasso, 1966), and schooling has been considered as an important variable in creating such differences (Deregowski and Serpell, 1971; Evans and Segall, 1969; Greenfield, Reich and Olver, 1966; Wassmann and Dasen, 1994).

Other studies have examined that the organization that subjects impose on individual objects, words and pictures. The dimensions in which the differences are interpreted included: taxonomic categorization (based on semantic classes), functional categorization (based on use, utility or function of objects), perceptual or structural categorization (based on colour, size or shape of objects), and idiosyncratic categorization (based on some peculiar features of objects obsessed by the subject). Population have been found to vary in the preferred dimensions of classification, the easiness or difficulty in the changing dimensions in categorization, the generality or fineness involved in its sorts, and the verbalization of the dimensions used in sorting (Glick, 1975; Jahoda, Deregowski and Sinha, 1974; Luria, 1976; Barbara, 1981; Mishra, Sinha and Berry, 1996).

A number of studies also suggested differences in people's classificational behaviour in terms of their acculturative experiences. These include influences due to schooling, literacy, participation in developmental change programmes, urbanization and industrialization. Differences due to acculturation are generally registered in terms of preferences in form over colour and of taxonomic groups over perceptual and functional groups (Mishra *et al.,* 1996). These differences are also interpreted with reference to the familiarity that people enduce to bear on the task material (Deregowski and Serpell, 1971; Okonji, 1971). The kinds of familiarity that might effect classification includes: familiarity in the mode of representation, familiarity in the objects, familiarity in the relevant features of objects, familiarity in a dimensions, and familiarity of an object-dimension relationship (Barbara, 1981). Anyone of these could be used for explanation of individual or group differences in classification other than the cultural features of the groups being compared.

Another problem in cross-cultural studies of classification is related with the language that is used for testing. Often the subjects' categorizations are assessed for the degree of abstractedness of conceptualization reflected by them. Such assessments may be unreliable if the subjects' descriptions are translated into Examiner's/ Experimenter's language (which is usually different from that of the subject), and if the subjects are asked to use a language which is not their native language of communication. To overcome these difficulties, constrains classificational procedure has been used (Cole, Gay and Glick, 1968; Mundy-Caste, 1967) where the subject has to infer the relevant features present in each stimulus based on the feedback provided by the examiner, but this procedure has also not worked well.

The purpose of the present study is to examine cognitive function in the children of Kharwar tribals which reflects a classification of a variety of objects. In a study where the subsistence sociey like that of the Kharwar where the people speak the same language, the use of highly familiar objects as test stimuli reduces the possibility to contribute in test-related factors in classification to almost a negligible level. On the other hand, it also enhances the probability of experience-based explanation in the objects classification. In the light of general findings, reported in this area, it was hypothesized that:

(1) Compared to the children of younger age and low acculturated families, children of elder age and high acculturated families has classified objects in categories, which were more similar to the experimenter-held categories.

(2) Compared to the children of elder age and high aculturated families the children of younger age and low acculturated families would classify objects on the basis of functional features of objects more often than on the basis of perceptual or conceptual features.

(3) In the regrouping of objects, children of elder age and of high acculturated families would show greater shift in categorization behaviour than children of younger age and low acculturated families.

Sample

The study was carried out on a group of Kharwar children living in village areas of Naugarh region in Chaundauli district. A group of 140 children between the age-group of 8-13 years served as subjects. They were randomly selected in equal number from high and low acculturated families. A measure of contact-acculturation (Mishra *et al.*, 1996) was used to assess the level of acculturation in the families. The indicators of acculturation included: knowledge of regional, official and English languages, nature of household goods (e.g., utensils, ornaments, clothes, furnishing), means of livelihood, usage of modern technology, religion, dressing styles, travel experiences, exposure to movies and other mass media. Median split on the contact-acculturation measure was used to distinguish between high and low acculturated children. There were 70 children of high acculturated and 70 of low acculturated parents equally divided into 8-10 and 11-13 year age brackets. Thus, the design of the study was the 2 (age) ×2 (acculturation) factorial design.

The Setting

The Kharwars represent a settled agricultural community in an elaborate village vicinity. They consider themselves as Rajput, and are engaged in many Rajput cultural practices (e.g., worshipping weapons). Their houses generally have mud walls and slanting roofs with enough room to store agricultural produce. They have a community *panchayat,* a village *pradhan* (the headman) and a *baiga* (the priest), who occupies a prominent place in their life.

In the absence of irrigation facilities, the Kharwars of Naugarh region grow only rainy season crops. Guarding crops against animals is a round-the-clock activity. The agricultural yield feeds them hardly for 3-4 months. For the rest the year, the families have to depend on forest resources.

The health status of the community generally appears to be poor. A few NGOs have started programmes for primary education and health care in some villages. The villagers have shown varied response to these programmes. The life of a Kharwar is still full of many difficulties and constraints. Due to the economic depravity, the new generation is moving out of the village in search of wages. Consequently, a number of changes are currently evident in some families, while many others continue to stay in their traditional life style.

Procedure

An object-assortment task (Mishra *et al.*, 1996) was given to children. It consisted of 29 familiar and locally salient objects, which were categorised in six groups, namely clothes, animals, cereals, stationery, households, and women's ornaments. The objects were selected on the basis of familiarity ratings by the group of children. The objects were placed before children one after another in a random order and the children were asked to name each one of them. Then they were asked to sort them in as many categories as possible putting all the objects at one place, which they thought could "go together". The children were given their own time. The number of categories and the objects put in each category were recorded.

Following the sorting of objects, the children were asked about the reason of putting more various objects in that "particular group". The reasons given by children for putting various objects together were recorded.

When this task was over, the children were asked to classify the same objects again in another possible way. They were allotted their own time for regrouping. After sorting out the objects, the objects put in various categories were recorded and the children were asked to reason for putting those objects in particular groups. The testing was carried out by two local assistants of the native language of the children.

Scoring

The assortments made by children were scored separately. The classification presented a number of features:

1. *Number of Categories.* This was represented by the number of groups in which the objects were assorted.
2. *Conforming Categories.* This represented the caegories in which the names given to categories as well as the items included in

them were almost the same as specified by the experimenter. Each instance of such a convergence was given one point.

3. *Sub-categories.* When items of an experimenter defined category were divided into two or more groups, or the items of different categories were put with items of other categories (whether they had a reasonable basis or not), the groupings were called sub-categories. One point was given for each such grouping.

4. *Nature of Groupings.* Different objects might be put together on the basis of their conceptual, functional, perceptual or other characteristics which may typically be perceived by a subject (called idiosyncratic). One point was given for each such grouping. In the conceptual grouping, various objects were put together on the basis of certain abstract similarities among them, already specified by the experimenter (e.g., assorting elephant, horse, dog and monkey in one group assigned them as "animals"). In the functional grouping, objects were put together on the basis of their common function, usage or utility (e.g., putting all cereals together assigned them as 'edibles' that "these were to be eatten" or "were used for cooking").

In the perceptual grouping, the items were put together on the basis of certain objective features present in stimuli such as height, size, colour and length (e.g., placing all animals in one group saying that they were "white" or "small").

In an idiosyncratic grouping, the objects were put together on the basis of certain peculiar characteristics typically perceived by a child (e.g., putting all cereals in one group saying that they were "sold in the market" or "grown in the field").

5. *Shifts in the Basis of Grouping.* Children were asked to assort the objects twice and explain each time the reason for putting various objects in particular groups. A shift represented a change in the reasoning for 'object grouping' in the second sort relative to the first one. Here the category was the same and the items were also almost the same, but a different reason for grouping of objects was given. One point was given to each such change.

Analysis of Results

The general findings pertaining to categorization behaviour are summarized in Table 2.1 according to various measures.

Table 2.1: Mean Scores, S.Ds. and F-ratios on various Measures of the Object Assortment Task

Measures	*Young*		*Old*	
	Acc. high	*Acc. low*	*Acc. high*	*Acc. low*
Assortment I				
Categories	5.71	6.57	7.34	8.05
	(1.45)	(2.25)	(1.53)	(4.42)
Conforming categories	4.71	4.23	5.06	4.51
	(0.97)	(1.17)	(0.98)	(1.50)
Sub-categories	1.09	2.34	2.43	2.74
	(1.18)	(2.68)	(1.95)	(2.99)
Assortment II				
Categories	5.83	6.40	6.74	6.71
	(1.25)	(2.10)	(1.34)	(1.77)
Conforming categories	4.80	4.34	5.06	4.66
	(0.95)	(1.07)	(0.75)	(1.45)
Sub-categories	1.14	2.00	1.83	2.20
	(1.10)	(2.29)	(1.50)	(1.95)
Shifts	0.37	0.43	1.37	1.03
	(0.83)	(0.87)	(1.15)	(2.24)

Note: Values in parentheses are S.Ds.

Number of Categories

Mean score of groups revealed that children of elder age group produced significantly more number of categories than those of younger age group (F = 11.59; df = 1,136, $p < .01$). Acculturation did not play any role in this context (F = 2.95; df = 1,138, $p > .05$). Similar results have been found in the regrouping of objects (Age F = 4.72; df = 1,136, $p < .05$; Acculturation F = 0.92; df = 1,136, $p > .05$).

Number of Conforming Categories

Mean score revealed that acculturation was a major influence on this aspect of categorization (F = 6.48; df=1,136, $p < .05$). The categories produced by high acculturated children showed greater conformity with experimenter it assigned categories than those given by the low acculturated children. The effect of age was not significant on this aspect (F = 2.34; df = 1,136, $p > .05$), although the evidence for conforming categories was greater in higher than lower age group children. A similar pattern of results was noted in the second assortment trial (Age $F = 2.34$; $df = 1,136$, $p > .05$; Acculturation $F = 5.27$; $df = 1,136$, $p > .05$). No significant interaction among variables was noted in this measure.

Number of Sub-categories

The Mean score in this measure indicated differences in the performance of children according to age and acculturation (Age $F = 4.85$; $df = 1,136$, $p > .05$; Acculturation $F = 3.94$; $df = 1,136$, $p > .05$). Sub-categories were noted more often in the sorting of higher than lower age children. In both age-groups children of high acculturated background produced more sub-categories than those of the low acculturated background, but in the second sorting, the difference was significant only due to acculturation (Acculturation $F = 4.09$; $df = 1,136$, $p > .05$).

Shifts in Grouping

The Mean score in this measure revealed a significant difference between the two age groups ($F = 9.82$; $df = 1,136$, $p > .01$), although there was a high degree of variability in the scores of all groups. Elder children changed their groups more than younger children. The effect of acculturation on this measure was not significant ($F = 0.31$; $df = 1,136$, $p > .05$), nor was the effect of interaction ($F = 0.61$; $df = 1,136$, $p > .05$).

Nature of Categories

The explanation given by children in each grouping was evaluated in terms of conceptual, perceptual, functional, or idiosyncratic rule of classification. The analysis revealed that sorting on the basis of perceptual features of objects (e.g., colour, size) was a rare phenomenon. Hence, this category was omitted. Findings with respect to other groupings are presented in Table 2.2. It is evident that the functional grouping was dominant in all groups, but elder children tended to group objects more on functional basis than younger children (Age $F = 6.19$; $df = 1,136$, $p > .05$). The effect of acculturation was not significant (Acculturation $F = 0.01$; $df = 1,136$, $p > .05$).

Although high acculturated children of the elder age group used functional categorization more than other groups, the interaction of age and acculturation did not reach the level of significance ($F = 3.82$; $df = 1{,}136$, $p > .05$).

Table 2.2: Mean Scores, S.Ds. and F-ratios for varieties of classification on the Object Assortment Task

Grouping	*Young*		*Old*	
	Acc. high	*Acc. low*	*Acc. high*	*Acc. low*
Assortment I				
Conceptual	1.26 (0.94)	1.26 (0.97)	2.34 (0.95)	1.14 (0.87)
Functional	2.80 (1.88)	3.46 (2.03)	4.23 (1.46)	3.63 (2.07)
Idiosyncratic	0.51 (0.73)	0.63 (1.02)	0.43 (0.80)	0.60 (0.90)
Unspecified	1.17 (1.86)	1.23 (2.13)	0.37 (0.83)	1.80 (3.12)
Assortment II				
Conceptual	1.20 (0.29)	1.29 (0.97)	2.29 (0.97)	1.23 (0.93)
Functional	2.80 (1.77)	3.34 (1.79)	3.77 (1.22)	3.46 (1.86)
Idiosyncratic	0.51 (0.73)	0.66 (0.90)	0.57 (0.93)	0.86 (1.10)
Unspecified	1.11 (1.86)	1.20 (2.14)	0.20 (0.52)	1.23 (1.59)

Note: Values in Parentheses are S.Ds.

In the conceptual grouping the findings indicated a significant effects of age and acculturation (Age $F = 9.28$; $df = 1{,}136$, $p < .01$; Acculturation $F = 14.15$; $df = 1{,}136$, $p > .01$). Elder children classified objects on conceptual basis more than younger children, and the high acculturated did more so than the low acculturated. The interaction effect revealed that the tendency for conceptual grouping was greater in the high acculturated elder children than in the low acculturated older children ($F = 14.15$; $df = 1{,}136$, $p < .01$).

All these groups presented some evidence for idiosyncratic grouping. Children's age and acculturation level did not present any significant difference in this respect (Age $F = 0.14$ $df = 1{,}136$, $p > .05$;

Acculturation $F = 0.91$; $df = 1,136$, $p > .05$). There was also an evidence of some unspecified categorization across groups. The tendency for this aspect was significantly greater in the low than high acculturated samples (Acculturation $F = 4.07$; $df = 1,136$, $p < .05$). These findings were replicated in the second assortment trial also.

Discussion

The findings of the study support some of the hypothesis fully and some only partly. While age influenced the number of categories in which the objects were sorted out and the number of sub-categories produced, acculturation tended to influence the conforming of categories with the experimenter it defined categories and the production of sub-categories (both increased with greater acculturation). Shifts in assortments were more evident in performance of elder than younger children. Acculturation did not play any major role in this context. All the groups assorted objects predominantly on functional basis, but the elder children did it more often than the younger ones. On the other hand, acculturation influenced conceptual grouping, particularly in the older children. The pattern of results remained almost unchanged in the second assortment trial.

Claims of differences in thoughts in abstract or general terms are often made in studies in which sorting tasks have been used on people from different cultural background. Doubts have been raised for such claim in view of the differences between the language used in testing and familiarity with stimuli used in the sorting tasks (Mishra *et al.*, 1996). There is some evidence which suggests that testing subjects in their primary language alters from the pattern of results. Similar findings have been reported in studies in which familiar and unfamiliar materials have been used for testing classification ability. That some children can sort objects predominantly on functional basis, and have less abstractedness or generality in their thought processes which are not substantiated by the findings of the present study.

A glance into the number of categories represented by the classification of objects would reveal that the categories produced by relatively younger children were of more inclusive (general) nature than those of the elder children. With increase in acculturation, the categorization behaviour of both young and elder children tended to be similar to the categories held by the experimenter. Both the groups produced certain new categories, although the elder children did it more often than the younger children. The low acculturated children framed their own rules of categorization more than did high acculturated children. The findings remained almost the same in the second assortment trial except that the elder children showed some difference from the younger children with regard to category explanation in this trial. These findings suggest that the use of familiar objects as test stimuli and children's own language as testing medium can substantially minimize age related differences in categorization behaviour among children, especially when they have entered into childhood in late years.

Grouping explanation across samples revealed that the objects were assorted in various groups more in functional level than on any other basis. However, the elder children offered functional explanations more than younger children. This suggests that even this basis of grouping was more characteristic of elder than younger children. With regard to the conceptual grouping, there were slight advantage with elder children, particularly those of high acculturation background, was noted. There was no difference due to acculturation in the case of younger children. Idiosyncratic and unspecified categorizations were represented in all groups. This pattern of results was almost similar in both assortment trials.

Thus the study reveals that while acculturation may influence some aspect of cognitive functioning of children, the child's age also presents an important variation in this respect. The consequences of acculturation at such basic level of cognitive functioning for classification needs to be examined in the context of eco-cultural characteristics of the groups undergoing acculturation. The findings also indicate that even children of a traditional group (e.g., Kharwar) living in remote rural, hilly and forest areas have the ability to engage in conceptual grouping of objects by abstracting their underlying semantic features. These abilities develop with age, and get partly influenced by family acculturation variables, but the basic structures of children's cognitive functioning do not get altered by the influences of acculturation.

REFERENCES

Berry, J.W., Segall, M.H., Poortinga, H.H., and Dasen, P.R. (2002), *Cross-Cultural Psychology: Research and Applications.* Oxford: Cambridge University Press.

Barbara, R. (1981), Schooling and the development of cognitive skills. In H.C. Triandis and A. Heron (Eds.), *Handbook of Cross-Cultural Psychology.* Boston: Allyn and Bacon.

Cole, M., Gay, J., and Glick, J. (1968), Some experimental studies of Kpelle Quantitative Behaviour. *Psychonomic Monograph Supplements,* 2, 173-190.

Dergowski, J.B. and Serpell, R. (1971), Performance on a Sorting Task: A Cross-Cultural Experiment. *International Journal of Psychology,* 6, 273-281.

Evans, J.L. and Segall, M.H. (1969), Learning to classify by Colour and by Function: A Study of Concept Discovery by Ganda Children. *Journal of Social Psychology,* 77, 35-53.

Pick, A.D. (1980), Cognition: Psychological Perspectives. In H.C. Triandis and W. Lonner (Eds.), *Handbook of Cross-Cultural Psychology,* Vol. 3. Boston: Allyn and Bacon.

Eysenck, H.J., Arnold, W.J. and Meili, R. (1975), *Encyclopaedia of Psychology.* London: Fontana.

Glick, J. (1975), Cognitive development in Cross-Cultural Perspective. In F. Hortwitz *et al.* (Eds.), *Review of Child Development Research.* Chicago: University of Chicago Press.

Greenfield, P.M., Reich, L.C. and Olver, R.R. (1966), On Culture and Equivalence: In J.S. Bruner, R.R. Olver and P.M. Greenfield (Eds.), *Studies in Cognitive Growth.* New York: John Wiley.

Jahoda, G., Dergowski, J.B. and Sinha, D. (1974), Topological and Euclidian Spatial Features Noted by Children. *International Journal of Psychology,* 19, 159-172.

Luria, A.R. (1976), *Cognitive Development: Its Cultural and Social Foundations.* Cambridge, Mass: Harvard University Press.

Mishra, R.C. (1977), Cognition and Cognitive Development. In J.W. Berry, P.R. Dasen and T.S. Saraswathi (Eds.), *Handbook of Cross-Cultural Psychology,* Vol. 2, pp. 147-179. Boston: Allyn and Bacon.

Mishra, R.C. (1998), Cognitive Processes. In NCERT (Ed.), *Fifth Survey of Educational Research,* pp. 128-146. New Delhi: NCERT.

Mishra, R.C. (2001), Cognition Across Cultures. In D. Matsumoto (Ed.), *Handbook of Culture and Psychology,* pp. 119-135. New York: Oxford.

Mishra, R.C. (2002), Cross-Cultural Perspectives on Cognition. In A. Agrawal and A.K. Saxena (Eds.), *Psychological Perspectives in Environment and Developmental Issues,* pp. 84-97. New Delhi: Concept Publishing Company.

Mishra, R.C., Sinha, D. and Berry, J.W. (1996), *Ecology, Acculturation and Psychological Adaptation: A Study of Adivasis in Bihar.* New Delhi: Sage.

Mundy-Castle, A.C. (1967), An Experimental Study of Prediction among Ghanaian Children. *Journal of Social Psychology,* 73, 161-168.

Okonji, M.O. (1971), A Cross-Cultural Study of the Effects of Familiarity on Classification Behaviour. *Journal of Cross-Cultural Psychology,* 2, 39-40.

Serpell, R. (1969), Cultural Differences in Attentional Preference for Colour Over Form. *International Journal of Psychology,* 4, 1-8.

Sinha, D. (1982), Socio-cultural Factors and the Development of Perceptual and Cognitive Skills. In W.W. Hartup (Ed.), *Review of Child Development Research,* Vol. 6. Chicago: University of Chicago Press.

Suchman, R.G. (1966), Cultural Differences in Children's Colour and Form Preference. *Journal of Social Psychology,* 70, 3-10.

Suchman, R.G. and Trabasso, J. (1966), Colour and Form Preference in Young Children. *Journal of Experimental Child Psychology,* 3, 177-187.

Wassmann, J. and Dasen, P.R. (1994), "Hot" and "Cold": Classification and Sorting Among the Yupno of Papua-New Guinea. *International Journal of Psychology,* 29, 19-38.

3

Spatial Cognition of Children

Shanta Niraula and *Ramesh Chandra Mishra*

Space refers to that aspect of the environment in which various objects are located and events are created. Spatial Cognition is a process with which an individual gain systematic knowledge of the location of the objects in the environment (Mishra, 1997). It refers to the knowledge of space either as a continuous and homogenous entity, or as discrete spatial categories, such as location, direction, distance and depth of objects (Bowerman, 1993).

Curiosity about various objects and events of the spatial world is a universal phenomenon children begin to acquire knowledge about it from a very early age. Spatial conceptualization is so centralised to human cognition that it is considered as the representative of the first intellectual domain to explore physical world in relation to the nature of human psycho-biology (Levinson, 1991, 2003). Changes in spatial knowledge and spatial behaviour takes place as the development proceeds. Many types of experience which children encounter in their environment are often associated with these changes.

Western developmental studies suggests that the spatial concept development starts with the child's own body, both at the sensori-motor level of action, and later at the representational level. Research had been carried out in the Piagetian tradition suggests that spatial concept development progresses through three different stages (e.g., Evans, 1980; Hazen, Lockman and Pick, 1978), which consisted of an egocentric stage, an allocentric stage and a geocentric stage. In the egocentric stage, all spatial knowledge is referred to the self-characterization of the features of sensori-motor and the early pre-operational periods. Here the child's body serves as a main reference point. The allocentric stage provides the understanding of the organization or layout of the environment independent of one's own point of view. This is generally characterized by the use of Situational Landmarks (SL) and Conventional Landmarks (CL) with reference to the objects. Geocentric stage is characterized by the use of cardinal directions of north, south, east, west (NSEW) to refer to objects. Piaget and Inhelder (1956, 1967) decribe spatial concept development in terms of the use of topological projective, and Euclidean features of the space. While it is well established that topological space comes first and is universal, the sequence between projective and Euclidean concepts is less clear and seems to be more logical than an empirical implication (Laurendeau and Pinard, 1968, 1970).

Theorists of spatial language development describes three kinds of reference frames: intrinsic or object-centred, deictic or viewer-centred, and extrinsic or environment centred (Taylor and Tversky, 1996). Levinson (1996) broadly distinguished between intrinsic, relative, and "absolute" (extrinsic) frames which seems to be most popular and widely accepted among researchers. The intrinsic frame of reference is object-centred; it describes the object in terms of its front, back or sides. In the relative frame, the location of objects is described in relation to a viewer's front, back, left, and right (FBLR); they are viewer-centred and require knowledge of the viewer's position and orientation in space. In the geocentric frame, objects are located according to a coordinate system (NSEW) that is external to the scene. It has also been noted that different language communities preferentially use different reference frames (Levinson, 1996, 2003; Taylor and Tverskey, 1996).

In the last few years, a number of studies have been carried out to explore infants' abilities to locate objects according to their body-orientation or geocentric landmarks in the sensorimotor period (e.g., Arcedolo, 1990; Bremmer, 1989; Lepecq and Lafaite, 1989). The findings indicate that babies first use their own body as a reference point, i.e., relative frame, before establishing geocentric reference systems, which occurs at an earlier stage than Piaget had described. Whether the same sequence of stages development occurs in other cultures is doubtful.

A couple of studies carried out in India and Nepal on the issue of spatial concept development has been seriously addressed (Mishra,

Dasen and Niraula, 2003; Dasen, Mishra and Niraula, 2004; Niraula, Mishra and Dasen, 2004). The samples included 4-14 year old children, both schooled and unschooled, in India and Nepal. The field sites were selected with consideration of how reference to the spatial locations is organized in the language as well as in the local cultural practices. In a village near Varanasi in India, people organize spatial locations mainly with reference to cardinal directions, but in the city of Varanasi, relative references are also used, although people in both the places speak the same language (i.e., Hindi). In a village in Nepal, on the other hand, the 'uphill-downhill' geocentric frame of reference is the most compelling one, where the relationship between ecology, culture, language, encoding of spatial information and performance on some Piagetian spatial tasks was tested, in which age and schooling were taken into account. The findings indicate that in the Indian villages children begin with a geocentric orientation to space and develop as more geocentric as they grew old in age, whereas in the village in Nepal the 'uphill-downhill' orientation (again a part of geocentric system) seems to be all pervasive. On the other hand, in the city of Varanasi, children use both the geocentric and ecocentric references to space. These findings indicate the role of ecological demands and cultural practices in the development of a geocentric or egocentric orientation to space.

Researchers who have investigated developmental changes in spatial memory and recall (Allen and Ondracek, 1995; Pezdek, Roman and Sobolik, 1986) have found that both tend to increase significantly with age. It has been pointed out that the nature of stimulus items is an important factor in producing developmental differences in spatial memory (Perlmutter, Metzger, Nezworski and Miller, 1981). A distinction has been made between memory of spatial location in objects and their cognitive representation. While the former seems to be present in early childhood, the latter (i.e., cognitive representation of location information) occurs between the age of 7 and 10 years (Piaget, Inhelder and Szeminska, 1960). Whether the same developmental trend could be found in other cultures is unknown.

In a study, Allen and Ondracek (1995) found that elder children acquired landmark knowledge more rapidly than the younger children, as they were more quick and skilful at encoding and retrieving information from complex visual arrays. Other studies suggest that as the children grow elder, memory retrieval becomes increasingly dominant with corresponding increase in accuracy (Ashcraft, 1982, 1990). On the other hand, Voyer and Voyer and Bryden (1995) suggest that the effect of age is difficult to evaluate because a variety of other factors are associated with the acquisition and development of spatial skills could not be examined along with age.

Studies have also provided evidence of gender difference in spatial cognition (Maccoby and Jacklin, 1974; Voyer, Voyer and Bryden, 1995). It has been indicated that these differences become consistent and significant only after early adolescence. Voyer, Voyer and Bryden, (1995) have pointed out that certain tests are more appropriate than others to study sex differences in spatial abilities. Several explanations have been offered on account for the prevalence of sex differences in spatial abilities. Variables such as choice of strategy (Bryden, 1980), rate of maturation (Waber, 1976), cerebral lateralization (Bryden, 1979; Levy, 1971), genetic complement (McGhee, 1982), sex hormones (Imperato-McGinley, Ricardo, Gautier, Voyer and Bryden, 1991; McGhee, 1979), differential experience and socialization (Baenninger and Newcombe, 1989), and sex role identification (Nash, 1975; Signorella and Jamison, 1986) have been proposed as the possible explanations for sex differences. The latter two have been more under discussion in recent years than others due to the proliferation of women studies.

Many studies have shown that acculturated individuals demonstrate cognitive skills quite different form those of unacculturated individuals (Cole and Scribner, 1977; Rogoff, 1981; Mishra, Sinha and Berry, 1996; Sinha, 1982). While acculturated individuals felt ease and work better in test situations, they also have more familiarity with test materials, which leads to differences in performance without transforming their cognitive skills or styles (Rogoff, 1981). Whether acculturation brings a change in a person's cognitive functioning to the extent that acculturated individuals become cognitively different from those who are unacculturated (Mishra, Sinha and Berry, 1996), and whether acculturation related differences at an early age facilitate a particular form of spatial orientation among children is not known.

In review of studies, Gauvain (1993) and Levinson (2003) suggest that findings in spatial cognition must be viewed and evaluated with reference to the environmental and socio-cultural situations in which they are acquired. Socio-cultural conditions provide children with different opportunities to acquire, organize, and use spatial knowledge. The cultural characteristics of groups not only influence the perception and description of space (Spencer and Darvizeh, 1983), but also the memory of objects and their location in space (Niraula, 1998; Niraula and Mishra, 2001).

The study reported in this paper aims to investigate the development of spatial cognition in rural and urban Newar children of Nepal. The focus is on the processes of spatial memory of object and the interpretation of their spatial location. It was hypothesized that elder children would have a better memory for object and object locations than younger children. It was also expected that boys would score higher than girls and urban children would score higher than rural with regard to memory for spatial location of objects.

Method

The Sample

The study was carried out with 240 children from 5 to 12 years of age group. The sample included urban and rural boys and girls in each age group. Rural children were drawn from the schools of Chhaling Village Development Committee (VDC) of Bhakatapur district; and urban children were selected from schools of Kathmandu city. The Nepalese government provided urban and rural distinction on the basis of several grounds that is physical facility, dependency on agriculture, less urban contact, other subsistence activities, settlement pattern, and life styles were the main indicators. Differences in these terms were quite evident between the rural and urban samples.

The Newar represent a fairly dominant cultural group in Kathmandu valley. They can be easily distinguished from other ethnic groups on the basis of several physical features, such as the fetures of their face, nose, eyes, and shoulders (Nepali, 1965). They are the mixture of Indo-Aryan and Mongoloid (Tibeto-Burman) cultures. They speak Nepali and Newari (Tibeto-Burman langauge), which includes about half a dozen dialects. Rural Newars in Chhaling mostly live in the hilly region with agriculture and animal husbandry as their main occupation, while urban Newars depends on wages, government jobs, small shops, and house rentals. Rural Newars generally have the joint family system compared to the urban Newars were extended and nuclear family systems are most prevalent. In the rural Newar group literacy rate is lower, and boys attend school more in numbers than girls. In urban Newar group literacy rate is higher, and both boys and girls equally attend school. Rural Newars represent a more egalitarian society than the urban Newar.

Tests/Tasks

Three tests were used in this study:

Story-Pictorial Embedded Figures Test (SPEFT)

This test is developed by Sinha (1984) consisted eight sets of test cards with three sets of practice cards (P1-P3). Each set has a simple and a complex card. Each simple card consisted of the picture of some objects familiar to children. Each complex card, on the other hand, consisted of the picture of a familiar setting that camouflages the objects in the simple card.

The test was administered as an "object search game". The child was presented with the complex card (P1) for about 10 seconds, and was asked to identify the contents. Then the simple card (P/1) was presented and the child was asked to identify and count the objects depicted therein. When the child encountered any difficulty, (s)he was helped to identify and count the objects. The child was told that the complex card (P1) presents a story, which describes the circumstances which lead to the hiding of the objects in complex picture, then the child was asked to identify the hidden figures. No time limit was imposed for this purpose. However, the child was asked to indicate as soon as possible all the hidden figures therein. The time taken and the number of the simple figures correctly disembedded were noted down.

Procedure for the test series was the same as for the practice series. The test series started only after the child had understood the task. The child was encouraged to look around and not to confine the search for a particular place in the card. The SPEFT had already been used with Gurung and Brahmin children of Nepal (Shrestha and Mishra, 1996; Sinha and Shrestha, 1992). However, some difficulty was encountered with Newar children in one practice card (rural children had difficulty with cricket bat and badminton shuttlecock) and in one test card (teacher's shoes and sticks). Hence, those were not used. With this change, the maximum disembedding score on the test was 34, and a minimum was zero. The number of figures disembedded correctly was the score of the child.

Contact Acculturation Measure

This measure was modelled on a scale developed by Mishra, Sinha and Berry (1996), which comprises such objective indicators of acculturation as the knowledge of local language, knowledge of the official language, knowledge of other languages (e.g., English), household items, means of livelihood, use of technology, religion, dressing style, travel experiences, and exposure to movies. The rating on different indices are aggregated to obtain acculturation score for a subject. Although the scale was developed for use with tribal people in Bihar, it appeared quite useful for measuring the level of acculturation of Newars with a slight modification. Mishra *et al.* (1996) scale consists of eleven items. A subject is rated with each of these scales, which ranged from 3 to 5 points. The maximum score on the scale is 36 with a minimum of zero score. This scale provides an index of an individual's acculturation. While some of the items on the scale require observation, others require an interview. The scale was given to the parents to obtain an index of acculturation at the family level.

Spatial Cognition Task

This task comprised the pictorial scene of a village in which sixteen objects were represented in a spatial layout along a road passing through the village. The child was shown the layout (10×12) for approximately 120 seconds, and was asked to point out all the objects on the picture (e.g., house, dog, car, hen, bicycle, etc.). Then the scene was covered and the child was asked to reach those various objects that were shown. The recalled items were noted down.

Following the recall trial, the test of spatial memory was given. The child was then to tell the location of objects with reference to the road. For each object one question was asked (e.g., where is the school from the road?). Sixteen such questions were asked, and the answers given by the child were recorded. With respect to location, a child could use several directional terms (e.g., east, west, north, south, back, right, left, up, down, etc.). For each correct recall of object location (irrespective of the term used), "one" point was given. This yielded a score range of 0-16 for relative (LRFB) as well as absolute directional (NSEW) terms.

Results

The data were analyzed separately on measures of disembedding (SPEFT), "object recall", and "spatial memory" as well as on the measures of the use of directional terms. The mean score of groups for SPEFT, object recall, and spatial memory are given in Table 3.1. There were clear differences according to age level of subjects. Urban children scored higher than rural and the scores of boys were generally higher than those of girls. The pattern was almost the same of SPEFT and the two measures of spatial cognition.

Table 3.1: Mean Scores of Groups on SPEFT (Disembedding Measure), Object Recall, and Spatial Memory

Age		*Rural*		*Urban*	
		Girls	*Boys*	*Girls*	*Boys*
SPEFT					
5-6 years	Mean	14.95	15.60	14.84	16.65
	SD	4.35	5.71	5.89	5.01
8-9 years	Mean	18.50	20.90	24.50	24.90
	SD	5.69	3.55	3.33	3.28
11-12 years	Mean	26.60	27.00	28.70	28.75
	SD	2.68	3.66	2.90	3.08
Object Recall					
5-6 years	Mean	8.50	9.20	8.95	9.60
	SD	1.32	2.12	2.21	2.14
8-9 years	Mean	11.35	11.85	12.05	12.20
	SD	1.[illegible]	2.25	1.32	1.67
11-12 years	Mean	12.40	12.75	12.55	13.15
	SD	1.31	1.77	1.76	1.18
Spatial Memory					
5-6 years	Mean	9.85	10.00	10.15	10.80
	SD	2.23	2.27	2.13	1.70
8-9 years	Mean	10.15	11.10	12.15	12.65
	SD	2.21	2.61	2.48	2.25
11-12 years	Mean	12.85	13.50	13.15	14.10
	SD	2.91	2.61	1.98	1.45

In order to examine if different cognitive measures showed any consistent pattern of relationship, inter-correlations across the measures of SPEFT and spatial cognition task were computed (Table 3.2). All values of correlation were found to be significant positive except those of the relative direction measure, which exhibited a negative correlation with all other measures. The values of these correlations ranged from. 21 to -.99.

Table 3.2: Correlations Across SPEFT and Spatial Cognition Task Measures

Variables	*SPEFT*	*Spatial Exploration*	*Spatial Recall*	*Spatial Memory*	*Direction Absolute*	*Direction Relative*
SPEFT	*	.35*	.61*	.53*	.67*	.64*
Spatial exploration		*	.39*	.21*	.28*	-.27*
Object recall			*	.44*	.50*	-.47*
Spatial Memory				*	.44*	-.41*
Direction Absolute					*	-.99*
Direction Relative						*

We had information about children's age, residence, gender, family background and level of acculturation. In order to examine the contribution of these variables the scores obtained by children on different measures were subjected to multiple regression analysis (MRA). Since it was difficult to determine the relative hierarchy of the predictor variables in terms of the degree of their effect on different measures, a stepwise regression analysis was preferred. The values of R, R^2, Beta weights and 't' for variables which made significant contributions to various cognitive measures are given in Table 3.3.

It could be noted that in the disembedding measure, age and acculturation made significant contributions to the variance in scores; they accounted for approximately 61 per cent of the variance in scores. Age contributed approximately 56 per cent and acculturation approximately 5 per cent to the variance in scores. Beta weight for age was higher than that for acculturation. On the spatial exploration measure only the contribution of age (12%) to the variance in scores was significant. On the object recall measure, the contributions of age, gender, and acculturation were found to be significant. Age contributed approximately 41 per cent to the variance in the scores, whereas gender and acculturation each contributed 1 per cent respectively. Again, the Beta weight for age was higher than for gender or acculturation.

Table 3.3: The Outcomes of MRA on Various Spatial Cognition Measures

Variables	*R*	R^2	*Beta*	*t*
Disembeding				
Age	.75	.56	.73	17.89
Accultration	.78	.61	.24	5.86
Object Recall				
Age	.64	.41	.63	12.70
Gender	.65	.42	.10	2.10
Acculturation	.65	.43	.09	2.03
Spatial Memory				
Age	.49	.24	.47	8.64
Acculturation	.53	.28	.19	3.49
Gender	.54	.29	.12	2.15
Absolute directional				
Age	.75	.56	.65	17.85
Residence	.76	.58	.16	3.75
Relative directional				
Age	.72	.51	-.72	-16.14
Residence	.73	.53	-.15	-3.39

On the spatial memory measure, the contributions of age, acculturation and gender were significant. Age contributed approximately 24 per cent to the variance in scores. Acculturation contributed 4 per cent and gender approximately 1 per cent to the variance in scores. Beta weight for age was higher than that of acculturation or gender.

It could also be noted that age and residence made significant contributions to the variance in scores on the absolute direction measure. Age contributed approximately 56 per cent, whereas residence contributed only 2 per cent to the variance in the scores. Beta weight for age was higher than that of residence.

On the relative direction measure, age and residence contributed significantly to the variance in scores. Age contributed 51 per cent and residence approximately 2 per cent to the variance in scores. Beta weights for age and residence were found to be negative which indicate that relatively older and urban children made less use of relative directional terms.

Discussion

The findings of the study were largely in the expected direction. The first hypothesis, which predicted an increase in spatial cognition with increasing age levels of children, was supported by the findings. Children of higher age levels (11-12 and 8-9 years) scored higher than their counterpart children of the lower age level (5-6 years) for the recall of objects and their spatial location. As children advanced in age, they became more capable or recall accurately the objects and their location in the spatial layout.

This developmental pattern noted on the spatial cognition task is in support of a general theory of development. A child at the pre-operational stage (2-7 years) begins to function symbolically with specific cognitive acquisition, but with limitations of reasoning capacity. With the attainment of concrete operational stage (7-12 years) some major changes, like spatial operations, allocentrism, etc., are evident (Piaget, 1952). The younger children's "perception bound" understanding, concentration (focus on one aspect of a situation and neglect for other important features), lack of rules of operation, and failure to apply certain strategies in the performance of tasks do not allow them to function skilfully. They fail to use strategy in situations where it could be helpful (called production deficiency) or fail to perform the mental strategy effectively (called control deficiency). On the other hand, the elder children seem to be relatively thorough and quicker at encoding and retrieving information from complex visual arrays, particularly the information concerning a central environmental object and its relationship to other objects or features of the background. They tend to encode and process information in the long-term memory, and employ a variety of internal retrieval cues to recall them later. These findings are in consonance with those of other studies that document the relationship between age and performance on spatial cognition tasks (e.g., Berk, 1994; Cornel *et al.*, 1989; Elkind and Flavell, 1969; Elkind and Scott, 1962; Piaget, 1950).

The hypothesis regarding gender difference in spatial cognition also supported by the findings, although they do not bring out results exactly the same way as generally reported in psychological literature. It may be noted that studies generally reported considerable sex differences in cognitive ability in favour of girls in early years, a small or non-existent difference during the pre-pubertal years and a major difference after adolescence, which generally remains stable throughout the life span (Maccoby and Jacklin, 1974). Our findings indicate a better performance by boys than girls from the early childhood period onwards.

Explanations offered to account for gender differences in spatial abilities have taken at least three different forms. One given in terms of *deficiency or nature theory,* is biologically based, and argues that the brains of males and females are structured differently. This explanation is tied to hemispheric specialization hypothesis (e.g., Annett, 1985; Bryden, 1979), sex hormones (Imperato-Meginley, Pichardo, Gautier, Voyer and Bryden, 1991; Kimura, 1989), and rate of maturation (e.g., Newcomb and Dubas, 1987; Waber, 1976). The second explanation, forwarded in terms of *difference or the nature theory,* argues that boys receive more encouragement from parents and teachers to engage in activities that promote cognitive skills (Vasta, Haith and Miller, 1992). The third explanation, advanced in terms of *international theory,* argues that boys innately prefer activities involving spatial relations, and as a result of it, they spend more time improving these skills (Vasta *et al.,* 1992). This theory asserts that cognitive abilities are placed approximately to the same level in both sexes, but performance and behaviour indicators often favour males on these tasks (Allen, 1974; Goldstein, Haldane and Mitchell, 1990; Linn and Pulos, 1983a, 1983b). This happens largely due to social and cultural expectations and stereotyping that produce less opportunities for females to develop spatial cognitive skills.

Although all these explanations have received due attention in research, the factors which are more important in producing gender difference in cognitive functioning are still not clear (Harris, 1978; Voyer, *et al.,* 1995). The pattern of gender difference noted in the present study seems to offer support to Interactional theory in which cultural and social conditions are largely held responsible for producing such differences. Greater participation of boys in wider community activities than girls (Whiting and Edwards, 1988) found in this study further supports this contention.

Our observations revealed that in the Newar community, boys were often asked to go for shopping and arrange things to meet the petty day-to-day needs of the family. They enjoyed greater choice and freedom than girls. They were also more conscious about the surrounding environment through interpersonal contacts and direct access to various places. The girls were more dependent, socially oriented and restricted in access due to strict parental discipline and severe control. Boys also participated widely in typical traditional male games, whereas girls were found to be more involved in domestic activities. These conditions seem to be associated with a low level of development in the spatial domain (Mishra, 1996; Nerloe and Snipper, 1981). The girls failed to develop spatial cognitive skills perhaps due to these cultural conditions (Harkness and Super, 1985; Whiting and Edwards, 1988). Studies suggest that sex difference is generally less evident in such societies where men and women share common roles and activities (Berry, 1976; Sinha, 1988). As far as the Newars are concerned, they represent a male dominated society in which gender differences are emphasized from early childhood. The role assigned to boys in this community provides them ample opportunities for environmental experience, exploration and learning as compared to girls.

The hypothesis, which predicted the development of object recall and their spatial memory to be related to residential background was not fully supported by the findings. It is only on the use of directional terms (relative or absolute) that the difference due to residence was significant. We believe that differences in socialization and acculturation experience of the groups were the main factor in their performance difference. The city of Kathmandu is full of intersecting roads, signs, symbols, and other crossings. In this context, mental mapping of spatial layouts and cognitive orientation for directions in a cardinal or absolute framework becomes essential to keep track of directions. The rural setting does not provide children with such a complex surrounding. Studies indicate that the characteristic features of environment with which children interact is a crucial factor in the acquisition and development of cognitive skills (Mishra, 1990, 1996; Munroe and Munroe, 1971; Sinha, 1982).

The hypothesis regarding gender differences in the use of directional terms did not find support in this study. Although boys used absolute terms more often than girls and girls used relative terms more often than boys, the difference between boys and girls was not significant. Regression analysis clearly showed that gender contributed significantly to object recall and spatial memory, not to the use of directional terms (except for the use of cast). Thus, while the use of spatial vocabulary remains more or less similar among boys and girls, the performance on spatial tasks is not really so. This indicates that linguistic and cognitive processes may not always show a close correspondence. This pattern has been evident in other studies also (Dasen, Mishra and Niraula, 2004; Mishra, Dasen and Niraula, 2003; Niraula, Mishra and Dasen, 2005).

Thus, the study reveals that while age is an important factor in spatial cognitive development, gender also plays some role in it and rural or urban residence is important with respect to the use of relative or absolute spatial terms.

REFERENCES

Acredolo, L. (1990), Behaviour Approaches to Spatial Orientation in Infancy. In A. Diamond (Ed.), *The Development and Neural Bases of Higher Cortical Functions* (pp. 596-612). New York: The New York Academy of Sciences.

Allen, M.J. (1974), Sex Differences in Spatial Problem Solving Styles. *Perceptual and Motor Skills,* 39, 843-46.

Allen, G.L. and Ondracek, P.J. (1995), Age-Sensitive Cognitive Abilities related to Children's Acquisition of Spatial Knowledge. *Developmental Psychology,* 31, 934-945.

Ashcraft, M.H. (1990), Strategies Processing in Children's Mental Arithmetic: A Review and Proposal. In D.I. Bjorklund (Ed.), *Children's Strategies: Contemporary Views of Cognitive Development* (pp. 185-211). Halsdale, NJ: Erlbaum.

Annet, M. (1985), *Left, Right Hand and Brain: The Right Shift Theory.* Hillsdale, NJ: Lawrence Erlbaum.

Baenninger, M. and Newcombe, N. (1989). The role of experience in Spatial Test Performance: A Meta-Analysis. *Sex Roles,* 20, 327-344.

Berk, E.L. (1994), *Child Development.* New Delhi: Prentice-Hall of India.

Berry, J.W. (1976), *Human Ecology and Cognitive Style.* New York: Sage/ Halsted.

Bowerman, M. (1993), The Origins of Children's Spatial Semantic Categories: Cognitive *versus* Linguistic Determinants. In J.J. Gumperz and S.C. Levinson (Eds.), *Rethinking Linguistic Relativity.* UK: Cambridge University Press.

Bremner, G. (1989), Development of Spatial Awareness in Infancy. In A. Slater and G. Bremner (Eds.), *Infant Development* (pp. 123-141). Hove, NJ: Lawrence Erlbaum Associates.

Bryden, M.P. (1979), Evidence of Sex related Differences in Cerebral Organization. In M.A. Wittig and A.C. Peterson (Eds.), *Sex related Differences in Cognitive Functioning* (pp. 121-143). New York: Academic Press.

Bryden, M.P. (1980), Sex Differences in Brain Organization. Different Brains or Different Strategies? *Behavioural and Brain Sciences,* 3, 230-231.

Cole, M. and Scribner, S. (1977), Cross-Cultural Studies of Memory and Cognition. In R.V. Kail and J.W. Hagen (Eds.), *Perspectives on the Development of Memory and Cognition.* Hillsdale, NJ: Erlbaum.

Cornell, E.H., Heth, C.D. and Broda, L.S. (1989), Children's Wayfinding: Response to Instructions to Use Environmental Landmarks. *Developmental Psychology,* 25, 775-764.

Dasen, P., Mishra, R.C. and Niraula, S. (2004), The Influence of Schooling on Cognitive Development: Spatial Language, Encoding and Concept Development in India and Nepal. In B.N. Setiadi, A. Supratiknya, W.J. Lonner and Y.H. Poortinga (Eds.), *Ongoing Themes in Psychology and Culture* (pp. 223-238). Yogjakarta, Indonesia: IACCP.

Elkind, D. and Flavell, J.H. (Eds.), (1969). *Studies on Cognitive Development. Essays in Honour of Jean Piaget.* New York: Oxford University Press.

Elkind, D. and Scott, L. (1962), Studies in Perceptual Development: The Decentring of Perception. *Child Development,* 33, 619-630.

Evans, G.W. (1980). Environmental Cognition. *Psychological Bulletin,* 88, 259-287.

Gauvain, M. (1993), The Development of Spatial Thinking in Everyday Activity. *Developmental Review,* 13, 92-121.

Goldstein, D., Haldane, D. and Mitchell, C. (1990). Sex Difference in Visual-Spatial Ability: The Role of Performance Factors. *Memory and Cognitive,* 18, 546-50.

Harkness, S. and Super, C. (1985), The Cultural Contexts of Gender Segregation in Children's Peer Role of Performance factors. *Memory and Cognition,* 18, 546-50.

Harkness, S. and Super, C. (1985), The Cultural Contexts of gender segregation in Children's Peer Groups. *Child Development,* 56, 219-24.

Harris, L.J. (1978), Sex Difference in Spatial Ability: Possible Environmental, Genetic, and Neurological Factors. Kinsbourne, M. (Ed.), *Asymmetrical Function of the Brain* (pp. 405-522). New York: Cambridge University Press.

Hazen, N.L., Lockman, J.J. and Pick, H.L. Jr. (1978). The Development of Children's Representations of Large-Scale Environments. *Child Development,* 48, 623-636.

Imperato-McGinley, J., Pichardo, M., Gautier, T., Voyer, D. and Bryden, M.P. (1991), Cognitive Abilities in Androgen Insensitive Subjects—Comparison with Control Males and Females from the Same Kindred. *Clinical Endocrinology,* 34, 341-347.

Kimura, D. (1989), How Sex Hormones Boost or Cut Intellectual Ability. *Psychology Today,* 23 (11), 62-66.

Laurendeau, M. and Pinard, A. (1970), *The Development of the Concept of Space in the Child.* New York: International Universities Press. (Originally published in 1968: *Les Premieres Notions Spatiales de Venfant.* Neuchatel: Delachaux and Niestle).

Levinson, S.C. (1991), Relativity in Spatial Conception and Description. In J. Gumperz and S. Levinson (Eds.), *Rethinking Linguistic Relativity* (3-11). Ocho Rios, Jamaica.

Levinson, S.C. (1996), Frames of Reference and Molyneux's Question: Cross-Linguistic Evidence. In P. Bloom, M. Peterson, L. Nadel and M. Garerett (Eds.), *Language and Space* (pp. 109-169). Cambridge, MA: MIT Press.

Levinson, S.C. (2003). *Space in Language and Cognition.* New York: Oxford University Press.

Levy, J. (1971), Lateral Specialization of the Human Brain: Behavioural Manifestations and Possible Evolutionary Basis. In J.A. Kiger, Jr. (Ed.), *The Biology of Behaviour* (pp. 159-180). Corvallis; Oregon: State University Press.

Lepecq, J.C. and Lafaite, M. (1989), The Early Development of Position Constancy in a no Landmark Environment. *British Journal of Developmental Psychology,* 7, 289-306.

Linn, M.C. and Pulos, S. (1983a), Aptitude and Experience Influence on Proportional Reasoning during Adolescence: Focus on Male-Female Differences. *Journal for Research in Mathematics Education,* 14, 30-46.

Linn, M.C. and Pulos, S. (1983b), Male Female Differences in Predicting Displaced Volume: Strategy Usage, Aptitude Relationship and Experience Influences. *Journal of Educational Psychology,* 75, 86-96.

Maccoby, E.E. and Jacklin, C.N. (1974), *The Psychology of Sex Differences.* Stanford, CA: Stanford University Press.

McGhee, M.G. (1979), Human Spatial Abilities: Psychometric Studies and Environmental, Genetic, Hormonal, and Neurological Influences. *Psychological Bulletin,* 86, 889-918.

McGhee, M.G. (1982), Spatial Abilities: The Influence of Genetic Factors. In M. Potegal (Ed.), *Spatial Abilities: Development and Physiological Foundations* (pp. 199-222). New York: Academic Press.

Mishra, R.C. (1990), Society, Ecology and Competence. In G. Mishra (Ed.), *Applied Social Psychology in India,* New Delhi: Sage.

Mishra, R.C. (1996), Perceptual Differentiation in Relation to Children's Daily Life Activities. *Social Science International,* 12, 1-11.

Mishra, R.C. (1997), Cognition and Cognitive Development. In J.W. Berry, P.R. Dasen and T. Saraswathi (Eds.), *Handbook of Cross-Cultural Psychology,* Vol. 2. Boston: Allyn and Bacon.

Mishra, R.C., Sinha, D., Berry, J.W. (1996), *Ecology, Acculturation and Psychological Adaptation: A Study of Adivasis in Bihar.* New Delhi: Sage.

Mishra, R.C., Dasen, P. and Niraula, S. (2003), Ecology, Language and Performance on Spatial Cognitive Tasks. *International Journal of Psychology,* 38, 366-383.

Munroe, R.L. and Munroe, R.H. (1971), Effect of Environmental Experience on Spatial Ability in East African Society. *The Journal of Social Psychology,* 83, 15-22.

Nash, S.C. (1975), The Relationship Among Sex Role Stereotyping, Sex Role Preference and Sex Difference in Spatial Visualization. *Sex Roles,* 1, 15-32.

Nepali, G.S. (1965), *Newars.* Bombay: United Asia Publications.

Nerlove, S.B. and Snipper, A.S. (1981), Cognitive Consequences of Cultural Opportunity. In R.H. Munroe, R.L. Munroe, B. Whiting (Eds.), *Handbook of Cross-Cultural Human Development* (pp. 423-474). New York, Garland Press.

Newcombe, N. and Dubas, J.S. (1987), Individual Differences in Cognitive Ability: Are they Related to Timing of Puberty? In R.M. Lerner and T.T. Foch (Eds.), *Biological-Psycho-Social Interactions in Early Adolescence: A Life Span Perspective* (pp. 249-302). Hillsdale, N.J.: Erlbaum.

Niraula, S. (1998), *Development of Spatial Cognition in Rural and Urban Nepalese Children.* Unpublished Doctoral Thesis, Banaras Hindu University, India.

Niraula, S. and Mishra, R.C. (2001), Spatial Orientation of the Newar Children in Nepal. *Social Science International,* 17, 36-48.

Niraula, S., Mishra, R.C. and Dasen, P. (2004), Linguistic Relativity and Spatial Concept Development in Nepal. *Psychology and Developing Societies,* 17, 99-124.

Perimutter, M. Metzger, R., Nezworski, T. and Miller, K. (1981), Spatial and Temporal Memory in 20 and 60 Years Olds. *Journal of Gerontology,* 36, 59-65.

Pedek, K., Roman, Z. and Sobolik, K.G. (1986), Spatial Memory for Objects and Words. *Journal of Experimental Psychology: Learning, Memory and Cognition,* 12, 530-537.

Piaget, J. (1950), *The Psychology of Intelligence.* London: Kegan Paul, Trench and Trubner. (Original Work Published in French in 1947).

Piaget, J. (1952), *The Origins of Intelligence in Children.* New York: International University Press.

Piaget, J. and Inhelder, B. (1956; 1967), *The Child's Conception of Space.* London: Routledge and Kegan Paul.

Piaget, J. and Inhelder, B. (1967), *The Child's Conception of Space.* New York: Norton.

Piaget, J., Inhelder, B. and Szeminska, A. (1960). *The Child's Concept of Geometry.* New York: Basic Books.

Rogoff, B. (1981), Schooling and the Development of Cognitive Skills. In H.C. Triandis and A. Heron (Eds.), *Handbook of Cross-Cultural Psychology,* Vol. 4, (pp. 233-294). NJ: Allyn and Bacon.

Shrestha, A.B. and Mishra, R.C. (1996). Sex Differences in Cognitive Style of Brahmin and Gurung Children from the Hills and Plains of Nepal. In J. Pandey, D. Sinha and D.P.S. Bhawuk (Eds.), *Asian Contribution to Cross-Cultrual Psychology.* New Delhi: Sage Publication.

Signorella, M.L. and Jamison, W. (1986), Masculinity, Feminity, Androgyny and Cognitive Performance: A Meta Analysis. *Psychological Bulletin.* 100, 207-228.

Sinha, D. (1982), Socio-Cultural Factors and the Development of Perceptual and Cognitive Skills. In W.W. Hartup (Ed.), *Review of Child Development Research,* Vol. 6, Chicago: University of Chicago Press.

Sinha, D. (1984), *Story Pictorial SFT and Indo-African EFT.* Varanasi: Rupa.

Sinha, D. (1988), Basic Indian Values and Behaviour Dispositions in the Context of National Development. An Appraisal. In D. Sinha and H.S.R. Kao (Eds.), *Social Values and Development: Asian Perspectives.* New Delhi: Sage.

Sinha, D. and Shrestha, A.B. (1992), Ecocultural Factors in Cognitive Style Among Children from Hills and Plains of Nepal. *International Journal of Psychology,* 7, 49-59.

Spencer, C. and Darvizch, Z. (1983), Young Children's Place Descriptions, Maps and Route Finding: A Comparison of Nursery School Children in Iran and Britain. *International Journal of Early Childhood,* 15, 26-31.

Taylor, H.A. and Tversky, B. (1996), Perspective in Spatial Descriptions. *Journal of Memory and Language,* 35, 371-391.

Vasta, R., Haith, M.M. and Miller, A.S. (1992), *Child Psychology: The Modern Science* (p. 23). New York: John Wiley and Sons.

Voyer, D., Voyer, S. and Bryden, M.P. (1995), Magnitude of Sex Differences in Spatial Abilities: A Meta-Analysis and Consideration of Critical Variables. *Psychological Bulletin,* 117, 250-270.

Waber, D.P. (1976), Sex Difference in Cognition: A Function of Maturation Rate? *Science,* 1992, 572-573.

Whiting, B.B. and Edwards, C.P. (1988). *Children of Differenct Worlds: The Formation ofSocial Behaviour.* Cambridge, M.A.: Harvard University Press.

4

Linguistic Profile of Kumaun

Aradhana Shukla

In these days considerable attention has been paid to understand the concept of culture and its consequences on the behavioural properties of the individual. In general, culture represents social integration and is revealed by the individual's action which perform in social settings for their social establishment. Thus, culture is the sum total of all that is manifested in the actions of people.

Concept of Culture

According to the historian Stocking (1968), the modern concept of culture emerged by the end of the 19th and in the beginning of the 20th century. The research of early anthropologists through their field studies in the cultural groups of the world sought to pinpoint the factors responsible for variation in thought process in various groups. In cross-cultural psychology, a widely cited definition of culture put forth by Geertz (1973) is as follows: "[*Culture is a*] historically transmitted pattern of meanings embodied in symbolic form by means of which men communicate, perpetuate, and develop their knowledge about and attitudes toward life".

According to Geertz (1973), culture and cognition are inseparable, and it seems that this notion of inseparability is widely accepted by the modern cultural psychologists now-a-days. Geertz (1973) held that the human brain is thoroughly dependent upon culture for its very operation. Gordon (1991) has extended Geertz's notion of culture to include "structured relationships, which are reflected in institutions, social status, and ways of doing things, and objects that are manufactured or created such as tools, clothing, architecture, and interpretative and representational art". Besides, in an attempt to portray culture as an overarching construct in the lives of any social group, Gordon (1991) conceives it as a multi-dimensional construct comprising at least five dimensions: (a) the judgmental or normative, (b) the cognitive, (c) the affective, (d) the skill, and (e) the technological.

Although the concept of culture has a very long tradition in the human sciences, yet there is a lack of consensus in its characterization. It appears to be a fuzzy, yet a relevant concept (Feilich, 1989). Nevertheless, some understanding has been achieved and the available theoretical perspectives suggest that culture may be viewed as a collective product constituted by values, beliefs, perceptions, symbols, and other man-made artifacts which are transmitted to generations through language and other mediums. In this way, culture reflects the value-seeking process of human beings and implicates a world-view or design for living. In an ultimate analysis, cultures emerges as a meaning systems which define, inform, and constitute the range of one's understanding and intelligibility. Efforts for the interpretation of behaviour become sensible only after taking constraints and capacity which a given culture possesses.

Scholars usually differentiate between culture (i.e. human construction) and nature (i.e., structures and processes that exist and occur independent of human action) since the domains which constitute culture are not genetically acquired. However, in traditions, cultures are also "given" in a concrete form as symbols and signs. Not only this, once the cultural process is in motion, cultural evolution also ensures the development of human nature. A moment's reflection on the contents of culture suggests that it is inescapably psychological in its composition. Perhaps, the two are intertwined in such a manner that it is not possible to think of human nature independent of culture. The difference between the two is only of the levels of analysis and abstraction; one focuses on individual level processes and its modifications, while the other goes further to unravel the pattern of structure at a global level. In this dialogue, biology and ecology also play an important role. Human beings are biological organisms too and have many genetically programmed dispositions which are expressed in behaviour in a specific ecological-environmental context. As Cole (1990) argued, "culture is the unique medium of human existence, a medium that acts both as constraint and tool of human action. This medium has co-evolved with the biological constitution of our species." In this way, culture becomes a co-determiner of behaviour in nature. Culture and behaviour, thus, are reciprocally related and the dichotomy is false (D'Andrade, 1990), created only for analytical convenience and disciplinary priorities. Against this background the cultural constitution of psychology will be examined. This would help to understand why culture is conceived in psychological discourse in the way it is.

Every culture has its own values, traditions, rituals, sanctions and norms. There has been an increasing realization that imperative changes due to dynamism of environment can be facilitated by understanding and recognition of cultural dimensions of the society. Cultural norms and values are deeply rooted and no fundamental change can be brought and stabilized by ignoring culture. The procedure and mechanism of introduction, acceptance and assimilation differs in every culture. It will be inappropriate to perceive all previling Indian values as wrong and to make an effort to change them. Rather there are certain values, which are needed to be reserved and nurtured. They can give us a cultural edge. Such differentiation requires vision, analysis of the cultural dimensions. This needs an identification of functional and dysfunctional aspects of our culture.

Thus, culture is an embodiment which an individual acquires in the process his/her development. It thus, grows, evolves and transforms itself with the passage of time, employ the instruments of abstractions and conceptualization which are essentially accepted as cognitive abilities. Generally, it maintains a continuity of time that may not be self-apparent as it tends to lose articulation in its evalution.

Nature of Culture

There are many characteristics of culture and they are as follows:

Culture is Man-made

Culture can only be seen in human society. There are some psycho-physical characteristics in human which discriminate him from other species. Because of his developmental intellect he discovers many new dimensions of human development and takes them into account. Due to cultural enrichment a person considered as a super organism.

Culture is Learned

Cultural is the sum total of behavioural standards that are learned by human being in the society prevailing around them. This process is called socialization. Although a person learns many things for his personal use as well as for general welfare but it can not be considered as culture. Behaviours that are meant for many groups, majorities or society, culture is formed by them. Group behaviour generate customs, traditions or stereotypes that can be seen only in human society.

Culture is Transmitted

Since culture can be learned hence, it is transmitted from older to younger generation. The young generations takes knowledge from the elder group and adds their own experiences and language which plays a major role in this context.

Every Society has its Own Culture

A society is found different from the other because of its geographical and social circumstances. Society invents many new ideas for the fulfilment of its demands and these inventions give a new culture to the society. Needs of one society are entirely different from the other and they cause cultural variation. But it is not the end. In spite of these cultural variations there is a general similarity that can be seen in all societies. Thus, it is opined that culture is a accompanied by the similarities as well as differentials of the societies.

Culture has Social Quality

Culture is entirely the contribution of society and it is emerged by group habits, behaviours and experiences. The components of culture, e.g. custom, language, art, tradition, religion, science, philosophy present not only the life style of a person but also represents the life style of the whole socicty.

Culture is Ideal for the Group

The people of a given culture follow the specific culture and shape themselves accordingly. When two cultures are compared it is very difficult for the psychologist to make the distinction.

Culture Satisfies Human Needs

It is the primitive quality of a culture to satisfies the needs of the persons living in that particular culture. There are many psychological and social needs of a person and he forms culture in order to meet the demands of his life.

Culture has Adaptability

Culture has a quality on the basis of which a person adjusts himself according to his society and other circumstances.

Culture has the Integrative Quality

Culture is comprised many, for example social units like culture trait and culture complex are embedded interpretation of units from a culture maintains its systems.

Culture is Fundamental in Forming Human Personality

The relative significance of cultured environment or ecology cannot be denied. After birth the person makes a close perusal of his environment and absorbs its properties into himself. The major influencing factors of culture are rituals, custom, religion, philosophy, art and science. They lay their imprint on the person's behaviour.

Culture is Both Super Individual and Super Organic

The meaning of super individual denotes that culture is not formed by any particular and it consumes not only one part of the culture but culture is formed by the total segment.

On the ground of this discussion its can be said that culture has its own consistency and it is comprised with so many features.

Concept of Cognition

In a global perspective cognition has received more attention by scientists, neuro-scientist and philosophers. According to Shaffer (1988) cognition is a term that developmentalists use to refer to the activity of knowing and the mental processes by which human being operate acquisition and use it to solve problems. The cognitive processes that help us to understand and adopt the environment include such activities as attention, information processing, learning, thinking and remembering *in toto,* the memorable events and undertaking which characterizes the human mind (Flavell, 1983). Thus, it can be opined that cognition is the activity of knowing and process through which knowledge is acquired. Vygotsky (1978) insisted that cognitive growth occurs in a socio-cultural context that influences the form it takes. He claimed that the growth of human cognition is inheritably socio-cultural because it is affected by the beliefs, values and tools of intellectual adaptations passed to individual through his culture.

Moreover, human cognition relates to, and describes, the mental activities which manipulate, translate, and transform, as it were, information represented in any modality. Thus, it can turn verbal information into spatial representation or pictorial information into numerical representation. Furthermore, the more commonly cited cognitions involved in intellectual activities are those which are related to short- and long-term memory, comprehension, vocabulary, reasoning, visual processing, auditory processing, and speed of processing. An important provision is that all these cognitions do not function in isolation but depend, in part, on certain kinds of experiences in contexts of their expression and development.

The Cross-cultural Structure of the Kumaon Region

"अस्त्युत्तस्यां दिशि देवतात्मा, हिमालयो नाम नगाधिराजः।
पूर्वा परौतोय निधीव ग्राहयः, स्थितः पृथिव्यामिवमानदण्डः"।

—कुमार संभव 1/1

Located in the lap of Himalaya and named as Dev Bhumi Uttarakhand has maintained its culture and social diversity along with

Geographical variation. If the racial socio-cultural heritage of this part of world is studied we can entitle it as MINI INDIA. The natural prosperity and the whole community reveal the uniqueness cf this part. There are many cultural groups and they have maintained their identity. But the interaction lies between the groups which has produced a cultural reminiscence. They are also correlated by deculturation, communization, westernization and modernization.

We in our everyday surrounding we see many social segments and their spatial mobility but there are many communities which are in a statue like position in relation to their social and spatial mobility. Due to rapid increase in science and technology and modernized materials and an advanced and sophisticated segment has emerged. This segment is the reverse side of those who are still living in scarcities and tied with the chains of stereotype and traditions. Between these poles is the middles who are not only traditional but also sophisticated.

Linguistic Profile of Kumauni Children

Although Kumauni is the regional language of Kumaun but it varies from one place (village) to another. In the villages and traditional families of cities people use to speak traditional Kumauni pertaining to their place but generally in cities people have adopted multi-dimensional approach to language in which they use English and Hindi terms along with other regional languages and the Urdu language is also discernible. A close perusal of the usage of different languages in Kumauni culture is presented in Table 4.1:

Table 4.1 (a): Linguistic Adaptability of Kumauni Language with Other Regional Languages

Kumauni	*Asamia*	*Hindi*	*English*
काण	कना	काना	One eyed
दानाक्	दानर	दान में	In charity
आड़ुबेलि	आड़ुलि	अँगुली, उंगली	Finger
लाठि	लाठि	लाठी	Stick

(contd.)

Kumauni	*Oria*	*Hindi*	*English*
पैरन	पहरन	पहनना	To wear
बल्दा	बल्दा	बैल	Ox
घ्यू	घिअ	घी	Ghee
चुपड़	चिक्कड़	चिकना-चुपड़ा	Greesy

Kumauni	*Gujrati*	*Hindi*	*English*
दि	दीवो	दिए	Earthen lamps
शरम	लाज	शर्म, लज्जा	Shame
करम	काज	कर्म, कार्य	Work, Action

Kumauni	*Punjabi*	*Hindi*	*English*
द्वि	दो	दो	Two
लौ	नवाँ	नया	New
बुड	बुड्ढा	बूढ़ा	Old
सैप	हाकम	साहब, हाकिम	Boss

Kumauni	*Bengali*	*Hindi*	*English*
चोर	चोर	चोर	Thief
डर	डरि	डर	Fear
अन्या	अंधकार	अंधकार	Dark
मिठ	मिश्टि	मीठा	Sweet

Kumauni	*Marathi*	*Hindi*	*English*
गोरू	गाइ	गाय	Cow
दछिन	दक्षिण	दक्षिण	South
चेलि	चलि	लड़की	Daughter
पाणि	पाणी	पानी	Water

Kumauni	*Sindhi*	*Hindi*	*English*
मैक	माउक	मां के	(Of) Mother
प्यट	पेटा	पेट से	Pregnant
पकि	पकी	पका	Ripe, well cooked
छोडि	छडिड	छोड़ना	To leave

Kumauni	*Rajasthani*	*Hindi*	*English*
राणि	राणी	रानी	Queen
मुट्ठि	मूठी	मुट्ठी	Grip
खुलि	खुल्ली	खुलना	To open
कामल	कामली	कम्बल	Blanket

In Kumauni language usage of regional language of South India is also apparent but due to linguistic specificity the magnitude of this linguistic approach is very limited.

Table 4.1 (b): Linguistic Adaptability of Kumuani Language

Kumauni	*Tamil*	*Hindi*	*English*
दुसरक	पररिच्छ	दूसरे की इच्छा	Others' wish
Kumauni	*Telugu*	*Hindi*	*English*
कुकुर	कुक्कनु	कुक्कुर, कुत्ता	Dog

However, Kumauni language is very close to Hindi language, many Hindi words in their *tatsam* form are most frequently used in this language. For example:

Table 4.2: Use of *Tatsam* Words of Hindi Language in Kumauni

Tatsam words of Hindi in Kumauni	*Pure Hindi*	*English*
तिरिया	त्रिया, स्त्री	Woman
कुकुरगति	बुरी दशा, कुत्ते जैसी दशा	Bad Condition
खिसैन	खिसियाहट	Shamefulness
द्योर	देवर	Husbands', Younger Brother
व्या	व्याह विवाह	Marriage
तिति	तीता, कड़वा	Bitter
ज्याढ़	जेठ (पति का बड़ा भाई)	Husbands' Elder Brother
क्याल	केला	Banana

Some persian words in Kuamuni language after a slight modification in pronounciation, like, Akhtiyar, Andaaz, Azmaish, Avaz, Asharfi, Asman, Asay, Asteen, Ada, Akhir, Amadani, Dustkhat, Ummeed, Ustad, Kangal, Kachhori, Kaddu, Kishti, Kushti, Khazanchi, Khaki, Khamosh, Khurpi, Kharab, Khushamad, Khushi, Kushki, Khunkhar, Gand, Gup, Gabaru, Gardish, Garam, Garden, Galicha, Gulaab, Chand, Chadar, Chalak, Chalbaaz, Zabardust, Zaban, Zamin, Zimmevar, Tankhwah, Dafter, Dushman, Dar, Nakhera, Nami, Nuksan, Nishan, Pari, Bakhsheesh, Numayashi, Payjaama, Besharam, Behosh, Barbaad, Bardasht, Bahal, Buzurgh,

Biradari, Mard, Yarana, Muzara, Rista, Sharab, Sabzi, Sardi, Hamesha, Restedari, Shaher, Razinama.

Table 4.3: Use of Arabic and Persian compound words in Kumaun language

Arzi (a) naviz (p)= Arzinavish
Gusal (a) khana (p)= Guslkhana
Dimag (a) dar (p)= Dimagdar
Ba (a) daulat (p)= Badaulat
Be (a) hal (p)= Behal
Be (p) dekhal= Bedekhal
Be (p)eman=Be-iman
Mal (a)Dar (p)=Maldar
Halaf (a) nama (p) = Halafnama
Haval (a)dar (p)=Havaldar
Khatar (a) nak (p)=Khatarnak
Khatir (a) dari (p)= Khatirdari
Takat (a) var (p)=Takatvar
Fauz (a) dari (p)=Fauzdari
Bad (a)mash (p)=Badmash
Be (a)an (P)= Bayan
Be (p) koof (a)=Bevakoof
Be (p)vakht (a)= Bevakht
Madad (a)gar (p)= Madadgar
Raz (a)dar (p)=Razdar

After a close observation of Kumaun societies it is appeared that mistakes in sentence formation and pronunciation are very common. Generally they use very typical regional words, like "***thahara***" (this word has no meaning but they use it at the end of the sentences ***e.g. Rama ka bhai kah raha thahara ki usaki bus chhoot gayi***) "***bal***" (narration of any event but boycott ones' participation from responsibility in regard to that particular event, ***e.g. Ramu ki dadi kah rahi thi ki Geeta ki beti Amarica se aye hai bal.*** It means that Ramu's grandmother has not seen the daughter of Geeta. She is telling whichever she has been told by she is not responsible for this statement. **हणि** (bechara), **सिबो-सिब** (alas, hay-hay), **असज** (inconvenience), **चिचाट** (noise), **उड़पचास** (49). In addition, typical villages usually do not discriminate between Sh and S. They usually employ Sh at the place of S ***(e.g. shashur*** in place of ***Sasur or Shash is place of Sas***).

However, Kumauni is not based only on such regional words. It is comprised of Hindi, English, Arabi, Persian, and other regional languages. It means that it is an exhaustive language.

Cognitive Spectrum of Kumauni Children

In general, it appears that in spite of many cultural complication and diversity in comparison to the plains area the cognitive competence of Kumauni children is almost similar to the plains. Najhoon (1993) studied the pattern of recall proficiency, memory knowledge and strategy use in children as affected by experiential deprivation and age. It resulted that the magnitude of recall and memory knowledge (meta memory) was relatively higher and in elder children as compared to their younger counterparts. In addition, it was also found that this cognitive component was high in low deprived children than high deprived children. Najhoon also noticed that the meta-memory—potential memory difference decreases with increase in age. Bora (1994) found that the high level of cognitive competence was shown by those children who had received tangible reward by the investigator. In addition, age-related and deprivational findings were found in close consonance with Najhoon. Pant (2000) aimed to find out the pattern of school related outcomes of Kumauni and Non-Kumauni children as influenced by age, sex and experiential deprivation. It was found that school related activity follow right path with increase in age and decrease in experiential deprivation, but the sex-related discrepancy was not significance. Pande (2001) studied tribal society in relation to their meta memory. It was found that children of tribal society were relatively less in comparison to non-tribal children. Kaur (2001) studied the pattern of self-esteem and ego-development in adolescents as a function in cultural context. She noted that self-esteem and ego-development were relatively lower in the adolescents of closed cultures. Dhami (2002) studied level I and level II intelligence in the children as affected by age, sex and emotional disturbance. It has found that levels of intelligence increase and emotional disturbances decrease with age. Agrawal (2007) is studying the pattern of study habits of boarders/non-boarders in developmental perspective. These findings in general, suggest that cognitive development is determined by chronological age and such other factors which help a person to enhance his/her personality.

Contributors of Cognitive Behaviour

Cognition is the art of knowing on the basis of which a person copes the environmental demands and actualizes his potentials. Similar to other type of development, cognitive development is also facilitated by many environmental forces like, demographic variables, environmental research, climatic, supportiveness, chronological age etc. They are described below.

Environmental Prosperity

Although the contribution of heredity and environment is equally seen in all over development but in true sense both acts in different way. Heredity influences the physical development and the early sensory development but environment plays a vital role later in socio-cognitive development. It has been found that memory proficiency and memory knowledge (Najhoon, 1993; Pande, 2001), attribution style (Agarwal, 1996; Joshi, 2004; Joshi, 2007) motivational pattern (Najhoon, 1993; Shrivastava, 1996; Bora, 1994) were found high in those children who were brought up or still being brought up in higher level of experiential amenities.

Parenting Style and Home Environment

If we have to observe parents as socializer could we identify the dimensions in which they differ ? Since the pioneering work of Diana Baumrind (1975, 1991) investigators have attempted to answer this question through studies employed interviews and questionnaires. They suggest that there are important variations in parenting style and these differences are significantly related to socio-cognitive personality development of children. Many explorations in Kumaun have been made and it is noticed that the children of authoritarian parents were relatively higher in motivational style (Srivastava, 1996) and social cognition (Latwal, 2002). It was also noticed that supportive family climate reveals potentiality in emotional tolerance (Bhandari, 2005; Adhikari, 2002) and academic stress and stress management (Dwivedi, 2000; Karnatak, 1998).

Age-Related Variation

As children grow older they develop more strategies and skills that help them to develop and enhance their cognitive framework. Definitely, experiences in higher magnitude play vital role in this regard. Since older people have more experience so they produce higher level of cognition. Studies done in Kumuan reveals that increase in recall, meta-memory and cognitive skills were caused by increase in age (Najhoon, 1993). Dhami (2002) found that Level I and Level II intelligence was highly pronounced in secondary graders as compared to primary graders. Agrawal (1996) and Joshi (2C04) had explored that attributional style modified with increase in age. Bora (1996) explored that perceptual differentiation was also shared by increasing age. Not only cognitive but personality variables also modified by age-related changes. Adhikari (2002), Bhandari (2005) and Joshi (2007) explored that the general problematic behaviour in children was higher upto late childhood but as they grew older they acquire normal behaviour. On the basis of this discussion it is surely fair to say that cognitive development is facilitated with increase in chronological age.

Cultural Context and Cognitive Behaviour

Culture is the full set of specific knowledge, attitude, behaviour and a product that characterizes an identifiable group of people. It appears that variations in culture causes variation in behaviour. Karnatak (1998) studied Tharus and Bhotia tribals and compared them with the children of non-tribal civilized society. It was found that tribals were lower in academic and achievement motivation as compared to the children of non-tribal society who evinced high level of concern for their future. Pande (2001) compared Bhotia and Tharu children with non-tribal children of urban society. She found that the cognitive competence of tribal children was extremely in comparison to the non-tribal children. In addition, inter-tribal comparison was also made and it was noted that Bhotias were relativity superior than Tharu children. Joshi (2004) studied the causal attribution of Tharu and Buxa children and compared them with the children of general Kumauni society. She explored the general Kumauni children stressed on internal causes and showed them responsible for their success and failure. On the other hand tribal children evinced themselves as dependant on external causes and they charge external forces for their achievements discrepancy has been registered. Not only in tribal-non-tribal society but also in rural-urban setting (Bhandari, 2005; Joshi, 2007) and town *versus* metropolitan city. Kaur (2001) studied the population of open culture city (New Delhi) and closed culture (Almora). She found that the metropolitan population was higher in self-esteem and ego development. Dwivedi (2001) studied culture in relation to affector as academic stress and stress management. She investigated that higher level of academic development was shown by the students of open culture. On the basis of this debate it is apparent that cognitive development is determined by many existing forces. These findings suggest that different socialization practices lay their influence on cognitive development. Cognitive development appears not as an inevitable progression structures but as an opportunistic process which make use of the products of obvious specialization to construct alternative pathways through specific context and thereby represent the metaphor of a "constructive web" (Biddel, 1991).

REFERENCES

Adhikari, S. (2002), Impact of Parenting Style on Disruptive Behaviour and School Related Outcome. Unpublished Ph.D. Thesis, Department of Psychology, Kumaun University, Nanital.

Agarwal, P. (2007) Study Habit as Affected by Environmental Pollution Grade and Residential Locale: An Empirical Analysis. Unpublished Ph.D. Thesis. Department of Psychology, Kumaun University, Nainital.

Agarwal, N. (1996), Attributional Analysis in Young Children: A Test of Wieners' Model Unpublished Ph.D. Thesis, Department of Psychology, Kumaun University, Nainital.

Baumrind, D. (1975), *Early Socialization and the Discipline Controversy,* Morriston N.J. General Larning Press.

Baumrind, D. (1991), Parenting Style and Adolescent Development. In R.M. Learner, A.C. Paterson and J. Brooks-Gunn (Eds.). *Encycholopaedia of Adolescence.* New York, Garland.

Bhandari, V. (2005), Disruptive Behaviour of Children and Urban Setting unpublised Ph.D. Thesis. Department of Psychology, Kumaun University, Nanital.

Bora, D.S. (1996), Developmental Impact of Experiential Deprivation and Motivational Feed Back on Some Behavioural Processes. Unpublished Ph.D. Thesis, Department of Psychology, Kumaun University, Nainital.

Cole, M.C. (ed.) (1990), Cultural Psychology: A Once and Future Discipline? In J.J. Berman (ed.). Nebraska Symposium on Motivation 1989: *Cross Cultural Perspectives.* Lincon: University of Nebraska Press.

D'Andrade, R.G. (1990), Culture and Personality: A False Dichotomy. In D.K. Jordon and M.J. Swartz (eds.) *Personality and Cultural Construction of Society.* To Scaloosa and London University of Alabave Press.

Dwivedi, V. (2002), Climatic Supportiveness, Sex and Grade as Affectors of Academic Stress and Atress Management. A Study of Open and Closed Culture Unpublished Ph.D. Thesis, Department of Psychology, Kumaun University, Nainital.

Dhami, S. (2002), Impact of Grade, Sex and Age Emotional Disturbance on Intelligence and Adjustment Pattern: A Factorial Analysis. Unpublished Ph.D. Thesis. Department of Psychology, Kumaun University, Nainital.

Freilich, M.C. (ed.) (1989), *The Reference of Culture.* New York, Bergen and Gravy.

Flavell, J.H. (1985), *Cognitive Development* (2nd ed.). Englewood Cliffs, N.J.: Practice Hall.

Greertz, C. (1973), *Interrelation of Cultures.* NewYork. Basic Books.

Gordon, E.W. (1991), Human Diversity and Pluralism, *Educational Psychologist,* 26, 99-108.

Joshi, A. (2004), Study of Familial Relation in Children as a Function of Grade and Sex: A Cross Cultural Study, Unpublished Ph.D. Thesis, Department of Psychology, Kumaun University, Nainital.

Joshi, U. (2007), A Study of Climatic Supportiveness and Disruptive Behaviour in Children as Affected by Grade Sex and Residential Locale. Unpublished Ph.D. Thesis, Department of Psychology, Kumaun University, Nainital.

Kaur, K. (2001), Self Esteem and Ego Development in Adolescents of and Closed Cultures as Affected by Their Grade and Sex. Unpublished Ph.D. Thesis Department of Psychology, Kumaun University, Nainital.

Karnatak S. (1998), Cross Cultural Analysis of Grade and Sex on Academic Motivation Academic Stress and Stress Management: A Study of Accepted and Rejected Children. Unpublished Ph.D. Thesis, Department of Psychology, Kumaun University, Nainital.

Latwal, A. (2002), Family Climate and Social Cognition. Unpublished Ph.D. Thesis. Department of Psychology, Kumaun University, Nainital.

Najhoon, S.K. (1993), Recall Proficiency, Memory Knowledge and Strategy Use in Children as a Function of Experiential Deprivation and Age. Unpublished Ph.D. Thesis, Department of Psychology, Kumaun University Nainital.

Pande, S. (2001), Meta Cognition and Achievement Motivation in Tribal and Nontribal Male and Female Students. Unpublished Ph.D. Thesis. Department of Psychology, Kumaun University, Nainital.

Pant, N. (2000), Impact of Deprivation, Grade and Sex on School Related Outcomes. Unpublished Ph.D. Thesis, Department of Psychology, Kumaun University, Nainital.

Shaffer, D.R. (1980), *Social and Personality Development.* Pacific Grave. Calif: Brooks/Cole.

Srivastava, P. (1996), Developmental Impact of Sex and Experiential Deprivation on Perceived Parenting Attitude and Personality Functioning. Unpublished Ph.D. Thesis, Department of Psychology, Kumaun University, Nainital

Stocking, G. (1968), *Race, Cultures and Evolution.* New York Free Press.

Vygotsky, L.S. (1978), Mind in Society: the Development of Higher Mental Process. In M. Cole, V. John Steiner, S. Scriber and E. Souberman (Eds.) Cambridge: Harvard University Press.

5

School Related Outcomes in Children Unity in Diversity

Aneeta Joshi

Children are the future of every society. It is upon them that the progress and advancement of the whole society depends. The personality of the child develops according to the cultural surroundings in which the child is brought up. It also determines his or her performance in school as well as in different institutions of society. A number of psychologists have tried to give a particular definition of culture.

Mazumdar and Madan have presented culture as the life style of the person. According to Tylor, "Culture is that complex whole which includes knowledge, belief, art, morals, law, custom and many of other capabilities and habits acquired by man as a member of society. It is apparent that culture is the social heritage, a gift to human being given by society. It is the total way of life and psychophysical and social means on which the particular life style is based.

Herskovits (1957) believes culture as the 'man-made part of the environment'. He follows Pidington and states two aspects of culture e.g. natural or god-gifted and materialistic or man-made culture. Linton defines culture, 'as the sum total of knowledge, attitude and natural behaviour patterns showed and transmitted by the members of a particular society'.

Thus, it is apparent that it is a very difficult job to provide an universally accepted definition of culture. "Culture in total could be defined as a particular life style, adjustment pattern and behavioural norms of a particular society. Cuiture is compared of all sorts of ideas and behaviour which is acquired.

We in our surrounding see many social segments and their spatial mobility but there are many communities which are in a state like position in relation to their social and spatial mobility. Due to advancement in science and technology and modernization at materials a sophisticated and advanced segment has emerged. This segment is the reversed side of those who are still living in scarcity and were tied in chains of stereotype and traditions. Between these poles are the middles who are not only traditional but also sophisticated.

In this study four sub-cultural groups (Hindu, Muslim, Sikh and Christian) have been taken in consideration and the access is to achieve the effect of culture over achievement motivation and school related fructification.

Achievement Motivation

The motivational tendency refers to the positive or negative anticipatory goal reactions aroused in situations which involve competition in terms of a standard of excellence, where performance may be evaluated on the basis of success or failure. According to Murray:

> "Need for achievement may be defined as a desire or tendency to overcome obstacles, to exercise power, to strive to do something difficult, as quickly as possible."

The theory of achievement motivation, formulated by Atkinson (1960) and his colleagues include individual differences in achievement needs with the determinant's behaviour. The theory specifies that the achievement related behaviour is a result of a conflict between a hope of success (approach motivation) and a fear of failure (avoidance motivation). The apporoach and avoidance tendencies in turn, are the function of achievement-related needs (need for achievement and anxiety about failure), the expectancy of success and failure. A special assumption of this model is that the incentive value of achievement tasks is determined by the probability of success.

The prominent focus of this theory is that individuals higher in resultant achievement needs are particularly attracted towards tasks of immediate difficulty, while those, of low in achievement needs, are inhibited by task whose probability of success approximates .50. Investigations by Atkinson, Litwin, the Feather and Marlton, respectively employed dependent variables of risk preference, persistence in behaviour following failure and choice. (aspiration level), support the general hypothesis that differential attraction towards tasks of intermediate difficulty are displayed by groups which are high and low in achievement motivation. In addition a wide array of education relevant studies especially related to the field of vocational aspiration (Katz, 1980), field of concentration (Isaacs, 1965) and ability grouping (Atkinson and Litwin, 1960) not only provide empirical support for the theory of achievement motivation, but, researches have also shown that achievement is closely related to gender, education and occupational level. Females have been associated with low achievement motivation. It is reported that majority of girls have low achievement. Bartal and Frieze (1977) pointed out that the attribution pattern of females can be equated with low achievers. They have noted that females attribute their performance more to external factors than males. However, individuals belonging to low educational and occupational level display low Achievement (Misra and Tripathi, 1978).

These studies share the implicit assumption that achievement motivation manifested similarly in the learning and the manifestation of Achievement motivation will therefore arise in different forms. Stimulated by different situational error and may be chanellised to accomplish different types of goals (Bhagat and McQubid, 1982).

The aim of the study was to find out the impact of cross-cultural variation, grade and gender on achievement motivation. Another attempt was made to assess the effect of all these variables in school related outcome. Keeping these things in consideration the objectives and hypotheses of the study are as follows:

1. The first objective of the study was to find out the impact of cross-cultural variation on school related outcome. It was hypothesized that cross-cultural variation would make a difference in school-related outcome.
2. The second objective of the study was to find out the impact of grade in school-related outcome. It was hypothesized that difference in grade would cause difference in school-related outcome.

3. The third objective of the study was to find out the effect of gender in school-related outcome. It was assumed that gender difference would affect school-related outcome.
4. The fourth objective of the study was to find out the effect of cross-cultural variation in achievement motivation. It was assumed that achievement motivation would be affected by cross-cultural variation.
5. The fifth objective of the study was to find out the effect of grade in achievement motivation. It was hypothesized that variation in grade would cause difference in achievement motivation.
6. The sixth objective of the study was to find out the effect of gender in achievement motivation. It was hypothesized that difference in gender would make difference in achievement motivation.

Keeping these objectives and hypotheses in consideration this study was planned in factorial perspective.

Method

Sample

The sample consisted of 160 students from VIII and X grades of Hindu, Muslim, Sikh and Christian communities, from different schools of Almora and Pithoragarh districts. Sample was arranged according to the requirements of 4×2×2 mixed model factorial design with 4 sub-cultured groups [(Hindu, Muslim, Sikh and Christian) ×2 gender (Boys and Girls) ×2 grades (VIII and X)] i.e. 10 participants per cell.

Table 5.1: Schematic Presentation of Experimental Design

	A								
	A1		*A2*		*A3*		*A4*		
	B1	*B2*	*B1*	*B2*	*B1*	*B2*	*B1*	*B2*	
C1	10	10	10	10	10	10	10	10	80
C2	10	10	10	10	10	10	10	10	80
	20	20	20	20	20	20	20	20	160

Legends

A. Cross-Cultural Variation

A1—Hindu. A2-Muslim A3—Sikh A4—Christian

B. Grade

B1—X B2—VIII

C. Gender

C1—Boys C2—Girls

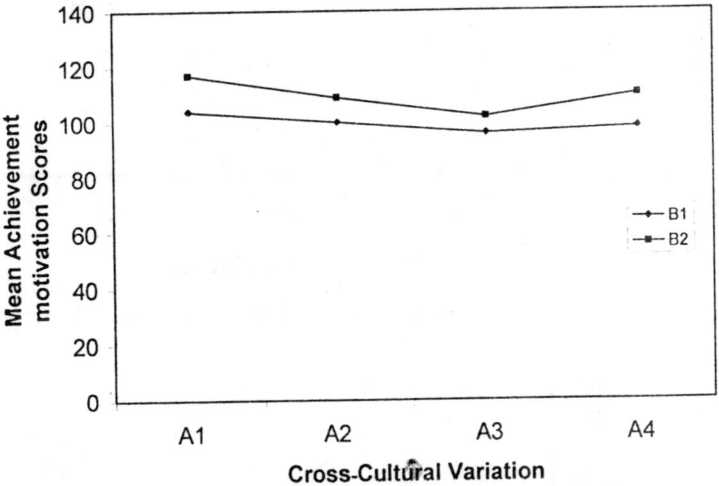

Fig. 5.1: Achievement Motivation Scores as affected by Cross-Cultural Variation and Grade

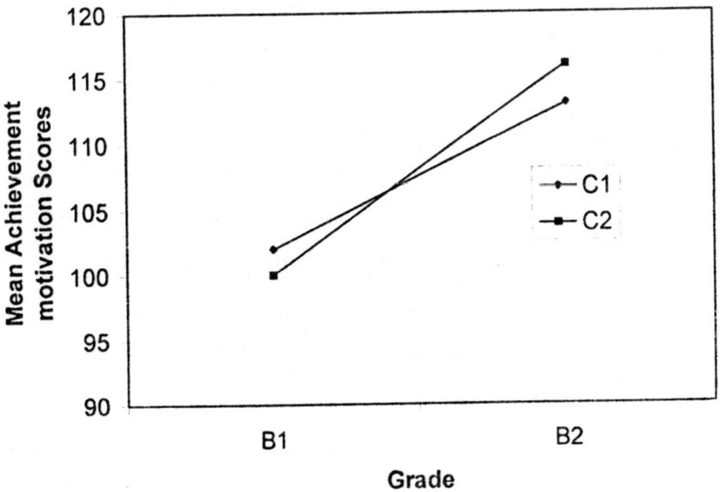

Fig. 5.2: Achievement Motivation Scores as affected by Grade and Gender

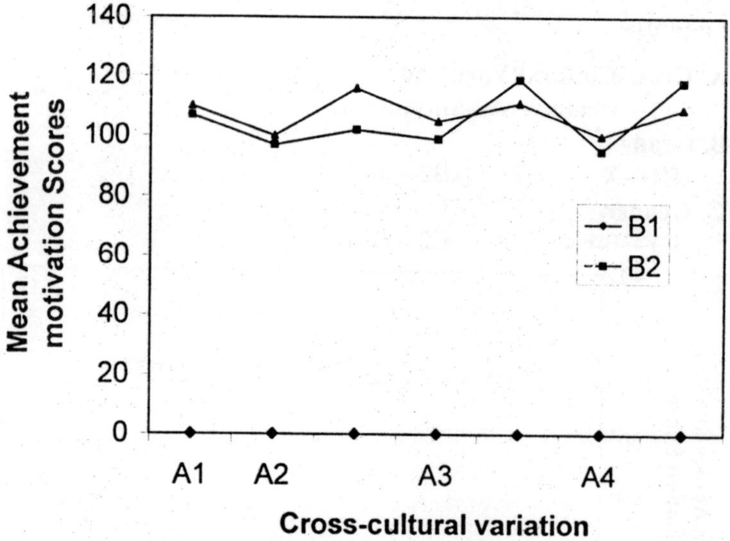

Fig. 5.3: Achievement Motivation Scores as affected by Cross-Cultural Variation, Grade and Gender

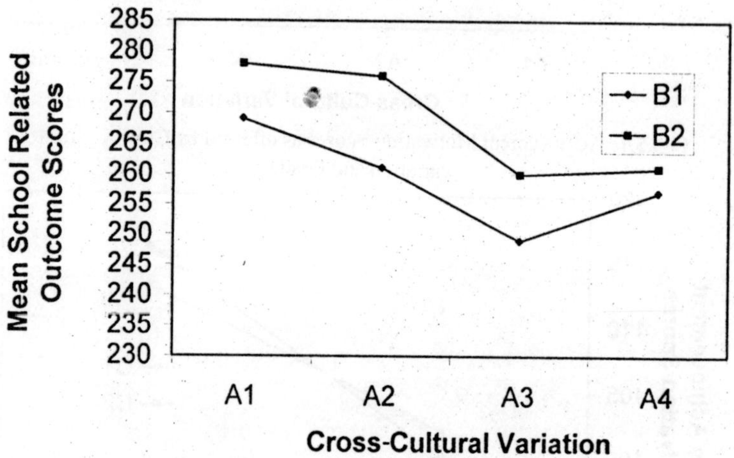

Fig. 5.4: School Related Outcome Scores as affected by Cross-Cultural Variation and Grade

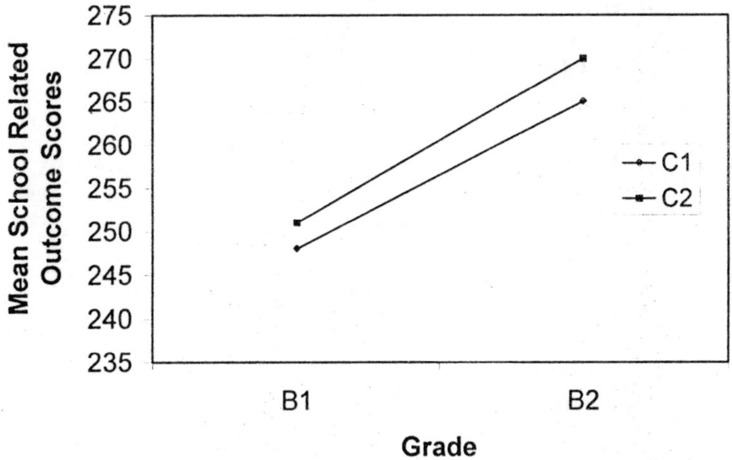

Fig. 5.5: School Outcome Scores as affected by Cross-Cultural Variation and Grade

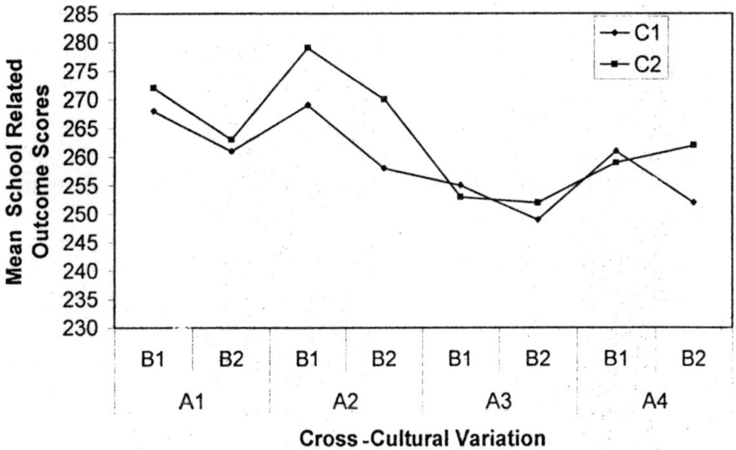

Fig. 5.6: School Related Outcome Scores as affected by Cross Cultural Variation, Grade and Gender

Legends

A. Cross-cultural variation

A1—Hindu.

A2—Muslim

A3—Sikh
A4—Christian

B. Grade
B1—X
B2—VIII

C. Gender
C1—Boys
C2—Girls

Tools

In order to measure school related outcome and achievement motivation two tools were taken into consideration.

1. *The Achievement Test*: In order to measure the achievement motivational pattern an achievement test (Shukla and Najhoon 1993) was employed. It consisted of forty, five point items and dealt with academic interest, academic concentration, deep study, feeling of competitiveness, punctuality, intelligence, peer selection, discussion, level of aspiration and self-evaluations. The score ranges from 40 to 200. Low score indicates high level of achievement motivation and *vice versa.*

In order to test the subjects in this measure the investigator instructed them as follows:

"प्रस्तुत परीक्षण का उद्देश्य यह जानना है कि आप अपने जीवन में क्या पाना चाहते हैं। आप सारे कथनों को ध्यानपूर्वक पढ़िये और अपनी प्रतिक्रिया कथनों के सामने दिये गये अनुक्रमों (बहुत अधिक, अधिक, सामान्य, कम, बहुत कम) में से किसी एक पर सही (√) का निशान लगाकर दीजिए। समय की पाबन्दी नहीं है। फिर भी कार्य शीघ्रता से ही करें।"

2. *The measure of school-related Outcomes*: In order to measure the patterns of school-related outcome a scale was constructed by Dr. Aradhana Shukla. It is based on Marjoribanks (1991) and it is consisted of 100 items, in five points and it deals with hard work, goal orientation, work interests, orientation towards reward; positive interaction with teachers and peers, helping behaviour, presence of individual work, leadership, self-confidence etc. the score ranges from 100 to 500 Low scores indicates higher level of school-related outcome and high score *vice versa.* Prior to the conduction of measures the SS were instructed as follows.

"मैं आपके सामने कुछ कथन रख रही हूँ, आप कथनों को ध्यानपूर्वक पढ़ें और प्रत्येक कथन पर अपनी सहमति या उक्त कथनों के समक्ष दिये पांच बिन्दुओं (बहुत अधिक, अधिक, सामान्य, कम, बहुत कम) में से किसी एक पर सही (√) का निशान लगाकर दीजिए। समय बन्धन नहीं है। फिर भी कार्य शीघ्रता से ही करें।"

Procedure

Data collection was made individually or in groups as per the availability of the participants and convenience. Best attempts were made to avoid external distractions.

Results

Obtained data were analyzed by 3-way analysis of variance and interpreted in terms of achievement motivation and school-related outcomes as affected by cultural variation grade and gender. Separate analysis was made for achievement motivation and school-related outcomes. Findings are given below:

Impact of Cross-Cultural Variation Grade and Gender on Achievement Motivation

Findings are reported in Table 5.2.

Table 5.2: Summary table showing the impact of Cross-Cultural Variation, Grade and Gender on Achievement Motivation

Souce of variance	*Ss*	*df*	*Ms*	*F*
A	40.71	3	13.58	4.31
B	10.78	1	10.78	5.43
C	3.00	1	3.00	1.20
AB	43.80	3	14.60	5.84
AC	9.30	3	3.10	1.24
BC	22.68	1	22.68	9.07
ABC	76.50	3	22.50	10.20
Error (within)	760.00	144	2.50	

Table shows that the main effect of cross cultural variation over achievement motivation is significant (F, 3, 144=4.31, p < 0.01). The next main effect of grade over achievement motivation is significant (F1, 144-5.43, p < .01) and it showed that grade had affected the pattern of motivation. Mean values pooled across cultural variation and sex were 110.12 and 101.75, respectively for VIII and X graders. The third main effect of gender was insignificant (F, 1, 144, 1.20 p>.05) and it revealed that boys (X=107.50) and girls (X=106.63) were more or less equal in his achievement motivation.

The 2-way interaction of cross-cultural variation and grade was significant (F3, 144, 5.84 p < .01) and it is given in Figure 5.1. a close perusal of the future indicates variation in achievement motivation by the variation in culture and grade. Achievement motivation of Sikh was found highest in comparison to others while the Hindu's were lowest and Christians and Muslims were almost equal. In addition it was also found that the culture related discrepancy was highest among Christians and Hindus. While Muslims and Sikh were almost equal. Moreover, it was also seen that cultural discrimination was rather evident in VIII class that 10th class. The two-way interaction of cross-cultural variation and gender was insignificant (F, 3, 144=1.24 p> .05). In addition to it is also clear that gender related variation was more pronounced in Muslims in comparison to Hindus and Christians while in Sikh it was lesser. The grade and gender interaction was also significant (F, 1, 144=9.07, p < .01) and it is given in Fig. 5.2. Figure shows grade related variation among both genders but it was more prominant in case of girls. Moreover, it was also seen that gender related discrepancy was more pronounced among VIII graders.

The 3-way interaction of cross-cultural variation X grade X gender was also significant (F3, 144=10.20, p < .01) and it is given in Fig. 5.3. The figure indicates that all variables in sum yielded their influence on achievement motivation significantly.

Impact of cross-cultural variation, grade and gender on school-related outcome

Results are given below in Table 5.3.

Table 5.3: Summary Table Showing the Impact of Cross-Cultural Variation grade and Gender on School Related Outcome

Source of variance	*Ss*	*df*	*Ms*	*F*
A	2.18	3	7.06	6.79
B	3.53	1	3.57	3.40
C	1.44	1	1.44	1.18
AB	21.75	3	7.11	6.84
AC	6.18	3	2.09	2.00
BC	12.26	1	12.26	11.79
ABC	34.92	3	11.64	11.19
Error (within)	149.76	144	1.04	

The effect of cross-cultural variation, grade and gender over school related outcome is given in Table 5.2. The table shows that the mean effect of cross cultural variation in school related outcome, is significant (F3, 144=6.79 $p < .01$). Mean values pooled across grade and gender were 249.75, 259, 170.65 and 228.65 respectively for Hindus, Muslims, Sikhs and Christians. It showed that the school related outcome of Sikh students was high and the outcome of Hindus was lowest.

The next main effect of grade was also significant (F1, 144= 3.40, $p < .05$) and it showed that VIII graders were different (X=235.72) from Xth graders (X=248.17.75) in their scores in school related outcome. The third main effect of gender was insignificant (F1, 144, 1.18 $p> .05$) and it showed that there was a little difference between boys (X=243.07) and girls (X = 240.87) in their scores as school related criterion.

The two way interaction of cross-cultural variation and grade was significant (F3, 144, 6.84 <.01) and it is given in Fig. 5.4. Figure shows that Sikh student, are highest in their school related outcomes. The next 2-way interaction of cross-cultural variation and gender was also significant (F3, 144, 2.00 $p>.05$). The next interaction of grade and gender was also significant (F1, 144=11.79 <.01) and it is shown in Figure 5.5. It shows that Xth graders were higher in their school related outcomes than VIII graders. Figure also shows that boys are higher in their school related outcomes than girls in both grades but the difference is higher in VIIIth graders.

The 3-way interaction of cross cultural variation X made X gender was also significant (F3, 144, 11.19 $p < .01$) and it is mentioned in Figure 5.6. Figure indicates that all variables in sum yielded their influence on school related outcomes significantly.

Findings in sum are as follows:

1. Cross-cultural variation was prominent everywhere
2. Grade related difference was also significant
3. Gender issue also yielded its impact on dependent variables but the magnitude was not so high.
4. All interactions were also significant and it was found that achievement motivation and school related outcomes were influenced by these variables jointly.

Discussion

Obtained findings were analyzed by analysis of variance and interpreted in terms of developmental impact in cross-cultural variation and gender in achievement motivation and school related outcome. Findings will be interpreted on the lines of notion on the basis of which the study was done.

Culture and Grade as Effectors of Achievement Motivation and School Related Outcome

Our first notion was that variation in culture would provide variation in achievement motivation. Our hypothesis was related with cultural impact on achievement motivation. It was found that variation in culture caused variation in achievement motivation. It has been seen that every culture has its own values, traditions rituals sanctions and norms. There has been increasing realization that imperative change due to dynamism of environment can be facilitated by understanding and recognition of cultural dimensions of the society. Cultural norms and values are deeply rooted and no fundamental change can be brought and stabilized by ignoring culture. Transition in procedure and mechanism of introduction, acceptance and assimilation are present in every culture. It will be inappropriate to perceive all. Indian value as wrong and futile to change them. Rather these are certain values, which need to be preserved and nurtured. They can give us a cultural edge. Such differentiation affects motivational pattern of children. Since culture holds its own surroundings and modes of life which enable the person to behave accordingly. Our findings appeared in such a way. As a result of cultural differentiation difference in achievement motivation was appeared. As culture affects achievement motivation, similarly grade would cause difference in achievement motivation. Our notion was related with developmental change. It was assumed that grade increment would make a lot of change in achievement motivation. Our findings supported our assumption and we found that elder subjects were higher in achievement motivation than their younger counterparts of VIII grade.

Similarly in other studies, it appears that as the child grows he/she gets many good qualities in himself/herself and they make good impression on others. It was the reason following which post-graduate students were higher than intermediate students. As a child shifts to adolescence the behaviour of his/her parents towards him/her is also changed, because they (parents) think that their son/daughter is no lower child so they should leave the rod and treat him/her friendly. It is the age when an adolescent comes across many tensions and career related problems. Educated parents think that their son/daughter is in tension and is facing many problems consuming his/her future so the home should be supportive and calm. Findings are in close consonance with Dwivedi (2002) and Dhami (2002) where the significance of home environment has been shown. In this way we can say that the impact of grade cannot be denied.

Gender Achievement Motivation and School Related Outcome

Our other notion was related with gender issue and an attempt was made to find out the impact of gender on achievement motivation and related outcome.

In almost every society socialization process for boys and girls is different. Socialization is more strict and rigid in the case of boys than girls so that boys strongly prefer the stereotyped male role and girls prefer the stereotyped female role (Palria and Dixit, 1994). As age advances, there is a steady change towards greater masculinity among boys which probably implies that boys receive relatively consistent reinforcement throughout early and middle childhood for imbibing the appropriate masculine roles and attributes. In the case of girls the change is not consistent. Das and Ghadially (1998) observed that parents with traditional sex role orientation promoted sex stereotyping among their children. Parents with non-traditional or more modern sex role orientation, on the other hand, encouraged their children to incorporate both masculine and feminine qualities. These androgynous children, the authors predicted, would be able to better adapt with the changing social order. Mother's sex role attitude was found to be associated with training for independence and need for achievement in children. Verma and Ghadially (1985a) observed that both boys and girls of mothers who support modern attitudes were high on wish and expectancy for success, compared to children of mothers who support traditional sex role attitudes. Further, they (Verma and Ghadially, 1985b) studied that modern mothers made significantly greater demands from their girls as compared to their counterparts. Thus, modern mothers encouraged their daughters to value independence early in life while stressing their care and other routine responsibilities at the same time. This early training of daughters for both achievement and motherhood sex role attitudes, explains Bharat's (1994) observation regarding the perception of Indian women in terms of both traditional and non-traditional traits by career women and their spouses.

Apart from parental characteristics, familial variables also influence sex role orientation among children. For example, Srivastava (1992) demonstrated the influence of family socio-economic status on sex role preference among boys and girls (age 3-9 year). Boys from higher socio-economic status preferred masculine items in comparison to boys from lower income groups but an inverse relationship was observed in the case of girls. The lower SES girls were more feminine than the higher SES girls. His findings point to the differential value systems with which girls and boys are raised in middle class Indian homes. Parents emphasise on early and clear-cut definitions of sex appropriate behaviour for boys—The finding was in conformity with Rao *et al.'s* (1992) observation that there is greater clarity about the typical Indian male. As for girls, parents in middle class homes desire more masculine traits for them not only because male attributes are more valued in society but also because they are closer to western culture and ethos. In the lower SES homes, rigid sex typing still prevails and hence both boys and girls express stereotyped sex preferences.

In accordance with these findings our study has also focused on the role of gender in achievement motivation and school-related outcomes. The school related outcome of boys was found higher than girls although the magnitude was not very high. Because of the changes in time, facilities and mentality of the parents gender could not strongly affect the achievement motivation of the children. In our study the achievement motivation of the girls of Xth grade has increased in comparison to their VIIIth grader counterparts.

Thus the study has confirmed the impact of cross-cultural variation, grade and gender upon achievement motivation and school related outcomes.

REFERENCES

Atkinson, W. and Litwin, G.N. (1960), Achievement Motivation, Test Anxiety and Motive to Avoid Failure, *Journal of Abnormal and Social Psychology,* 60, 52-63.

Bharat, S. (1994), Perception of Indian Women: A Comparison of Career Women. *Psychology,* 37.

Bhagat, R.S. and McQubid, S.J. (1982), Role of Subjective Culture in Organizations, A Review and Diversion for Future Research. *Journal of Applied Psychology,* 67. 653-685.

Bartal, D. and Fricze, J. (1977), Achievement Motivations for Males and Females as a Determinant of Attribution for Success and Failure. *Journal of Sex Roles.* 3, 301-313.

Dwivedi, V. (2002), "Impact of Family Climate and School Climate on Academic Stress and Stress Management in Adolescents." A Study of Open and Closed Cultures. Unpublished Ph.D. Thesis. Department of Psychology, Kumaun University Nainital.

Dhami, S. (2002), "Developmental Impact of Sex and Emotional Disturbance on Intelligence and Personality Adjustment. A Factor Analytic Study." Unpublished Ph.D. Thesis, Department of Psychology, Kumaun University Nainital.

Das, S. and Ghadially, R. (1988), Parental Sex Role Orientation and Sex Stereotypes of Children. In R. Ghadially (Ed). *Women in Indies Society: A Reader* (pp. 124-135), New Delhi: Sage.

Katz, J. (1980), A New Approach to the Study of School Motivation in Minority Groups Children. In U.L. Allan (Ed). *Psychological Factors in Poverty,* New York: Academic Press.

Misra, G. and Tripathi, L.B. (1978), *Prolonged Deprivation Scale.* Agra National Psychological Corporation.

Palaria, J.V. and Dixit, R.C. (1994), Sex Role Preferences in 3-5 Years Old Boys and Girls as a Function of Birth Order. *Indian Journal of Psychology,* 69, 71-78.

Rao, S., Gupta, G., Murthy, V.N. and B.S. Rai. (1992), An Indian Adaptation of the Bem Sex Role Inventory. *Personality Study and Group Behaviour,* 2, 1-10.

Srivastava, S. (1992), The Effect of Socio-economic Status on Sex Role Preferences of the Children. *Journal of Clinical Psychology,* 36, 59-63.

Taylor, E.B (1871), *Primitive Cultures: Research into the Development of Mythology, Philosophy, Religion and Custom.* (Vol. 1) Origins of Culture, Gloncesten, Mass: Smity.

Verma, R.K. and Ghadially, R. (1985), Effect of Mothers Sex Role Attitudes on Need for Achievement and Expectancy for Success in Children, *Psychological Studies,* 30, 1-4.

Verma, R.K. and Ghadially, R. (1986), Mothers Sex Role Attitudes and Demands for Independence Training in Boys and Girls. *The Indian Journal of Social Work,* 46, 105-111.

6

Dynamics of Educational Development of Tribal Children

Shobhna Joshi

Introduction

Education has been widely described and intensively analyzed by philosophers, educationists and social scientists for a long time. It has been a theme of continuous debate among scholars. Education has been conceived of as a process that trains people for better life and effective adjustment within a given community or social context. The present paper attempts to discuss the dynamics of educational development in the tribal community in general, and among the Kharwar of Naugarh region of UP in particular. Focusing on their cultural and socio-economic background, parents' and children's attitudes towards school education, the role of teachers in imparting education, the reasons for children's lack of interest in and drop-out from school, and parents' perception in the value of education in general, an attempt will be made to examine why education has not been able to deliver goods to the Kharwar community which inhabits villages of Naugarh region in Chandauli district of Uttar Pradesh.

The Kharwar represent a tribal group which has always been in the focus of developmental activities for a long time. The term 'tribe' is derived from Latin word "tribus", which means "a group of persons forming a community and claiming descent from a common ancestor" (Oxford English Dictionary, ix. 1993, p. 339). Over the years, the meaning of the term has been expanded to include the systems of social organization that comprises several local villages, bands, districts, lineages, or other groups sharing a common ancestry, langauge, culture and name. The process of relating groups or organizations to phenomenal growth which in the present days are referred to as "the time of tribes" (Maffassoli, 1996). In a common man's vocabulary, the term "tribal" is applied to a group of people who live a primitive life usually in remote forest and hilly areas. They have been subjected to several kinds of experiences including colonization prior to the Independence of the country, and of developmental changes after the Independence.

Historically or developmentally a tribe consists of a social group that existed before the development of, or outside of, status. Some modern theorists hold that contemporary tribes can only be understood in terms of their relationship with the states. Tribes also refer to social division within a traditional society which consists of a group of interlinked families or communities with a common culture and dialect. Current research suggests that tribal structures consist of one type of adaptation to situation providing plentiful yet unpredictable resources. Tribe is also used for all sorts of smaller units of such larger nations, people or ethnic groups. The followers of a particular local leader may also be called as a tribe. By tribe, we also mean a social or political unit, a shared religious tradition, a similar economic system, and common cultural practices and such a group found in the real world. These characteristics almost never correspond precisely with each other today, nor did they at any time in the past.

The population of different tribal groups varies enormously in our country. According to Census reports there are only six tribes that have got more than one million populations. These tribes are Bhil, Gond, Santhal, Oraon, Mina and Hunda. The Bhils, numerically the largest one among tribes in India, are found mostly in Madhya Pradesh, Maharashtra, Rajasthan and Gujarat. Gond is numerically the second largest tribe. A large population of these tribals lives in fairly remote forest and hilly areas and in isolated hamlets generally cut off from the world. The other tribes generally live as distinct groups of the population with their political and judicial systems, customs and rituals. Many of them have their distinct languages too. They engage in traditional occupations such as hunting and gathering of forest produce and rudimentary farming and remain underdeveloped economically as well as educationally. They seem to be quite happy with their own subsistence level of economy and traditional life style.

Great interest in many tribes and tribal groups around the world is emerging from remarkably diverse areas but with major difference in focus or theme. Within India, the tribal people are treated as an "outcaste" group, and the Constitution of India identifies them as 'scheduled tribes' or *'anusuchit janjati'*. Reports indicate that tribals represent the most neglected group of the Indian society (Sivanand, 2001). After several changes in their life patterns, habits and culture, the criteria to distinguish them from other groups of the population have become more difficult that the previous decades.

No development initiative should be aimed to bring about violent upheaval in the established socio-economic milieu of a community. Change is inevitable, but it should be gradual, smooth and beneficial. Therefore, socio-economic development should be pushed through the gamut of existing economy and culture of the beneficiaries. Adaptation would necessitate a new set of technology and a fresh body of knowledge. Living in a harsh environment, tribal communities exhibit a typical ideological adaptation to the nature. The dismal scenario evinced in tribal development is due to the lack of an understanding of tribal societies and culture (Behura, 1992, 1993).

The tribal communities are dispersed all over the country and differ widely from one another in their social organization, social relations, cultural patterns, attitudes and world-views. On the basis of several indicators of socio-economic development and cultural transformation in their life, tribal people have been classified in a number of ways. A dominant classification distinguishes tribals on the basis of economic activities in four distinct categories, viz., hunting-gathering group, rudimentary agricultural group, irrigation agricultural group and urban industrial wage earning group. In recent years, many people from irrigation agricultural group are engaged in business or wage employment in a variety of organizations. Such people altogether different from those tribal people who still pursue their traditional life style. They have adopted many cultural and psychological qualities with a number of other groups.

In the last decades of India's independence, the tribal society has undergone a considerable change. Education through schooling has played a vital role in this process. As a social process education has nurtured the tribal society by preparing its members to function more effectively than before. Ideally it is believed to promote a harmonious development in an individual in context of the community and culture to which he belongs. For generations, tribal people have been found concerned and satisfied their basic needs and for their economic needs they are mainly dependent on forest resources. In the absence of any formal education system, the tribal people in India had their traditional institutions for educational purposes, which catered to the needs of their culture. Such an education was usually imparted through one's family. As the smallest unit it played a very important role in the formation of personality by providing culturally meaningful and economically viable education to children.

The importance of education to bring a change, development and source of employment for tribal people was emphasized in the national plans long time ago. Since majority of the tribal population distinctly stood below the poverty line facing problems of debt, illiteracy, malnutrition and exploitation, in tribal communities, only the informal education could make its way through the processes of socialization. This kind of education was possible only through interactive learning and guided participation. This stood as a sound base for them to manage livelihood. In this context it may be noted that education can be viewed as valuable as long as it can serve a constant motivating force in socio-economic transformation of tribal society. Any kind of expected change in the tribal community has to be viewed from this perspective. For this reason, the parent's point of view is equally important as the child's point of view.

When a child becomes the part of formal education system, he/she has to coordinate and cope with a new kind of setting, which earlier was never a part of his/her life. These types of changes are difficult and challenging. The roles of male and female are well defined in their lifestyle. As the male child accustomed to grazing the cattle, the female helps her mother in cleaning house and collecting firewood from the forest. In a tribal community parents socialize their children at very early age for the management of these activities without any support from elders.

In the formal education system school plays an important role for the tribal children. Studies done on tribal children have tried to assess their performance in school settings and test settings. In studies related to school settings Singh (1996), Singh and Jayaswal (1981) have argued that low levels of parent education, occupational income and depravity characteristics at home and neighbourhoods are mainly responsible for poor performance of tribal children in the school. Research related to cognitive characteristics of tribal has received great attention as it is directly linked with the educational development of an individual. All the factors such as sociological correlates and familial correlates have been studied (Jayaswal, 1981, Jayaswal and Singh, 1978; Rath, Dash and Das, 1979; Singh, 1981) and it has been found that it is rather difficult to assess the cognitive functioning simply by assessing tribal children on the basis of school performance. A non-ethnocentric approach is required for their assessment according to their day-to-day life activities and also in relation to their eco-cultural settings (Mishra, Sinha and Berry, 1990; Sinha, 1984; Sinha and Shrestha, 1992).

Sinha and Mishra (1997) have indicated that tribal children can perform fairly well in schools if the intervention programmes directed to them. It can modify their living conditions and provide rich experiential inputs. Encouraging appropriate motivations and pattern in the parent-child interaction at home and implementation of the abilities, with which tribal children are highly suffered for educational purposes can also ensure their optimal performance in schools.

Studies conducted in tribal children to assess their performance at school as well as in test settings indicates that the cognitive abilities are relevant to their day-to-day life activities and livelihood. On the other hand, in a number of studies related to motivational patterns of Kharwars it has been found that they are confined only to the satisfaction of their primary needs, which ensure their survival. Other needs, for example, health, education, etc., are secondary, and do not occupy any prominent place in their life (Mishra and Vajpayee, 1995).

A number of studies related to personality characteristics of tribal people suggest that a number of personality variables seem to have a positive impact upon tribal education. Most of the research work related to personality has been conducted upon Tharu tribal group (Srivastava, 1991, 1992, 1993).

It is very difficult to compare that teaching style adopted for tribal children and the style that should be used for a child who lives in a different types of setting. In tribal life the child does not have a fixed routine, because he/she is primarily oriented towards making livelihood. Kharwar children neither have money to spend on educational materials, nor do they have literate parents to give them formal education at home. In schools also, frequent absence of teachers for considerable periods of time and lack of guidance make the child's future uncertain. Education as an agency (media) of cultural change like urbanization and industrialization can affect the CHANGE in the tribal way of life at three levels, (i) changes which are already occurring in their ethos, (ii) changes which are in the process, and (iii) changes which are set for the future.

The teacher is the most important person in the whole system of education. Non-tribal teacher in the community of tribal people exploits the simplicity of tribal people. A teacher who does not know the tribal language cannot engage into effective communication with tribal children.

Course curriculum/content is another important factor related with education for the tribal child. The curriculum prescribed for tribal children is the same as for children of the general population. Such a curriculum appears meaningless in the context of Kharwar life because it tells them nothing that is useful for their life. Curriculum, school schedule, teachers, and their teaching skills need an adjustment according to the local contexts. Tribal parents cannot presume that the need of education of their children could become the part of their occupation in future. It is also difficult to convince them that education would serve their needs of livelihood. Tribal culture satisfies tribal instinct in a way that it provides a dependable environment for all members. Schools are not socially and culturally neutral. Rules which describe human interaction in a tribal setting do not include language, dress, ethical values, life philosophy, family structure, etc. Education is a base for cultural modification and knowledge. Carrying on this principle, the growth of a new culture could be made possible. Hence, the educational principle environment should not be restrictive or biased in any direction.

The Kharwar

The word 'Kharwar' has been used in two different ways. In one respect it refers to a group of people whose origin is traced in the Palamau region of Bihar. In another respect, Kharwar refers to a group of people who earlier used to reside in Sone valley, and in the course of time, migrated to many places. The Kharwars of Naugarh claim their origin from Palamau. They are of Dravidian origin and dependent on agriculture. Raja Harishchandra is known as the ancestor of this tribe. They are of dark complexion and normal structure and they do not have their own language.

The Kharwar villages of Naugarh region are situated within the radius of 10-25 kms. from the Naugarh block head quarter. Their villages also have the populations of Yadav and Harijan groups; however, the Kharwars are in majority compared to Yadavs and Harijans almost in all villages. The families of Kharwars are generally located in the middle of the village, while the families of Harijans are scattered on outskirts of the village. Due to a hilly landscape it is characterized by acute shortage of water, people of these villages earn their livelihood from jungle resources largely through the collection of *tendu patta* (leaves used for making *Bidi* or indigenous cigarettes). Due to the seasonal nature of work, little land and lack of education the Kharwars of Naugarh region live in extremely poor conditions. During the summer and early monsoon seasons, they do not have enough to feed their families.

Kharwars consider themselves as tribal, but they are not considered so by the State Government. They are classified as "scheduled castes" in the government records. Despite being declared as scheduled castes, they have great concerns for untouchability. They do not accept food or water offered by Musahars or harijans, who inhabit the same villages. This feelings is reinforced by the fact that they consider themselves as Kshatriyas and claim to belong to the Suryavanshi Rajput. They nurture a strong identity of a tribal.

The total population of Kharwars is about 61,692, which is spread in Deoria, Ballia, Gazipur, Varanasi (Chandauli) and Sonbhadra districts (Census of India, 1991). The state government has not paid much attention to Kharwars, and even today they are deprived of many advantages available to other tribal communities. Kharwars life is very simple. They have mud houses. The projected areas of roofs are covered with carvings. They use straw with mud in the construction of the house which prevents the houses from cracking. The village head man is known as *mahto.* Hunting and gathering forest products are pursued as a substantial part of economic activity. Forest provides them with timber wood, herbal medicines and firewood. Children equally participate with their parents in forest based activities. Rice is their main agricultural produce.

Education of Kharwar Children

In order to understand the dynamics of educational development among Kharwars, it is necessary to examine how education has been related to the development of tribal communities in general. It should be noted that education for tribals has become a matter of great concern today. A large amount of money has been spent on the education of tribal people, especially of those who are underdeveloped and neglected. Studies indicate that the educational condition of tribal children is highly discouraging (Sinha and Mishra, 1997). The condition of Kharwar group is more pathetic than many other groups. The pressures on day-to-day economy are so strong that there is hardly time to consider any other aspects of life. Preparing them for education and arranging educational facilities has been a challenging task for all those who have shown concern to the development of Kharwar people of Naugarh region. Lack of motivation is responsible for low level of literacy among them. Schools in backward tribal areas are mostly neglected, and the standard of teaching is deplorable. In spite of the school facility now made available in villages, the number of school going children is fairly low, although in almost every village, one can easily notice slogans of education written on the walls of the house. These slogans may be taken as indicators of the efforts made by government and non-government sectors with respect to the education of Kharwar children. As a result of these initiatives, many families have started sending their children to schools. The number of schools are very few and the condition of schools is also not good. There is very little space for holding classes, and the strength of teachers is inadequate. Sometimes a single teacher has to manage four to five class rooms. The poor quality of education in schools hamper their masses adversely and affects the employment prospects in a long-run.

Survey reports indicate that Kharwars have very good knowledge about forest and its products. They are also known as wise veterinarians beside farmers. An average Kharwar seems to have knowledge of about 80-90 plants along with their usages. Some aged

Kharwars have excellent knowledge of herbs that carry great medicinal value.

Dynamics of Kharwar Education

Researchers in the field of education believe that education of any group, whether tribal or non-tribal takes place through the interaction between an individual and the society. It plays a vital role in shaping the life style of individuals. It could also play the role of a catalyst for socio-economic transformation. Education is viewed as a group process by which knowledge store in a culture is transmitted from one generation to another. It has a great bearing in social structure, modes of living, thoughts, behaviour patterns and personality of an individual. It is the most powerful tool in shaping one's future. Education creates trends in the society to prepare future generations for change. On one hand, it imparts specific knowledge and develops general reasoning skills (called cognitive effect), on the other hand it also induces changes in beliefs, values and attitudes towards work and society (called non-cognitive effects). Economic growth can be accelerated by investing more and more in education. It could also be viewed as an experience, which prepares individuals through the process of learning to take many social responsibilities as adults in a society. The main aim of education is to present, transfer and enrich culture. It emerges as an instrument to bring social transformation. The entire culture including values, norms, ideas, beliefs, customs, skills and techniques, etc., is transmitted through education from one generation to another.

There are many maladies of the education in the Kharwars at the Naugarh region. The absence of schools is one of them. Not many schools are available for the education of children in this region. Those, which are there, remain generally closed because of the absence of teachers who often go to their homes for personal work and engagement in agriculture. The Kharwar children also do not like non-tribal teachers because they belong to different community and have no understanding of tribal language and culture. Firstly, for the teacher it becomes difficult to adapt in the tribal cultural setting. Secondly, they have to travel long for teaching for which there are no arrangements. Language is also one of the important barriers in the teaching of tribal children, who are confined largely to their mother tongue.

Another important reason for the failure of Kharwar children is the poor socio-economic condition of their family and inability to afford the cost of education. The home conditions of a majority of children are not congenial for schooling. In the absence of pre-school educational experience, they are not able to cope with the demands of education. School timing is another big factor. It overlaps with their economic activities, such as cultivation or forest activities. Majority of the families are poor. They possess meagre resources, and are largely dependent on forest produce and agriculture and part-time wages. Subsistence level of economy, accessibility of good educational institutions, communication barriers, lack of committed teachers, culturally meaningless school curriculum, and lack of proper facilities are some of the factors responsible for poor enrolment and heavy drop-out rate of Kharwar children from school. That is why there are many difficulties in the promotion of education in the Kharwar community. Girls help their mothers in almost all possible ways in household activities, whereas during agricultural season, the boys work in the fields with their parents. The male children pick up the general duties performed by males in the family, whereas female children pick up the roles and responsibilities of female members of the family. For example, the male child gets involved in cattle grazing, whereas the female child helps her mother in cleaning house and collecting firewood from the forest. Many parents also have a latent fear that school attendance may weaken their tribal cultural identity. This serves as another negative factor in child education in the Kharwar community.

Certain physical conditions also serve as barriers. The village school buildings are very poor. There is hardly any furniture. There are only one-room schools to manage teaching of five classes. In some residential schools the children are provided with free boarding, lodging, clothes and stationery but this type of schooling puts tribal children so apart from non-tribal children that they miss the opportunity of interaction and learning from them. This separation also culminates into poor adjustment of Kharwar children with other groups of children. Later the adjustment between them become difficult. Tribal parents do not seem to link children's education with their occupational expectations.

Thus, any planning for Kharwar children's education calls for a number of considerations. Some of them are listed below. The list can be made exhaustive by adding many more.

Adjustment with Teachers and Schools Schedule

While recruiting the teachers, attempts should be made to recruit more teachers from tribal community. As far as possible, teachers should be posted in the schools which are nearer to their village, and the school schedule of the children must be able to accommodate their economic activities.

Adjustment with Teaching and Adequate Number of Teachers

The teachers should belong to tribal community. If they are from the non-tribal community, they must have adequate knowledge of the tribal community. There should be adequate number of teachers in the school so that proper attention could be given to the students. The tribal teachers should be given proper incentives for motivating tribal children and their families about education.

Educational Background of Family

The background of family is also important for educational process. We know that most of the Kharwar families are illiterate. If a brighter future of the child, family and community could be displayed in their minds through counselling and also through incentives, they would feel tempted to send their child to schools.

Curriculum

Curriculum is very important issue in the education of tribal children. Culturally sensitive programme are important for the education of tribal children so that they can have economically viable options in their life (Sinha and Mishra, 1997). Dave (1997) has suggested for serious research in this regard.

Language

Language is the most important medium of communication. Studies indicates that a tribal child spends a lot of energy in learning school langauge. In view of this, some researchers (Mohanty, 1994; Mohanty and Perregaux, 1997) have emphasized bilingualism in the education of tribal children in general.

Family Economic Conditions

Family's economic condition depend entirely on the source of family's income. Expenditure of money by person on education of children indicates that he is able to fulfil their basic needs. It is expected that with optimal economic conditions even uneducated parents will encourage their children to attend schools.

Attitude Towards Education and Tuition Facility

Need-based education should be facilitated. Teacher has always been a motivating factor in the education of tribal children. Tuition facilities may also attract more Kharwar children to schools. Such an approach is likely to facilitate educational processes in Kharwar children.

Conclusions

The eco-cultural settings of the tribal children have generally been ignored in designing educational plans for them. It is an essential aspect that needs a careful attention in any discussion of the barriers of Kharwar education. Adoption of a culture-specific approach would go a long way in educating Kharwar children.

Study reveals that the literacy among the tribal population in general is very low as compared to the general population. The drop-out among tribal children has been found to be the highest. This appears to be largely a motivational problem. Hence, tribals need to be motivated properly to participate in educational programmes in order to derive its fruitful results. More effort is needed to strengthen school facilities in the tribal areas. Since, the teacher plays a key role in imparting education to these children, ensuring his motivation and regularity can reduce the dropout rate of tribal students.

As far as the education of Kharwar tribal children is concerned, few important points need special consideration.

(1) Community awareness is very important for which they should be sensitized. Their participation in developmental activities related to the educational programmes should be encouraged at all levels.

(2) Readiness of family is another important domain to deal with. Families will have to come forward for not only taking decisions for their children's education, but also for providing them with education in such a manner so that their future could be safe.

(3) Child's preparedness is a must from every point of view. Children should be trained in such a manner that they should their willingness to participate in each kind of programme associated with education. In this context the fulfilment of their economic needs will have to be ensured.

(4) Teacher's motivation, involvement and commitment are key factors for tribal education. Therefore, it may be a good exercise to consider their views about various aspects of children's education. Questions pertaining to need of better living, search for better economic prospects, satisfaction in the present living conditions, satisfaction with the existing system of education and curriculum, etc., may provide deep insight into the dynamics of Kharwar education.

Use of mother tongue as school language, cultural tailoring of syllabus/curriculum in tune with the demands of the life of Kharwar children, dissemination of education through the use of stories and video film, etc., are likely to add to the interest of children in school education. There is an urgent need to reflect on what has been accomplished so far in the direction of Kharwar children's education. Seasonal nature of economic activities, children's participation in those activities, low land holdings of families, and a general lack of education in Kharwar villaers leave enough scope for planning for education of the community.

Much has been said about improvement of socio-economic condition of Kharwar people to encourage educational processes in the community. It seems that their education needs to be oriented to accommodate their agricultural patterns. Teachers can make a valuable contribution in this respect by attempting an integration of education with agricultural and other developmental needs of Kharwar children. These measures will promote education in the community at large and contribute to its overall well-being.

The major findings of a research on Kharwar Tribals by Mishra and Joshi (2001), also suggest that the life of Kharwar seems very much concerned with the survival needs (e.g., food, water and money). It is highly desirable now to explore the cultural and parental factors which could best explain the different educational barriers of tribals in general and Kharwars in particular.

The important question arises here that can we compare Kharwars with general tribal. The major problems related with tribal people is the socio-economic status, literacy, education, health etc. which are more or less the same. If the problems of one type-sample of tribe could be explored deeply from different perspective then it would become much easier to investigate the other important problems of the tribal community as a whole.

Long time ago Nehru (1965) had said, "The people of the tribal areas and the hills attract me greatly and deserve our very special care. I am anxious that they should not lose their artistry and joy in life and the culture that distinguish them in many ways. I am not at all sure which is the better way of living, the tribal or our own. In some respects I am quite certain theirs in better. Therefore, it is grossly presumptuous on our parts to approach them with an air of superiority, to tell them how to behave or what to do and what not to do. There is no point in tying to make how to behave or what to do and what not to do. There is no point in tying to make of them a second rate copy of ourselves". It is rather unfortunate that the vision of our great leader has yet remained largely unfulfilled during the last four decades of our concerted efforts to educate tribal people.

Acknowledgements

The author is grateful for the constant encouragement and critical review of the manuscript by Prof. R.C. Mishra, Department of Psychology, Banaras Hindu University, Varanasi.

REFERENCES

Census of India, (1991), www.census.india map.net. www.education.nic.in.

Dave, P.N. (1997), Primary Education in National Council of Educational Research and Training (Ed.), *Fifth Survey of Educational Research,* Vol. 1 (pp. 273-312). New Delhi: NCERT.

Department of Women and Child Developments, Ministry of HRD. (2002). *The Indian Child: A Profile.*

Jayaswal, M. and Singh, A.K. (1978), Parental Attitudes and Behaviour, and Academic Achievement in Tribal School Students. *Indian Journal of Psychiatric Social Work,* 8, 1-7.

Jayswal, M. (1981), Familial Correlates of Academic Achievement in Tribal School Students. Unpublished doctoral thesis, Ranchi University.

Maffasoli, M. (1996), *The Time of the Tribes.* Thousand Oaks: Sage.

Mishra, R.C., Sinha, D. and Berry, J.W. (1990), 'Some Aspect of Cognitive Functioning of Birhor and Oraon Children in Relation to Acculturation'. Paper presented at the 10th IACCP Congress, Nara, Japan.

Mishra, R.C. and Vajpaee, A. (1995), 'Mental Health Problems of Women in Changing Community', unpublished manuscript, Department of Psychology, Banaras Hindu University.

Mishra, R.C. (1996), 'Cognitive Process, Cultural Adaptations and Education of Children of Some Tribal Groups'. Project Report, New Delhi, National Council of Education Research and Training.

Mishra, R.C., Sinha, D. and Berry, J.W. (1996), *Ecology, Acculturation and Psychological Adaptation: A Study of Adivasis in Bihar.* New Delhi: Sage.

Mishra, R.C. (1999), Research Education in India, *Prospects,* 29, 335-347.

Mishra, R.C. and Joshi, S. (2001). 'Some Psychological Barrier to the Education of Kharwar Children of the Naugarh Region'. Unpublished Report. Deptt. of Psychology, Banaras Hindu University.

Mohanty, A.K. (1994), 'Bilingualism in a Multilingual Society: Implication for Cultural Integration and Education'. Keynote address at the International Congress of Psychology, Madrid, Spain.

Mohanty, A.K., Perregaux, C. (1997), Language acquisition and Bilingualism. In J.W. Berry, P.R. Dasen and T.S. Saraswati (Eds.), *Handbook of Cross-Cultural Psychology,* Vol. 2 (pp. 217-254). Boston: Allyn and Bacon.

Nehru, J.L. (1965), Adibasi. *Journal of the Scheduled Castes and Scheduled Tribes,* No. 2. *Psychological Adaptation: A Study of Adivasi in Bihar,* New Delhi: Sage.

Rath, R., Dash, A.S. and Das, U.N. (1979), *Cognitive Abilities and School Achievements of Socially Disadvantaged Children in Primary Schools.* Bombay: Allied.

Singh, A.K. (1981), 'Poverty and Prejudice in India; God that Failed', Paper presented at the National Seminar on Psychology in Indian Context, CAS in Psychology in Indian Context, Utkal University.

Singh, A.K. and Jayaswal, M. (1981), Correlates of Scholastic Achievement in Socially Disadvantaged Students. *Social Change,* 11, 23-28.

Singh, A.K. (1996), "Improving the Educational Status of the Tribal in India", Paper presented at the National Seminar on Research in Tribal Education, National Institute of Educational Planning Administration, New Delhi.

Sinha, D. (1977), Social Disadvantages and Development of Certain Perceptual Skills. *Indian Journal of Psychology,* 52, 115-132.

Sinha, D. (1984), *Mannual for Story—Pictorial E.F.T. and INDO-African E.F.T.* Varanasi: Rupa.

Sinha, D. and Shrestha, A.B. (1992). Eco-Cultural Factors in Cognitive Style among Children from Hills and Plains of Nepal. *Internatinal Journal of Psychology,* 27, 49-59.

Sinha, D. and Mishra, R.C. (1997), Some Personality, Motivational and Cognitive Characteristics of Tribal and Their Implications for Educational Development of Children. *Journal of Education Planning and Administration,* 11, 283-295.

South Asian Human Right Documentation Centre. (September 2001), *Racial Discrimination: The Record of India,* New Delhi.

Srivanand, M. (2001), The Good Doctors of Sittilingi. *Reader's Digest,* 159, 110-117.

Srivastava, R.K. (1991), 'Cross-Cultural Comparisons of Tribal and Non-Tribal Adolescent's Perception of Maternal Behaviour', Paper presented at teh 78th sessions of the Indian Science Congress, Indore.

Srivastava, R.K. (1992), 'Acculturation and Perceived Socialisation Practices: Evidence from Tharu Tribe'. Paper presented at the 79th Session of the Indian Science Congress, Varodara.

Srivastava, R.K. (1993), 'Cultural Contexts and Identity Styles'. Paper presented at the 80th session of the Indian Science Congress, Panaji.

Tribe (1933). (Lower tribus, originally, a third part of the Roman people, afterwards, a division of the people, a tribe; of uncertain origin: cf. F. tribu). *Oxford English Dictionary,* IX, pp. 339.

7

Contextual Factors in Memory

Yogesh Kumar Arya

Introduction

The existence of human beings depends on their ability to retain a large variety of information and experiences, which help them in making adjustment with day-to-day life. This ability is termed as memory. It is one of the important cognitive processes centralised to all other cognitive processes. Psychologists have studied memory for over hundred years. Within this field, the area of eyewitness memory has received a great deal of attention in the last three decade. Researchers working in the area of real life memory adopt an accuracy-oriented approach. This approach concerns with the correspondence between recalled events and actual events that have been personally experienced by an individual. Researchers have mainly concentrated on eyewitness testimony because of its significance in legal processes. Issues related to eyewitness testimony have been an important concerns for police officers, judges, lawyers, and other members of the judicial systems who utilize witnesses' memory in legal processes. Eyewitness testimony is different from eyewitness memory in the sense that the former is conducted within the framework of judicial processes, while the latter represents a large segment of episodic memory. Another difference is that eyewitness memory is directly concerned with understanding of essential features of episodic memory and includes eyewitness identification and eyewitness testimony.

Eyewitness memory refers to the memory of other's action, or the recollection of events that have been personally witnessed either as a victim or as a bystander. It provides an incredible useful tool for people associated with judicial system and police. Memory can store unlimited information over a period of life time and has an ability to reconstruct past experiences as if they are recently experienced. However, recent studies shows that it is also prone to contaminate from various sources, which lead to memory distortions or false memories (Brainerd and Reyna, 2002; Lindsay, Allen, Chan and Dahl, 2004; Loftus, Miller and Burns, 1978; Schacter, 1996). A false memory or "memory illusion" is a mental experience that is believed to be a veridical representation of a personally experienced event (Lindsay and Johnson, 2000). Eyewitness memory has gained attention because of the fact that recollection of personally experienced events has very little correspondence with the original event due to a number of factors. An extensive body of literature supports the hypothesis that eyewitness memory is often inaccurate (Christianson, 1989; McCloskey, Wible and Cohen, 1988; Neisser, 1982; Wagenaar and Groeneweg, 1990). Neither emotionality nor vividness provides any guarantee of memory accuracy.

Among numerous important issues of eyewitness testimony, the memory reliability of the witness has been the most important issue. The question is how and why the witness recalls incorrect information. In other words, the eyewitness memory research emphasizes on the underlying mechanisms and factors, which threaten the accuracy of eyewitness memory. Factors affecting eyewitness memory are classified broadly in two categories, *system variables* and *estimator variables.* System variables are factors that are under the direct control of the justice system. These include—(a) line up identification procedure in which a criminal suspect or a picture of the suspect is shown with pictures of other people and the eyewitness is asked to identify the suspect as the culprit, (b) post-event information which is considered to be a part of system variable when the information comes from an interview during judicial process, (c) time delay which occurs due to the judicial process, (d) type of questioning (open ended or forced choice) during the judicial process, (e) repeated questioning which exploits the suggestibility of a witness. Estimator variables, on the other hand, are factors over which the justice system exerts little or no control. These variables include—(a) characteristics of the offender, such as sex, appearance, disguise, and clothing, (b) characteristics of the victim or bystander, such as age, sex, stress, mood, anxiety, suggestibility and personality, (c) characteristics of the event, such as the period or span of time the culprit is in view, the lighting conditions, whether the culprit wears a disguise, the distinctiveness of the culprit's appearance, the presence or absence of a weapon, afective aspect of the event, and the timing of knowledge that one is witnessing a crime. This paper focuses mainly on factors which provide a context that lead to inaccuracy to recall events that are personally experienced or witnessed.

Eyewitness Memory and the Context

Tulving and Thomson's (1973) theory of encoding specificity specifies that overlapping contextual features present at the time of encoding and retrieval can facilitate recall of an event by activating the related parts of memory representation and by providing additional retrieval cues. By presenting the time of retrieval the physical context cues that had been presented at the time of encoding, memory can be facilitated (Salmon, Bidrose, and Pipe, 1995). A number of studies on improving eyewitness' memory have emphasized on reinstatement of the environmental context surrounding an event (e.g. Eich, 1985; Godden and Baddeley, 1975, 1980; Memon, Wark, Holley, Bull and Koehnken, 1997; Parker, Gellatley and Waterman, 1999). Researchers believe that contextual stimuli can provide cues to episodic memory. Context effect is so strong that it triggers memories of remote past, sometimes even children memories, which have not been recollected for many years. Sometimes individuals report that language abilities left unused for many years have returned when they came back to their old environment after a long period of time. This phenomenon has been termed as "context-dependent-memory". Every event takes place in a context, which operates in the encoding and recollection of the event. Contextual stimuli not only facilitate encoding and recollection of an event, but they also inhibit or distort the content of an event being encoded or recalled. Studies focused on factors, which provide strong influential context have revealed that context can distort information at the time of encoding or at the time of recall of an episode (Loftus and Palmer, 1974; Loftus, 1992; Loftus *et al.* 1978; Glibling and Davis, 1988; Loftus, 1975). Several conditions can affect the magnitude of context effect on recollection of an episode, such as confidence of the witness, retention interval, central *versus* peripheral details, etc. Context also affects the face recognition, for example, own race bias, gender and similarity between target face and otehr faces in the lineup identification. Several other contextual factors, such as the way the questions are raised in the interview, can have a profound impact on eyewitness memory and can at times lead to eyewitness "suggestibility" (e.g., Loftus *et al.* 1978; Loftus and Palmer, 1974).

Misinformation as a Context

Witnesses' memory has been the source of important information about the criminal act in the court room trials. However, the reliability of the witnesses' memory is questioned. Recent research substantiates the view that recollecting an episode in the misinformation context, which is not compatible with the original event, leads to distortion in memory. Consequently, eyewitnesses are likely to make unintentional false reports. Earlier studies (Loftus, 1979a) on the contaminating effects of misleading post-event information (MPI) have led several researchers to focus their attention on the accuracy of recalled event and reconstructive nature of episodic memory. In a classical study conducted by Loftus and Palmer (1974), 195 students viewed clippings of films of automobile accidents and then answered questions about events occurring in the films. The question, "about how fast did the cars run when they smashed each other?" elicited higher estimates of speed than questions which used verbs like "collided", "bumped", "contacted", or "hit" in place of "smashed". After a week, all students were asked the question, "Did you see any broken glass?" Subjects who received the word "smashed" were more likely to say "yes" to the question, although the broken glass was not present in the film. The result supported the view that the context of subsequent question can lead to reconstruction of memory for an event.

In a series of studies Loftus *et al.* (1978) exposed subjects to consistency, misleading, or irrelevant information after the accidental event. It was found that the misleading information produced less accurate responses in both a Yes-No and a two-alternative forced-choice recognition test. It was also found that the misleading information was greater if introduced just prior to a final test rather than immediately after the initial event. In many other studies it has been found that, after exposure to misinformation, subjects have been reported having seen a variety of non-existent objects, such as yield signs (Loftus *et al.,* 1978), hammers (Glibling and Davies, 1988), and even something as large as a barn (Loftus, 1975).

These studies suggest that misinformation can distort the accuracy of eyewitness testimony and report of actual event. McClosky and Zaragoza (1985) argued that misleading information did not distort memory, distortion occurred due to lack of subjects' confidence about their memory. The effect of misinformation context is not similar in all conditions. It has been found that misinformation effect is stronger in peripheral details than with central details (Cassel and Bjorklund, 1995; Heath and Erickson, 1998), when retention interval is longer (Belli, Windschitl, McCarthy and Winfrey, 1992; Higham, 1998), when the misleading information is prosecuted in context of a statement (Zaragoza and Lane, 1994), and when the question is persecuted in a presupposition format ("what was the colour of the...") (Fiedler, Walther, Armbruster, Fay and Naumann, 1996) rather than in an open format. Many researchers have contended that false information during the interval plays an important role in the distortion process (Jankins and Davis, 1985). Distortion of recalled information by misleading post-event information is affected by several other factors among which the suggestibility of the subject is the one. Studies have shown that more suggestible participants are more likely to be affected by misleading information in eyewitness memory task. It is also found that induction of anxious mood reduces the suggestibility in misinformed group (Ridley and Clifford, 2004). Burgess (2000) examined the effect of positive and negative mood on children's memory and suggestibility. The results revealed that children were less suggestible to leading questions when happy than when angry or sad, particularly when they attempted to recall information concerning the outcomes and consequences described in the stories. Comparison between angry and sad children indicated that sadness was associated with greater suggestibility for all types of story information except consequences. In addition, elder children were found to be less suggestible and showed better overall performance in most types of story information, than younger children.

In another study Frost, Ingraham and Wilson (2002) investigated stubjects' memory for the source of misinformation at different retention intervals. The results showed that after the longer retention interval, participants were more likely to agree that they had seen misleading information and were also more likely to associate the misinformation with the event incorrectly. These findings were also supported by the findings obtained by Mudd and Govern (2004), who showed a video clip to the participants. After viewing the clip the subjects interacted with the confederate who either introduced misinformation about the video or introduced unrelated information. Participants' memories were tested immediately after the video show. The confederates were interacted again after 2 weeks. The results showed that the misinformation provided by the confederate was incorporated into participants' memories, and this effect increased its magnitude over time. Participants exposed to misinformation became more confident of their memories in the period of 2-weeks, participants in the control condition became less confident over this interval.

A number of explanations have been given for suggestibility effect. According to "alteration hypothesis" (Loftus, 1979), misleading postevent information changes the trace of original memory (Belli, Lindsay, Gales and McCarthy, 1994; Loftus, 1977, 1979; Tversky and Tuchin, 1989), which leads to memory distortion. "Coexistence hypothesis", however, suggests that original information and misleading information coexist independently in the memory, but the misleading information is more accessible (Christiansen and Ochalek, 1983). The factors that make misleading information more accessible are not very clear and needed to be studied.

Both alteration and coexistence hypothesis suggest that misleading information leads to memory impairment of some sort. The memory "impairment hypothesis" states that misinformation can either alter or make less accessible to the original memory of the event. This hypothesis is supported by a number of experimental studies (Loftus, 1975); Loftus *et al.,* 1978; Loftus and Palmer, 1974). This hypothesis remained accepted for several years until McCloskey and Zaragoza (1985) criticized the memory impairment hypothesis. They argued that misinformation effect found in earlier studies was due to misinformation acceptance. That is, in the absence of memory for event item due to ordinary (non-impairment) mechanisms, subjects accept the possibility that post-event item may have been shown during the event show (Rubin, 1996).

In a later study, however, Tversky and Tuchin (1989) used modification for the recognition test ("Yes"/"No" instead of forced choice as in earlier studies) and obtained evidence for impairment hypothesis. They found that misleading information distorted the memory for original information.

Schema and Memory

Almost all cognitive processes take place in an influential context of generic knowledge structures or expectancies that are developed through experience. These general knowledge structure of expectancies are called schema. It has been used as the most general framework to explain a wide array of issues concerning the accuracy and distortion of memory. Schemas have been shown to affect the correspondence between the input and remembered material in a variety of ways at different stages of the memory process. Schema theory holds that people's recall is the outcome of an interaction between the input information and pre-existing schemas. Alba and Hasher (1983) identified schema processes such as selection, abstraction, interpretation, and integration, which affect memory process during encoding and reconstruction. Most of these schema processes are concerned with the ways in which memory could go wrong.

Selection is a kind of effect that concerns the amount of remembered information rather than its accuracy. Selection refers to the process in which information consistent with the active schema is more likely to be assimilated and recalled than schema-irrelevant information. That is, when there is no relevant activated schema or background knowledge is available at the time of encoding, information is encoded less efficiently and is less like to be recalled (e.g. Bransford and Johnson, 1972). Also, information that is more central to an activated schema will be recalled better than information that is less central (e.g., Johnson, 1970). However, the opposite has also been reported. For example, Davidson (1994) found that inconsistent information is often remembered better than schema-consistent information.

Abstraction is another kind of effect concerned with the amount of remembered information. It refers to the process in which semantic content or gist of textual messages are encoded and remembered better rather than their verbatim format. This effect reduces the amount of encoded and remembered information. These effects can lead to errors and distortion in recalled information. When subject are asked to recall details that are not available in the schematic representation, they may try to reconstruct the missing details using schema-based inference processes at the time of remembering (Bartlett, 1932; Neisser, 1967). The process of reconstruction replaces the original information about an event from the schema, leading to errors or schema-consistent distortions.

Unlike selection and abstraction, interpretation effects involve actual changes and addition to the input information during encoding. Activated schematic knowledge is used to make inferences and suppositions that go beyond the actual input event, which then becomes incorporated as a part of the event's memory representation (Johnson, Bransford and Solomon, 1973; Dooling and Cristiaansen, 1977).

Integration effects result when various pieces of information are combined into a unified schematic whole either during or after the initial encoding. Integration increases misinformation effect and leads to inaccuracies in recalled information.

Mood and Emotions as Context

Mood of the person at the time of encoding and recall provides a strong physiological context and has profound effect on remembering past experience. Current moods and emotions also have strong effects on perception and thought (Forgas and Bower, 1987; Forgas, Bower and Moylan, 1990). Mood is similar to emotion in all respects; except that it is long term in nature. There has been considerable research on how one's emotional feelings affect acquisition or recall of information. Two phenomena related to this issue have been studied extensively. One is "mood state-dependent effect" and the other is the "mood congruence effect" (Blaney, 1986; Ellis and Ashbrook, 1989).

Mood State-Dependent Effect

Mood state-dependent effect suggests that memory is enhanced when there is a match between individual's mood state at the time of encoding and at the time of retrieval, but memory is impaired if there is a mismatch between the mood at the time of encoding and retrieval (Leight and Ellis, 1981). State-dependent effect assumes that mood acts as a critical context cue, irrespective of the nature of material to be learned or recalled. A number of studies have clearly indicated mood state-dependent effect (Blaney, 1986; Bower, 1981; Ellis and Ashbrook, 1989; Kuiken, 1989; Ucros, 1989). On the other hand, some studies have failed to replicate mood state-dependent effect (Bower and Mayer, 1985, 1989). The contradiction in the results may be due to the possibility that mood acts as relatively weak cue for learning and retrieving neutral information. Mood state-dependent effect should be more likely when mood is integrated with to-be-remembered information (Gage and Safer, 1985; Bower, 1987, 1992; Eich and Metcalfe, 1989). In autobiographical memory, the to-be-remembered information naturally causes the rememberer to feel a pleasant or unpleasant emotion. In this case, mood state-dependent and mood congruent effects are combined (Bower, 1987).

Eyewitness Memory as State-Dependent Memory

Eyewitness memory, particularly for traumatic criminal events, is assumed to be state-dependent as these events induce a state of mild to intense emotional as way in the victim or bystander. Janet (1989, 1993) has argued that memories for these events are highly state-dependent and cannot be evoked at will. Being state-dependent, these memories are difficult to be retrieved in ordinary circumstances (non-emotional situations). In most of these cases traumatic events are recalled under ordinary circumstances, either in a legal setting or in a lab setting. These settings do not provide actual physical or physiological state which result in low correspondence between actual and recalled traumatic events. Whitfield (1995) has argued that state dependence "is usual" (p. 45) in traumatic amnesia, and that "getting back into the original state can appear to be a catalyst to recalling an otherwise forgotten event or experience" (p. 46). Similarly, Van der Kolk, and Fisler, (1995) have asserted that "recall is triggered by exposure to sensory or affective stimuli that match sensory or affective elements associated with the trauma" (p. 509). So far there is no evidence that memory for traumatic event is state dependent. It is perhaps, difficult to induce the same affective state in the individual that had been present at the time of original traumatic event.

Mood Congruence Effect

Mood congruent effect suggests that information is better acquired or recalled if the information itself is congruent with the current affective state at acquisition or recall. Thus, the information which is congruent or matches in the affective tone with the current mood of the individual is processed more efficiently than incongruent information (Bower, 1981; Nasby and Yando, 1982). Fiedler and Stroehm (1986) suggest that in sad mood there is a tendency to recall sad events even though these events have been experienced during happy mood. It suggests that mood evokes memories consistent with current mood. A number of studies suggest that current mood can produce selective retrieval of mood-congruent memories (Blaney, 1986; Eich, 1989). Recall is facilitated by the exposure to sensory or affective stimuli that match sensory or affective element associated with the trauma. Thus, the content of an event would be more accurate if it matches with the mood state of the witness at the time of retrieval. Conversely, inaccuracies are likely if there is mismatch between the current mood of the witness and the affective nature of content of the event to be recalled.

Emotional Arousal and Memory

Emotional arousal provoked by ongoing traumatic event provides an influential context that has profound effects on the way in which the ongoing event is encoded. Traumatic memories are encoded differently than other personal events. These memories are initially imprinted as sensations or feeling states that are not immediately transcribed into personal narratives due to lack of a coherent semantic component. Consequently, individual finds it difficult to recollect these memories as verbal narratives.

Terr (1994), Van der Kolk and Fisler (1995) and McGaugh (1992) agree that memories of traumatic event are encoded by processes, such as repression and dissociation that make them difficult to retrieve as coherent, verbal narratives. The result is that traumatic memories are primarily available as isolated, non-verbal, sensory, motor, and emotional fragments. Despite a number of researches on the effect of arousal on memory, there remains a considerable controversy concerning the effects of arousal. One view posits and increased arousal and fear will facilitate subsequent recognition because this arousal will lead to a permanent memory for the event. This view has been supported by a number of studies concerning eyewitness memory that have ascertained that a high level of arousal enhances memory (Burke, Heuer and Reisberg, 1992; Yuille and Cutshall, 1986; Yuille and Tollestrue, 1992).

On the other hand, recent research demonstrates that the high levels of arousal that are induced in the laboratory can interfere with later recognition (Christianson and Hubinette, 1993; Christianson and Loftus, 1987, 1991; Christianson and Nilson, 1984; Leweis and White, 1997; Wessel and Merckelbach, 1998). Arousal also causes attention to be focused on a particular aspect of the ongoing event while ignoring its other important aspects. This "narrowing of attention" phenomenon has been demonstrated in a number of studies. For example, phenomena of "weapon focusing", that demonstrates that certain critical stressful objects, (e.g., a gun or a knife) being used in crime, can capture people's attention, and thus promote memory for the weapon at the cost of other details in the event (Cutler, Penrod and Martens, 1987a; Kramer, Buckhout and Eugenio, 1990; Loftus, Loftus and Messo, 1987; Maass and Kohnken, 1989).

This interference effect has also been established in "weapon focus" literature (Brigham, 1990; Cutler, *et al.*, 1987b; Cutler, Penrod, O'Rourke and Martens, 1986; Loftus, *et al.*, 1987; Narby, Cutler and Penrod, 1996; Stebley, 1992), and the memory of concentration camp survivors (Wagenaar and Groeneweg, 1990). A number of studies have found that arousal has an adverse effect on memory for details (e.g., Clifford and Hollin, 1981; Clifford and Scott, 1978; Deffenbacher, 1983; Loftus and Burns, 1982). Loftus and Burn (1982) showed high and low arousing versions of a video clip depicting a bank robbery to their subjects. They found that the subjects who had seen the low arousing version remembered more detail in both recognition and recall memory test than the subjects who were shown high arousing version of the video clip. Few studies, on the otherhand, have revealed that arousal benefits memory for details (Andrews, 1990; Dorman, 1989; Heuer and Reisberg, 1990). The evidence obtained from laboratory studies indicates that memory is more likely to be enhanced than impaired by high levels of emotion and stress, so that memories for traumatic events are distinctive, long lasting, and easily retrieved.

Culture as a Context

Virtually every definition of culture (e.g., Hofstede, 1980; Mead, 1955) considers that it is a collection of discrete behavioural norms and cognitions shared by individuals within some definable population that are distinct from those shared within other populations. This view is different from the view of British empiricist who believed that cognitive processes were same for all normal adults. This assumption of universality of cognitive processes was adapted by mainstream psychology of 20th century. It is strengthened by the analogy of computer in which the brain equals hardware, inferential rules and data processing procedures equal the universal software, and output equals belief and behaviour. The output may be different depending upon the nature of input available in the context. However, "basic" processes such as categorization, learning, inductive and deductive inference, and causal reasoning are generally presumed to be the same in all human groups (Mishra, 1997).

There have been two schools of thought regarding the development of cognitive processes: the nativists, and the empiricists. Nativists believe that perceptual and cognitive processes are innate, and the stimulus itself provides complete information about the organization. Thus, the perceptual process is independent from the active construction of the organism. It seems that nativists emphasized the "bottom up" nature of the perceptual organization. Empiricists on the other hand argue that the role of learning and experience is exemplified by the way organisms respond to stimuli in the environment.

The functional approach is one of the most frequently employed empiricist theory in cross-cultural research on cognition. It emphasizes the adaptive aspects of organism-environment interaction. This approach has been used to explain a variety of perceptual and cognitive phenomena (Berry, 1976; Berry, Van de Koppel, Senechal, Annis, Bahuchet, Cavalli-Sforza and Witkin, 1986; Mishra, Sinha and Berry, 1996).

Learning, Memory and Culture

Since learning and memory have great significance in day-to-day activity of an individual efforts have been made to understand the role of cultural factors in acquisition and recollection of stimuli. In one such efforts, Stephenson and Calker (1982) tested U.S. and Australian Aboriginal women to recall two stories about a child for sickness. In one story, the child was treated by Western medicine and by native medicine in another story. It was found that recall of these stories were consistent with people's own cultural knowledge. These findings have also been reported by Harris, Schoen and Lee (1986) to recall stories in American and Brazilian subjects, and by Harris, Schoen and Hensley (1992) to recall of stories in U.S. and Mexican cultural groups.

Earlier some researchers found very few differences in story recoll by U.S. and Liberian children and adult. They argued that story recollection was a culturally universal process (Mandler, Scribner, Cole and De forest, 1980). Harris, *et al.* (1992) argued that cultural knowledge affects the recollection of culturally discrepant stories or story-like events rather than organization of that knowledge in particular culture. Mishra (1997) argued that in the recollection of stories in other cultures people tend to use assimilation of a discrepant knowledge, which provides familiar codes to unfamiliar objects or events. Thus, while recalling stories of other cultures, people replace their own cultural contents with the unfamiliar aspects of the stories.

Results obtained from these studies can be taken into consideration for understanding cultural influence on episodic memory, particularly eyewitness memory, as it is similar to story recollection in many respects. For example, assimilation may lead to inaccuracies in eyewitness memory as is evident in story recollection experiments mentioned above. It is also likely that when one recalls a story which belongs to other's culture, the level of confidence about the memory specifically for unfamiliar elements in the story is challenged, which makes the individual more susceptible to report misinformations. It is hypothesized that subjects accept the misleading information because they have no memory of the original event and suggestibility effects reflect gap-filling strategies in which misleading post-event information is used to fill the gaps of the memory for original event (McCloskey and Zaragoza, 1985).

Eidetic Imagery

Eidetic imagery is also supposed to be an important factor in the accuracy of eyewitness memory. Eidetic images are visual images that persist for a period following stimulation, that are fairly accurate and detailed, and can be scanned by the viewer (Rogoff, 1981). The incident of eidetic memory is believed to be higher in illiterate people as compared to literate, who place emphasis on verbal memory. Doob (1964) found that more eidetic imagery was associated with less schooling. In the light of the findings obtained by Doob (1964), it may be assumed that people in illiterate cultures emphasize that eidetic imagery would be more accurate in eyewitness memory recall and face identification than people of literate cultures.

Culture, Cognitive Styles and Eyewitness Memory

Cognitive style refers to the dimension of individual difference, which involves a particular form of cognitive functioning. It is an individual's characteristic and consistent approach to organise and process information. In other words, it refers to a person's preferred way of thinking, perceiving, remembering or solving problems. Riding and Rayner (1998) have defined cognitive style as "an individual's preferred and habitual approach to organise and represent information" (Riding and Rayner, 1998, p. 25).

A number of researchers have studied ecological, social and cultural factors involved in the origin and development of cognitive styles. It is indicated that cultures that encourage separate autonomous functioning, sense of personal agency, and have less social constraints foster the development of differentiation, in general, and more particularly, a field-independent (FI) cognitive style. In contrast, cultures that encourage reliance, interdependence, sense of reciprocal social obligation or collectiveness lead to the development of (FD) cognitive style (Berry, 1994).

The descriptors field dependence and field independence were used by Witkin, Oltman, Raskin and Karp (1971) to describe the extent to which an individual's perception or attainment of information are affected by the surrounding contextual or perceptual field. Field dependents find it difficult to extract information from the surrounding, tend to perceive objects as a whole (global field approach), rely more on external referents, have limited analytic and structuring skills in perception and cognition, show greater orientation towards people and sensitivity to social situations, and respond passively to the environment and leave stimulus material "as it is" (Witkin and Goodenough, 1976). The overall analysis indicates that FD individuals adopt a 'global field approach' that involves submission to the dominant organization of the field and the tendency to experience items as 'fused' with their background. Field independents, on the other hand, find it easier to extract the relevant information from the surrounding, focuses more on individual parts of the object; rely on internal references (Witkin and Goodenough, 1977), use analytical approach for perceptual and cognitive materials, have limited sensitivity to social context, are less influenced by the organization of the prevailing field, and tend to have inner orientation, i.e., maintain boundaries between their inner sphere of experience and distracting external social influences.

With respect to the role of ecology, it has been indicated that groups which pursue a subsistence level economy of hunting and gathering with a nomadic settlement pattern and low population density develop a higher level of psychological differentiation or FI cognitive style. In contrast, groups which pursue an agricultural pattern with a sedentary settlement and a high population density develop a lower level of differentiation (Berry, 1976; Berry, Van de Koppel, Annis, Senechal, Bahuchet, Cavalli-Sfroza and Witkin, 1986; Mishra *et al.,* 1996). Other researchers have also reported the effect of culture on the development of psychological differentiation (Bagley, 1984, 1988; Bagley and Young, 1983; Sinha, 1979). In a later work Mishra (1996) found hunting, gathering and wage earning groups generally score higher in tests measuring differentiation in cognition, whereas agricultural groups generally scored higher in tests measuring connectedness in cognition.

Triandis (1994, 1995) proposed the hypothesis that collectivism is high in cultures that are simple and strict. That is, in cultures where social norms are imposed strictly, people are more dependent on each other and where the population density is relatively high. Carpenter (2000) obtained empirical support for the correlation of collectivism and strictness. In collectivist cultures people are interdependent on their in-groups (family, tribe, nation, etc.), give priority to the goals of their in-groups, shape their behaviour primarily on the basis of in-group norms, and behave in a communal way (Mills and Clark, 1982). Individualism on the other hand, is related to the cultures where competitiveness, self-reliance, independence, and uniqueness are encouraged (Trandis and Gelfand, 1998).

There is a link between FD-FI cognitive style and individualism and collectivism (Berry, 1994). Literature on eco-cultural factors lead to the development of FD-FI and individualism-collectivism dimensions makes it clear that the same eco-cultural factors are shared in both these dimensions. This supports the idea that individualistic societies are more likely to promote the development of the FI cognitive style and collectivistic societies are more likely to promote the development of FD cognitive style.

Through the difference in behavioural characteristics and way of cognitive functioning, it is likely that FD-FI individuals would perform differently on eyewitness memory tasks. FD-FI cognitive style may affect the memory for an event by tuning the attention of an individual to a particular aspect of onging event (stimulus selection). For example, attention may be focused on central or peripheral aspects of the event, or it may be focused on human, objects, or on place related details in an event.

Being analytical, good at restructuring skills, more individualistic and having limited sensitivity to social context the FI individuals should focus more on the details of an event in general, should be able to separate central details from peripheral details of an event, and should be better at processing information related to objects and places as compared to human related information. Whereas, being holistic, more collectivistic, having highly developed interpersonal competencies, greater orientation towards people and sensitivity to social situations, the FD individuals should focus on entire event, should be influenced by the peripheral aspects of an event while recalling central details, and should be better at processing human-related information than other details. FD individuals are also likely to perform better in recognition of faces presented in a social context than their counterparts FI individuals.

Another behavioural characteristic in which FD and FI individuals differ is suggestibility. FD individuals tend to show more suggestibility and modify their own opinions with greater ease after reading texts attributed to very well-known authors. In an earlier study on female psychiatric patients by Sangiuliano (1951) it was found that FD subjects tended to respond more to suggestions. Other studies shows that FD individuals are more easily hypnotized (Goldenberg and Watchlel, 1973), and are more sensitive to Rosenthal effect (McFall and Schenkein, 1970) support the idea that FD individuals are more suggestible than FI individuals. Social compliance up to a considerable extent is an indicator of suggestibility. Witkin's hypothesis is that FD individuals are socially compliant and is supported by a study conducted by Solar, Davenport and Bruehl (1969). It seems that due to FD-FI individuals' tendencies to rely on external or internal referents, the degree to which they differ with respect to suggestibility should vary considerably. Suggestibility is considered to be an important factor in the accuracy of eyewitness memory because more suggestible individuals are highly susceptible to misinformation effect discussed earlier in this chapter.

Conclusions

The research literature available on eyewitness memory indicates that eyewitness memory is subject to forgetting and is prone to contamination from a variety of sources. As a result, the accuracy of eyewitness memory cannot be taken for granted. Factors such as mood, suggestibility, schema and emotional arousal provide a variety of contexts that influence encoding and recall of a witnessed event, and have profound effects on accuracy of eyewitness memory. On the other hand, the presence of contextual cues at the time of retrieval seems to have facilitating effect on witnesses' memory (Salmon, *et al.*, 1995).

In spite of the fact that immense literature focuses on the effects of different contextual factors on eyewitness memory accuracy, studies examining the role of cultural factors in eyewitness memory have not been reported. A lack of direct evidence regarding the influence of culture on eyewitness memory makes this field lively for cultural as well as cross-cultural research. The review presented above suggests that different behavioural characteristics, such as individualism-collectivism, field dependence-independence, degree of suggestibility, and schema of an individual, significantly influence the memory and accuracy of the witness. Since, all these variables seem to have stong cultural roots, one may argue that eye witness memory will also be significantly under the influence of other cultural factors that seem to characterize other aspects of memory in particular and overall cognition of individuals in general.

Acknowledgements

The help rendered by Professor R.C. Mishra, Department of Psychology, Banaras Hindu University, Varanasi in the preparation of this chapter is gratefully acknowledged.

REFERENCES

Alba, J.W. and Hasher, L. (1983), Is Memory Schematic? *Psychological Bulletin*, 93, 203-31.

Andrews, K. (1990), *The Effects of Emotion on memory Accuracy.* Unpublished Bachelor's thesis. Reed College, Portland, OR.

Bagley, C. (1984), Cultural Diversity, Migration and Cognitive Styles. In R. Samuda, J.W. Berry and M. Laferriere (Eds.), *Multiculturalism in Canada: Social and Educational Perspective.* Toronto: Allyn and Bacon.

Bagley, C. (1988), Cognitive Style and Cultural Adaptation in Blackfoot, Japanese, Jamaican, Italian and Angloceltic Children in Canada. In G. Verma and C. Bagley (Eds.), *Cross-Cultural Studies of Personality, Attitudes and Cognition.* London: McMillan.

Bagley, C. and Young, L. (1983), Class, Socialization and Cultural Change: Antecedents of Cognitive style in children in Jamaica and England. In C. Bagley and Verma (Eds.), *Multicultural Childhood.* Aldershot: Gowet.

Bartlett, F.C. (1932), *Remembering: A Study in Experimental and Social Psychology.* New York: Cambridge University Press.

Belli, R.F., Lindsay, D.S., Gales, and McCarthy, T.T. (1994), Memory Impairment and Source Misattribution in Postevent Misinformation Experiments with Short Retention Intervals. *Memory and Cognition,* 22, 40-54.

Belli, R.F., Windschitl, P.D., McCarthy, T.T. and Winfrey, S.E. (1992), Detecting Memory Impairment with a Modified Test Procedure: Manipulating Retention Interval with Centrally Presented Event Items. *Journal of Experimental Psychology: Learning, Memory and Cognition,* 18, 356-367.

Berry, J.W. (1976), *Human Ecology and Cognitive Style.* New York: Sage/ Halstead.

Berry, J.W., Van de Koppel, J.M.H., Annis, R.C., Senechal, C., Bahuchet, S., Cavalli-Safroza, I.I. and Witkin, H.A. (1986), *On the Edge of the Forest.* Lisse: Swets and Zeitlinger.

Blaney, P.H. (1986), Affect and Memory: A Review. *Psychological Bulletin,* 99, 229-246.

Bower, G.H. (1981), Mood and Memory, *American Psychologists,* 36, 129-148.

Bower, G.H. (1987), Invited Essay: Commentary on Mood and Memory. *Behavioural Research and Therapy,* 25, 443-455.

Bower, G.H. (1992), How Might Emotions Affect Learning? In S.A. Christianson (Ed.), *The Handbook of Emotion and Memory: Research and Theory* (pp. 3-31), Hillsdale, NJ: Lawrence Erlbaum.

Bower, G.H. and Mayer, J.D. (1985), Failure to Replicate Mood-Dependent Retrieval. *Bulletin of Psychonomic Society,* 23, 39-42.

Bower, G.H. and Mayer, J.D. (1989), In Search of Mood-Dependent Retrieval. In D. Kuiken (Ed.), *Mood and Memory: Theory, Research and Applications.* Special Issue of *Journal of Social Behaviour and Personality,* 4, 121-156.

Brainerd, C.J. and Reyna, V.F. (2002), Fuzzy-Trace Theory and False Memory. *Current Directions in Psychological Science,* 11, 164-169.

Bransford, J.D. and Johnson, M.K. (1972), Contextual Prerequisites for Understanding: Some Investigations of Comprehension and Recall. *Journal of Verbal Learning and Verbal Behaviour,* 11, 717-726.

Brigham, J.C. (1990), Target Person Distinctiveness and Attractiveness as Moderator Variables in the Confidence-Accuracy Relationship in Eyewitness Identifications. *Basic and Applied Social Psychology,* 11, 101-115.

Burgess, S.L. (2000), The Effects of Specific Emotions on Memory and Suggestibility in Young Children. *Dissertation Abstracts International. Section B—The Sciences and Engineering,* 60 (8-B), 4271.

Burke, A., Heuer, F. and Reisberg, D. (1992), Remembering Emotional Events. *Memory and Cognition,* 20, 277-290.

Carpenter, S. (2000), Effects of Cultural Tightness and Collectivism on Self-Concept and Causal Attributions. *Cross-Cultural Research,* 34, 38-56.

Cassel, W.S. and Bjorklund, D.F. (1995), Developmental Patterns of Eyewitness Memory and Suggestibility: An Ecologically based Short-term Longitudinal Study. *Law and Human Behaviour,* 19, 507-532.

Christiansen, R.E. and Ochalek, K. (1983), Editing Misleading Information from Memory: Evidence for the Existence of Original and Post Event Information. *Memory and Cognition,* 11, 467-475.

Christianson, S.-Å. and Nilsson, L.G. (1984), Functional Amnesia as Induced by a Psychological Trauma. *Memory and Cognition,* 12, 142-155.

Christianson, S.Å. (1989), Flashbulb Memories: Special, but not so Special. *Memory and Cognition,* 17, 435-443.

Christianson, S.Å. and Hubinette, B. (1993), Hands up! A Study of Witnesses' Emotional Reactions and Memories Associated with Bank Robberies. *Applied Cognitive Psychology,* 7, 365-379.

Christianson, S.Å. and Loftus, E.F. (1987), Memory for Traumatic Events. *Applied Cognitive Psychology,* 1, 225-239.

Christianson, S.Å. and Loftus, E.F. (1991), Remembering Emotional Events: The Fate of Detailed Information. *Cognition and Emotion,* 5, 81-108.

Clifford, B.R. and Scott, J. (1978), Individual and Situational Factors in Eyewitness Testimony. *Journal of Applied Psychology,* 63, 352-359.

Clifford, B. and Hollin, C. (1981), Effects of the Type of Incident and the Number of Perpetrators on Eyewitness Memory. *Journal of Applied Psychology*, 66, 364-370.

Cutler, B.L., Penrod, S.D. and Martens, T.K. (1987a), Improving the Reliability of Eyewitness Identification: Putting Context Into Context. *Journal of Applied Psychology*, 72, 629-637.

Cutler, B.L., Penrod, S.D. and Martens, T.K. (1987b), The Reliability of Eyewitness Identifications: The Role of System and Estimator Variables. *Law and Human Behaviour*, 11, 223-258.

Cutler, B.L., Penrod, S.D., O'Rourke, T.E. and Martens, T.K. (1986), Unconfounding the Effects of Contextual Cues on Eyewitness Identification Accuracy. *Social Behaviour*, 1, 113-134.

Davidson, D. (1994), Recognition and Recall of Irrelevant and Interruptive A typical Actions in Script-based Stories. *Journal of Memory and Learning*, 33, 757-775.

Deffenbacher, K.A. (1983), The Influence of Arousal on Reliability of Testimony. In S.M.A. Lloyd-Bostock and R.B. Clifford, (Eds.), *Evaluating Witness Evidence. Recent Psychological Research and New Perspectives.* Chichester: John Wiley and Sons.

Doob, L.W. (1964), Eidetic Images Among the Ibo. *Ethnology*, 3, 357-363.

Doob, L.W. (1970), Correlates of Eidetic Imagery in Africa. *Journal of Psychology*, 76, 223-230.

Dooling, D.J. and Cristiaansen, R.E. (1977), Episodic and Semantic Aspects of Memory for Prose. *Journal of Experimental Psychology: Human Learning and Memory*, 3, 428-436.

Dorman, C. (1989), *The Effects of Emotional Arousal on Memory.* In Press.

Eich, E. and Metcalfe, J. (1989), Mood dependent memory for internal *versus* external events. *Journal of Experimental Psychology: Learning, Memory and Cognition*, 15, 443-456.

Eich, J.E. (1985), Context, Memory and Integrating Item/Context Imagery. *Journal of Experimental Psychology: Learning, Memory and Cognition*, 11, 764-770.

Ellis, H.C. and Ashbrook, P.W. (1989), The "State" of Mood and Memory Research: A Selective Review. In D. Kuiken (Ed.), *Mood and Memory: Theory, Research and Applications.* In Special Issue of the *Journal of Social Behaviour and Personality*, 4, 1-21.

Fiedler, K. and Stroehm, W. (1986), What Kind of Mood Influences What Kind of Memory? The Role of Arousal and Information Structure. *Memory and Cognition*, 14, 181-188.

Fiedler, K., Walther, E., Armbruster, T., Fay, D. and Naumann, U. (1996), Do You Really Know What You have Seen? Intrusion Errors and Presuppositions Effects on Constructive Memory. *Journal of Experimental Social Psychology*, 32, 484-511.

Forgas, J.P. and Bower, G.H. (1987), Mood Effects on Person-Perception Judgements. *Journal of Personality and Social Psychology*, 53, 53-60.

Forgas, J.P. and Bower, G.H. and Moylan, S.J. (1990), Praise or Blame? Affective Influences on Attributions for Achievement. *Journal of Personality and Social Psychology*, 59, 809-819.

Frost, P., Ingraham, M. and Wilson, B. (2002), Why Misinformation is More Likely to be Recognized Over Time: A Source Monitoring Account. *Memory*, 10, 179-185.

Gage, D.F. and Safer, M.A. (1985), Hemisphere Differences in the Mood State-Dependent Effect for Recognition of Emotional Faces. *Journal of Experimental Psychology: Learning, Memory and Cognition*, 11, 752-763.

Glibling, F. and Davies, G. (1988), Reinstatement of Context Following Exposure to Post Event Information. *British Journal of Psychology*, 79, 129-141.

Godden, D.R. and Baddeley, A.D. (1975), Context-Dependent Memory in Two Natural Environments: On Land and Underwater. *British Journal of Psychology*, 66, 325-331.

Godden, D.R. and Baddeley, A.D. (1980), When Does Context Influence Recognition Memory? *British Journal of Psychology*, 71, 99-104.

Harris, R.J., Schoen, L.M. and Hensley, D.L. (1992), A Cross-Cultural Study of Story Memory. *Journal of Cross-Cultural Psychology*, 23, 133-147.

Harris, R.J., Schoen, L.M. and Lee, D.J. (1986), Culture-based Distortion in Memory of Stories. In J.L. Armagost (Ed.), *Proceedings of the Twentieth Annual Mid-American Conference*. Manhattan: Kansas State University Press.

Heath, W.P. and Erickson, J.R. (1998), Memory for Central and Peripheral Actions and Props After Varied Postevent Presentation. *Legal and Criminological Psychology*, 3, 321-346.

Heuer, F. and Reisberg, D. (1990), Vivid Memories of Emotional Events: The Accuracy of Remembered Memory. *Memory and Cognition*, 18, 496-506.

Higham, P.A. (1998), Believing Details Known to have been Suggested. *British Journal of Psychology*, 89, 269-283.

Hofstede, G. (1980), *Culture's Consequences: International Differences in Work-Related Values*. Beverley Hills, C.A. Sage.

Janet, P. (1989), *L'automatisme Psychologique*. Paris: Alcan.

Janet, P. (1893), L'Amnesie Continue. *Revue Generale Des Sciences*, 4, 167-179.

Jankins, F. and Davis, D. (1985), Contamination of Facial Memory Through Exposure to Misleading Composite Pictures. *Journal of Applied Psychology*, 70, 164-176.

Johnson, M.K., Bransford, J.D. and Solomon, M.K. (1973), Memory for Tacit Implications of Sentences. *Journal of Experimental Psychology*, 98, 203-205.

Johnson, R.E. (1970), Recall of Prose as a Function of the Structural Importance of the Linguistic Units. *Journal of Verbal Learning and Verbal Behaviour*, 9, 12-20.

Kramer, T.H., Buckhout, R. and Eugenio, P. (1990), Weapon Focus, Arousal and Eyewitness Memory: Attention Must be Paid. *Law and Human Behaviour,* 16, 167-184.

Kuiken, D. (Ed.), (1989), Mood and Memory: Theory, Research and Applications. *Journal of Social Behaviour and Personality,* 4, (2).

Leight, K.A. and Ellis, H.C. (1981), Emotional Mood States, Strategies and State-Depdendency in Memory. *Journal of Verbal Learning and Verbal Behaviour,* 20, 251-266.

Lewis, S.F. and White, H. (1997), Remembering details in Stories about Childhood Sexual Abuse. *The Journal of Generic Psychology,* 158, 377-379.

Lindsay, D.S., Allen, B.P., Chan, J.C.K. and Dahl, L.C. (2004), Eyewitness Suggestibility and Source Similarity: Intrusions of Details from One Event into Memory Reports of Another Event. *Journal of Memory and Language,* 50, 96-111.

Lindsay, D.S. and Johnson, M.K. (2000), False Memories and Source Monitoring Framework. *Learning and Individual Differences,* 12, 145-161.

Loftus, E.F. and Burns, T. (1982), Mental Shock can Produce Retrograde Amnesia. *Memory and Cognition,* 10, 318-323.

Loftus, E.F. (1975), Leading Questions and the Eyewitness Report. *Cognitive Psychology,* 7, 560-572.

Loftus, E.F. (1977), Shifting Human Colour Memory. *Memory and Cognition,* 5, 696-699.

Loftus, E.F. (1979), The Malleability of Memory. *American Scientist,* 67, 312-370.

Loftus, E.F. (1992), When a Lie Becomes Memory's Truth: Memory Distortion After Exposure to Misinformation. *Current Directions in Psychological Science,* 1, 121-123.

Loftus, E.F. and Palmer, J.C. (1974), Reconstruction of Automobile Destruction: An Example of the Interaction between Language and Memory. *Journal of Verbal Learning and Learning Behaviour,* 13, 585-589.

Loftus, E.F., Loftus, G.R. and Messo, J. (1987), Some Facts about "Weapon Focus" *Law and Human Behaviour,* 11, 55-62.

Loftus, E.F., Miller, D.G. and Burns, H.J. (1978), Semantic Integration of Verbal Information into Visual Memory. *Journal of Experimental Psychology: Human Learning and Memory,* 4, 19-31.

Maass, A. and Kohnken, G. (1989), Eyewitness Identification: Simulating the "Weapon Effect". *Law and Human Behaviour,* 13, 397-408.

Maccoby, E.E. (2000), Parenting and Its Effects on Children: On Reading and Misreading Behaviour Genetics. *Annual Review of Psychology,* 51, 1-27.

Mandler, J.M., Scribner, S., Cole, M. and De forest, M. (1980), Cross-Cultural Invariance in Story Recall. *Child Development,* 51, 19-26.

McGaugh, J.L. (1992), Affect Neuromodulatory Systems and Memory Storage. In S.A. Christianson (Eds.), *The Handbook of Emotion and Memory: Research and Therapy* (pp. 245-268). Hillsdale, NJ: Lawrence Erlbaum.

McCloskey, M. Wible, C.G. and Cohen, N.J. (1988). Is there a Special Flashbulb-Memory Mechanism? *Journal of Experimental Psychology: General,* 117, 171-181.

McClosky, M. and Zaragoza, M. (1985), Misleading Post Event Information and Memory for Events: Arguments and Evidence Against Memory Impairment Hypothesis. *Journal of Experimental Psychology: General,* 114, 3-18.

Mead, M. (1955), *Cultural Patterns and Technical Change.* New York: Mentor Books.

Memon, A., Wark, L., Holley, A., Bull, R. and Koehnken, G. (1997), Context Effects and Event Memory: How Powerful are the Effects? In D. Payne and F. Conard (Eds.), *Intersections in Basic and Applied Memory Research* (pp. 175-191), Mahwah, NJ: Erlbaum.

Mills, J. and Clark, M.S. (1982), Exchange and Communal Relationships. In *Review of Personality and Social Psychology,* (ed.), L. Wheeler, 3: 121-144. Beverly Hills, CA: Sage.

Mishra, R.C. (1997), Perceptual Differentiation in Relation to Children's Daily Life Activities. *Social Science International,* 12, 1-11.

Mishra, R.C. Sinha, D. and Berry, J.W. (1996), *Ecology, Acculturation and Psychological Adaptation: A Study of Adivasi in Bihar.* New Delhi: Sage.

Mudd, K. and Govern, J.M. (2004), Conformity to Misinformation and Time Delay Negatively Affect Eyewitness Confidence and Accuracy. *North American Journal of Psychology,* 6, 227-238.

Narby, D.J., Cutler, B.L. and Penrod, S.D. (1996), The Effects of Witness, Target and Situational Factors on Eyewitness Identifications. In S.L. Sporer, R.S. Malpass and G. Koehnken (Eds.), *Psychological Issues in Eyewitness Identification,* (pp. 23-52). Lawrence Erlbaum Associates.

Nasby, W. and Yando, R. (1982), Selective Encoding and Retrieval of Effectively Valiant Information. *Journal of Personality and Social Psychology,* 43, 1244-1253.

Neisser, U. (1967), *Cognitive Psychology,* New York: Appleton-Century-Crofts.

Neisser, U. (1982), *Memory Observed: Remembering in Natural Contexts.* San Francisco: Freeman.

Parker, A. Gellatley, A. and Waterman, M. (1999), The Effects of Environmental Context Manipulation on Memory: Dissociation between Perceptual and Conceptual Implicit Tests. *European Journal of Cognitive Psychology,* 11, 555-570.

Riding, R.J. and Rayner, S.G. (1998), *Cognitive Style and Learning Strategies.* London: David Fulton Publisher.

Ridley, A.M. and Clifford, B.R. (2004), The Effects of Anxious Mood Induction on Suggestibility to Misleading Post-Event Information. *Applied Cognitive Psychology,* 18, 233-244.

Rogoff, B. (1981), Schooling and the Development of Cognitive Skills. In H.C. Triandis and A. Heron (Eds.), *Handbook of Cross-Cultural Psychology: Developmental Psychology,* 4, (pp. 233-294). Boston: Allyn and Bacon.

Rubin, D.C. (Ed.), (1996). *Remembering Our Past: Studies in Autobiographical Memory.* NY: Cambridge University Press.

Salmon, K., Bidrose, S. and Pipe, M.E. (1995). Providing Pros to Facilitate Children's Event Reports: A Comparison of Toys and Real Items. *Journal of Experimental Child Psychology,* 60, 174-194.

Sangiuliano, I.A. (1951), *An Investigation of the Relationship between the Perception of the Upright in Space and Several Factors in Personality Organization.* Unpublished Doctor's Dissertation, Fordham University.

Schacter, D. (1996), *Searching for Memory: The Brain, the Mind and the Past.* Basic Books.

Sinha, D. (1979), Perceptual Style Among Nomadic and Transitional Agriculturalist Birhors. In L. Eckensberger, W. Lonner and Y.H. Poortinga (Eds.), *Cross-Cultural Contributions to Psychology* (pp. 83-93), Lisse: Swets and Zeitlinger.

Solar, D., Davenport, G. and Bruehl, D. (1969), Social Compliance as a Function of Field Dependence. *Perceptual and Motor Skills,* 29, 299-306.

Steblay, N.M. (1992). A Meta-Analytic Review of the Weapon Focus Effect. *Law and Human Behaviour,* 16, 413-424.

Stephenson, M.S. and Calker, L. (1982), Intercultural Misunderstandings about Health Care: Recall of Descriptions of Illness and Treatments. *Social Science and Medicine,* 16, 1949-1954.

Terr, L. (1994), *Unchained Memories: True Stories of Traumatic Memories, Lost and Found.* New York: Basic Books.

Triandis, H.C. (1994), *Culture and Social Behaviour.* New York: McGraw-Hill.

Triandis, H.C. (1995), *Individualism and Collectivism.* Boulder, CO: Westview.

Triandis, H.C. and Gelfand, M. (1998), Converging Measurements of Horizontal and Vertical Individualism and Collectivism. *Journal of Personality and Social Psychology,* 74, 118-28.

Tulving, E. and Thomson, D.M. (1973), Encoding Specificity and Retrieval Processes in Episodic Memory. *Psychological Review,* 80, 352-373.

Tversky, B. and Tuchin, M. (1989). A Reconciliation of the Evidence on Eyewitness Testimony: Comments on McCloskey and Zaragoza. *Journal of Experimental Psychology: General,* 118, 86-91.

Ucros, C.G. (1989). Mood State-Dependent Memory: A Meta-Analysis. *Cognition and Emotion,* 3, 139-167.

Van der Kolk, B.A. and Fisler, R. (1995). Dissociation and the Fragmentary Nature of Traumatic Memories: Overview and Exploratory Study. *Journal of Traumatic Stress,* 8, 505-525.

Wagenaar, W.A. and Groeneweg, J. (1990), The Memory of Concentration Camp Survivors. *Applied Cognitive Psychology, 4,* 77-88.

Wessel, I. and Merckelbach, H. (1998), Memory for Threat-Relevant and Threat-Irrelevant Cues in Spider Phobics. *Cognition and Emotion,* 12, 93-104.

Whitfield, C.L., (1995), *Memory and Abuse: Remembering and Healing the Effects of Trauma.* Deerfield Beach, FL: Health Communications.

Witkin, H.A. and Goodenough, D.R. (1976). *Field Dependence Revisited.* Princeton, NJ: Educational Testing Services.

Witking, H.A. and Goodenough, D.R. (1977). Field-Dependence and Interpersonal Behaviour. *Psychological Bulletin,* 84, 661-689.

Witkin, H.A., Oltman, P.K. Raskin, E. and Karp, S.A. (1971), *A Manual for the Group Imbedded Figures Test,* Consulting Psychologists Press, Palo Alto, C.A.

Yuille, J.C. and Tollestrop, P.A. (1992). A Model of Diverse Effects of Emotion on Eyewitness Memory. In S.A. Christianson (Eds.), *The Handbook of Emotion and Memory: Research and Theory* (pp. 201-215). Hillsdale, NJ: Exlbaum.

Yuille, J.C. and Cutshall, J.L. (1986), A Case Study of Eyewitness Memory of a Crime. *Journal of Applied Psychology,* 71, 291-301.

Zragoza, M.S. and Lane, S.M. (1994), Source Misattributions and the Suggestibility of the Eyewitness. *Journal of Experimental Psychology: Learning Memory and Cognition,* 20, 934-945.

8

Culture and Knowledge

Rekha Singhal

In the past decade, the relationship between culture, knowledge systems and environmentally responsible behaviour have received a great attention, resulting in, the identification of 'intricate link' between cultural and biological factors. Environment is recognized as an essential resource at all levels ranging from family, community, nation and future generations. Biologists, ecologists, conservationists and social scientists have recognized now that solutions of environmental problems extends the boundaries of technical solutions and can be addressed through the socio-cultural systems. This chapter aims to contribute a better understanding between culture, knowledge systems, and psychological factors in encouraging pro-environmental behaviour and inter-relationship among them.

The Context

The concern of environmental quality in our planet and its impact on our behaviour has necessitated tremendous interest among environmental and social scientist towards culture. Knowledge systems and its implications for pro-environmental behaviour combines the understanding of scientific and indigenous knowledge system, and challenge in developing environmentally responsible behaviour embedded in the culture. The scientific knowledge focuses towards centralized, technically-oriented generalized elucidation, while Indigenous Knowledge (IK) highlights micro level, local, area-specific solutions. In this backdrop, the ultimate goal of environment-behaviour and knowledge system (approach) is the development of environmentally responsible citizens. Pro-environmental behaviour includes *awareness of consequences.* This concept may roughly be equated with environmental concern or attitude (Fransson and Gärling, 1999). Behaviour is considered environmentally responsible when the actions of an individual or group or group are environmentally compatible for sustainable or diminished use of environmental (natural) resource. Today sustainable environmental conservation and management is considered as pivotal for quality of life and balanced development. This realization has resulted in active involvement of behavioural scientists in efforts to develop environmentally responsible behaviour and techniques for measuring the same (Scott and Willits, 1991).

Against this background the present paper focuses on the knowledge system in general and indigenous knowledge in particular and the role of culture in it. The background of indigenous knowledge and its relationship with environment, need to integrate indigenous and scientific knowledge for stimulating pro-environmental behaviour is delineated with the help of examples relating psychological factors. Thus, this article attempts to contribute our understanding towards the relationship between the components of environmental concern on one hand, and their relationship to "psychological variables" on the other.

Culture and Knowledge System

Broadly, culture is defined as the human-made part of the environment. It can be divided into material and subjective culture. Material culture consists of elements as dress, food, houses, highways, tools, and machines. Subjective culture is a society's "characteristic way of perceiving its social environment" (Triandis, 1972, pp. viii, 3). It consists of ideas about what has worked in the past and, thus, is worth transmitting to the future generations. Language, economic, educational, political, legal, philosophical and religious systems are important elements of culture. Ideas about aesthetics, and how should people live with others are also important elements. The most important are unstated assumptions, standard operation procedures, and habits of sampling information from the environment.

Knowledge systems are related with the way people understand the world, interpret and apply meaning to their experiences. Knowledge is built through the complex process of selecting, analyzing, testing, rejecting, creating, and transforming information, and is inextricably linked to the social, environmental, institutional and cultural contexts in which it occurs (Arce and Long, 1992). Broadly, it has been categorized into: (i) indigenous and (ii) scientific knowledge systems.

Indigenous knowledge (IK) is the local knowledge—knowledge that is unique to a given culture or society. It forms the base for local decision making with respect to agriculture, water, health, and management of other natural resources. It is the base for local-level decision making in agriculture, health care, food preparation, education, natural-resource management, and a series of other activities in rural communities (Warren, 1991). Recognising the importance and place of environment in the life of indigenous people, the term Traditional Ecological Knowledge (TEK) is used to refer those aspects of IK which directly relates with the conservation and management of environment (Johnson, 1992). IK contrasts with the Scientific Knowledge (SK) also referred as international knowledge system postulated by universities, research institutions and private firms.

According to Agarwal (1995) Scientific and IK systems can be distinguished on the basis of three grounds:

- *Substantive grounds*: IK and SK differ with respect to their history and distinctive characteristics in the subject matter.
- *Methodological and epistemological grounds*: The two forms of knowledge employ different methods to build knowledge. Science is open, systematic, objective and analytical. It advances by building rigorously on prior achievements. IK, however, is closed, non-systematic, holistic rather than analytical, without an overall conceptual framework, and advances on the basis of new experiences.
- *Contextual grounds*: IK is often seen to exist in a local context, anchored to a particular social group in a particular setting at a particular time. SK, on the other hand, has been divorced from an epistemic framework in the search for universal validity (Banuri and Apffel-Marglin, 1993:11/13). Hence, traditional/indigenous knowledge is more deeply rooted in its environment (Banuri and Apffel-Marglin, 1993; Chambers, 1980:2; Dei, 1993; Howes and Chambers, 1980:330; Warren, 1989 and 1990:1).

At the same time it is also believed that knowledge systems can never be so separated or fixed. Evidences suggest that contact, diversity, exchange, communication, learning and transformation differ as per systems of knowledge and belief), however, it is difficult to adhere to a view that separates IK and SK (Wolf, 1982). Agrawal (1995), therefore, concludes that the distinction between indigenous and scientific knowledge separates 'us' from 'them.' When we recognize how these two types of knowledge are similar, we can begin a "productive dialogue to safeguard the interests who are maltreated. In this regard adaptive learning, detailed in the following section, can provide useful background to integrate the knowledge systems.

Culture, Knowledge and Pro-environmental Behaviour

The linkage between IK system, people, and pro-environmental behaviour can be noticed in their way of life. In many tribal areas, indigenous knowledge is a major element in local decision-making processes relating to the use and management of natural resources, which is the major constituent of the environment. Indigenous knowledge reflects a society's intimate understanding of its ecological and social environment (Warren, 1991). According to Haverkort and David (1996), the general world-view of indigenous communities about environment is of a holistic nature, implying that human life is considered to be a part of, and is in complete harmony with the environment. Ideally, all resource management activities are compelled to be in harmony with nature too. Umans (1992) describes four ways of how indigenous people construe their world:

- Giving environment
- Reciprocating environment
- Disposable environment
- Prohibiting environment

(1) The *giving environment,* where nature is seen as continuously and unconditionally provides their subsistence needs. This is reflected in their management and economic activities. Ecological balance is maintained only when population density is below the critcial level.

(2) The *reciprocating environment,* where nature requries a continuous investments, in response to provisions. Traditional

management systems have been developed together with a reciprocal economic system. In this system ecological balance is pursued, but not always attained.

(3) When a shortage occurs behaviour adapts for survival reasons. This third world view develops, which is based on the perception of a *disposable environment* because it will eventually destroy the resources.

(4) Opposite to the "disposable" world-view is the non-materialistic perception of the environment/nature for religious purposes. In these situations the environment/nature is completely protected. This is called the *prohibiting environment.*

Based on giving and reciprocating perceptions of environment, indigenous people consider their behaviour primarily with the environment which is a part of their way of life. Thus, different cultures and people perceive and appreciate environment in different ways because of their distinct heritage and experience (Posey, 1999).

Most discussions on complex relationship between cultures and conservation of environment centre to argue that the cultural diversity can sustain a wide variety of practices, therefore, conservation of natural resources/environment (Posey, 1999; Macmillan, 2000). Examples of how 'indigenous' and 'local' people around the world have protected both individual species and entire habitats have led to the interest in linking biodiversity to human diversity and knowledge systems. In many parts of the world, natural features and habitats are often protected by religious taboos and are considered sacred by community members, have survived due to strong cultural forces and today practiced as reservoirs of local biodiversity (Laird, 1999). For example, in a more general perspective, they contribute to a people's sense of place (Kusel, 2001; Wiersum *et al.*, 2004). For instance, the Menominee tribes have a spiritual relationship with their forest which represents a twin identity for both the tribe and the forest (Groenfeldt, 2003). Similarly, Tulsi, Mahua, Neem trees are considered sacred in various parts of India, thus, conserved and protected by different social groups. Hence, 'indigenous' and 'local' people are understood to ascribe symbolic significance to their surrounding landscapes and consequently perceive and value nature differently than ecologically trained conservationists and biologists (Posey, 1999; Infield, 2001).

Psychology of Pro-environmental Behaviour

As the human population continues to expand, the role of conservation has become critical. Conservationists, who are usually trained in the natural sciences, have concentrated their efforts on technological or biological solutions to environmental crises. Biological (scientific) researches in life histories, habitat requirements, and minimum viable populations have provided extremely valuable information for the recovery of endangered wildlife. New methods to reduce pollution, dioxin emissions from mills, creating more fuel-efficient vehicles, and installing water treatment systems, have undoubtedly contributed for a cleaner environment.

Despite these advances, there is a steady rise in the realization that technology alone cannot solve environmental problems. Maloney and Ward (1973), describes ecological crisis as a "crisis of maladaptive behaviour" (p. 583). Accordingly, it has been recognized that the root cause of environmental problems is human behaviour and the possible solution for today's environmental problems besides technology and various political and economical instruments, individual's environmental concern and environmentally responsible behaviour too is equally important factor. For example, for selected environmental problems, such as littering behaviour, there are no technical solutions. The World Commission on Environment and Development (WCED, 1987) and the 1992 United Nations Earth Summit in Rio de Janeiro also reiterated that citizens must take a participatory role in environmental protection.

In the light of the above view in recent years, a shift can be observed in the discussions about environmental problems and their solutions. During 1970s an insight developed which says that the environmental problems are the consequences of 'maladaptive human behaviour' (Malony and Ward, 1973) which is harmful to the environment (Stern and Oskamp, 1987). This analysis motivated social scientists to engage in the analysis of individual motives and conditions underlying pro-environmental behaviour. Consequently, to understand how to encourage environmentally responsible behaviour, it is important to identify factors that promote or govern such behaviour. In this regard, psychology can play an important role to understand human behaviour and the change in the "maladaptive behaviour" which is harmful to the environment (Galler, Winett and Everett, 1982; Oskamp, 1983; Stern and Oskamp, 1987). Pertaining to the central role played by the psychologists, in recognition, besides environmental psychology and environmental cognition, related sub-fields like conservation psychology, eco-psychology, psychology of sustainability, conservation behaviour, ecological psychology, nature psychology, and of course, conservation psychology have emerged to the surface. However, there is general feeling that "environmental psychology" is chiefly convicted to build environment, focuses mostly on the impact of environment on people and not the other way around, limits the interdisciplinary are studying the connections between psychology and conservation issues, and more specifically how to influence human behaviour to protect the environment across cultures. However, most people agreed that the name should at the minimum clearly convey the message that it refers to psychology to promote conservation. Beside the naming issue. There is a need to maximize application of existing knowledge and theory from all areas of psychology, psychology's contribution to the problems of conservation and quality of environment.

Human Dimensions in Pro-environment Behaviour

Three different basic dimensions to assess the role of human in ecological context (Clark, 1988):

1. The interaction between human and environmental systems (resources, the sources of change, the consequences of these changes).
2. The choices that individuals, communities, governments, and organisations make in order to manage the interaction (Peoples perception, attitude, awareness, motivation).
3. The underlying elements of social structure of culture that shape these interactions and choices.

In the contemporary world there are numerous cases, particularly in the developing regions which indicate that natural resources are being destroyed for immediate and short-term benefits. Sustained and effective measures on these factors requires human interventions which may enable it to counter such effects and provide antidote and facilitate positive action. This demands promotion and encouragement in pro-environmental actions. Such actions are products of psychological variables and possesses part of complex interactive systems consisted of attitudes, awareness, motivation, and the socio-cultural context. They jointly determine pro-environmental action.

What important variables involved in natural resource management with a socio-psychological perspective and how could these variables be placed in a unified theoretical framework are the questions that need reflection and deliberation: what follows is an outline of a conceptual framework which delineates some of the related components.

Basics of Human Action

Kurt Lewin (1951) has given the very basic formula of action (behaviour). According to him:

$$B = f(P \times E)$$

Where B = Behaviour
P = Person (individual)
E = Environment

Based on this conception, Lewin contented that person and environment are interdependent parts of the total field.

Elaboration of the above conception, Figure 8.1 presents a conceptual structure of relationship between individuals, social-psychological, variables, cultural factors and human action.

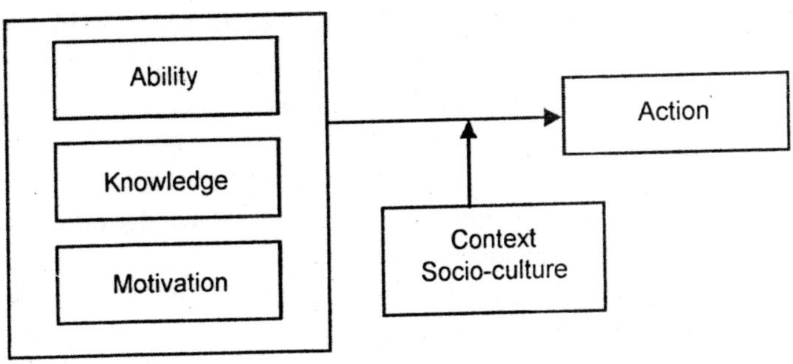

Fig. 8.1: Relationships between human action, individual and environment

The model of behaviour presented here considers that human actions are planned, intentional and rational steps based on evaluation of the probable consequences of actions in terms of their likelihood as well as their valence. The likelihood and valence of any action is solely determined by the meaning of actions held by the people. Meaning involves (a) knowledge of the domain, (b) goals involved, and (c) understanding of pertinent skills.

Determinants of Environmentally Responsible Behaviour

In the light of above mentioned basics of human action it will be pertinent, now to depend on the psychological factors in determinants the pro-environmental behaviour. Healthy environment is one of the essential prerequisites of human life and has a far-reaching implications in determining quality of life. Environment refers to natural things around us, which sustain human life. It may be defined as the outer physical, biological and psycho-social system in which man and other organisms live with many interacting components.

Knowledge

Knowledge of an issue is clearly a prerequisite for appropriate action. However, knowledge of the problem is only part of the catalyst required; a person must also know what he can do in the given situation. Thus, environmental knowledge can be categorized into three levels: (a) knowledge about the issue, (b) knowledge about the action strategy, and (c) action skill (Boeschig and Deyoung, 1993). These different levels of knowledge are considered to influence responsible people. Volk (1990), for example, categorized environmental behaviour-related variables further subdivided into three categories: entry level, ownership level, and empowerment level. They suggested that knowledge about a general concept is considered an important variable for entry-level, in-depth knowledge about issues for the ownership level, and knowledge about skill and action strategy for the empowerment level. Cotterll and Graffe (1997) in their study related with the determinants of the environmental responsible behaviour and found that knowledge and awareness of consequences contributed to the most variance explained.

For the environment policy question, the due basic fundamental scientific knowledge of relevant environmental issues has been cited as a factor linking value orientation, specific attitudes (Tarrant Bright, and Cordell, 1997) and as a factor influencing environmental behaviours (Stern, 1992). This thought process suggests that if people become more conscious about the environment and its associated issues, they will, in turn, become more aware of environment and its problems, will motivated to act towards the environment in more responsible ways (Hungerford and Volk, 1990, p. 9). Although the effect of knowledge is not conclusive the studies suggests that knowledge plays a vital role in enhancing the value-attitude-behaviour relationship by providing individuals an ability to better formulate alternative views and present arguments to support their beliefs and behaviours (Pierce, Lovrich, Tsurutani, and Abe, 1989).

Education

Education is regarded as a key factor in the prevention of natural resources and environmental depletion (Disinger, 1982). Researches in the field of environmental education have claimed that they can change behaviour by enhancing human knowledge about environmental issues. They also suggest that if one has more knowledge about the environment, the awareness level would be higher, as well as the favourable attitude (Hungerford and Volk, 1990). However, more environmental knowledge does not necessarily mean more responsible for environmental behaviour. A major difficulty in imparting enviromental literacy lies in the simple fact that researchers has not yet satisfactorily identified the knowledge components to procure a responsible environmental behaviour (Sivek and Hungerford, 1989). Nevertheless, many researchers have used change in knowledge as an effective variable for explaining the change in the responsible environmental behaviour (Armstrong and Impara, 1991; Gillett *et al.*, 1991; Guiterrez de White and Jacobson, 1994; Roth and Perez, 1989; Sivek and Hungerford, 1989; Smith-Sebasto, 1995; Wendling and Wuensch, 1986). Education programmes are basically conducted by conveying of certain information (knowledge) from Experts, Educationist, Analysts etc. (i.e., teachers or interpreters) to receptors (i.e. students or visitors).

Most environmental psychologists and educators believe that Environmental Education (EE) is linked to pro-environmental behaviour [e.g. Borden, 1984-85; Bowers, 1993; Cortese, 1992; Cowan and Stapp, 1982; Giglotti, 1990; Gray, 1985; Milbrath, 1989; Olson Lodwick and Dunlap, 1992; Smith, 1992). One assumption in this perspective is that education leads to greater awareness and attitude change which ultimately improves environmentally responsible behaviour (Bruvold, 1973; Oriordan, 1976)]. "The primary goal of environmental education should be to encourage people to engage in more pro-environmental behaviours" (Leeming Dwyer, Porter and Cobern, 1993, p.8). However, critics of Environmental Education have argued that few EE interventions actually encourage responsible environmental behaviour because they do not actively involve students in environmental issues (Volk, Hungerford and Tomera, 1984). Others have argued that educational interventions in general are ineffective in their ability to change behaviour (Cone and Hayes, 1980). Gardner and Stern (1996 p.91), however, contradicted/refuted this argument. They reported that education interventions which were successful in changing pro-environmental intentions and behaviour presented credible environmental information and actively involved participants. Through, the meta-analysis of the published studies between 1971 to 1996, Zelezny (1999) has concluded that the effect of environmental education on pro-environmental behaviour depends on the method of education. Interventions most effectively improved environmentally responsible behaviour used by young participants who were actively involved.

Locus of Control and Group Perspective

Almost all researches on Locus of control in the West have been focused on individual. In developing countries, in collectivist societies (contrast with Western individualistic societies), both individual and collective perspectives are also significant for locus of control (Pareek, 2003; Sia, Hungeford and Tomera, 1985; Sivek and Hungerford, 1989, 1990). Other categories used by some researchers are individual locus of control and group locus of control Individual locus of control refers to an individual's perception of his or her ability to carry out actions as an individual acting alone, whereas group locus of control refers to actions resulting from working within a group (Marcinkowski, 1988).

With regard to the impact of locus of control in relation to pro-environmental behaviour it has been noted that when it comes to protect environmental faith and confidence in the people so their actions can make a difference (Clark, Kotcherld, and Moore, 2003; Osbadistion, 2003) and government alone cannot achieve the desired results to preserve environment.

Perceived Outcomes

A number of factors can influence an individual's behaviour. People's perception in terms of that their own behaviour is responsible for environmental crisis and, hence, can be managed and controlled by them than by government or others. Models of social psychology suggests that behaviour of the people is influenced by what people perceive as outcomes of behaviour or characteristics of objects (Anderson, 1971:1991; Fishbein and Ajzen, 1971, 1975). The perception of outcome relationship has been applied in a variety of specific environment related areas such as, attitudes towards prescribed burns (Manfredo *et al.*, 1990), trapping (Fulton *et al.*, 1995), villagers to extinguish participation to extinguish forest fire, poaching (Singhal *et al.*, 1999), and limitation for firewood and grass collection (Singhal, 2000).

Motivational Orientation

Individuals' possess different motivational orientations and these motives are related are related to differences in individual's choice behaviour (Pruitt, 1967). To examine the effect of motivational orientation on choice behaviour, Liebrand (1984) distinguished four motivational orientations: (1) *altruistic*, the motivation to maximize others outcome ; (2) *individualistic*, the motivation to maximize one's own outcome; (3) cooperative, the motivation to maximize the sum of one's own and others joint outcome; and (4) *competitive*, the motivation to maximize the difference between one's own and others outcome have been identified. On the basis of an experimental study by Librand and Van Run (1985) and Loomis, Samuelson, and Sell (1995), it was found that there is a strong relationship between cooperative behaviour and pro-environmental behaviour. In this context, a related concept "Tragedy of Commons" (Hardin, 1968) is perhaps the most cited publication on overuse of common property resources (i.e., grazing land, lake, pond, fishing etc.), whereby individual attempts maximize individual gains.

Similarly Deci's (1980) writings on self-determination provide insight on distinction between action and behaviour. Deci described three types of behavioural responses: (i) Non-self determining; (ii) automatize or habit; and (iii) self-determined—involving human capacity to decide how to behave. Emmons (1997) in a variety of pro-environmental settings ranging from recycling of garbage to specific environment resource conservation, such as water, forest, use of energy have found that people with the self-determined behaviour have more knowledge and are significantly more involved in pro-environmental behaviour in comparison to others.

Value Orientation

Values tend to be widely shared by all members of a culture. Value orientation towards natural resources can be arrayed along a continuum ranging from anthropocentric to bio-centric (Shindler *et al.*, 1993; Steel *et al.*, 1994; Vaske and Donnelly, 1999). On this scale these orientations are not mutually exclusive rather, they can be arranged along a continuum with bio-centric viewpoints on one end and anthropocentric orientations on the other. An anthropocentric value orientation represents a human centred view of the non-human world (Eckersley, 1992). The approach assumes that providing human usage and benefits is the primary aim of environmental resource allocation and management. The environment is seen as material to be used by humans as they find fit (Scherer and Attig, 1983). Thus, an anthropocentric value orientation emphasizes the instrumental importance of forests for human society, rather than their inherent worth (Vaske and Donnelly, 1999). In contrast, a bio-centric value orientation is a nature-centred approach (Ekersley, 1992). Ecosystems, species, and natural organisms are elevated to centre stage. Human desires are still important, but are viewed in a large perspective. This approach assumes that environmental objects have inherent as well as are of instrumental worth and that human economy and benefits are not necessarily the most important centre of natural resources. In matters of natural resource management, these inherent qualities are to be equally respected and preserved, even if they conflict with human-centred ideals (Thompson and Barton, 1994).

The foundation of intrinsic motivation and attitude-behaviour linkages are provided by values. Basic values are chacterised as being few in number, they are widely shared in society, and transcend to specific situations and experiences. While values are typically learned early in childhood and remain stable throughout life, there is increasing evidence that we are in a period where are rapidly and significantly change with regard to environmental value orientation (Bengston, 1994). Researchers have attributed this shift to population growth (Cromartie and Wardwell, 1999; Manfredo and Zinn, 1996) and changing demographics (Steel *et al.,* 1994). Generally, it has been found that bio-centric-oriented individuals tend to be more motivated towards environment protection-oriented management strategies like aiming protection and are less supportive to economic development (McFarlane and Boxall, 2002, 2003; Vaske and Donnelly, 1999; Singhal, 2000; Sinha and Suar, 2003). Misra (2003) found environmental awareness is a prerequisite for environmentally responsible behaviour. Similarly, involvement in environmentally responsible behaviour has been found associated with age, education, place of residence, gender (Hobley, 1996; Poffenberger, 1996; Ostrom, 1990; Singhal, 1999).

Cognitive Hierarchy Model

Determinants of pro-environmental behaviour has been summarized through cognitive hierarchy model, which recognizes environmental activism as a function of social psychological variables (e.g., value orientation, attitude towards natural resource and knowledge), social structural variables, and social influences. Several studies have shown that a cognitive hierarchy framework consists of basic values, general beliefs, specific attitudes, and behaviour provides a suitable basis for understanding environmentalism (Stern, Dietz, and Guagnano, 1995; Dietz, Stern, and Guagnano, 1998; McFarlane and Boxall, 2003). The conceptual framework of the cognitive hierarchy model is presented in Figure 8.2. Several layers of cognitions are represented with the basic values which provides the foundation for higher order attitudes and behaviours (Rokeach, 1973).

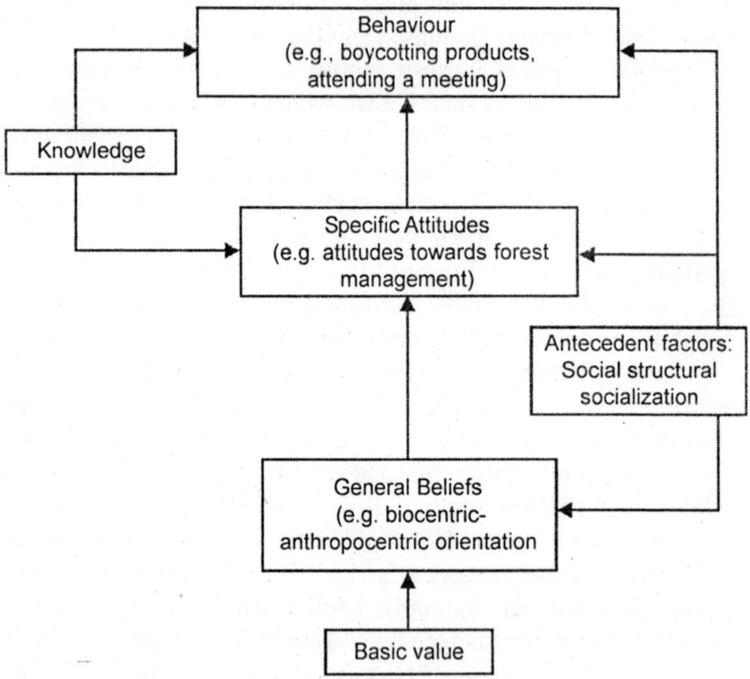

Fig. 8.2: Conceptual Representation of a Cognitive Hierarchy Model of Values, Attitudes and Behaviours.

The figure shows that the basic values serve as the foundation of behaviour. They are fewer in number and shared in the society, and transcend specific situations and experiences. Thus, they are generally poor explantors of specific attitudes and behaviours. The precise number or types of basic values are not known.

In the backdrop of cognitive hierarchy model and review of determinants of pro-environmental behaviour it can be said, the most important factor from psychological point of view, in this regard is, lack of people's concern in environmental protection in their day-to-day behaviour. For example, there is a need to bring about desirable changes in the attitude of the people towards these problems, because environmental attitudes have been found to be an important and powerful predictor of ecological behaviour (Kaiser *et al.*, 1999). In order to bring about permanent changes in people's environmentally destructive behaviour through intervention, it is essential to increase their environmental concern and knowledge about the effects and consequences of the ongoing environmental degradation (Fransson *et al.*, 1999). Unless there is mass awareness about the negative consequences of continuous and accelerating overuse and destruction of natural resources, environmentally responsible behaviour cannot be expected. One line of research in the field of environmental psychology has, therefore, been oriented towards studying the ways in which people perceive and evaluate the various forms of environmental problems.

Indigenous Approach to Sustainable Environment Development

To understand the role of culture in determining pro-environment behaviour it would be worthwhile to consider indigenous approach to study sustainable environment development, specifically for Indian conditions. People of India have spiritual and socio-cultural affinity with Himalayas, Ganges and Bhagirathi. Besides, symbolizing cultural significance they determine human survival, quality of life and development. Kulkarni (1991) has shown that the ancient India people belonging to various cultures were more concerned to the environment in which they breathe in. Attitude of these people was based on the relationship between (hu)man and nature. Vedic people interacted with nature by treating them as a part, and wished well-being of other creatures and plants along with themselves. Similarly, they regarded rivers as life-bestowing and themselves pulsating with life (Lal, 1991). Several contemporary Indian thinkers (Chaitanya, 2000; Dharmpal, 1993; Misra, 1994; Thakar, 1989) have indicated that mysterious East has a potential to contribute various field of psychology but is not interesting enough to a large section of psychologists. Unfortunately, they have even neglected the environmental issues troubling its people (Sinha, 1997).

Recently, based on the experience of struggle to save Himalaya, Pirta (2003) has developed an indigenous approach to sustainable development (refer Figure 8.3).

A view at the figure makes it evident that in this paradigm, the development of both individual and community is important along with harmony among head, heart and hand. This approach explains that besides physical encompasses its social, psychological and spiritual aspects are deeply rooted in Hindu Worldview. The importance of cultural factors in community interventions have also been highlighted by Roy (1993), Sheth (1994) and Tripathi (2003).

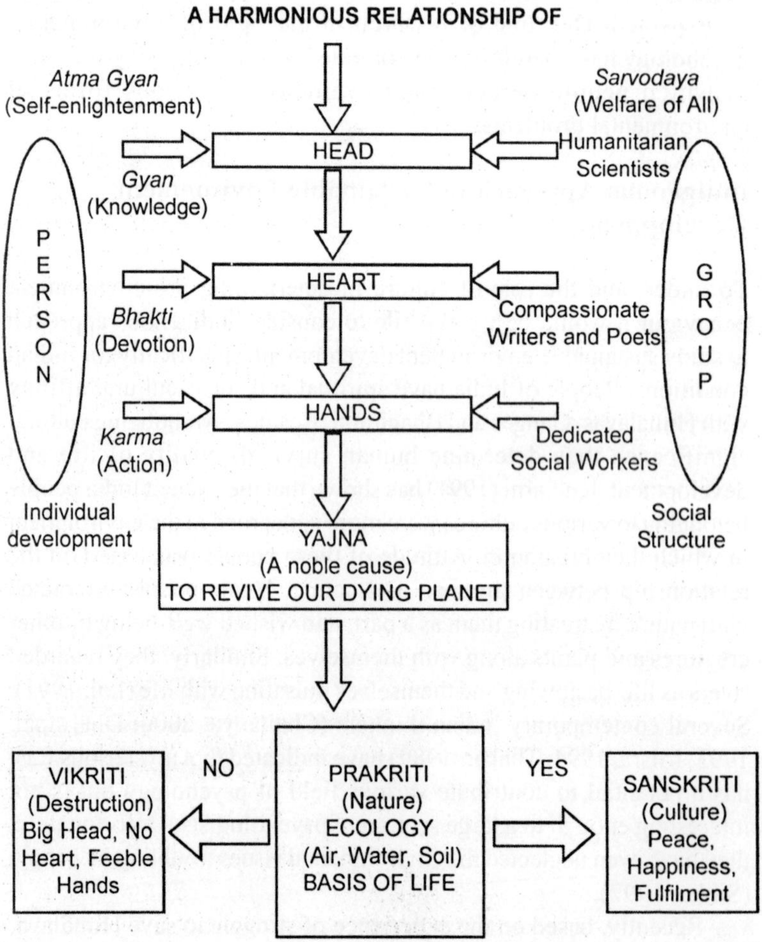

Fig 8.3: The Native Cognitive Model of Sustainable Environment Development (after Pirta, 2003)

Conclusion

In the backdrop of culture, knowledge systems and determinants of pro-environmental behaviour it can be concluded that the studies of behavioural and psychological factors have profound implications for pro-environmental action. Ultimately, human action will be the basis for success or failure of sustaining the diversity of life. It is however, very difficult to change behaviour (short of coercion) without changing people's attitude, motivation and awareness. Therefore, in a collective society like India the intervention for mobilising people and engaging them in pro-environmental action would demand interpersonal coordination. Interpersonal coordination for social and individual action necessitates bridging the gap between existing conditions and goals, redefinition of the boundaries of self, and society. An effective strategy in this regard would be promotion of common goals, interdependencies, joint activity, and linking life goals with natural resource management goals. It is hoped that this framework can help as a guide for future action-oriented programmes in the field of education and management of environment for quality of life.

REFERENCES

Agrawal, A. (1995), "Dismantling the Divide between Indigenous and Scientific Knowledge." *Development and Change*. 26, 413-439.

Arce, A. and Long, N. (1992), The Dynamics and Knowledge-Interfaces between Bureaucrats and Peasants. In Long, N. and Long A. (eds.). *Battlefields of Knowledge: The Interlocking of Theory and Practice in Social Research and Development*. Routledge, London.

Armstrong, J.B. and Impara, J.C. (1991), The Impact of an Environmental Education Programme on Knowledge and Attitude. *The Journal of Environmental Education*, 22 (4), 36-40.

Berkes, F. and Folke, C. (1998), Linking Social and Ecological Systems for Resilience and Sustainability. In Berkes, F. and Folke, C. (eds.) *Linking Social and Ecological Systems: Management Practices and Social Mechanisms for Building Resilience*, Great Britain; Cambridge University.

Boerscjog, S. and De Young, R. (1993), Evaluation of Selected Recycling Curricula: Educating the Green Citizen. *The Journal of Environmental Education*, 24 (3), 17-22.

Bonnes, M. and Sechiaroli, G. (1995), *Environmental Psychology*. New Delhi, Sage Publication.

Borden, R.J. (1984-1985), Psychology and Ecology: Beliefs in Technology and the Diffusion of Ecological Responsibility. *The Journal of Environmental Education*. 16 (2), 14-19.

Borden, R.J. and Schettino, A. (1979), Determinants of Environmentally Responsible Behaviour: Facts or Feelings? *Journal of Environmental Education* 10, 35-37.

Bos, A.H. (1974), *Oordeelsvorming in Groepen: Willens en Wetens, Wikken en Wegen: Polariteit en Ritme als Sleutel tor Ontwikkeling Van Sociale Organismen*. (Ph.D. Dissertation: Wageningen Agricultural University, WAU Dissertation Abstract No.586, The Netherlands).

Bowers, C.A. (1993), *Education Cultural Myths and the Ecological Crisis* Albany: Suny Press.

Bright, A.D. and M.J. Manfredo (1996), Conceptual Model of Attitudes Toward Natural Resource Issues. *Hum Dimensions Wildi* 1 (1), 21.

Bright, A.D., Barro, S.C., and Burtz, R.T. (2002). Public Attitudes Toward Ecological Restoration in the Chicago Metropolitan Region. *Society and Natural Resources*, 15, 763-785.

Bruvold, W.H. (1973), Beliefs and Behaviour as Determinants of Environmental Attitudes. *Environment and Behaviour* 5:202-218.

Carr, S. and J. Tait (1991), Differences in the Attitudes of Farmers and Conservationists and Their Implications. *Journal Environmental Management*, 32:281-291.

Clarck, C.F., Kotchen, M.J. and Moore, M.R. (2003), Internal and External Influences on Pro-environmental Behaviour: Participation in a Green Electricity Program. *Journal of Environmental Psychology*, 23 (3), 237-246.

Clark, W.C. (1988), The Human Dimension of Global Environmental Change. In Committee on Global Change: Toward an Understanding of Global Change. Washington. D.C.: National Academy Press.

Cone, J.D. and Hayes, S.C. (1980), *Environmental Problems and Behavioural Solutions*. Monterey. CA: Books/Cole.

Cortese, A. (1992), Education for an Environmentally Sustainable Future. *Environmental Science and Technology*; 26, 1108-1114.

Cottrell, S.P. and Graffe, A.R. (1997). Testing a Conceptual Framework of Responsible Environmental Behaviour. *The Journal of Environmental Education*, 29 (1), 17-27.

Cowan, M. and Stapp, W. (1982), *Environmental Education in Action: International Case Studies in Environmental Education*. Columbus. OH: ERIC Clearinghouse.

Donnelly, M.P., J.J. Vaske, D. Whittaker and B. Shelby, (2000). Toward an Understanding of Norm Prevalence: A Comparative Analysis. *Journal of Environmental Management*, 25:403-414.

Eckersley, R. (1992). *Environmental and Political Theory: Toward an Ecocentric Approach*, Albany: State University of New York Press.

Fishbein, M. and Ajzen, I. (1971, 1975), *Belief, attitude, intention, and behaviour: an introduction to theory and research*. Reading. MA: Addison-Wesley.

Fransson, N., and Gärling, T. (1999), Environmental Concern: Conceptual Definitions, Measurement Methods, and Research Findings, *Journal of Environmental Psychology*, 19, 4, 369-408.

Fulton, D.C., J. Pate and M.J. Manfredo, (1995), *Colorado residents' attitudes toward trapping in Colorado* (Project Report No.23) Project Report for the Colorado Division of Wildlife Fort Collins, Co., Colorado State University, Human Dimensions in Natural Resources Unit.

Fulton, D.C., M.J. Manfredo and J. Lipscomb, (1996), Wildlife Value Orientations: A Conceptual and Measurement Approach. *Hum Dimensions Wild* 1:24-27.

Gagnon-Thompson, S.C. and Barton, M.A (1994), Ecocentric and Anthropocentric Attitudes Toward the Environment. *Journal of Environmental Psychology*, 14, 149-157.

Gardner, G.T. and Stern, P.C. (1996), *Environmental Problems and Human Behaviour Boston*: Allyn and Bacon.

Garling, T., Fujii, S., Garling, A. and Jakobsson, C. (2003), Moderating Effects of Social Value Orientation on Determinants of Pro-Environmental Behaviour Intention. *Journal of Environmental Psychology*, 23, 1-9.

Geller, E.S., Winettt, R.A. and Everett, P.B. (1982), *Preserving the Environment*, New York: Pergamon.

Giglotti, L.M. (1990), Environmental Education: What Went Wrong? What Can be Done? *The Journal of Environmental Education* 22 (1), 9-12.

Gray, D. (1985), *Ecological Beliefs and Behaviour: Assessment and Change* Westport, CT: Greenwood Press.

Guiterrez deWhite, T. and Jacobson, S.K. (1994), Evaluating Conservation Education Programs at a South American Zoo. *The Journal of Environmental Education*, 25 (4), 18-22.

Hardin, G. (1968), The Tragedy of the Commons. *Science*, 162, 1243-1248.

Hines, J. Hungerterd, H. and Tomera, A. (1986), Analysis and Theses of Research on Environmental Behaviour: A Meta-analysis, *Journal of Environmental Education* 18, 1-18.

Holling, C.S. (1998), Science, Sustainability and Resource Management. In: Berkes, F. and Folke C. (eds.) *Linking Social and Ecological Systems: Management Practices and Social Mechanisms for Building Resilience*. Cambridge University. Great Britain.

Johnson, M. (1992), *Lore: Capturing Traditional Environmental Knowledge*. Ottwa: Dene Cultural Institute/IDRC.

Jordan, J.R., Hungerford, H. and Tomera, A. (1986), Effects of Two Residential Workshops on High School Students. *Journal of Environmental Education* 18: 15-22.

Kaiser, F., G. Wolfing, S. and Fuhrer, U. (1999), Environmental Attitude and Ecological Behaviour. *Journal of Environmental Psychology*. 19, (1), 1-19.

Kaiser, F.G. and Simoda, T.A. (1999), Responsibility as Predictor of Ecological Behaviour. *Journal of Environmental Psychology*. 19, 3, 243-253.

Lewin, K. (1951), *Field Theory in Social Science,* New York: Harper.

Maloney, M.P. and Ward, M.O. (1973), Ecology: Let's Hear in From the People. An Objective Scale for the Measurement of Ecological Attitudes and Knowledge. *American Psychologists*, 28. 583-586.

Manfredo, M.J., Fishbein, M., Haas, G.E. and Watson, A.E. (1990), Attitudes Toward Prescribed Fire Policies, *J. For* 88 (7): 19-23.

McFarlane, B.L. and Boxall, P.C. (2000), Factors Influencing Forest Values and Attitudes of Two Stakeholder Groups: The Case of the Foothills Model Forest, Alberta, Canada. *Society and Natural Resources*, 13, 649-661.

Milbrath, L. (1989), *Envisioning a Sustainable Society: Learning Our Way Out.* Albany: State University of New York Press.

Osakamp, S. (1983), Psychology's Role in the Conserving Society. *Population and Environment Behaviour and Social Issues.* 6, 255-293.

Pirta, R.S. (2003), Native Cognition of Sustainable Development in the Western Himalaya. *Psychological Studies*, 48 (2) 32-42.

Roth, R.E. and Perez, J. (1989), Twelfth Grade Student Knowledge and Attitudes Toward the Environment in the Dominican Republic: An Assessment. *The Journal of Environmental Education*, 20 (3), 10-14.

S.J. 'O'berg, L., (1988), Psychological Perspective on Environmental Problems. In U. Svedin and B. Heurling, (Eds), *Swedish Perspective on Human Response to Global Change.* Stockholm: Swedish Council for Planning and Coordination of Research.

S.J. 'O'berg, L., (1989), Global Change and Human Action: Psychological Perspectives. *International Social Science Journal.* 121, 413-432.

Schoenfeld, C., and Griffen, R.J., (1981), Communication: A Human Factor. In R.J. Dunke, G.V. Burger, and J.K., March (Eds.) *Wildlife Management on Private Lands Madison,* Wisconsin: The Wildlife Society (Winconsin Chapter).

Scott, D. and Willits, F.K. (1991), *Environmental Concern of Pennsylvania Citizen's: Data from a Statewide Survey (Technical Report, A.E. and R.S. 219).* University Park. PA: The Pennsylvania State University, Department of Agricultural Economics and Rural Sociology.

Shindler, B.P. List and Steel, B.S. (1993), Managing Federal Forests: Public Attitudes in Oregon and Nationwide. *Journal of Forestry,* July: 36-42.

Sia, A.P. Hungerford, H.R. and Tomera, A.N. (1985), Selected Predictors of Responsible Environmental Behaviour: An Analysis. *The Journal of Environmental Education*, 17 (2), 31-40.

Singhal, R. (2000), A Model for Integrating Indigenous and Scientific Forest Management: Potentials and Limitations for Adaptive Learning in A. Lawrence (Ed.). *Forestry, Forest Users and Research: New Ways of Learning.* 133-138. The Netherlands: ETFRN.

Sinha, S. and Suar, D., (2003), Forest and People: Understanding the Institutional Governance, Social Identity and Peoples Participation in Indian Forest Management. *Journal of Rural Development,* 22 (4), 425-454.

Sinha, S. and Suar, D., (2003), Values and Peoples Participation in Community Based Forest Management. *Journal of Human Values,* 9 (2), 141-151.

Sivek, D.J. and Hungerford, H. (1989), Predictors of Responsible Behaviour in Members of Three Wiscosin Conservation Organization. *The Journal of Environmental Education,* 21 (2), 35-40.

Stern, P.C. (1992), Psychological Dimensions of Global Environmental Change. *Annual Review of Psychology,* 43, 269-302.

Stern, P.C. and Oskamp, S. (1987), Managing Scarce Environment Resources. in. D. Stokols and I. Altman (Eds.) *Handbook of Environmental Psychology* (vol. 2. pp. 1043-1088). New York: Wiley.

Stern, P.C., Dietz, T. and Guagnano, G.A. (1995), The New Ecological Paradigm in Social-Psychological Context. *Environment and Behaviour,* 27, 723-743.

Thompson, S.C.G. and Barton, M.A. (1994), Ecocentric and Anthropocentric Attitudes Toward the Environment. *Journal of Environmental Psychology,* 14:149-158.

Tripathi, J.P. (2003), *Time Management and Choice Behaviour Among Eastern* UP villagers. Unpublished Thesis work, Department of Psychology, D.D.U. Gorakhpur University, Gorakhpur.

Umans, Laurent, (1992), *Analysis and Typology of Indigenous Forest Management in the Humid Tropics of Asia.* IKC-NBLF and BOS Foundation, Wageningen, Netherlands.

Vaske, J.J. and Donnelly, M.P. (1999), A Value-Attitude-Behaviour Model Predicting Wildland Preservation Voting Intentions. *Society and Natural Resources,* 12, 523-537.

Warren, D.M. (1991), *Using Indigenous Knowledge in Agricultural Development.* World Bank, World Bank Discussion Paper No.127. Washington DC, USA.

WCED, (World Commission on Environmental and Development). (1987). *Our Common Future,* Oxford, Oxford University Press.

Weirsum, K.F., Singhal, R. and Benneker, C. (2004), Common Property and Collaborative Forest Management: Rural Dynamics and Evolution in Community Forestry Regimes. *Forests, Trees and Livelihoods*, 14, 281-293.

SECTION-III

CULTURE AND PERSONALITY

9

Family and Socialization

Aradhana Shukla

In our daily life we generally observe that the human behaviour is not independent. It is always governed and decided by the rules of the society in which she resides. Whiting (1977) and Bronfen Brenner (1977) have shared the view that human activity can best be understood within the context in which it develops and takes place. Also, s/he receives many experiences which help him/her in vital development and teaches him/her how to live in a society as an active member. Socialization is the set of events and processes by which children as well as adults acquire the belief, view and knowledge about the particular society, and the subgroups in which they are born.

Ochs (1986) has defined socialization in terms of language and socialization as, "Socialization through language and socialization to use language". It comes from interaction, sequence of exchange in behavioural term and which appears in terms of one's response. Interactional routines level to strudel the situation.

The concept of socialization was at first emerged and developed as a disciplines of Sociology, Social psychology and Social Anthropology refers to the process of deliberate shaping, by conscious and active training of an individual to imbibe and adopt the models, values and expectations of the society (Berry, Poortinga Segall and Dasen, 1992/2002). Jahoda (1995) and Johoda and Lewis (1988) have compiled many definitions of socialization and defined as the process whereby children become effectively as the member of a particular society and they have described three models of socialization. They are as follows:

(1) The unfolding model (it is based on the internal attributes of person),
(2) The clay moulding model (which emphasizes the process of development, and
(3) The interactive model (it deals with the interaction between nature and nurture.

The interactive model is the ground of socialization research and deals the interactions of child with his family and other features of environment. Bruner and Bornstein (1989) draw attention to the significant aspects of socialization, namely, symbolic representation and meaning making. To quote as anthropologist's and that concern with socialization it can be said that they are fond of reminding us much of development that has taken place in culture in which symbolic encounters and symbolic representations therefore are at a level of nature encountered confrontationally. A great deal of early transmission undoubtedly consists of getting the child ready to play a part in symbolic exchanges that, in their pattern entirely constitute a culture. Thus, socialization is viewed here as a life long process continuous throughout the life span, till death.

Herskovitz (1948) and Berry *et al.* (1992-2002) have established the fact that an individual is always surrounded by his culture which motivates him to learn about the environment which are directly related to his culture. Learning occurs without informal training and it is generally through apprenticeships and exposures to daily experiences in which seasoned adults, e.g. parents, relatives, teachers and neighbours, and even peers act as agents of socialization. This process is called enculturation. The end product of successful enculturation is a person who can competently function in a given culture.

According to Berry *et al.* (1992/2002), the study of both the enculturation and socialization processes focuses on two aspects: the cultural content or substance that is being transmitted and the means of style of cultural transmission (child reading or child training practices). Thus, it can be said that socialization is an ontogenetic process which continues till death.

Family Network and the Process of Socialization

In dealing with the process of socialization the importance of family cannot be denied. The term environment has been regarded as a network to provide form and factors, which surround, engulf and play with an individual (Bloom, 1968). According to Stott (1974) the term environment in its usual sense, encompasses all of the influences, upon development which come from outside to the individual.

Different authors have defined home and family. Murdock (1949) states that, "The family is as social group characterized by common residence, economic cooperation and reproduction. It includes both sexes, who maintain a socially approved social relationship and one or more children, own or adopted of the sexual co-habituating pair". The international dictionary of education mentions that, "family is a primary social group of parents, offsprings and possibly other members of household".

Dealing with the significance of family climate Malm (1952) has characterized, "A good house with affection, democracy, lack of conflict, comradeship, good personal adjustment, scarcity and appropriateness of attitude". The family is considered good where child is allowed a fair degree of autonomy and a share in familial matters.

Thus, it is surely fair to say that a good home seems to be one is which the child is given fullest opportunity for self-expression within the limit of parental affection, protection and supervision. A child is allowed a fair degree of autonomy, is included in important discussions and controlled by reasoning and verbal disciplines. Danesh (1978) pointed out, "authoritarian families are power oriented, tend to have dichotomous conceptions and have emotional and intellectual rigidity. In contrast, democratic homes and permissive homes bow to the whim of the child".

With regard to the developmental surroundings that play vital role were suggested by psychologist. Super and anthropologist Harkness (Harkness and Super, 1983, 1996; Super and Harkness, 1986; 1997). They suggested that the surroundings of a child has three components or subsystems: first the setting, or the physical and social context in which the child lives. It is the family with its basic attributes. The second subsystem is the customs or culturally determined rearing and educational products. It is customary and is culturally influenced by school environment. The third and last component is psychological characteristics of the caretakers including the impact of parental behaviour on children as well as parent child interaction. These subsystems cover all aspects and dimensions which are covered by people throughout the life. In addition, they deal major early sensory experiences which play important role in life. They are universal and occur everywhere.

Social Context of Kumaun

Kumaun is known as the north zone of central Himalayas and entitled as Uttaranchal earlier and Uttarakhand later on. On the 9th November, 2000, it received the prestige of 27th state of India. The Uttarakhand is divided in two regions namely, Kumaun and Garhwal. Six districts have constituted Kumaun. They are Almora, Bageshwar, Champawat, Nainital, Pithoragarh and Udham Singh Nagar. According to census 1991 the total population of Kumaun is 29,43,199, which increased rapidly. The social segment residing in these six districts is termed as Kumauni. These traditional Kumauni people are found somewhat different with the people of other segments of society because of their family structure and social system. In order to find out the difference in the family patterns many attempts have been made. Srivastava (1996) studied personality profile of children as correlated with perceived parental attitude. It was found that democratic parenting was highly prominent among Kumauni and the structure of self was quite higher. Moreover, she investigated that achievement level was relatively higher among non-Kumauni children migrated from plains. Karnataka (1998) pointed out that academic stress and stress management skills were relatively higher in Kumauni children as compared to Bhotia—a notable tribal of Kumaun. Also, she studied the pattern of parent child relation in Kumaun and it was found that parent child network was quite supportive for each other. Perhaps, it may be the reason that the self of Kumauni children was found more high. Family climate was also studied by Dwivedi (2001) and Bhandari (2005) and it was found that supportive family climate facilitated school related activities. In addition, it was also seen that those who had supportive climate at their homes were highly efficient in cognitive functioning and personality structure.

In addition, positive views for school and interest towards school related activities were also noted. Dhami (2002) studied the pattern of level-I and level-II intelligence in Kumauni children of various grades and found grade related change in level-II intelligence. Adhikari (2002) studied the pattern of disruptive behaviour and compared it with family climate. She found that decrease in the supportiveness of family climate causes disruption in behaviour.

Keeping these views in considerations it is surely fair to say that the family structure of Kumaun is not so traditional. It is modern. In addition, it is composed of higher order psychological practices that are implemented by the parent on their children. These studies were generally conducted in urban setting where almost couples were highly educated and both were employed. It can be argued that an employed couple does not spend much time with their children so when parent and child come on a platform (in every situation). They deal their children very softly and try to fulfil their all demands that are reasonable. Many parents help their children to shape their career and provide proper guidance. But in almost families parents expect love discipline, good academic career and obedience from their children. On the other hand, children expect love, care demand filler guide of life and counseller wherever required (Joshi, 2004). If it is present in the family, parent-child relationship is always appreciable.

Impact of Family Network on Personality

As it has been studied earlier that family is such type of network where a couple (one male and one female) lives along with their children. The couple is called parents by their children. These parents have a high responsibility on their shoulders and this is to bring-up their children properly and shape them according to their own demand and demands of the society. Also, it is the responsibility of the parents that they provide a platform to their children where they shape their personality either by their own endeavour the situations given by their parents. So, it is surely fair to say that parents laid an important role to build the personality of their children. For the fulfilment of this purpose supportive and favourable home environment is essential.

Pattern of Parenting Style

Going through the familiar network in Kumaun it is noticed that variation in parenting style causes variations in personality. Srivastava (1998) has opined that positive rearing practices from a family produce a sense of self-respect and personal identity in a child. Children brought-up in authoritative environment (Baumirind, 1975, 1991), Macoby and Martin (1983) develop positive image for themselves and shape their personality properly because they learn the difference of "good and bad", "acceptable/rejectable" and "desirable/ unbearable" from their parents and live accordingly. Moreover, it was also noticed that the children of authoritative parents were cognitively better than the children of authoritarian, democratic and permissive-indulgent parents. On the basis of Srivastava's (1998) findings it appears that authoritarian, democratic, and permissive-indulgent parenting is not suitable for the proper development of the child. Authoritarian parenting is very harsh while in the democratic and permissive-indulgent practices, parents loose their control over their children. Expectation of good rearing from these rearing devices is relatively impossible. Thus, it can be said that supportive family climate is necessary for overall development of the child (Dwivedi, 2001; Adhikari, 2002; Karnataka, 1998). Joshi (2004) studied the pattern of causal inference in children cross-cultural perspective. She studied Tharu, Buxa and general Kumaun children and found that the perception of causal inference was quite similar in these children. Also, she studied the pattern of within family expectation in six ways, namely:

(i) expectation from mother to child.
(ii) expectation from father to child.
(iii) expectation from child to mother.
(iv) expectation from child to father.
(v) expectation from husband to wife.
(vi) expectation from wife to husband.

Joshi explored that the magnitude of familiar expectation was relatively higher in general Kumauni children's followed by Tharu and Buxas, respectively. She also found that parents expect higher from their sons as compared to their daughter.

Summing up, certainly it may be said that variation in family climate causes variation in the personality pattern of children.

Not only in childhood but also for adults family climate plays important role. Kumari (2005) explored the pattern of life satisfaction, temperament and emotional disturbance between husbanded and widow women of varying SES and residential local and she found that widows were more emotionally disturbed and dissatisfied with life than husbanded women. Also, she studied that urban women were more dissatisfied from their life than rural women. She concluded that husbanded and widow women do not perceive their family climate. A husbanded woman finds supportive network of family and complete security from her husband but widow woman has to carve out her destiny and future of her children. She has to carry out the responsibilities within home and outside home. Therefore, higher level of emotional disturbance and dissatisfaction from life is obvious for her. In addition, it was also noted that the high level of emotional disturbance was shared by young adult women. This finding is in close consonance with Kakkar (2005). She also found that variation is that level of employment plays an important role in the development of emotional disturbance. Also, she resulted that the magnitude of well-being was higher and resulted and emotional disturbance was lower is middle class employed women. Moreover, it was also visited that women were more disturbed than men. Actually, Kakkar (2005) has taken the sample from the rural area where the condition of women is vary pathetic. She works hard for home and agriculture system is also based on her shoulders. On the other hand male society is very lethargic and spent the time in playing cards and drugs. In addition, they impose very cruel practice with their women and children's i.e. beating, abusing and harsh control over financial expenses. Therefore, it is vary obvious that women are highly emotionally disturbed than men in Kumauni society.

Although the participation of women is conspicuously low in the Indian labour force, a trend towards feminization of the labour market was seen in urban India by the 1980s (Deshpande and Deshpande, 1992). In the manufacturing sector in particular, the participation rate of women increased from 13 per cent in 1977-78—1983 to 29.3 per cent in 1983—1987-88 (Visaria and Minhas, 1991). In the other sectors, both finance and services, registered a slight increase in women's participation from 1.9 to 3.0 per cent and from 28.5 to 30.4 per cent during the same period. Acharya (1996) reported a significant rise in the number of women in professional, administrative and clerical staff between 1977-78 and 1987-88. Some trades also indicate a small but growing number of women opting for professional which was considered male dominated, for example, engineering, commerce, management and marketing (Narasimha Reddy, 1979). As a result, despite an overall low participation of women in labour activity, the visibility of women employed in regular salaried jobs in the formal sector are gradually increasing. With the Indian government's commitment to education of the girl child, the expansion of the industrial and service sector, and the rising cost of urban living, Indian women are expected to enter the organized labour market in large number in the coming years.

From this discussion it appears that women's employment is stratified in three ways and it determines the socio-economic status of the family where women live. Kakkar (2005) selected doctors, university teachers, bank officers, class three clerks and maids and sweepers in her study and compared them with unemployed women. She found that the pattern of well-being was higher in middle class employed women followed by lower class and higher class respectively. In order to prove her results she argued that middle class women are satisfied with their life because they in general are in salaried employment and they have to be satisfied with their salary. In their limited financial structure they have to maintain their status. So far as the matter of women of class fourth employment was concerned it was noticed that they had no complaint with their life. In this regard it can be stated that a person who gets less money and finds difficult to get his needs fulfil is entirely concern with the present. He has less care about his future and believes in eat, drink and be marry policy. So, it appeared that the life of middle class society is more tensed as compared to higher and low people.

Thus, it is surely fair to say that employment of women affects in two ways. It yields rewards as well as cost. It is by and large accepted by the researchers [Thaker and Mishra (1999); Karnatak (2003)]. It is the main quest that whether employed cause changes in the quality of stress in women's life. Joshi (2007) studied the impact of family structure on the daily hessels of employed and unemployed women. She noted that since the subjective well-being was relatively higher in the employed women of joint family and residing in nuclear family. Joshi in this regard stated that women's employment in nuclear family plays an important role because here salary is considered as an additional income. If in a joint family a woman is permitted in employment it is supposed that family members will share her responsibilities and try to give her every possible comfort. But economic independence of women causes many other stresses on her life. They are related with her own health inability of social functioning less care for her children and unsatisfactory marital relations. Although it has created a sense of ego development and self-esteem (Kaur, 2001) in women yet they have gained it on the cost of their own family. Since, the psyche of Indian and western people is entirely different, so Indian women get many problems while confronting home and office. So it is a doubtless fact that in spite of economic independence of life the employed women of Kumaun are not so healthy.

Impact of Family Climate on School Climate and Scholastic Behaviour

As it has been stated that family plays an important role in child development it has also been described that early experience of family makes direct influence on early scholastic experiences and school related behaviour of the child. In case, parents help the child in school readiness the adjustment of child in school becomes very easy, but if they threat the child by name of school reversed situation is appeared which blackens the adjustment of the child. Karnatak (1998) studied that the children who experienced themselves as rejected in their homes experienced much academic stress and they were unable to get the devices stress management. In a cross-cultural perspective she found that where the children were less adjusted to schools there they had more sense of rejection from their parents. Pant (1999) studied family-school relationship in developmental perspective and she noted that with increase in age the children got more facilitation in scholastic adjustment. Perhaps, it is due to peer group interaction and good teacher-taught relationship. Dwivedi (2000) and Adhikari (2002) carried family climate and school environment at one platform and studied their consequences on academic stress, management and disrupted behaviour. It was found that supportiveness provided by family results supportiveness in school and helps in school related activities. Children brought up in such environment are able to use positive coping behaviour to get rid of from school related hassles as well as familial complications. Findings are in close consonance with Bhandari (2005) who compared home and school climate with emotional disturbance and found that variation in both climates causes variation in the magnitude of emotional disturbance and disruptive behaviour which was defined in terms of depressive behaviour, obsessive-compulsive behaviour, hyper activity, somatic complaints, anxiety and social withdrawal, so on.

On the basis of this discussion it can be suggested that healthy family matrix is needed for harmonious development of the child. There is a need for longitudinal researches which produce long-term pattern of disruptive behaviour.

Although attempts have been made to cover many variables that emerges in the family and lay their impact on behaviour patterns yet many other variables are remained that need to be explored like, broken home, single parenting, family size ordinal position of the child behaviour and in case, studied properly can help in minimizing the behavioural complication of the child may be caused by disturbed family environment.

REFERENCES

Acharya, S. (1996), Women is the Labor Force: A Temporal and Spatial Analysis. In S. Harton (Ed), *Women and Industrialization in India*, Landon: Routledge.

Adhikari, S. (2002), Effect of Climate Supportiveness and Parenting Style on Disruptive Behaviours. Unpublished Ph.D. Thesis. Department of Psychology, Kumaun University, Nainital.

Baumrind, D. (1951), Parenting Style and Adolescent Development. In R.M. Hesner, A.C., Pelisson and J. Brooks. Gunn (Eds.), *Encyclopedia of Adolescence*. New York: Gailand.

Baumrind, D. (1975), *Early Socialization and the Discipline Controversy.* Morristown N.J: General Lessening Press.

Berry J. W., Poortinga, Y.H., Segall, M.H. and Dasen P.R. (1992/2002), *Cross-Cultural Psychology: Research and Applications.* New York: Cambridge University Press.

Bhandari, V. (2005), A Study of Disruptive Behaviours in Children of Rural and Urban Setting, Ph.D. Thesis Submitted. Department of Psychology, Kumaun University, Nainital.

Bloom, M. (1968), *Stability and Change in Human Characteristics*, New York: John Willy and Sons.

Brenfenbrenner, U. (1977), Towards an Experimental Ecology of Human Development. *American Psychologist* 32, 513-531.

Bruner, J.S. and Bornstein, M.H. (1989). On Interactions. In M.H. Bornstein and J.S. Bruner (eds). *Interactions in Human Development.* Hillsdale N-J: Lawrence-Erlbaum.

Danesh, H.B. (1978). The Authoritarian Family and Its Developments. *Canadian Psychiatric Association Journal*. 23, 7, 479-485.

Deshpande, S. and Deshpande, L.K. (1992), New Economic Policy and Female Employment. *Economic and Political Weekly*, 27, 2248-2252.

Dhami, S. (2002), A Study of Level I and Level II Intelligence as Affected by Age, Sex and Emotional Disturbance a Factor Analytic Approach. Unpublished Ph.D. Thesis, Department of Psychology, Kumaun University, Nainital.

Dwivedi, V. (2001). Impact of Climateric Supportiveness on Academic Stress and Management as Affected by Sex and Grade. A Study in Open and Closed Cultures. Unpublished Ph.D. Thesis, Department of Psychology, Kumaun University, Nainital.

Harkness, G. and Super, C.M. (1983), The Cultural Construction of Child Development. *Ethos,* 11, 221-231.

Harkness, S. and Super, C.M. (1996), *Parents Cultural Belief System and Their Origins, Expression, and Consequences*, New York: Guilford.

Herskovits, M.J. (1948), *Man and His Works: The Science of Cultural Anthropology,* New York: Knopf.

Jahoda, G. (1995), *The Ancestry of a Model. Culture and Psychology,* pp. 11-24

Jahoda, G. and Lewis I.M. (Eds) (1988) *Acquiring Culture: Cross Cultural Studies in Child Development.* London: Croom Helm.

Joshi, A. (2003), Life Satisfaction and Adjustment Problems in Kumauni Women. Paper Presented in IAAP Congress held at Department of Psychology, JNV University, Jodhpur, Oct. 10-13.

Joshi, A. (2004), A Cross-Cultural Analysis of Casual Attribution in Children as Affected by Age and Gender: A Study of Accepted and Rejected Children. Unpublished Ph.D. Thesis, Department of Psychology, Kumaun University, Nainital.

Joshi, K. (2007) Pattern of Well-being and Daily Hassels in Kumauni Women of Joint and Nuclear Families as Affected by Their Job Status and Age. Unpublished Ph.D. Thesis. Department of Psychology, Kumaun University, Nainital.

Kakkar, R. (2005), A Development Analysis of Emotional Disturbance and Well-being as Affected by Gender and Level of Employment. Unpublished Ph.D. Thesis, Department of Psychology, Kumaun University, Nainital.

Karnatak, S. (1998), Cross-Cultural Analysis of Academic Stress and Stress Management in Developmental Perspective: A Study of Accepted and Rejected Children. Unpublished Ph.D. Thesis, Department of Psychology, Kumaun University, Nainital.

Karnatak, K. (2003), Life Satisfaction Among Dual Earners. Paper Presented in IAAP Congress held at Department of Psychology, JNV University, Jodhpur. Oct. 10-13.

Kaur, K. (2002), Patterns of Self-Esteem and Ego Development in Adolescent as Affected by Age, Sex and Cultural Context. Unpublished Ph.D. Thesis, Department of Psychology, Kumaun University Nainital.

Kumari, K. (2005), A Study of Temperament and Life Satisfaction as Affected by Emotional Disturbance in Kumauni Women of Varying SES. Unpublished Ph.D. Thesis, Department of Psychology, Kumaun University, Nainital.

Liederman, S.R., Tulkin and A. Rasenfield (Eds) *Culture and Infancy: Variations in the Human Experience.* New York: Academic Press.

Lin, C.C. and Fu, V.R. (1990), A Comparison of Child Rearing Practice among Chinese. Immigrant Chinese and Caesarian-American Parents. *Child Development,* 61, 429-433.

Maccoby, E.E. and Mastin, J.A. (1983), Socialization in the Context of the Family: Parent-Child Interaction. In P.H. Mussen (Ed.), *Handbook of Child Psychology,* Vol. 4, New York: Wiley.

Murdock, G P. (1949), *Social Structure.* New York, Macmilan Weekly.

Narsimha Reddy, D. (1979), Female Work Participation in India: Facts, Problems and Policies. *Indian Journal of Industrial Relations*, 15, 197-212.

Ochs, E. (1986), From Feeling to Grammar: A Samoan Case Study. In B. Scheiffelin and E. Ochs (Eds.) *Language Socialization Across Culture*, Cambridge: Cambridge University Press.

Pant, N. (1991), Development Patterns of Experimental Deprivation and Sex as Family Climate and School Related Outcomes. Unpublished Ph.D. Thesis, Department of Psychology, Kumaun University, Nainital.

Srivastava, P. (1996), Development Impact of Expressional Deprivation and Parental Attend on Personality Functioning of Children. Unpublished Ph.D. Thesis Department of Psychology, Kumaun University, Nainital.

Stott, L. H. (1974), *The Psychology of Human Development.* New York: Holl, Rinehart and Winston.

Super, C.M. and Harkness, S. (1986), The Developmental Niche: A Conceptualization at the Interface of Child and Culture. *International Journal of Behavioural Development*, 9, 4,545-570.

Super, C.M. and Harkness, S. (1997), The Cultural Shuttering of Child Development. In J.W. Berry, P.R. Dasen and T.S. Saraswathi (Eds). *Hand Books of Cross-Cultural Psychology*, Bostan: Allync Bacan.

Visaria, P. and Minhas, B.S. (1991). Evolving an Employment Policy for the 1995: What Do the Data Tell Us ? *Economic and Political Weekly,* 26, 969-982.

Whiting, J.W.M. (1977) A model for psychic cultural research. In P.H. Liederman., S.R., Tulkin and A. Rosenfield (eds.). *Culture and Infancy: Varifications in the Human Experience,* New York: Academic Press.

10

Culture and Identity Style Preferences

Contexts and Consequences

Rakesh Kumar Srivastava

The several intervening factors in formation of identity have been targeted in a broad body of theoretical and empirical literature. Erikson saw the formation of a personal sense of identity (verses identity diffusion) as one of the cornerstones of ego development (Erikson, 1982). Defined as "the accrued confidence (in) the inner sameness and continuity of one's meaning for others" (Erikson, 1950), identity is considerd to be of central concern during late adolescence. Building upon Erikson's work, James Marcia (1966) developed the identity statuses approach for studying the process of identity formation. Marcia's four identity statuses occupy unique positions along the dimensions of explanation and commitment. Identity statuses are both outcomes of the proces of identity formation and structural properties of personality, and each portrays a dominant mode of experiencing the world. Identity status at late adolescence should thus affect and shape future identity formation as well as person's passage through subsequent life stages.

Berzonsky (1989) presented a model of identity development that highlighted individual differences in the process by which self-relevant experience is encoded, represented, and utilized. He argued that individuals within Marcia's (1966) identity statuses differ in the social-cognitive processes they use to make decisions, cope with problems, and negotiate identity issues (Berzonsky, 1990). More specifically, three processing orientations (information, avoidant, and normative) were proposed to underline the four statuses. Berzonsky's model derived from the promise in larger run, information based decision will maximise adoption. In order to investigate three processing orientations or identity styles more directly, Berzonsky (1986, 1990) constructed a self-report measure of identity style. This process is assumed to have at least three levels. The most general level, identity style, refers to the strategy that individuals characteristically use or would prefer to employ. Berzonsky (1989) described that these orientations encompass the mechanism by which self-relevant information within specific identity domins is processed, structured, utilized, and revised (Srivastava, 1993; Berzonsky, 1994).

Given the importance of understanding the effect of social context on identity formation and the need for a workable multi-dimensional conceptual framework, Cote (1996) offered a series of interrelated postulates regarding some broad contextual parameters affecting identity formation. Identity, like other constructs of development, is thought to occur through the course of normal maturational processes within appropriate supportive social context. Contextual factors pertinent to identity formation encompass issues that close social relationships and the socio-cultural milieu present to the adolescent. Identity formation is not wholly an individualistic process; rather the social environment exerts its forms of power and influence. The certain important social contextual factors identified in relation to identity include family relationships, religiosity, ethnic and racial group membership, residence, and few others. The overview of researches conducted in the area of ego-identity and identity style suggests that several attempts have been made in the West (Adam, Montemayor and Gullotta, 1996; Phinney, 1990; Taylor and Oskey, 1995; Nesler, 1995) and also in India (Sinha, 1979; Srivastava, 1996, 1998; Bhusan, 1993) to correlate identity with a number of social and psychological variables.

In an earlier study (Srivastava, 1993) using the 39-item Identity style inventory ISI revised version (Berzonsky, 1992; Srivastava, 1992) found that tribal adolescents had significantly more information oriented and norm oriented style but less avoidant/diffuse style than the non-tribal adolescents. Results on a separate index of identity commitment show that tribal and non-tribal adolescents were not found to be significantly different. Howevr, no reported research has studied identity style of tribal and non-tribal boys, using an Indian adaption of the short form of Berzonsky's Identity style inventory short ISI-2 (Berzonsky, 1989; Srivastava, 1995). The main goal of the present research was to compare the identity style preferences of tribal and nontribal boys. Thus the purpose of the present paper was to study linkages between culture and identity style preferences as proposed by Berzonsky (1992).

The present study was conducted on Tharu tribals of Lakhimpur-Kheri district of Uttar Pradesh. In the 1991 census the five tribes (Bhotia, Buxa, Jaunsari, Raji and Tharu) were treated as scheduled tribes in Uttar Pradesh. The total population of scheduled tribes in India is 67,758,380 (Males = 34,363,271 and females = 33,395,109), in Uttar Pradesh 287,901 (Males = 150,420 and females = 137,481) and in Lakhimpur-Kheri district 28,856 (Males = 14,958 and females = 13,898). The Tharus live mainly in the *terai* regions of Lakhimpur-Kheri, Gonda, Gorakhpur and Behraich districts of Uttar Praesh, Dehradun, Nainital district of Uttaranchal and also in the terai regions of Nepal. There are also some pockets of Tharus in Bihar, Orissa, Maharashtra, Mizoram and West Bengal (Srivastava, 1988, 2000).

Method

Participants

The participants were 50 tribal (Tharu) and 50 non-tribal boys. Age range of the participants was 18-22 years. The tribal boys were sampled from the Tharu tribe of Lakhimpur-Kheri district in the state of Uttar Pradesh. The non-tribal boys were taken from the closest geographical regions from where the Tharu tribal boys were sampled. The participants were also matched on the variable of their educational level.

Measure

Identity style Inventory (ISI-2, Revised version, short form) developed by Berzonsky (1989) and as adapted in Hindi by the present researcher (Srivastava, 1995a) was used in the present study for studying identity styles of tribal and non-tribal boys. Like its original English version of ISI-2 (short form) the Hindi adaptation also consists of three subscales (*i.e.*, Information, Normative and Avoidant/Diffuse orientation) comprising 17 items. The score on a subscale was obtained by summing up the total for items of particular subscale rated on a scale of 1 to 5. This inventory yields a score for each of the three identity styles. Like original scale of short ISI-2 the adapted form also had the same scoring procedure. The adapted form of the short ISI-2 was also found to be a reliable and valid measure of identity style (Srivastava, 1998).

Results and Discussion

The Means, SDs and t-ratios obtained by tribal and non-tribal boys on three identity styles are given in Table 10.1.

Table 10.1: Showing Means, SDs and t-ratios obtained by tribal and non-tribal boys on adapted form of Short ISI-2

Identity Style	*Tribal Boys (N=50)*		*Non-Tribal boys (N=50)*		*t*
	M	*SD*	*M*	*SD*	
Informational	21.78	2.68	16.08	3.67	8.88*
Normative	23.38	3.15	16.14	3.80	10.37*
Diffuse/Avoidant	17.16	2.40	22.90	3.52	9.54*

* $p < 0.01$

Results as shown in Table 10.1 clearly reveal that tribal and non-tribal boys were found to be significantly different on all the three identity styles, i.e., information, normative, and diffuse/avoidant. The tribal boys scored significantly higher on information and norm oriented identity styles than non-tribal boys. On the other hand, non-tribal boys scored significantly higher on diffuse/avoidant oriented identity style than their tribal counterparts. In other words, the tribal boys had significantly more information and norm oriented identity style than the non-tribal boys. The non-tribal boys had significantly more diffuse/avoidant identity style orientation than their tribal counterparts.

Results further reveal that the tribal boys were found to have more information-oriented style than the non-tribal boys. This shows that tribal boys deal with personal decisions and problems by deliberately seeking out, elaborating and testing self-relevant information. They are most likely to employ a balanced mix of assimilative and accommodative processes. The results on information-oriented style are also in conformity with the findings of other studies (Srivastava, 1981, 1983) that young tribal (Tharus) are simple, accommodative and peace loving. The higher score of tribal boys on normative oriented style indicates that tribal boys are significantly more concerned with conformity to the normative standards and prescriptions held by significant reference other such as parental figures than non-tribal boys. Normative scores have been found to be positively associated with a socially-defined identity, and with the tendency to defend against new information relevant to "core" areas of the self such as values and belief systems. However, the non-tribal boys scored significantly higher than the tribal boys on diffuse/avoidant style scale which indicate that nontribal boys had significantly more diffuse/avoident style orientation than the tribal boys. The non-tribal boys were found to be more uncommitted and diffused individuals and are likely to avoid facing up to and dealing with problems and decisions than tribal boys (Srivastava, 1999, 2002a, b, 2003a, b).

Results of the present study reveal that cross-cultural difference in identity style of tribal and non-tribal boys may be attributed to the different type of cultural contexts (tribal and non-tribal cultures) including social norms, socialization practices, frustration-aggression patterns, personality characteristics and some other factors (Srivastava, 2002a, b, 1995a, b, 1993b, c, 1985; Sen, 2001; Roy, 2001; Naidu, 2001). Therefore, findings of the present study suggest that cultural contexts are important in determining the identity style preferences used by tribal boys which would be useful in understanding their life span identity crises. In particular, it may provide a framework within which life span identity crises of tribals may be interpreted. Results also suggest that short version of identity style inventory (ISI-2) is also a reliable and valid measure of identity style like its original version ISI-2 (Srivastava, 1995).

The results of the present research suggest that cultural contexts are important external correlates of identity style among tribals and non-tribals in India. However, for drawing wider generalizations similar studies need to be replicated on larger sample with more rigorous research designs and representing samples from different states of India. However, the knowlede of these correlates the identity styles of tribal and non-tribal boys may be found to be useful in understanding the life-span identity crises of Indian adolescents and also relevant for contemporary social life (Srivastava, 1989, 1990, 1997; Pandey, Sinha, Bhawuk, 1996; Shanmugam, 1988; Saho, 1999). The findings may also be useful from community psychologists' viewpoint. It should be borne in mind that the community psychology is about understanding people and using this understanding to improve people's well-being (Asthana, 1992; Srivastava 1995a, b, c). The findings of the present research may prove to be useful in achieving above objectives of the community psychology (Srivastava, 1992, 2000, 2001; Orford, 1992). Results are also in agreement with Cote (1996) that it is not necessarily the identity crisis that guards our future; rather, what guards our future is the welcoming each new generation into the adult community by helping them develop viable, nonexploited identities in that community. Findings confirm the view of Berzonsky that identity develops within a given cultural context and cannot be divorced from environmental constraints and interpersonal influence (Srivastava, 2005a, b; Ungar, 2005).

REFERENCES

Adams, G.R., Montemayor, R. and Gullotta, T.P. (1996) (Eds.). *Psychosocial Development During Adolescence: Progress in Developmental Contextualism.* Thousand Oaks, California: Sage Publications.

Asthana, H.S. (1992, Sep.), *Community Psychology: Issues, Relevance and Directions,* Presidential Address Delivered at First Biennial Conference of the Community Psychology Association of India, Kanpur.

Berzonsky, M.D. (1996, March), A Measure of Identity Style: Preliminary Findings. Paper presented at the Meeting of the Society for Research on Adolescent, Madison, and WI.

Berzonsky, M.D. (1989). Identity Style: Conceptualization and Measurement. *Journal of Adolescent Research,* 4(3), 268-282.

Berzonsky, M.D. (1990), Self-Construction Over the Life-Span: A Process Perspective on Identity Formation. In G.J. Neimeyer and R.A. Neimeyer (Eds.), *Advances in Personal Construct Theory.* (Vol. 1, pp. 155-186). Greenwich, CT: JAI Press.

Berzonsky, M.D. (1994), Self-Identity: The Relationship between Processes and Content. *Journal of Research in Personality,* 28, 453-460.

Bhusan, R. (1993), Ego-Identity Research: A Review and Examination of the Indian Viewpoints. *Indian Journal of Clinical Psychology,* 20(2), 113-118.

Cote, J.E. (1996), Identity: A Multi-dimensional Analysis: In G.R. Adams, R. Montemayor and T.P. Gullotta (Eds.), *Psychosocial Development During Adolescence.* Thousands Oaks: California; Sage Publications.

Erikson, E.H. (1950), *Childhood and Society,* New York: W.W. Norton.

Kao, H.S.R. and Sinha, D. (1997) (Eds.), *Asian Perspectives in Psychology.* New Delhi: Sage Publications.

Marcia, J.E. (1966), Development and Validation of Ego-Identity Status. *Journal of Personality and Social Psychology,* 3, 551-558.

Naidu, R.K. (2001), Personality, Self and Life Events. In J. Pandey (Ed.), *Psychology in India Revisited: Developments in the Discipline (Vol. 2).* New Delhi: Sage Publications.

Nesler, M.S. (1995), Context Effects, Self-Presentation and the Self-Monitoring Scale. *Journal of Research in Personality,* 29, 273-284.

Orford, J. (1992), *Community Psychology: Theory and Practice.* Chichester: Wiley and Sons Ltd.

Pandey, J. Sinha, D. and Bhawuk, D.P.S. (1996) (Eds.), *Asian Contributions to Cross-Cultural Psychology.* New Delhi: Sage Publications.

Phinney, J. (1990), Ethnic Identity in Adolescents and Adults: A Review of Research. *Psychological Bulletin,* 180, 499-514.

Roy, B. (2001), Child Health and Human Development: A Discussion. Paper presented at the 88th Session of the Indian Science Congress, New Delhi, January 3-7.

Sahoo, F.M. (1999), The Hindu-Muslim Relationship in Indian Plural Society. In U.N. Dash and U. Jain (Eds.), *Perspectives on Psychology and Social Development.* New Delhi: Concept Publishing Company.

Sen, A.K. (2001), *Environmental Deprivation and Malnutrition and Mental Retardation: Challenges for Psychology and Educational Sciences.* Presidential Address, the 88th Session of the Indian Science Congress, New Delhi, January 3-7.

Shanmugan, T.E. (1998), *Community Psychology,* Madras: Utsav Shanmugam.

Sinha, J.B.P. (1979), The Hindu (Indian) Identity. *Dynamic Psychiatry,* 15, 148-160.

Srivastava, R.K. (1981), Psychological Characteristics of Tharus and Non-Tharus: A Cross-Cultural Study. *Journal of Psychological Researches,* 25, 154-158.

Srivastava, R.K. (1983). *A Cross-Cultural Study of Depression and Ego-Identity in Tribals and Non-Tribals.* Proceedings of the International Conference on Man and Environment, Calcutta, December 6-9.

Srivastava, R.K. (1984), Rural-Urban Differences in Authoritarianism among the Hindus in India. *Journal of Social Psychology,* 122, 291-292.

Srivastava, R.K. (1988), Psychological Perspective on Tharu Tribals in Uttar Pradesh. Paper Presented at the National Seminar on Tribal Situation in Uttar Pradesh, Yojana Bhawan, Lucknow.

Srivastava, R.K. (1989), Acculturation and Frustration-Aggression Patterns of Indian Tribals. *British Journal of Projective Psychology,* 34(2), 12-30.

Srivastava, R.K. (1990), Culture-Contact and Child-Rearing Attitudes of Indian (Tharu) Tribals. *Indian Journal of Social Work,* 51, 425-436.

Srivastava, R.K. (1992), Community Psychology: Current Research and Trend. Paper Presented at the 1st Biennial Conference of the Community Psychology Association of India, Kanpur, September 27-28.

Srivastava, R.K. (1993a). Cultural contexts and identity style. *Indian Journal of Psychology*, 68, 35-44.

Srivastava, R.K. (1993b), *Some Sociodemographic Correlates of Ego-Identity among Tharu Tribal Youth*. Research Project Report, New Delhi: University Grants Commission.

Srivastava, R.K. (1993c), Socio-Cultural Deprivation and Ego-identity of Indian Adolescents. *Purvanchal Journal of Social Sciences*, 1, 41-54.

Srivastava, R.K. (1995a), *An Indian Adaptation of Identity Style Inventory (Short-Form)*. Ghazipur: Shivam Publications.

Srivastava, R.K. (1995b), Community Problems in India: Some Issues and need for Indegenisation. In H.S. Asthana (Chair), *Community Problems: Issues and Psychological Interventions*. Symposium conducted at the 2nd Biennial Conference of the Community Psychology Association of India, Ayodhya, April 13-15.

Srivastava, R.K. (1995c), Socio-Familial Correlates of Identity Style. Paper Presented at the 82nd Annual Session of the Indian Science Congress, Calcutta, January 3-8.

Srivastava, R.K. (1996a), Identity Style and Traditional Family Ideology. Paper Presented at the 83rd Session of the Indian Science Congress, Patiala, January, 3-7.

Srivastava, R.K. (1996b), *Tribal Ego-Identity in India*. New Delhi: Classical Publishing Company.

Srivastava, R.K. (1998), Rural-Urban Differences in Identity Style of Indian Adolescents: A Process View of Identity Development. Paper presented at the 85th Session of the Indian Science Congress, Hyderabad, January 3-7.

Srivastava, R.K. (1999), Psychology and Social Problems: Some Issues and Challenges for Making Psychology Relevant for the Masses. Paper Presented at the 10th Annual Conference of the National Academy of Psychology, Lucknow, December 3-5.

Srivastava, R.K. (2000), Ethnic Psychology of Tharu Tribals of Uttar Pradesh: Some Issues and Current Status. Paper presented at the International Seminar on Development of Tribal and Native Peoples in India and Canada, Canadian Studies Development Programme, B.H.U., Varanasi, February 12-13.

Srivastava, R.K. (2001), Acculturation and Perceived Parental Behaviour. In M. Bhargava and S. Aurora (Eds.), *Parental Behaviour*, (Chapter 18, pp. 173-179). Agra: H.P. Bhargava Book House.

Srivastava, R.K. (2002a), Ethnic Psychology of Tharu Tribals: Some Issues and Current Status, *Journal of Community Guidance and Research*, 19, 15-24.

Srivastava, R.K. (2002b), Social Disadvantages and Identity Style of Indian Adolescents, *Indian Psychological Review*, 59, 121-125.

Srivastava, R.K. (2003a). Identity Style Preferences of Adolescents of Hindu and Muslim Communities in India. *Journal of Community Guidance and Research,* 20, 323-329.

Srivastava, R.K. (2003b), Traditional Family Ideology and Identity Style of Adolescents. *Praachi Journal of Psycho-Cultural Dimensions,* 19, 71-75.

Srivastava, R.K. (2005a), Consequences of Acculturation on Mental Health of Tharu Tribals. In A. Shukla (Ed.), *The Indian Tribals,* New Delhi: Kanishka Prakashan.

Srivastava, R.K. (2005b), Consequences of Socio-Cultural Deprivation on Mental Health of Indian Adolescents. *Indian Journal of Community Psychology,* 1, 79-89.

Taylor, R.D. and Oskay, G. (1995), Identity Formation in Turkish and American Late Adolescents. *Journal of Cross-Cultural Psychology,* 26, 8-22.

Ungar, M. (2005) (Ed.), *Handbook of Working with Children and Youth: Pathways to Resilience Across Cultures and Contexts.* New Delhi: Sage Publications.

11

Social Identity Awareness in Hindu and Muslim Children

Shabana Bano and *Ramesh Chandra Mishra*

Psychological studies indicate that very early in life, we begin to learn who we are. We develop a social identity, or a self-definition, that includes how we conceptualize and evaluate ourselves (Deaux, 1993; Ellemers, Wike and VanKnippenberg, 1993). Social identity seems to evolve from the knowledge of one's membership of a social group together with the value and emotional significance attached to that membership (Tajfel, 1978), where social represents two or more individuals who perceive themselves as members of the same social category (Turner, 1982).

The theoretical model developed by Tajfel (1959) suggests that social categorization is a cognitive process of dividing the social world into "Us" and "Them". According to this model, members of different groups are likely to be seen as more different from each other than they really are, while members of the same group are likely to be seen as more similar. Categorization leads not only to stereotypical perception of in-group and out-groups, but it also leads to some degree of accentuation of inter-group differences. The accentuation effect in largely accounted for by social comparisons, because it occurs mainly on the self-enhancing dimensions through the exaggeration of inter-group differences and in-group similarities.

One offshoot of social identification is prejudice, which is reflected in a low preference for and low interpersonal attraction among the members of different groups. Prejudice is an expression of unfavourable attitudes towards an individual or individuals because of their membership of a particular group (Augoustious and Walker, 1995; Brown, 1995). Prejudice involves not only negative evaluations, but also beliefs about others. These are often reflected in stereotypes, which influence the processing of social information in ways that make them self-confirming.

Social psychologists have explained children's preference for members of the in-group in terms of the processes of self-categorization and identification with the in-group (Bennet, Lyons, Sani and Barrett, 1998). Studies show that from a very young age, children are aware of categorical distinction among people. In an early attempt to study category awareness, Clark and Clark (1947) found that even at the youngest age, over 75 per cent of the children correctly identified the ethnicity of the doll, and by the age of five, over 50 per cent of children were doing so.

Aboud (1988) has proposed a three-stage model of the development of social identity. Stage-I (up to 5 years) is dominated by perceptual and affective processes. According to this approach, originally articulated by Piaget (Piaget and Weil, 1951), children's social attitudes (e.g., about gender and race) are critically affected by their acquisition of cognitive skills. Children classify the world into broad categories and associate these categories with different emotional responses, presumably derived from a mixture of their own personal experiences and the vicarious observation of the experiences of others. Thinking at this stage is ego-centric and dominated by perceptual cues provided by the appearance of things and people (Piaget, 1954). Young children below the age of six generally do not develop a conception of the invariance of physical properties. This may be true even in the case of social objects. The identities that people have should be viewed by children as being just as impermanent as mass, weight or number. The combination of these affective and cognitive processes provides the basis for the an early emergence of own ethnic preferences.

In stage-II (5-7 years) children's thinking becomes more sophisticated as it progresses through the concrete operational period (Piaget, 1954). The concept of social grouping based mainly on physical attributes. At this point, paralleling the achievement of conservation in physical domain, children recognize that many major social category memberships are relatively stable, and do not change with superficial changes of appearance or with age. At about the same time (5-7 years), early group preferences in terms of simple likes and dislikes evolve into full-fledged stereotypes in which less obviously observable attributes and traits are associated with particular categories. According to Aboud (1988), the coupling of these social and cognitive changes is likely to facilitate a particularly high degree of ethnocentrism among children of 5-7 years.

Finally appears stage-III. As children are capable of operational thinking, there is a recognition of the possibility of individual variation within groups. At this stage the initially rather rigid stereotypes become more flexible and amenable to change in response to counter stereotypic or individuating information. Aboud (1988) suggests that as children mature, they become more sensitive to the norms of adult society and, hence, more aware of the social undesirability of expressing certain kind of prejudices too overtly.

Aboud (1993) indicates that although the prejudice of children under 12 years of age does not seem to be similar to that of their parents or friends, these people may be best able to facilitate reduction in prejudice through open discussion. Other studies suggest that prejudice appears to decline with age on some measures (e.g., positive and negative attribution), but it tends to increase with age on other measures (e.g., playmates' preferences) (Sigelman and Singleton, 1986). However, this advanced cognitive ability leads to greater flexibility of attitudes and, hence, a decline in prejudice (Doyle and Aboud, 1991; Doyle, Beaudet and Aboud, 1988).

A partial explanation is provided by Vaughan (1987) by adding the process of social comparison in the cognitive developmental model. It is argued that children's understanding and evaluations of their identity stems largely from their comparison of that in-group with relevant out-groups. When such a comparison reveals their group to be superior or at least roughly equal to others, there is some accentuation of positive self-regard from ethnicity, usually in the case of dominant group children. For subordinate group children, on the other hand, such comparisons may be unacceptable in the sense that their own group appears obviously inferior on a number of dimensions. There is still much to be understood in this respect.

Research suggests that cognitive-developmental factors may influence the average level of prejudice displayed by children, but individual experiences appear to determine the targets of prejudice for a given child at a given age. Social learning theory also focuses on individual differences (Allport, 1954; Mischel, 1966; Bandura,

1977). Prejudice arises from child's specific learning experiences. Hence, its developmental pattern is likely to vary among children depending on their specific experiences in the family, school, or the community at large.

Studies searching for age-related development provide with inconsistent results. While some studies reveal decline in prejudice with advancement of age, others indicates an incrase in prejudice with advancing age. What are the psychological processes through which social identity and prejdice develop in children? At which age does social identity become internalized? What effect is exerted by children's emerging cognitive abilities upon their acquisition and retention of social identity and prejudice? There is currently little agreement on these issues. Developmental studies are also spare in our country.

The study reported in this paper aimed at addressing some of these issues with respect to the development of social identity and prejudice in Hindu and Muslim children. The objective was to examine those processes by which children come to know about the social groups they belong to. A related objective was to assess the relationship between social identity and prejudice.

Method

Sample

The study was carried out with 100 Hindu and 100 Muslim children, aged 3 to 12 years. They were selected from some schools of Varanasi city using a quasi-randomization method. In order to study the developmental trend, children were divided into five age groups: 3-4 years, 5-6 years, 7-8 years, 9-10 years, 11-12 years. To fulfil the requirements of the sample design the schools in which Hindu and Muslim children were available, were identified. Twenty children of both Hindu and Muslim groups in each age group were selected randomly from the available pool of children. Although they were selected from both the modern and traditional schools (*Madarsa* and *Matha*), in the present paper, data were pooled for these two school groups.

Tasks

Two tasks, namely Model Identification Task and Projective Prejudice Task were used. Children were administered these tasks individually.

The Model Identification Task (MIT)

This task was designed to elicit responses without asking children about their social identity directly. Highlighting the traditional features and dressing styles two toy models were used to represent the members of the Hindu and Muslim groups. Children were administered the task individually. They were shown the models simultaneously, and were asked to identify the individuals represented in the models. The identification was attempted a second time by interchanging the dressing of the models. Liking and preferences of children for these models and several behavioural characteristics of individuals represented in the models were also studied by asking a series of questions.

The Projective Prejudice Task (PPT)

This task consisted of 8 pictures, each depicting Hindu and Muslim children in situations that involved some degree of ambiguity. The children were shown the pictures and were told a background story about each one of them. Children in the story were given either a Muslim or a Hindu name. The children were described as the initiators of an action that led to a positive or negative consequence. After listening to the story, the children were asked to choose the child who initiated the action in the picture and tell who should be rewarded or punished for the outcome of that action. Four of the pictures depicted positive situations (e.g., winning a trophy), the other four pictures depicted negative situations (e.g., stealing, quarrelling). Children in the picture were named, and the questions were always referred to their names.

Results

In the present study, prejudice was measured in terms of general liking, preference to one's own group members and non-preference to other group members. Biased attitude was measured as a tendency to consider one's own group for positive outcomes (reward) and prevent it from negative outcomes (punishment).

Table 11.1 presents the frequency of responses of Hindu and Muslim children on the MIT. No significant difference between Hindu and Muslim children on measures of social awareness, basis of awareness, sources of awareness, and preference was noted. Both Hindu and Muslim children were quite aware of their own social identity as well as that of others. They identified the model of their own and other group member more often on the basis of internal features than on the basis of external features. In both the groups, parents or family appeared to be the main source of knowledge of their social identity. An overall preference for own group model over the other group model was also evident in both the groups.

Table 11.1: Distribution of Children's Responses on Awareness Measures of the MIT

No.	*Variables*	*Responses in Frequency*		*Chi-Square*
		Hindu Children (N=100)	*Muslim Children (N=100)*	
1.	*Social Awareness*			
	(a) Yes	92	100	0.24
	(b) No	08	—	
2.	*Basis of Awareness*			
	(a) External Features	32	34	0.00
	(b) Internal Features	60	66	0.38
	(c) No Response	08	—	
3.	*Sources of Awareness*			
	(a) Parents/Family	75	88	0.92
	(b) Others	17	12	
	(c) No Response	08	—	
4.	*Preferences*			
	(a) Own-group	89	92	0.02
	(b) Other-group	11	08	

Analysis of developmental trend with respect to the use of external and internal features to identify the model is presented in Table 11.2. A similarity in the way of identifying own as well as other group on the basis of external and internal features was noted for Hindu and

Muslim children at all age levels. None of the chi-square values reached the level of significance.

Table 11.2: Age-wise Distribution of Children's Responses with Respect to the Basis of Ethnic Awareness on the MIT

Age Group	Basis of Social Group Awareness					
	External Features			Internal Features		
	Hindu	Muslim	Chi-square	Hindu	Muslim	Chi-square
3-4	12	14	0.02	00	06	2.08
5-6	15	15	0.00	05	05	0.00
7-8	05	04	0.00	15	16	0.00
9-10	01	00	0.00	19	20	0.00
11-12	01	01	0.00	19	19	0.00

Table 11.3 presents the values of chi-square across age groups with regard to the basis of awareness. External features appeared to be an important basis of social awareness up to the age of 5-6 years. From 7 years onwards, internal features became increasingly obvious referents of social awareness in both groups of children. Chi-square values revealed that 7-12 year age groups differed significantly from 3-6 years age groups.

Table 11.3: Chi-square Values for Age Comparison on "the Basis of Awareness" Measure of the MIT

Age Groups	3-4 Years	5-6 Years	7-8 Years	9-10 Years	11-12 Years
3-4 Years	—	2.36	21.91**	33.36**	37.59**
5-6 Years	—	—	22.66**	35.87**	39.84**
7-8 Years	—	—	—	4.50	4.30
9-10 Years	—	—	—	—	0.52
11-12 Years	—	—	—	—	—

Results obtained on the PPT are given in Table 11.4. Although both the Hindu and Muslim children generally considered that positive outcome of the situation (reward) should go to their own group members, the tendency was significantly stronger in Hindu than Muslim children ($t = 2.43$, $p < .01$). Hindu children (Mean = 8.94) scored higher in comparison to Muslim children (Mean = 8.24). A significant difference ($t = 3.88$, $p < .01$) between Hindu and Muslim children was noted on the negative outcome measure suggesting that the tendency to prevent own group from negative outcomes (punishment) was slightly more compelling among Muslim (Mean = 8.64) than Hindu children (Mean = 7.60).

Table 11.4: Mean, SD and Significance of Difference (t-values) of Groups on the PPT Measures

Responses	*Hindu*		*Muslim*		*t-value*
	Mean	*SD*	*Mean*	*SD*	
Positive Outcome	8.94	2.04	8.24	2.04	2.04**
Negative Outcome	7.60	1.93	8.64	1.87	3.88**

** $p < .01$

Discussion

The present study was designed to examine the development of social identity and prejudice in Hindu and Muslim children. The findings demonstrated that both Hindu and Muslim children were aware of own as well as of other group's identity even at the age of 3-4 years. At this age, children of both the groups had also learnt some of the ethnic ABCs, i.e., the words and concepts used to describe the members of other groups. For example, the children had developed the idea that they were good because they belonged to one group, whereas others were bad because they belonged to another group. This clear "Us"—"Them" distinction was present in the cognition of children at this early age. Children had also developed liking for the members of their own social group and disliking for those who belonged to the other group. In a study with religious groups in India, Singh (1985) had found that religious identity began to take shape in the nursery schools and it got crystallized quite early in childhood. Research evidences from other cultural settings seem to suggest more or less a similar trend (Horowitz, 1939; Lehrer, 1946; Hartley, Rosenbaum and Schawartz, 1948; Clarke and Clarke, 1958; Hassan, 1984). Our results also indicated that children of both the social groups acquired knowledge of their social identity from their parents indicating the social identification is largely an outcome of the social learning process.

Analysis of developmental trend in data revealed similarity in the way social identity and prejudice developed among Hindu and Muslim groups. Children in both the groups were clearly aware of their social identity, and both expressed their bias towards each other to some extent. In a study with Hindu and Muslim students, Mohsin (1984) had indicated the existence of strong ethnocentrism and prejudice among them. Our results suggested that both Hindu and Muslim children tended to produce increasingly biased responses with advancement in age. Children's recurrent experiences of conflicts between the two groups, which occasionally take the form of communal riots in different parts of our country, may be held responsible for this kind of results. Research also suggests that the tendency for children to develop ethnic prejudice increases as competition, tension and conflict increase between members of the dominant and ethnic minority group. Under these circumstances, in-group identification and bias increase with commensurate increase in out-group rejection, dislike and hatred (Brown, 1995).

The results of the study also indicated some differences in the developmental pattern of Hindu and Muslim children. It may be noted that in Muslim children social identity and prejudice became evident at an early age than in Hindu children. Studies indicate that due to their minority status, the Muslim tend to be more conscious of their own as well as others' social identity. Some studies have reported that low status or threatened groups exhibit greater inter-group bias than do high status or non-threatened groups (Branscombe and Wann, 1994; Corneille *et al.*, 2001; Hogg and Suderland, 1991; Turner, Hogg, Turner and Smith, 1984).

Our findings suggest that in identifying groups, children's emphasis was generally more on internal than external features of the model. The basis of awareness showed considerable variation according to age. The young children (3-6 years) mainly focused on external features (e.g., dressing style) in identifying their own group member on the MIT, whereas slightly older children (7-12 years) focused mainly on internal features (Psychological characteristics) in identifying the models. The latter features became more salient at the higher age levels, suggesting a kind of shift from the use of external (e.g., dressing/clothing, appearance) to more internal features (e.g., perceptions, religious beliefs) to describe the differences between groups. This finding seems to be consistent with those reported by others in respect of the development of social thinking in children. Piaget (1958) has indicated that thinking of a child in early years is dominated by the physical attributes (e.g., clothing, colour) of stimuli. Children at this stage generally believe in the invariance of physical properties. At a later age (5-7 years), children's thinking becomes more sophisticated, abstract and internal when they seem to recognize that category memberships (be they social or otherwise) are relatively stable, and do not change with superficial changes, such as of appearance (Aboud, 1988; Piaget, 1954). The latter features become salient particularly at the higher age levels, suggesting a kind of shift from the use of external (dressing/clothing, appearance) to more internal features (e.g., perceptions, religious beliefs) to describe the differences between groups. Such cognitive developmental changes are implicated in the acquisition and expression of many social behaviours (Durkin, 1995).

In our study, the children of both Hindu and Muslim groups tended to have great admiration for their own social identity, which sounded more like "own group glorification". A negative feeling towards the member of the other group may be explained on the basis of this tendency of self-glorification. A positive correlation noted between social identity and prejudice in this study is in accordance with the prediction of Berry *et al.* (1977) made in terms of the definition of social identity. They have suggested that confidence in one's own individual identity can provide a basis for respect for others. However, if this confidence in one's ethnic identity leads to "own group glorification", then the outcome is a strong positive attitude towards the in-group with a strong negative attitude towards the out-group (Le Vine and Campbell, 1972).

Our results revealed that Hindu and Muslim children generally considered that positive outcomes (reward) of the situation should go to their own group members suggesting that a tendency for 'topenism' was evident among them from an early age. Similarly, in tendency to prevent the own group from negative outcomes (punishment) was also present among children from the same early age. Working for the norm violation theory, DeReider and Tripathi (1992) have noted that group members with a strong own group identification attribute the other group's behaviour to negative disposition of the group and react negatively to the out-group because they perceive the other group's behaviour as a possible threat to their own group integrity. Islam and Hewstone (1993) indicated that such attributions validate one's own social position with respect to the out-group. Hence, it is not surprising to find that majority and minority groups show positive in-group evaluation and negative out-group evaluation (Verkuyten, 2005).

The overall results of the study suggested that the development of social identity followed the same developmental pattern in Hindu and Muslim groups. Children became aware of their ethnic identity at an early age (around 3 years), preferred their own group members and expressed negative feelings towards the other ethnic group on the basis of more internal than external features. The basis of awareness varied according to age. While up to 6 years, children's emphasis was largely on external features, after this age, the emphasis shifted to internal features for identifying own as well as the other group. Children's prejudice increased as they advanced in age.

The findings of the study have several implications for understanding and managing inter-group relations in a culturally plural society. They suggest the need for intervention early in childhood, starting from pre-school years, because religious identity develops primarily during these years. The period of 6-7 years appears to be critical for the development of social identity and prejudice. Since children's identities become fairly internalized around age 6-7, there is a need to modify their thinking style by giving appropriate exposure prior to this age. As parents appear to be the main source of knowledge about one's social identity, a correctional programme for parents also seems to be important.

REFERENCES

Aboud, F.E. (1988), *Children and Prejudice.* New York: Basil Blackwell.

Aboud, F.E. (1993), The Developmental Psychology of Racial Prejudice. *Transcultural Psychiatric Research Review,* 30(3), 229-242.

Allport, G.W. (1954), *The Nature of Prejudice.* Readng, MA: Addison-Wesley.

Augoustinos, M. and Walker, I. (1995), *Social Cognition: An Integrated Introduction.* London: Sage.

Bandura, A. (1977), *Social Learning Theory.* Englewood Cliffs, NJ: Prentice Hall.

Bennett, M., Lyons, E., Sani, F. and Barret, M. (1998), Children's Subjective Identification with the Group and In-group Favouritism. *Developmental Psychology,* 34(5), 902-909.

Berry, J.W., Kalin and Taylor, D.M. (1977), *Multiculturalism and Ethnic Attitudes in Canada.* Ottawa: Ministry of Supply and Services.

Branscombe, N.R. and Wann, D.L. (1994), Collective self-esteem consequences of out-group derogation when a valued social identity is on trial. *Euroean Journal of Social Psychology,* 24, 641-657.

Brown, R. (1995), *Prejudice: Its Social Psychology.* Cambridge, MA: Blackwell.

Clark, K.B. and Clark, M.P. (1947), Racial identification and preference in Negro Children. In: H. Proshansky and B. Seidenberg (Eds.), *Basic Studies in Social Psychology,* New York: Holt Rinehart and Winston.

Clarke, K.B. and Clarke, M.P. (1958). Racial Identification and Preference in Negro Children. In E. Maccoby, T. Newcomb and Hartley (Eds.), *Reading in Social Psychology,* New York: Holt, Rinehart and Winston.

Corneille, O., Yzerbyt, V.Y., Rogier, A. and Buidin, G. (2001), Threat and the Group Attribution Error: When Threat Elicit Judgements of Extremity and Homogeneity. *Personality and Social Psychology Bulletin,* 27, 437-446.

Deaux, K. (1993), Reconstructing Social Identity. *Personality and Social Psychology Bulletin,* 19, 4-12.

DeRidder, R. and Tripathi, R.C. (1992), *Norm Violation and Inter-group Relations.* Oxford: Clarendon Press.

Doyle, A.B., Beaudet, J. and Aboud, F. (1988), Developmental Patterns in the Flexibility of Children's Ethnic Attitudes. *Journal of Cross-Cultural Psychology,* 19, 3-18.

Doyle, A.B. and Aboud, F. (1991), Prejudice as a Social Cognitive Development. Unpublished Manuscript.

Durkin, K. (1995), *Developmental Social Psychology: From Infancy to Old Age.* Oxford: Blackwell.

Ellemers, N., Wike, H. and VanKnippenberg, A. (1993), Effect of the Legitimacy Low Group or Individual Status as Individual and Collective Status-Enhancement Strategies. *Journal of Personality and Social Psychology,* 64, 766-778.

Hassan, M.K. (1984), Parental Behaviour, Authoritarian and Prejudice. Paper presented at the International Conference on Authoritarianism and Dogmatism, Postdam, New York.

Hartley, E.L., Rosenbaum, M. and Schwartz, S. (1948), Children's Perceptions of Ethnic Group Membership. *Journal of Psychology,* 26, 387-398.

Hogg, M.A. and Sunderland, J. (1991), Self-esteem and Inter-group Discrimination in the Minimal Group Paradigm. *British Journal of Social Psychology,* 30, 51-62.

Horowitz, R.E. (1939), Racial Aspects of Self-Identification in Nursery School Children. *Journal of Psychology,* 7, 91-99.

Islam, M.R. and Hewstone, M. (1993), Inter-group Attributions and Affective Consequences in Majority and Minority Groups. *Journal of Personality and Social Psychology,* 64, 936-950.

Lehrer, L. (1946), The Jewish Elements in the Psychology of the Jewish Child in America. *YIVO Annual Jewish Social Science,* 1, 195-216.

Le Vine, R.A. and Campbell, D.T. (1972). *Ethnocentrism: Theories of Conflict, Attitudes and Group Behaviour.* New York: Wiley.

Mischel, W. (1966), A Social Learning View of Sex Differences in Behaviour. In E.E. Maccoby (Eds.) *The Development of Sex Difference* (pp. 25-55). Stanford. CA: Stanford University Press.

Mohsin, S.M. (1984), *Securalism and Ethnic Prejudice on the Indian Scene.* Presidential Address at the National Seminar on Psychology and Secularism in India. Ranchi University, Ranchi.

Piaget, J. (1954), *The Construction of Reality in the Child.* New York: Basic Books.

Piaget, J. and Weil, A.M. (1951), The Development in Children of the Idea of the Homeland and of Relations to Others Countries. *International Social Science Journal,* 3, 361-378.

Sigelman, C.K. and Singleton, L.C. (1986), Stigmatization in Childhood: A Survey of Developmental Trends and Issues. In: S.C. Ainlay, G. Backer and L.M. Coleman (Eds.), *The Dilemma of Difference: A Multidisciplinary View of Stigma* (pp. 185-208). New York: Plenum Press.

Singh, A.K. (1985), *Developing Secularism and National Integration in India.* Presidential Address to the Section of Psychology and Educational Sciences, 72nd Session of Indian Science Congress, Lucknow.

Tajfel, H. (1978), *Differentiated between Social Groups: Studies in the Social Psychology of Inter-group Relations.* London: Academic Press.

Tajfel, H. (1959), Quantitative Judgement in Social Perception. *British Journal of Psychology,* 50, 16-29.

Turner, J.C. (1982), Towards a Cognitive Redefinition of the Social Groups. In H. Tajfel (Eds.), *Social Identity and Inter-group Relations.* Cambridge: Cambridge University Press.

Turner, J.C., Hogg, M.A., Turner, P.J. and Smith, P.M. (1984), Failure and Defeat as Determinants of Group Cohesiveness. *British Journal of Social Psychology,* 23, 97-111.

Vaughan, G.M. (1987), A Social Psychological Model of Ethnic Identity Development. In J.S. Phinney and M.J. Rotheram (Eds.), *Children's Ethnic Socialization.* London: Sage.

Verkuyten, M. (2005), Ethnic group identification and group evaluation among Minority and Majority Groups: Testing the Multiculturalism Hypothesis. *Journal of Personality and Social Psychology,* 88, 121-138.

12

Socio-Cultural Construction of Mind and Language

Minati Panda and *Ajit K. Mohanty*

Human mind (or the mental life and processes) must be understood as deeply connected to objects of human manufacture in the world around us. Human beings live in a world of human artifacts—tools, words, routines and rituals—changing objects that are, at one and the same time, things the indivudal deals with and the repository of prior human thought and judgment (Cole, 1995). The cultural psychologists consistently argued for an emphasis on mediated action in a context and the use of genetic method understood broadly to include historical, ontogenetic, and microgenetic level of analysis grounded in everyday life events. The assumption that mind emerges in the joint activity of people and is, in an important sense, "co-constructed" is based on the assumption that individuals are active agents in their own discursive environments.

The initial premise of cultural historical school is that human psychological processes emerge through culturally mediated historically developed, practical activity. Human mind and the associated psychological processes emerge simultaneously with a new form of behaviour in which humans modified the material objects as means of regulating interactions with the world and one another. Such mediational devices were called tools by the Soviet psychologists like Luria and Vygotsky whereas Cole preferred the term artifact. "When Luria and Vygotsky wrote about "tool" mediation, they did not have only such artifacts as hoes and plates. They considered language (more aptly described as the tool of tools) to be an integral part of the overall process of cultural mediation and they had a decided two-sided notion of how such tool mediation operates and its specific influences on human thought processes" (Cole, 1996). Language as cultural artifact is both a cultural product and also influences thought and, therefore, the culture. According to Cole, in addition to using and making cultural tools like language, human beings arrange for the rediscovery of the already created tools in each succeeding generation. "Becoming a cultural being and arranging for others to become cultural beings are intimately linked parts of a single process called enculturation" (Cole, 1996). In such a perspective, culture is understood as the entire pool of artifacts accumulated by the social group in the course of its historical experience. Here, the accumulated artifacts of the group—*i.e.* the culture—are then seen as the species specific medium of human development. And the culture is conceived as an even changing phenomenon that undergoes both quantitative change in terms of the number of artifacts and the qualitative change in terms of mediational potential they embody.

Origins of cultural mediation of language and thought in relation to phylogeny and cultural history can be found in several of the key publications of Vygotsky and Luria who tried to schematically present the path of psychological evolution from the ape to cultural man. The schema here includes evolutionary, the historical and the ontogenetic. Each has its own turning point that critically shapes the mind and thought. Every critical turning point is viewed primarily from the stand point of something new introduced by this stage as a starting point for furthr processes of evolution of human mind and thought. According to them, the turning point in phylogeny is the appearance of tool use by apes. The turning point in human history is the appearance of labour and symbolic mediation (language and other forms of discursive acts and, later, the system of writing). The apes can use tools (as in the case of Kohler's experiment) but cannot use the same for creating or organizing labour which the human being can do. The major turning point of ontogeny, therefore, is the coming together of cultural history and phylogeny with the acquisition of language.

Thought and language, which reflect reality in a way different from that of mere perception, is the key to the nature of human consciousness. Words and sentences play a central role not only in the development of thought but in the historical development of mind and consciousness as a whole. The relationship between words and thought is a living process where thought is borne through words. The connection between them is not a performed and constant one; it evolves in the course of development (Vygotsky, 1962).

Language and Construction of Mind

Formation of mind is a complex process which is necessarily integrated with the socio-cultural system and interpersonal relations (Vygotsky, 1978). The immediate social system in which the children develop is itself a product of historical processes, through which cultures evolve. Individuals are socio-historically situated. According to Vygotsky, all higher mental functions are mediated by a variety of cultural tools. Language is held to be the most fundamental (and also most potent) of the cultural tools which include many other symbolic and psychological means of mediation such as counting systems, works of art, maps, agricultural tools, social rituals and routines or repeated modes of social activities. Such mediating tools as forms of cultural representations alter "the entire flow and structure of mental functions" (Vygotsky, 1981, p. 137) and they do so by allowing the individual to engage in complex operations in the objective world. Further, these mediations are *social* (not organic or individual) in nature; they are used in inter-psychological processes. Speech, for example, functions as tool for communication, social interaction, and as a mechanism of influencing the social world. At the same time, speech is necessarily situated in the socio-cultural context; like other psychological tools, it is a social and not an individual product.

The socio-cultural approach views all forms of higher mental functions—the human mind itself—as a jointly constructed process. "The goal of social cultural approach is to explicate the relationship between the human mental functioning, on the one hand, and the cultural, institutional and historical situations in which this functioning occur, on the other" (Wertsch, Rio and Alvarez, 1995, p. 3). Human action has to be understood as a culturally situated meaning seeking process and as intentional acts (Bruner, 1990). In Vygotskyan socio-cultural and socio-historical approach, action is mediated by the speech process that uses language as a means. Language is viewed as semiotic means capable of shaping thought and speech. The focus on speech as opposed to language is characteristic of Vygotsky and post-Vygotskyan cultural psychology. Bakhtin (1986) also maintained the distinction between language and speech, sentences and utterance. He viewed metalinguistic analysis as necessary for understanding mental processes.

Discursive Practices and Meaning Making

How is reality created depends on how meanings are made (and also how meanings are negotiated). The role of discursive practices in a given culture is crucial in the given context as it embodies complex cultural processes like the nature and the way activities are organized, the scaffolding provided by the adult members to the novice in the society, the power relationship between the adult and the novice, the discursive contexts in which the adult and the child operate etc. Beside this, the term meaning postulates a quality or property of linguistic units that mediates between communicating people. If we know the meaning of the relevant word or the sentence, we are able to understand. If we do not know, we do not understand. The crucial point here is to understand the process of arriving at a meaning which is socially produced, validated and shared.

The social constructivists' position on this would be that everything that enhances an individual's induction into a given discourse is taken as contributing to that person's construction of meaning. Further, it is only by participating in the discourse that individuals can receive enough feedback to assure themselves of having constructed the socially accepted meaning. Thus, according to this perspective, developing a theory of meaning is an attempt to explain how we can successfully participate in a discourse. Many psychologists use theoretical notions of prototypes, protocols and *as-if* attitudes to elaborate on meaning negotiation processes. Panda (in press)'s study on "*As-if* discourse and mathematics learning among Saora children" documents various mathematical discourses that the children and adults from the Saora community (a linguistically and culturally distinct tribe from southern Orissa in India) engage in different eco-cultural settings and routine daily life activities. Many *as-if* assumptions underlying these discursive acts are analyzed to understand the development of mathematical thinking among the

Saoras. Some real buying activities (carried out by the researcher in the real village market place) were recorded and analysed later using discourse analysis technique. The discourse analysis of the conversations revealed that the specific world-view of the Saoras, their values and norms, their economic engagement etc. provide the context within which the specific *as-if* attitudes develop among the Saora children. These *as-if* attitudes play a crucial role in Saora children's acceptance or rejection of certain mathematical discourses. Analysis of two folk games and the conversations carried out by the children while playing these games revealed how the process through which understanding of the concept of 'probability' develops among uneducated Saora youths. The crucial point here is that the game itself was not used as prototype for understanding the concept of probability by the Saora adults and children. Rather, the prototype for understanding probability was a particular way of interpreting and talking about how the game should be played and how the points are to be distributed in the game, etc. Here the meaning of the concept of probability did not come from outside. The discourse itself created its meaning in a collaborative context. In other words, this game could not have served as an intra-discursive source of mathematical meaning for concepts like probabilities and relative weightage system unless children developed these ways of interpreting it. This study clearly shows that the shared experiences with prototypes and the protocols enhance the compatibility of these two cognitive structures for the individual. Here communication, even if deficient or fragmentary, is an important social framework of and support for being introduced into a discourse and its means. Therefore, verbal communication and other forms of discursive acts provide the social medium for the individual construction of prototypes and protocols and many *as-if* attitudes that regulate meaning making processes.

Acquisition of symbolic and representational systems of the culture is a significant aspect of children's mental development. Learning of and within the culture is made possible by learning of such symbolic systems including language. Olson (1995) goes further to argue that "learning of various notational systems of the culture—that is, the cultural means of storing and communicating information in a variety of written and ritualised forms" (p. 95) plays a significant role adding a new structure to the world.

Role of Mediation in Socio-Cultural Approach

As has been noted earlier, the construct of mediation (with particular emphasis on semiotic mediation) occupied a central place in Vygotsky's socio-cultural theory. In fact, action and mediation are undifferentiated in the process of construction of mind, even if, they are sometimes treated separately for theoretical analysis and clarity. Our encounter with the world is indirect and mediated. Thus, relating concrete actions of individuals and groups to the cultural-historical settings is essential for understanding the process of construction of mind. The mediation by the cultural tools or artifacts is not a passive but an active process. It does not cause action or behaviour in a mechanistic way, but it plays a central role in shaping actions by which mind is jointly constructed. Mediation can be viewed "as a *process* involving the potential of cultural tools to shape action, on the one hand, and the unique use of these tools, on the other" (Wertsch *et al.,* 1995, p. 22). Vygotsky emphasised the transformatory role of mediational means such as language and other cultural tools. "The psychological tool alters the entire flow and structure of mental functions. It does this by determining the structure of a new instrumental act, just as a technical tool alters the process of a natural adaptation by determining the form of labour operations" (Vygotsky, 1981, p. 137). In this respect, Vygotsky's socio-cultural approach makes a departure from Piaget and other similar approaches. For Piaget, mastery of symbolic functions and of the natural world go together and "language did not create representational and symbolic functions; rather the representational function that was based on the ability to hold objects in mind in their absence made language learning possible" (Olson, 1995, p. 97).

The mediated nature and social origin of mind is reflected in Vygotsky's notion of the Zone of Proximal Development (ZPD). According to Vygotsky, ZPD is the distance between a child's "actual developmental level as determined by independent problem solving" and the higher level of "potential development as determined through problem solving under adult guidance or in collaboration with more capable peers" (Vygotsky, 1978, p. 86). Thus, human development is a process of socially guided transformation of mind and language, as well as other psychological tools, plays a major mediating role in such transformation. Bakhtin (1981; 1986) placed even greater emphasis on the social situatedness of language as mediational tool. According to him, speech is a social act; even utterances by a single individual is "inherently responsive in nature" (1986, p. 68) and all forms of speech are dialogic or a part of a social langauge which is "a way of speaking that is characteristic of particular group in a particular socio-cultural setting" (Wertsch, 1991, p. 95). Bakhtin (1986) emphasised the integral nature of language, mind and culture. "The study of mind, of culture, and of language (in all its diversity) are internally related that is, it will be *impossible* to render anyone of these domains intelligible without essential reference to the others" (p. 39). Recently, scholars working on "culture, mathematics and cognition" treat mathematics as a special form of semiotic activity that includes all forms of discursive acts such as language use in a particular culture (Dorfler, 2000; Panda, 2004a; Panda, 2004b; Sfard, 2000). According to them, in any society, social exchanges with others constitute the primary occasion in which children represent a reality, mathematise it and manipulate it. Therefore, mathematical objects come into being (into the realm of experiential reality) exclusively within a discourse that attributes it the properties and the character of an object (Cobb, 2000; Dorfler, 2000; Panda, *in press*). The children learn mathematics by willingly indulging in discourses/discursive practices of a community. The meaning of symbols, words and sentences cannot be isolated and described in the same way as the properties of the physical objects.

Through their participation in social interactions, children learn the social language and, at the same time, they jointly construct their knowledge. "Language, thus, is both a tool and a product of a social process" (Babu and Mohanty, 2001, p. 5). Babu and Mohanty (2001) have argued that knowledge structures are co-constructed socially as children participate in the cultural activities. This is possible because cultural knowledge and world-views are themselves shared and are based on social transmission of knowledge as well as individual knowledge construction (which, in itself, is embedded in the social context). In the socio-cultural approach, the shared activities can be analysed in three planes of focus—personal, interpersonal and communicative processes (which are inseparable except for different levels of focus) (Rogoff, 1995). Rogoff (1995), Lave (1988) and Lave and Wenger (1991) speak of three forms of participation in socio-cultural activities, viz., apprenticeship, guided participation and participatory appropriation. In her analysis of cultural practices in Girl Scout cookie sales, Rogoff (1995) shows how, through these processes of participation, "individual, groups and communities transform as they together constitute and are constituted by socio-cultural activities" (p. 161). Panda's (*in press*) study shows how Saora children learn the concept of probability and determine the complex weightage system used in the game through participatory appropriation. In another study, she (Panda, 2004b) examines how children learn various physico-mathematical concepts (such as different kinds of measurements, angles, force, gravity etc. and their relationship) embedded in the cultural activities like house construction and agricultural tool making through apprenticeship (see also Panda, 2004a), where interaction among adults, children and the culture determine the nature of both scientific cognition and the knowledge. An ethnographic study of a Garhwali village by Panda and Pasbola (2005) explored the manner in which the Garhwali villagers perceive, interpret and adjust to their environment and how these determine their notional understanding of the physico-mathematical concepts embedded in everyday practices. Their house designs, agricultural practices and tool making were found to be related to the availability of resources, climatic conditions, and other ecological considerations in the region. Learning here is highly context bound and the knowledge generated was situated in the adults' knowledge of the larger eco-cultural conditions of Garhwal, the new challenges the community faces and the needs of younger generation and a host of other cultural and social factors. What determines the nature of knowledge is the interface or the discursive exchanges between the cognitive construction of eco-cultural conditions among the adults and the young children.

According to Babu and Mohanty (2001), such cognitive construction of culture is mediated by language and other cultural tools which are products of cultural transmission. "Language makes it easier or, even possible for people to share cultural norms, values and meanings by transmission of experiences and abstractions from such experiences" (Babu and Mohanty, 2001, p. 5). Thus, learning to communicate is inseparable from the processes of learning a culture.

Studies of the process of language socialisation (e.g. Gardner, 1984; Ochs, 1986) show how children's use of language for communication and other social functions is shaped through their participation in social interaction. Brunner (1975; 1978), like many others, has suggested the notion of *scaffolding* or adults' structuring of communicative acts to facilitate children's socio-cultural and linguistic competence. Stern (1985) pointed to the significant roles of mothers in bringing "the infants' behaviour to her framework of created meanings" (p. 134). The structural and functional aspects of maternal speech use has been shown to be reflected in children's participation in a similar situation (Shukla, 1988) when they were asked to teach a game (which their mothers had taught them earlier) to another younger child. Thus, participation in cultural activities seem to be essential in socio-cultural regulation of speech. Specific regulatory mechanisms and socialisation strategies, however, do vary from one culture to another. For example, cultural activities, in which children participate, involve various interactional routines through which they develop competence in social use of language (Peters and Boggs, 1986). These interactional routines involve set patterns of language use, repeated linguistic forms and structures which provide children with necessary practice for refinement of their language as a cultural tool. "Verbal behaviours, speech acts and communicative functions are culturally coded. The use of language, therefore, has to be viewed within a holistic framework in which the cultural context and the form and structure of language are necessary parameters" (Mohanty, 2000, p. 209).

Language, Culture and Language Use: Limitations of the Contextual Models

A somewhat gross model of the relationship between culture, language and language use was proposed earlier by Mohanty (2000). In this conceptual model, culture is viewed as providing the context in which language and its structure are embedded and functional priorities in language use are set. Language is viewed as being situated in the total cultural context or the total ethos which are crucial in setting the social goals (and, hence, functional priorities) of languae use. A variety of sociological, psychological and formal linguistic conditions (such as the dominant monolingual or multilingual character of the society, language policy and planning, social psychological processes of language contact and use etc.) form aspects of the cultural context of language use. According to this model, linguistic behaviours and processes at the individual level, including the mode of development of language and literacy, awareness and mental representation of language as a formal as well as a cultural tool, psycholinguistic proficiency, social and communicative competence, and processes of linguistic identity etc. can only be understood within their cultural context. The distinction, in this model, between cognition and social processes or between the linguistic processes and their cultural context is, however, questionable in a Vygotskyan socio-cultural framework of constructivism which views cognition and socio-cultural processes as necessarily integral to each other. "Recent theories of *situated cognition* are challenging the view that the social and the cognitive can be studied independently, arguing that the social context in which cognitive activity takes place is *an integral part of that activity, not just the surrounding context for it*" (Resnick, 1991, p. 4). Thus, any assumption of mutual independence (as well as interdependence) of cognition and social context does not further the socio-cultural perspective to the relationship between language and mind in terms of Vygotskyan constructivism.

Knowledge construction and sharing inevitably take place in group interactions in cultural settings making all such group interactions constructive processes. Hatano and Inagaki (1991) show that constructive group interactions involve collective invention of knowledge which may not be available to any single member of the group. They discuss some experimental findings of collective comprehension in classroom learning activities and point two processes involved in the construction of knowledge through such interactions—"(a) individual invention of knowledge, motivated by group interaction; and (b) assimilation of information proposed by others in the preceding interaction, with some individual editing" (p. 346). Such collective comprehension activity, however, does not necessarily lead to "uniform representations"; individual contributions and individual cognitive processes are not completely ignored in the processes of joint construal of cognition. However, collaborative cognitive activity has been specially emphasised under the influence of Vygotsky's emphasis on social construction of mind. Mathematical thinking and generation of mathematical knowledge in any particular culture can be taken as a case in point. Cobb (1995), Sfrad (2000), Dorfler (2000) and Panda (in press) asserted that mathematical activities emerge from socio-semiotic practices in early childhood that embody different kinds of symbolic representations of mathematical concepts and notions. The semiotic activities differ from culture to culture and hence, the nature of mathematical discourse and object mediation of mathematical concepts also differ across cultures (Dorfler, 2000). Children from different cultures vary in their experiential basis of mathematical knowledge, use of specific language (e.g. use of specific linguistic categories, metaphors and metaphorical projections of reality) and symbols (Harris, 1999) and also the process of mathematical enquiry (Barber and Estrine, 1995; Ernest, 1991; Harris, 1999; Schmittau, 2003). Studies exploring the social nature of mathematics reveal that the implicit rules of everyday mathematical cognitions are shaped to a good extent by non-mathematical considerations like social values, beliefs, expectations, experiences, relations and social institutions in an adult-child-culture interaction context (Abreau, Bishop and Presmeg, 2002; Atweh, Bleicher and Cooper, 1998; Lave, 1988; Lave and Wenger, 1991). Cross-cultural variations in such interactive practices give rise to different kinds of discursive practices and therefore, different kinds of mathematical knowledge systems (Cobb, 1995).

Social Processes in Knowledge, Language and Theory of Mind

Children's knowledge construction is fundamentally a social process involving all levels of social interaction with adults as well as peers. Quite early in development, infants (less than 3 years) are influenced by peer social contexts (Brownwell and Carriger, 1991). The social process of knowing seems to be closely related to children's ability to participate in collaborative activities with their peers. Social communicative skills and ability to influence other's behaviour are found to develop along with the ability to understand other's behaviour and intentions or mental states. According to Brownwell and Carriger (1991) "age related social and cognitive skills contributing to peer collaboration influence what and how children learn from these collaborations" (p. 381). It seems that children are able to co-regulate each other's behaviour even in the absence of adult support. Thus patterns of interaction with adults as well as peers influence social sharing of knowledge leading to common conception of reality and effective use of cultural tools such as language to mediate thought processes. Further, children's ability to benefit from social interaction also depends on their ability to comprehend the intentions and the mental states of others. In other words, development of a theory of mind and social cognition do have common trends. In their analysis of the relationship between language, theory of mind and the cultural construction of knowledge, Babu and Mohanty (2001) show that in the process of development, children come to impute mental states to self and others. This, in turn, forms the basis of a theory of mind. Development of a theory of mind becomes evident in predictions and explanations based on intentional states (such as beliefs, desires and intentions) which are mental representations, attitudes and also the meta-representations. According to Olson (1988), intentionality develops through three stages—a pre-linguistic stage in which behaviour is characterised by habits or expectancies, an intentional stage emerging with development of language and a stage of theory of mind which brings the child's action under control of the representation of self and others' mental representations. As children's conception of mind develops and changes (approximately between 3-6 years of age), they show concurrent developmental changes in understanding of belief states, lie and deception, mental state verbs (*belief, desire, know, think etc.*) and appearance-reality distinction. Review of research (Babu and Mohanty, 2001) shows that the development of theory of mind is closely linked to the development of language including its semantic, syntactic and pragmatic aspects. Further, research also shows that theory of mind can be viewed as a product of cultural processes and social experience.

Summing Up

In the social cultural perspective, cognition is a socially shared process of joint construal of reality. Through their participation in their social activities, children develop culturally based common conceptions of reality mediated by a variety of cultural tools including language. Abstractions from individual experiences as well as social encounters reach a different higher plane as the child develops linguistic skills. Innate propensities as well as experiences integrated in the socio-cultural milieu interact in complex ways leading to cognitive development and onset of representational and communicative symbolic functions. Use of language, as well as increasingly complex cognitive functions, facilitates children's understanding of intentionality of self and others and their concept of mind. It seems social sharing of knowledge is significantly influenced by the development of theory of mind. Both of these, in turn, act together to boost the development of cognition and language. "Thus, beyond the prelinguistic phase of development, a theory of mind including mental representations, attitudes and metarepresentations, cognition and linguistic/communicative processes become mutually interdependent, overlapping and synergistic social acts. Social relationships, both vertical (e.g. adult child with different levels of knowledge and power) and horizontal, (e.g. peer group with similar levels of knowledge and power) constitute the context in which such synergistic interplay between theory of mind and language development is possible" (Babu and Mohanty, 2001; p. 35).

The role of social interaction within a given culture seems to be particularly significant in development of language as well as joint construction of mind. With development of language and communicative skills, higher mental functions are increasingly regulated and mediated by langauge and other cultural tools. With language, social interactions become predominantly, if not exclusively, communicative and conversational discourses which are culturally organised carrying information about the socio-cultural order, the knowledge of which the child comes to share through repeated participation in cultural activities. Culturally appropriate communicative acts involve integration of knowledge of the formal linguistic codes as well as socio-cultural knowledge. The processes of language socialisation involve learning of linguistic forms and structures, social convention of language use and construction of common cultural concepts. Through several routine cultural practices involved in the use of language such as turn taking, prompting, announcing and similar other practices, adults guide the child through higher levels of cultural constructions and language socialisation. Social speech act, conversations and interactions invariably seek to establish and maintain common grounds in communications leading to shared cognitions. Several researches have documented the processes of a variety of collaborative efforts through which such common groundings are achieved.

REFERENCES

Abreu, G. de, Bishop, A. and Presmeg, N.C. (2002), *Transitions between Contexts of Mathematical Practice.* Dordrecht: Klewer Academic Publishers.

Atweh, B., Bleicher, R.E. and Cooper, T.J. (1998), The Construction of the Social Context of Mathematics Classrooms: A Sociolinguistic Analysis. *Journal for Research in Mathematics Education,* Vol. 29(1), 63-82.

Babu, N. and Mohanty, A.K. (2001), Language Theory of Mind and Cultural Construction of Knowledge: A review, *Indian Psychological Abstracts and Reviews.* Vol. 8(1), pp. 3-47.

Barber, S.N. and Estrin, E.T. (1995), Bringing Native American Perspectives to Mathematics and Science Teaching. *Theory into Practice.* Vol. 34, No. 3, pp. 174-185.

Bakhtin, M.M. (1981), *The Dialogical Imagination.* Austin: University of Texas Press.

Bakhtin, M.M. (1986). *Speech Genres and Other Late Essays.* Austin: University of Texas Press.

Brownwell and Carriger (1991), Collaborating among Toddler Peers: Individual Contribution to Social Contexts. In L.R. Resnick, J.M. Levine and S.D. Teasley (Eds), *Socially Shared Cognition.* Washington D.C. American Psychological Association, pp. 365-385.

Bruner, J. (1975), The Ontogenesis of Speech Act. *Journal of Child Language,* 2, pp. 1-19.

Bruner, J.S. (1978), The Role of Dialogue in Language Acquisition. In A. Sinclaire, R.J. Jarvella W.J.M. Levelt (Eds). *The Child's Conceptions of Language.* New York: Springer-Verlag.

Bruner, J.S. (1990), *Acts of Meaning.* Cambridge, MA: Harvard University Press.

Cobb, P. (1995), Cultural Tools and Mathematical Learning: A Case Study. *Journal for Research in Mathematics Education,* 26, 362-385.

Cobb, P., Yackel, E. and McClain, K. (2000). *Symbolizing and Communicating in Mathematics Classrooms: Perspectives on Discourse, Tools and Instructional Design.* London: Lawrence Erlbaum Associates, Publishers.

Cole, M. (1995), Socio-Cultural-Historical Psychology: Some General remarks and a Proposal for a New Kind of Cultural Genetic Methodology. In J.V. Wertsch, P.D. Rio and A. Alvarez (Eds.), *Socio-Cultural Studies of Mind.* Cambridge: Cambridge University Press, pp. 187-214.

Cole, M. (1996), *Cultural Psychology: A Once and Future Discipline.* Cambridge, Mass: Harvard University Press.

Dorfler, W. (2000), Means for Meaning. In P. Cobb, E. Yackel and K. McClain (Eds). *Symbolizing and Communicating in Mathematics Classrooms: Perspectives on Discourse, Tools and Instructional Design.* London: Lawrence Erlbaum Associates, Publishers.

Ernest. P. (1991). *The Philosophy of Mathematics Education.* London: The Falmers Press.

Gallimore, R. and Goldenberg, C. (2001), Analyzing Cultural Models and Settings to Connect Minority Achievement and School Improvement Research. *Educational Psychologist,* 36(1), 45-56.

Gardner, H. (1984), The Development of Competence in Culturally defined Domains: A Preliminary Framework. In R.A. Shweder and R.A. Levine (Eds). *Culture Theory: Essays on Mind, Self and Theory.* Cambridge, M.A.: Cambridge University Press.

Hatano, G. and Inagaki, K. (1991). Sharing Cognition through collective comprehension activity. In L.R. Resnick, J.M. Levine and S.D. Teasley (Eds), *Socially Shared Cognition.* Washington D.C.: American Psychological Association, pp. 331-348.

Harris Mary (1999), *Gender Sensitivity in Primary School Mathematics in India.* United Kingdom: Commonwealth Secretariat.

Lave, J. (1988), *Cognition in Practice: Mind, Mathematics and Culture in Everyday Life.* New York: Cambridge University Press.

Lave, J. and Wenger, E. (1991), *Situated Learning: Legitimate Peripheral Participation.* New York: Cambridge University Press.

Mohanty, A.K. (2000). Language Behaviour and Processes. In J. Pandey (Ed.) *Psychology in India Revisited, Vol. 1: Psychological Foundations and Human Cognition.* New Delhi. Sage, pp. 208-255.

Ochs (1986), Introduction. In B.B. Schieffelin E. Ochs (Eds). *Language Socialisation Across Cultures.* Cambridge, M.A.: Cambridge University Press.

Olson, D.R. (1988), On the Origins of Beliefs and the Other Intentional States in Children. In J.W. Ashington, P.L. Harris and D.R. Olson (Eds), *Developing Theories of Mind.* New York: Cambridge University Press, pp. 414-426.

Olson, D.R. (1995), Writing and the Mind. In J.V. Wertsch, P.D. Rio and A. Alvarez (Eds.), *Socio-Cultural Studies of Mind.* Cambridge: Cambridge University Press, pp. 95-123.

Panda, M. (2000), Mathematics Learning by Saora Children: A Case Study. Unpublished Research Report, NCERT, New Delhi.

Panda, M. (2004a), Culture and Mathematics: A Case Study of Saoras. In Karuna Chanana (ed.), *Transformative Links between Higher Education and Basic Education: Mapping the Field.* New Delhi, Sage.

Panda, M. (2004b), *Why Don't Saoras Mass Produce Agricultural Tools: Cultural Situatedness of Physico-Mathematical Concepts.* In International

Conference on "Cognitive Sciences". Centre for Behavioural and Cognitive Sciences, December 16-18. Allahabad University, Allahabad. (Under Publication in the Proceedings of the Seminar).

Panda, M. and Pasbola, H. (2005). Physico-Mathematical Concepts in Everyday Activities: A Study. Unpublished Manuscript. Jawaharlal Nehru University, New Delhi.

Panda, M. (In Press). Saora Culture, *As-if* Discourse and Mathematics Learning. In Gang Zheng, Kwok Leung and John Adair (Eds.). *Perspectives and Progress in Contemporary Cross-Cultural Psychology*. Beijing: China Light Industry Press.

Peters, A.M. and Boggs, S.T. (1986), Interactional Routines as Cultural Influences Upon Language Acquisition. In B.B. Schieffelin and E. Ochs (Eds.), *Language Socialisation Across Cultures*. Cambridge, MA: Cambridge University Press.

Resnick, L.B. (1991), Shared Cognition: Thinking as a Social Practice. In L.B. Resnick, J.M. Levine and S.D. Teasley (Eds.), *Perspectives on Socially Shared Cognition*. Washington, DC: American Psychological Association. pp. 1-22.

Rogoff, B. (1995), Observing Socio-cultural Activity on Three Planes: Participatory Appropriation, Guided Participation and Apprenticeship. In J.V. Wertsch, P.D. Rio and A. Alvarez (eds.), *Socio-Cultural Studies of Mind*. Cambridge: Cambridge University Press, pp. 187-214.

Schliemann, A.D. (1998), Logic of Meanings and Situated Cognition. *Learning and Instruction*, 8(6), 549-560.

Sfard, A. (2000), Symbolizing mathematical Reality into being—Or How Mathematical Discourse and Mathematical Objects Create Each Other. In P. Cobb, E. Yackel and K. McClain (Eds). *Symbolizing and Communicating in Mathematics Classrooms: Perspectives on Discourse, Tools and Instructional Design*. London: Lawrence Erlbaum Associates, Publishers.

Shukla, S. (1988). *Effect of Some Environmental Factors on Individual Differences in Language Development*. Unpublished Doctoral Dissertation, Utkal University, Bhubaneswar.

Stern, D.N. (1985), *The Interpersonal World of Infancy*. New York: Basic Books.

Vygotsky, L.S. (1962). *Thought and Language*. Cambridge, Mass: MIT Press. pp. 91-92.

Vygotsky, L.S. (1978), *Mind in Society, the Development of Higher Psychological Processes*. Cambridge: Harward University Press.

Vygotsky, L.S. (1981), *The Instrumental Method in Psychology*. In J.V. Wertsch (Ed.), *The Concept of Activity in Soviet Psychology*. Armonk, NY: Sharpe, pp. 134-143.

Wertsch, J.V., Rio, P.D. Alvarez, A. (1995). Socio-Cultural Studies: History, Action and Mediation. In J.V. Wertsch, P.D. Rio and A. Alvarez (Eds.), *Socio-Cultural Studies of Mind*. Cambridge: Cambridge University Press, pp. 1-34.

13

Developmental Impact of Type of Race and Experiential Deprivation on Achievement Motivation

Vidya Singh and *Aradhana Shukla*

Achievement motivation is a tendency which refers to the positive or negative anticipatory goal reactions in situations that involve competition with a standard of excellence where performance may be evaluated as success or failure. The experimental studies on achievement motivation have their origin in Murray's taxonomy of need systems and his concentration that fantasy behaviour *(The magic Apperceptions Test Imagery)* provides an index of an individual's motivation concerns. The TAT was adopted by McClelland and his colleagues for the measurement of achievement needs and was shown to relate a variety of achievement behaviours, such as the speed of learning and intensity of performance (Rosen, 1959), task recall (Atkinson, 1958) and work partner selection (French, 1972).

Delineating the relationship between social disadvantage and motivation Pareek (1970) argued that the structure of poverty leads to three-fold motivational pattern characterized by low n'ach, low extension and high dependency and expectancy that can be called the frame of powerlessness. The line of reasoning suggests that the motivational characteristics linked to social disadvantage are consequences of disadvantage which reduce the capacity to cope with environmental demands and therefore, accentuate the condition of disadvantage. The empirical studies on diverse motivational consequences of socio-economic deprivation are extensively wide (Misra, 1982; Sinha and Misra, 1982; Misra and Tripathi (1978 b, 1982).Tiwari and Misra (1977) have resulted that deprivation is negatively related to n'Ach. Agarwal and Misra (1986) observed that the gratification of basic needs and the desire to earn money were emphasized by the disadvantaged group as most important achievement goals while advantaged group was more concerned with the goals pertaining to the domains of career, prosocial and positive experiences.

Thus, it is surely fair to say that these studies share the implicit assumption that achievement motivation can be manifested similarly across cultures and within subcultures in the form of competitive effect and individualistic striving consequently. They levelled different cultures/groups/individuals along the same continum on the scale of achievement motivation. They had over looked the importance of fact that the culture provides the basis for learning and the manifestation of achievement motivation will therefore, arise in different forms, stimulated by different situational errors and may be channeled towards accomplishing different types of goals," (Bhagat and Mcquaid, 1982). Keeping these views in consideration, this study was planned in three way factorial design. The objectives and hypotheses were as follows:

1. The first objective of this study was to find out the pattern of achievement motivation as affected by chronological age. It was hypothesized that increase in age would cause increase in the magnitude of achievement motivation.
2. The second objective of this study was to ascertain the impact of race on achievement motivation. It was contended that variation in race would appear in terms of variation in the magnitude of achievement motivation.
3. The third objective of this study was to find out the pattern of achievement motivation as affected by experiential deprivation. It was thought that low and high deprived participants would evince variation in the magnitude of the level of achievement motivation.

Sample

Four hundred-eighty participants were taken and they were arranged according to the requirements of three-way factorial design with three levels of age (10-11, 12-13, 14-15 yrs), two types of races (tribal and non-tribal) and two levels of experiential deprivation (low and high), i.e. 40 participants per cell. The participants were termed as low and high deprived on the basis of their scores on Experiential Deprivation Scale.

The schematic presentation of experimental design is as follows:

Table 13.1: Schematic Presentation of Experimental Design (before Sample Selection)

A								
	A1			*A2*			*A3*	
	B			*B*			*B*	
B1	*B2*	*B3*	*B1*	*B2*	*B3*	*B1*	*B2*	*B3*
K	K	K	K	K	K	K	K	K

Legends:

A Chronological age	B Type of race	C Level of experiential deprivation
A1 10-11 years	B1 Tribal	C1 Low
A2 12-13 years	B2 Non-tribal	C2 High
A3 14-15 years		

Measures

The detail of the measure is as follows:

The Experiential Deprivation Scale

This scale is the revised version of experiential deprivation scale (Shukla, 1988) and it deals with six major areas of life where deprivation is experienced or at least felt. They are: housing conditions and home environment, familial relation, peer group relation, scholastic and economic experiences and motivational experience. It is consisted of 58 five-point items. Score ranges between 58-290. Almost items are scored positively and very few are negatively scorable. Low score indicates low level of experiential deprivation and high score *vice versa.* Split half reliability of this measure is .74 and test retest reliability is .68. This test is being successfully used in other studies (Ojha, 2006).

Achievement Test

In order to achieve the achievement pattern of participants the achievement test (Shukla and Najhoon, 1993) was employed. It consists of forty-point terms and deals with academic interest, academic concentration, deep study, feeling of competition, punctuality, selection of intelligent peer, selective discussion, level of aspiration, self-confidence, self-development and self-evaluation. The scores range between 40-200. Low score indicates higher level of achievement and high score *vice versa.*

Procedure

At first the investigators contacted the target places where they could get the sample. It was followed by a rapport with villages/residents of the places and then they got the target universe. The experiential deprivation scale was administered on 1000 participants and the participants scoring upto Q1 of the total score were termed as low deprived and above Q3 were termed as highly derived. In this way 40 participants were placed in each cell and thus, 480 participants were remained. They constituted the sample. Data was collected individually and/or in group and best attempts were made to avoid external distractions.

Results

Obtained data were analyzed by analysis of variance and interpreted in terms of chronological age, type of race and experiential deprivation as effectors of achievement motivation. The analysis was done in three phases. In first phase participants were termed as high/low deprived on the basis of their scores on experiential deprivation scale. In second phase impact of chronological age, type of race and experiential deprivation on achievement motivation was found. The third phase was consisted of correlational analysis of the data.

Findings are given below:

Phase I

Classification of participants as low and high deprived

The aim of this analysis was to classify the participants as low and/or highly deprived so, extreme group strategy was made and participants were termed as high and low deprived. The score of participants is given below:

Table 13.2: Distribution of participants as low and high deprived

	A1			A2		
	B1	B2	B3	B1	B2	B3
C1	78.54	85.56	86.72	110.46	121.56	129.76
C2	79.08	76.00	91.69	106.91	137.59	136.79

Legends:

A Chronological age	B Type of race	C Level of experiential deprivation
A1 10-11 years	B1 Tribal	C1 Low
A2 12-13 years	B2 Non-tribal	C2 High
A3 14-15 years		

Table clearly indicates that deprivation related discrepancy was highly evident.

Phase II

Impact of chronological age, type of race and experiential deprivation on achievement

Data were analyzed by three-way analysis of variance and findings are given in Table 13.3.

Table 13.3 reveals that impact of chronological age was significant *(F, 2, 468=7.79 P < .01)*. Mean values pooled across type of race and levels of experiential deprivation were 115.87, 98.85 and 95.82, respectively for young to old participants.

Table 13.3: Summary table of ANOVA showing the impact of chronological age, type of race and experiential deprivation on achievement motivation

Source of variation	*SS*	*df*	*MS*	*F*
A	25.52	2	12.77	7.79
B	1.21	1	1.21	.71
C	1.61	1	1.16	.73
AB	21.54	2	10.92	6.66
AC	24.54	2	12.27	7.48
BC	1.57	1	1.57	.96
ABC	31.64	2	15.80	9.64
Error (within)	767.52	468	1.64	

The next main effect of type of race was insignificant *(F, 1, 468=.71 P>.05)*. It revealed that tribals *(X=104.08)* were less sufficient in achievement motivation as compared to their non-tribal counter-parts *(X=103.60)*. The third main effect of levels of experiential deprivation also insignificant *(F, 1, 468=.73 P>.05)* and it revealed that high deprived participants *(X=105.98)* were relatively less in achievement motivation as compared to their low deprived counter parts *(X=105.98)*.

The chronological age* type of race interaction was significant *(F, 2, 468=6.66 P < 0.1)* and mentioned in Figure 13.1. Figure reveals that increase in age caused increase in the magnitude of achievement motivation. The F-ratio of chronological age * levels of experiential deprivation interaction was also significant *(F, 2, 468=7.48, P < 0.1)*. This interaction is appeared in Figure 13.2. Figure reveals significant pattern of age and levels of experiential deprivation on achievement motivation.

The type of race * levels of experiential deprivation was insignificant *(F, 1, 468=.96 L>.05)*. The three-way interaction of chronological age * type of race * levels of experiential deprivation was also significant *(F, 2, 468=9.64 P < 0.1)* and it is manifested in Figure 13.3. Figure reveals that all variables yielded their impact on achievement motivation.

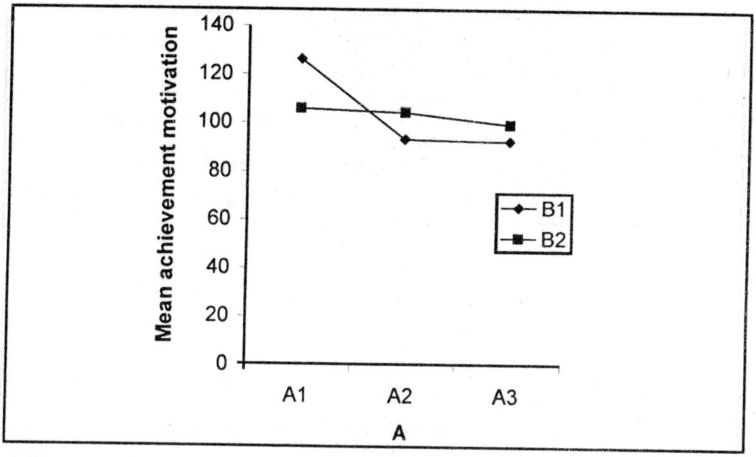

Legends:

A Chronological age	B Type of race
A1 10-11 years	B1 Tribal
A2 12-13 years	B2 Non-tribal
A3 14-15 years	

Fig. 13.1: Mean Values Showing the Impact of Chronological Age and Type of Race on Achievement Motivation

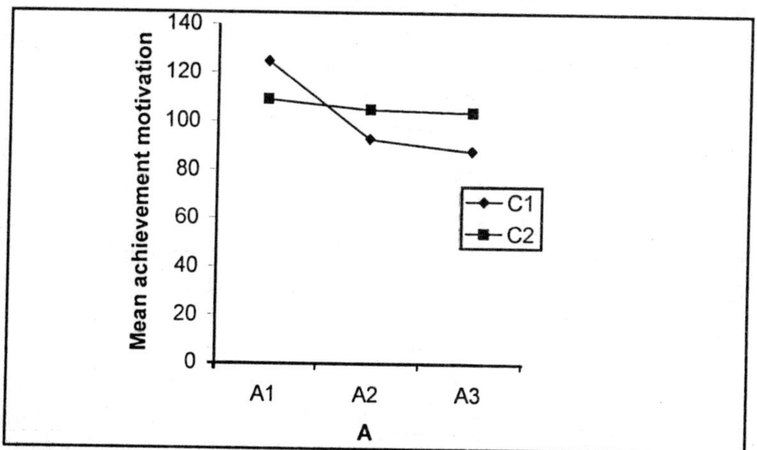

Legends:

A Chronological age	C Level of experiential deprivation
A1 10-11 years	C1 Low
A2 12-13 years	C2 High
A3 14-15 years	

Fig. 13.2: Mean Values Showing the Impact of Chronological Age and Levels of Experiential Deprivation on Achievement Motivation

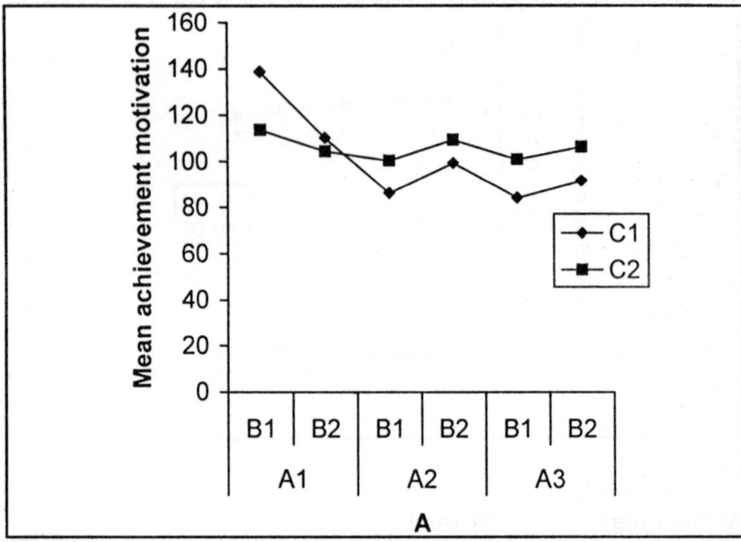

Legends:

A Chronological age	B Type of race	C Level of experiential deprivation
A1 10-11 years	B1 Tribal	C1 Low
A2 12-13 years	B2 Non-tribal	C2 High
A3 14-15 years		

Fig. 13.3: Mean Values Showing the Impact of Chronological Age Type of Race on and Levels of Experiential Deprivation on Achievement Motivation

Phase III

Correlational analysis of achievement scale as revealed through chronological age, types of race and levels of experiential deprivation

As it has been already mentioned in measure section, the achievement motivation scale was consisted of eleven areas namely, academic interest, academic concentration, deep study, feeling of competition, punctuality, selection of intelligent peer, selective discussion, level of aspiration, self-confidence, self-development and self-evaluation. A perusal of these areas indicates that there is a strong relationship among these areas and they serve as mediators to shape the pattern of achievement motivation. In order to renew this relationship an endeavour was made to ascertain the pattern of within group relationship. Data of each area was separated and correlation coefficient between each area was done. Findings are given in Table 13.4.

Table 13.4: Inter-correlational analysis of data

S. No.	Name of the areas	Correlation values										
		1	2	3	4	5	6	7	8	9	10	11
1.	Academic interest	—	.56	.52	.49	.58	.61	.69	.52	.61	.49	.46
2.	Academic concentration		—	.51	.48	.68	.71	.65	.55	.67	.52	.49
3.	Deep study			—	.47	.55	.65	.68	.56	.72	.59	.56
4.	Feeling of competition				—	.46	.57	.67	.61	.65	.54	.51
5.	Punctuality					—	.51	.61	.58	68	.51	.65
6.	Selection of intelligent peer						—	.62	.67	.57	.56	.66
7.	Selective discussion							—	.61	.56	.58	.69
8.	Level of aspiration								—	.66	.56	.71
9.	Self-confidence									—	.64	.74
10.	Self-development										—	.76
11.	Self-evaluation											—

Obtained findings, in sum, were as follows:

1. Achievement motivation was highly influenced by chronological age but type of race and level of experiential deprivation were unable to yield their impact an achievement motivation.
2. All areas of achievement motivation were highly related.

Discussion

Obtained data were analyzed by 3-way analysis of variance and interpreted in terms of chronological age, type of race and experiential deprivation as determinants of achievement motivation. Prior to the inception of this study same hypotheses were formulated and the findings will be discussed accordingly.

(i) Increase in chronological age would cause increase in the magnitude of achievement motivation

Our first and foremost notion was concerned with the developmental impact of achievement motivation. It was hypothesized that magnitude of achievement motivation would be enhanced with increase in chronological age.

In this study an attempt was made to ascertain the impact of age and it was assumed that achievement is a developing need so it would be matured with advancing age. Fortunately, our hypothesis was confirmed that age related enhancement in achievement was shown by participants though it was not uniform.

So far as the matter of age related development of achievement is concerned it may be argued that increase in age provides better chance to deal. With increasing age a child gets more insight and takes more inspiration from his past results. These factors facilitate him/her to do better. In addition, it can also be argued that with increasing age child comes in the context of more intelligent peers and he/she starts to compare him/her with his/her peers. This competence enables a child to compete with them. This time he gets more chance to meet various peer groups having different personalities. They also foster achievement tendency in him. Findings are in close consonance with Mishra (1993) who have pointed that with advancement in grade the tendency itself increases. In addition, Sohi (1976) has emphasized the significant role of teacher to raise the achievement of pupils. Therefore, it can be said that achievement tendency increased with increase in age although this discrepancy was not similar at each age. Here, it can be assumed that this study was conducted on children's and adolescents; so it is very possible to have a shift in the achievement pattern from childhood to adolescence. Actually, when a child passes from childhood and enters in the adolescence period he gets a lot of changes in him/her. As a result, he/she perceives the world in a new perspective. In addition he/she becomes more matured and able to deal the world so it is very reasonable to say that a shift may occur.

In sum, it seems that age is an important variable and it is closely related to the need for achievement. Also, increases in the grade do provide increase in the achievement patterns.

(ii) There would be variation in tribal and non-tribal relation to achievement motivation

The second objective was aimed to find out the impact of sub-cultural variation on achievement motivation. It was hypothesized that tribal and non-tribal would be different in their achievement motivation. Luckily our hypothesis was confirmed by our findings and it was found that achievement motivation was comperatively higher in tribal than non-tribal. Indeed, it was an interesting but commonly accepted truth. It has gives support to the fact that the goal and goal directed behaviour are entirely regulated by the living conditions prevailing assumed the person (Charon and Kati Back, 1991; Marjoribanks, 1979; Karnataka, 1999). What a person does, what he wants to do and what he should do all these questions are related to his/her environmental condition as well as entire thrust. In addition, TS × PS × IS (Tendency to Achieve Success × Probability of Success × Incentives of Success) also play an important role in this area. The general Kumaoni sample was taken from Almora city where cultural enrichment can be seen. Here people have many avenues to shape their life so they shape their children harmoniously. In addition, Almora city is near to big, privileged and career promoting cities like Lucknow and Delhi so it is very easy for the people of Almora to move there and decide their career in these cities. So far as the matter of tribal sample was concerned they were the residents of remote area of Northern Himalaya where scarcities of experiential enrichment prevail and they have very less opportunities to shape their future. Although numbers of attempts have been made by government to raise the life of tribal yet they have not been reached to the place where they should be. They have utilized by the high SES tribal.

It is fact that personal experiences and drive to achieve something higher in life also serve as a media for better 'n' achievement. Thus, it is appropriate to say that 'n' achievement may be affected by them. Since 'n' achievement is an outcome of cognitive-motivational-personality's process hence, it can be compared with other studies related with the environmental attributes as effectors of cognitive competence and personality characteristics. Findings are in close consonance with Shukla (1988), Misra (1998), Singhal and Misra (1990), Najhoon (1994), Srivastava and Muralidharan (1998) in which deprivational effect of environmental attributes on cognitive and personality variable have been presented.

Our findings also revealed a close shift in the achievement pattern from general Kumaonies to tribal sample. It may be due to sub-cultural gap, goal orientation and way of career formation. However, our hypothesis is confirmed.

(iii) Increase in experiential deprivation would retard the magnitude of achievement

Our third hypothesis stated that the variations in achievement would be caused by variation in experiential setting. Therefore, higher magnitude of n'achievement would be produced by people living in higher experiential amenities as compared to those who had been brought up in scarcity.

Our findings confirm the hypothesis and suggest that experiential surrounding provide a major role to develop the need for achievement. It has been proved as mediation variable and impresses the n'achievement pattern. Though achievement is a trade based dispositions but it also varies according to the variation in experiential set-up.

Thus, it is apparent that varying conditions of experience whether they are psychological, social or physical do provide variation in 'n' achievement tendency. It is true that the experiences stems from the environment and the environment provide the necessary sensory inputs, stimulations and experiential basis and this base serve as the fundamentals of n'achievement. A child as he grows old broadens his experiential set-up. He sees persons having ample resources and more gratified than him. He follows their ways and works harder and harder to achieve the things that are still dream for him. In a plethora of studies it has been noted that in lower social classes the achievement tendency was significantly lower than higher social classes' counterparts (McCleland, 1960; Nygard, 1969; Rosen, 1956). It has also been observed that SES is positively related to need for achievement. Lott and Lott (1963) have reported that in whites there was relatively stronger n'achievement than the Negros.

These findings support our findings and state that increase in the level of experiential deprivation retards the n'achievement pattern.

Our findings are also supported by some investigations (Tewari, Kumar and Morbhatt, 1980; Rao and Shanhar, 1977) and they clearly indicate that low deprived group indicated more achievement tendency than high deprived group. Though the data of this study were not equivocal but they do show deprivational influences.

On the basis of these findings it is surely fair to say that achievement motivation is highly determined by grade, deprivation and type of race.

REFERENCES

Atkinson, J.W. (ed) (1958), *Motives in Fancy Fantasy, Action and Society.* Princet N.J. Van Nostrand.

Bhagat, R.S. and Mcquvied, S.T. (1982), Role of Subjective Culture in Organizations: a Review and Dissertations for Future Research. *Journal of Applied Psychology*. 67, 653-685.

Chiron, A.T. and Katiback, M.S. (1991), Home Environment Nutritional Status and Maternal Intelligence as Data Ruminants of Intellectual Development in Rural. (Philippine Preschool Children). *Intelligence*. 15, 145-78.

Karnatak, S. (1999), Impact of Experimental Deprivation and Grade on Academic Motivation. Academic Stress and Stress Management. Unpublished Ph.D. Thesis, Department of Psychology, Kumaun University, Nainital.

Lott, A.J. and Lott, B.E. (1963), *Negro and White Youth*; New York: Hall Rinehart and Winston.

Majoribanks, K. (1978), Personality and Environment at Correlates of Cognitive Performance and School Elated Effective Characterstics. A Regression Surface Analysis. *Journal of Education Research*, 24, 230-243.

McCleland (1960), *The Achieving Society*, Princeton N.J. Van Notrand.

Misra, B. (1998), Revisiting Educational Day Tradition Across Cultures. *National Seminar on Environment and Cognition*, Department of Psychology D.D.V. Gorakhpur University, April 24-25.

Misra G. (1982), Deprivation and Cognitive Competence In D. Singh, R.C. Tripathi and G. Misra (Eds.) *Deprivation, Its Social Roots and Psychological Consequences*, New Delhi: Concept Publishing Company.

Misra, G. and Tripathi, L.B. (1978), *Deprivation Scale*, Agra National Psychologist Corporation.

Mishear, G. (1993), A Study of Elimaleter Variation is Children an Affiliated by there Chronological Age and Experiential Deprivation. Unpublished Thesis.

Najhoon, S. (1994), Recall Proficiency Memory and Strategy Use in Children as a Function of Chronological Age and Experiential Deprivation Unpublished Doctoral Dissertation, Department of Psychology. Kumaun University, Nainital.

Nygard, R. (1969), Motive to Approach Success and Motive to Avoid Future in Boys from Different Social Groups. *Scandinavian Journal of Educational Research,* 4.222-232.

Ojha, N. (2006), A Study of Emotional Disturbance and Frustration Tolerance among Kumaunies Tribal as a Function of Levels of Deprivation. Unpublished Ph.D. Thesis, Department of Psychology. Kumaun University, Nainital.

Rao, N. and Shankar, B. R. (1977), Sociological Background Variables of Self-Esteem in Adolescents, *Indian Journal of Behaviour,* 12-22.

Rosen, B.C. (1959), Race Ethnicity and the Achievement Syndrome. *American Social Review,* 24-4: 60.

Shukla, A. (1988), *Development of Representational Competence in Children.* Agra National Psychological Corporation.

Singhal, R. and Misra, G. (1989), Variation in Achievement Cognition: Role of Ecology, Age and Gender. *International Journal of intercultural Relation.* 13, 93-107.

Sinha, D. and Misra, G. (1982), Deprivation and Its Motivational and Personality Correct. In D. Sinha, R.C. Tripathi and G. Misra (eds.) *Deprivation: Its Social Roots and Psychological Consequences,* New Delhi, Concept Publishing Company.

Soni, A.S. (1976), Effects of Reinforcement as Motivational Technique on Level of Aspiration and Motor Performance. *International Journal of Sport Psychology.* 7 (2), 113-19.

Srivastava, A.K. and Muralidharan, R. (1998), Ecology and Cognitive Development: A Study of Children Growing in Temple Villages of South. India National Seminar on Environment and Cognition, D.D.U. Gorakhpur April, 24-25.

Tiwari, G.; Kumar, R. and Morbhatt, K.K. (1980), Level of Aspiration as a Function of Anxiety and Sex. Among High and Low Academic Achievers. *Indian Psychological Review,* 19 (4).

SECTION-IV

CULTURE AND HEALTH

14

Illness Beliefs and Coping Strategies

Poornima Awasthi and *Ramesh Chandra Mishra*

Psychological states generate physical reactions and lead to serious illness or even death if they are prolonged. Modification of behavioural sources of illness can greatly alleviate suffering and increase life expectancy. The interdisciplinary field of behavioural medicine integrates behavioural and medicinal knowledge to fight against disease and promote health. The field makes great promise for people suffering from chronic diseases, such as cancer, diabetes and cardiovascular diseases.

Cancer is a disease of the cells characterized by unrestricted cell proliferation that usually forms a malignant neoplasm (Williams, 1990). The prevalence rate of cancer has increased during the last decades. Dalal (1999) has noted that chronic diseases such as cancer, arthritis, asthma, tuberculosis, and diabetes cause death of almost 70-75 per cent of the cases worldwide. Cervix cancer has figured in most of the female registries in India (Rao and Ganesh, 1998). Studies have reported that cancer creates a unique stress among patents. While some patients become psychologically paralyzed by the attendant fear (Mages and Mendelsohn, 1979), others find medical procedures more aversive than the disease itself (Redd, Silberfrab, Andersen and Andrykowski, 1991).

Diabetes mellitus is a clinical syndrome characterized by hyperglycaemia due to an absolute or relative deficiency of insulin. Lack of insulin, whether absolute or relative, affects the metabolism of carbohydrate, protein, fat, water and electrolytes. Death may result from acute metabolic decompensation. A long-standing metabolic derangement is frequently associated with permanent and irreversible functional and structural changes in the cells of the body. These changes lead to the development of well-defined clinical entities, called "complications of diabetes", which most characteristically affect the eye, the kidney and the nervous system (Edwards, Baird, Frier, Shepherd and Toft, 1995).

The number of diabetics in India has shown staggering rise from 19 to 57 million during the last few years (Shah, 1998). According to an estimate, approximately 150 million people are affected by diabetes today. This number is likely to touch 300 million by the year 2025 if successful strategies are not implemented for its prevention and control (King, 1999). It is also estimated that by the year 2025, approximately 75 per cent of the total diabetic population will be living in developing countries. India will have a large majority of this number (approximately 220 million), and by the year 2025, diabetic population of India will be equal to the diabetics living in the entire world. The present India has got approximately 20 million identified diabetic patients, while an equal number of diabetic patients remain undiagnosed (Shah, 2001).

Several investigators have reviewed the importance of psychological factors in the causation of and the recovery from physical illness (Cohen and Herbert, 1996). A variety of beliefs about causes, controllability and outcomes of various diseases prevail in the society. Individuals acquire these beliefs as they grow up in their socio-cultural milieu. As an integral part of the cognitive system of individuals (Gilbert, 1990) beliefs determines not only their health cognition, but also treatment strategies, perceived treatment outcomes as well as coping with illness. Herzlich (1993) observes that when people suffer from a long-term illness, their self-perception becomes blurred. To regain self-sensibility, they need to make sense out of their illness. Patients extend their formulations about illness beyond medical explanations to embrace social-psychological implications for themselves and their family. Research carried out in India reveals that when people observe unusual symptoms, they confide it to their close relatives and friends to arrive at a naïve diagnosis with their help (Singh, 1987). It has been reported that in a large number of cases diagnosis is made in the absence of a formal medical check-up (Chandrasekhar, Isaac, Kapur and Parthsarathi, 1981; Mishra, 2001). Reliance on diagnosis made by elders, priests and others present in the social context of individual has been reported in other cultures as well (see Lambart, 1997).

Lay theories of illness (Furnham, 1988; Helman, 1990) reveal that all people have certain mental representations of illness. When their symptoms closely match with the pre-existing mental representations they exhibit appropriate illness behaviour (such as seeking treatment and demonstrating effective treatment follow-up). On the other hand, a mismatch of symptoms with the illness conception results in delay in seeking treatment, faulty or inappropriate behaviours, and poor adherence to health recommendations (Baumann and Leventhal, 1985; Turk, Rudy and Saovey, 1985). Such illness representations and their role in health behaviour have not been systematically analysed in the Indian cultural context while psychological studies of health behaviours have been carried out quite extensively in western countries (Ingledew, Hardy, Cooper and Jemal, 1996). In terms of the prediction of attribution theory (Kelly and Michael, 1980), it may be argued that in the Indian cultural context, in which concepts of gods, goddesses, spirits, and *karma* are transmitted to children as indispensable lessons, individuals are likely to consider external factors to be more responsible for health problems than internal or individual factors. The attribution of causality to external factors is likely to lead to a strong belief in controllability of illness by external agents.

Moos-Morris, Petrie, and Weinman (1996) studied the relationship between illness cognition, coping and adjustment in a sample of patients with chronic fatigue syndrome. Illness perceptions explained a greater per cent of variation in the level of an individual's psychological well-being than the coping strategy used to manage illness. Findings indicated that of the five illness components, illness identity, causality and controllability components, had serious consequences for individuals. A positive interpretation of health problems was positively related to internal control and self-oriented health beliefs. Radley (1994) has demonstrated that people not only seek medical explanations of their disease, but also try to understand the disease within their social and cultural context. A commonsense understanding of illness is often a social construction derived from the cultural models of illness. Family members, friends, social networks, and medical practitioners play their role in the formation of health beliefs and behaviour to combat the chronic disease.

Research indicates that the relationship between stressful events and indicators of adaptation status such as somatic health and psychological symptoms is mediated by coping processes. The coping processes are moderately stable across diverse stressful situations and they affect adaptation outcomes over the long-term. Studies have demonstrated the influence of beliefs about health and illness on behaviour of mental patients (Herzlich, 1986; Jodelet, 1990a), physically handicapped people (Echebarria and Paez, 1989; Weiner, Perry and Magnusson, 1988) and people's coping strategies towards the first symptoms of illness (Leventhal and Cameron, 1987; Leventhal, Meyer and Nerenz, 1980; Leventhal, Prohaska and Hirschman, 1985; Leventhal, Safer and Panagis, 1983). It has also been pointed out that a broad range of factors such as beliefs in the ability of some health practices to prevent illness and representations of illness, can promote health strategies (Prohaska, Leventhal, Leventhal and Keller, 1985). Ideas about illness, health and medicines vary, and it appears that these ideas are shaped by the information people get from social sources (Moscovici, 1990) and by their own past experiences with illness. These commonsense theories play an important role in directing the subject's behaviour (Leventhal *et al.*, 1980). Thus, in order to understand the reasons why people enage in self-promoting and self-mediating behaviours, it is essential to know how subjects construct their own representations of health and illness. Against this backdrop the present study attempted to examine illness consequences and controllability beliefs of women suffering from cancer and diabetes. It also attempted to analyze the role of coping strategies in perceived controllability and consequences of chronic illness. In the light of the general findings in this area it was hypothesized that:

1. Patients who would consider self and doctor as more effective agents of illness control would perceive less severe consequences of illness than those who believe in supernatural control.
2. Patients who would use more approach strategies of coping would perceive less severe consequences of illness than those would use avoidance strategies.
3. Patients who would use approach strategies of coping would consider self and doctor as more effective agents of illness control than supernatural factors.

Method

Design and Sample

The sample comprised 100 cervix cancer patients and 100 diabetic patients. The patients were selected taking into consideration whether they were educated or uneducated, and whether they came from a rural or urban background. A 2 × 2 × 2 factorial design was employed by sampling educated, uneducated, urban, and rural cancer and diabetic patents. The patients were selected from various medical centres and hospitals of Varanasi. The age group of women was 30-65 years. The social and demographic features of the two patient groups were almost homoenous.

Measures

Three measures were used in the study

Illness Consequences Belief Measure

It comprised 15 items related to physiological, psychological, and interpersonal consequences of disease. They were extracted from Factor Analysis of data (Awasthi, Mishra and Shahi, 2006) and explained approximately 77 per cent of the variance in scores with Alpha values of .91. The participants were asked to rate each item on a 5-point scale ("vary much" = 5, "very little" = 1). The score range for each consequence measure was 5 to 25. Test-retest reliability of the measure ranged between .69 and .89.

Illness Controllability Belief Measure

It consisted of 3 items that assessed the degree to which the participant believed that the disease was controllable by "self", "external agents" or a "doctor" (Awasthi *et al.,* 2006). Each item was rated on a 5-point scale, ranging from "not at all" (1) to "very much" (5). Test-retest reliabilities of the scales were .90, .93 and .91 respectively.

Coping Strategies Measure

It was a single item measure. The women were asked to list five things they considered important for managing cancer or diabetes. Following the usual categorisation of coping patterns, answers were categorised to represent either "approach" or "avoidance" coping strategy. The probable score range for each coping strategy was 0-5. The inter-coder reliability on the measure was .98.

Results

Illness Consequences Beliefs

The mean scores of the groups on this measure are given in Table 14.1. The scores were generally higher for physiological and psychological consequences than for interpersonal consequences.

Table 14.1: Mean Scores of Groups on Illness Consequences Belief Measure

Illness Consequences	*Disease Groups*		*Educated Groups*		*Uneducated Groups*	
			Urban	*Rural*	*Urban*	*Rural*
(a) Interpersonal						
	Cancer	Mean	15.76	19.68	19.04	15.68
		S.D.	4.70	3.03	5.14	4.90
	Diabetes	Mean	13.92	15.24	14.56	15.12
		S.D.	4.53	3.99	5.28	3.94
(b) Physiological						
	Cancer	Mean	15.00	15.12	16.12	16.16
		S.D.	4.23	3.44	4.14	4.11
	Diabetes	Mean	17.60	18.68	20.08	17.36
		S.D.	4.08	4.53	3.24	4.80
(c) Psychological						
	Cancer	Mean	17.68	17.92	14.40	17.48
		S.D.	4.48	4.92	5.53	5.96
	Diabetes	Mean	17.68	16.84	17.32	19.60
		S.D.	5.75	5.90	6.10	4.91

ANOVA (Table 14.2) revealed that the main effect of disease was significant for interpersonal and physiological consequences. Cancer patients scored higher than diabetic patients on interpersonal consequenccs, whereas diabetic patients scored higher than cancer patients on physiological consequences. The effects of education and residence were not significant.

Table 14.2: ANOVA Outcomes on Illness Consequences Belief Measure

Illness Consequences		*Interpersonal*		*Physiological*		*Psychological*	
Source of Variations	*df*	*MS*	*F*	*MS*	*F*	*MS*	*F*
Disease (D)	1	400.45	20.79**	400.44	24.75**	2.88	.10
Education (E)	1	00.13	00.01	34.44	2.13	8.82	.29
Residence (R)	1	18.61	.97	6.84	.42	9.68	.32
D × E	1	4.80	.25	3.13	.19	30.42	1.01
E × R	1	202.00	10.49**	47.05	2.91	27.38	.91
D × R	1	5.45	.28	10.13	.63	3.92	.13
D × E × R	1	132.84	6.90**	43.20	2.67	33.62	1.12
Replications	24	33.57	1.74	26.87	1.66	39.42	1.31
Error	168	19.26		16.18		30.02	
Total	199						

* $p < .05$, ** $p < .01$

The interaction of education and residence for interpersonal consequences suggested a significant difference between urban and rural patients only for educated samples where rural patients scored higher than urban patients. A significant disease × education × residence interaction for interpersonal consequences suggested that in educated sample difference between the scrores of cancer and diabetic patients was significant in the rural groups, whereas in uneducated sample the difference was significant in the urban groups. None of the interaction effect was found to be significant for physiological and psychological consequences. All the groups held more or less uniform beliefs about these consequences.

Illness Controllability Beliefs

The mean scores of groups on this measure are given in Table 14.3. In general, the mean scores of the groups were higher on doctor than on self and supernatural controls.

ANOVA (Table 14.4) yielded a significant effect for self-control. The mean scrore of diabetic group was higher than that of the cancer group. The main effect of education was significant on self, doctor and supernatural control measures. While educated women scored higher on self-control, uneducated women scored higher on doctor and supernatural controls. The mean score of rural women was higher than that of the urban women on supernatural control with a significant residence effect.

Table 14.3: Mean Scores of Groups on Illness Controllability Belief Measure

Types of Control	*Disease Groups*		*Educated Groups*		*Uneducated Groups*	
			Urban	*Rural*	*Urban*	*Rural*
(a) Self						
	Cancer	Mean	1.60	1.28	1.16	1.40
		S.D.	.94	.83	.46	.80
	Diabetes	Mean	2.84	1.96	1.72	1.60
		S.D.	1.46	1.37	1.00	.89
(b) Doctor						
	Cancer	Mean	3.88	3.36	3.64	4.24
		S.D.	1.03	1.05	1.16	.91
	Diabetes	Mean	3.72	3.52	3.65	4.12
		S.D.	1.00	.94	1.32	.86
(c) Supernatural						
	Cancer	Mean	1.16	1.40	1.52	2.12
		S.D.	.54	.80	1.02	1.58
	Diabetes	Mean	1.15	1.56	1.32	1.64
		S.D.	.46	1.13	.68	.97

Table 14.4: ANOVA Outcomes on Illness Controllability Belief Measure

Illness Controlability		*Self Control*		*Doctor's Control*		*Supernatural Control*	
Source of Variations	*df*	*MS*	*F*	*MS*	*F*	*MS*	*F*
Disease (D)	1	22.45	21.07**	.05	.04	.85	.90
Education (E)	1	10.13	9.50**	4.51	3.95*	5.45	5.80*
Residence (R)	1	3.65	3.42	.10	.09	7.61	8.11**
D × E	1	4.21	3.95*	.04	.04	2.21	2.35
E × R	1	5.45	5.11*	10.13	8.88**	.25	.26
D × R	1	2.65	2.48	.13	.11	.05	.05
D × E × R	1	.12	.12	.61	.53	.61	.64
Replications	24	1.11	1.05	1.12	.98	1.14	1.21
Error	168	1.07		1.14		.94	
Total	199						

* $p < .05$, ** $p < .01$

Disease × education effect of self-control revealed significant difference between cancer and diabetic patients only in the educated sample. Educated diabetic patients scored significantly higher than educated cancer patients. Education × residence effect was significant on self and doctor's control. With respect to self-control, educated urban patients scored significantly higher than uneducated urban patients. With respect to doctor control, a significant difference between educated and uneducated women was noted in the rural sample, where uneducated patients scored significantly higher than educated patients.

Illness Consequences and Illness Controllability

Table 14.5 shows that attribution for interpersonal consequences was positively correlated with physiological and psychological consequences as well as beliefs in supernatural control, and negatively with belief in self and doctor controls. It suggests that a strong belief in interpersonal consequences is linked to severe physiological and psychological consequences, and a strong belief in supernatural control. Physiological consequences were positively correlated with psychological consequences and belief in supernatural control and negatively with belief in self and doctor control. Psychological consequences were positively correlated with belief in supernatural control and negatively with belief in self and doctor control.

Table 14.5: Inter-correlation of Cancer and Diabetic Groups Across Various Measure

Variables	*Interper.*	*Physiol.*	*Psychol.*	*Self*	*Doctor*	*Supernat.*
Interper.	—	0.43**	0.66**	-0.22**	-0.44**	0.20*
Physiol.	0.55**	—	0.51**	0.06	-0.32**	0.38**
Psychol.	0.47**	0.56**	—	-0.24*	-0.39**	0.19*
Self	-0.41**	-0.48**	-0.53**	—	0.28**	0.00
Doctor	-0.14	-0.21*	-0.30**	0.15	—	0.10
Supernat.	0.23*	0.22*	0.19*	-0.25**	-0.05	—

* $p < .05$, ** $p < .01$

Note: Diabetic group above the diagonal
Cancer group below the diagonal

Coping Strategies, Illness Consequences and Illness Controllability

With respect to the role of coping strategies in illness consequences and controllability, the findings revealed (Table 14.6) that patients who used avoidance strategies of coping, not only believed in severe interpersonal, physiological and psychological consequences of disease, but also believed less strongly in doctor or self-control over illness. On the other hand, patients who resorted to approach strategies of coping believed in less severe interpersonal, physiological and psychological consequences. They also had a strong belief in doctor and self-control over illness. In the cancer group, the difference due to approach and avoidance strategies was significant only with respect to interpersonal consequences whereas in the diabetic group the difference was significant for interpersonal, physiological, and psychological consequences and belief in self and doctor control.

Table 14.6: Comparison between Avoidance and Approach Coping Strategies on Illness Consequences and Illness Controllability Scores

Diseases		*Illness Consequences (A)*			*Illnes Controllability (B)*		
Groups		*Inter-personal*	*Physio-logical*	*Psycho-logical*	*Self*	*Doctor*	*Super-natural*
			Cancer Group				
Avoidance Strategies of Coping							
	Mean	18.37	15.96	17.88	1.33	3.69	1.57
	SD	4.63	3.80	5.01	.87	1.09	1.03
Approach Strategies of Coping							
	Mean	16.32	14.79	16.71	1.34	3.92	1.55
	SD	4.92	3.96	5.58	0.69	1.04	1.07
	t	1.99*	1.40	1.03	0.09	0.98	0.08
			Diabetic Group				
Avoidance Strategies of Coping							
Escape	Mean	17.84	21.37	21.63	1.32	3.16	1.68
	SD	2.11	3.10	4.23	0.92	1.09	0.80
Approach Strategies of Coping							
	Mean	13.95	17.79	17.02	2.21	3.86	1.35
	SD	4.62	4.44	5.91	1.37	1.02	0.93
	t	3.55**	3.27**	3.16*	2.65**	2.58**	1.42

* $p < .05$, ** $p < .01$

Multiple Regression Analysis

Multiple regression analysis attempted using illness controllability beliefs as predictor variables and illness consequences beliefs as criterion variables. Since no theoretical hierarchy of the variables were established, a step-wise regression analysis was carried out. Findings revealed that in the cancer group, doctor control and supernatural control accounted for approximately 10 per cent of variance in interpersonal consequences scores (F 1, 168 = 22.44, $p < .01$, $b = -0.30$). Here, doctor's control made negative predictions (of less serious consequences). Supernatural control, accounted for approximately 11 per cent of variance in physiological consequences scrores (F 1, 168 = 9.38, $p < .01$, $b = 0.29$). Here supernatural control made positive prediction (of more serious interpersonal and physiological consequence). With respect to psychological consequences, results indicated that doctor control explained approximately 6 per cent of variance in scores (F 1, 168 = 19.21, $p < .01$, beta = -0.27). Doctor control emerged as a negative predictor of psychological consequences (of less serious consequences).

In the diabetic group, self-control explained approximately 6 per cent of variance in physiological consequences scores (F 1, 168 = 11.15, $p < .01$, beta = -0.28) and self-control also explained approximately 5 per cent of variance in psychological consequences scores (F 1,168 = 23.63, $p < .01$, beta = -0.24). Here, self-control made negative predictions (of less physiological and psychological consequences). Doctor's control accounted for approximately 5 per cent of variance in psychological consequences scores (F 1,168 = 8.14, $p < .01$, beta = -0.20) and emerged as a negative predictor of psychological consequences.

Discussion

This study examined illness consequences and controllability beliefs of cancer and diabetic women. A comparison of the groups revealed that cancer patients believed in interpersonal consequences more strongly than diabetic patients, who believed more in physiological consequences than the cancer patients. With respect to illness controllability, the findings revealed that diabetic patients believed more strongly in self-control than cancer patients. Educated patients believed more strongly in self-control, whereas uneducated women held stronger belief in doctor and supernatural control.

The hypothesis that the patients who believed in and doctor as effective agents of illness control would perceive less severe illness consequences than those who believed in supernatural control was fully substantiated by the findings. Those who believed in self and doctor as control agent reported less severe illness consequences. This provides support to the findings of other studies in which people with a strong sense of self-control have been found to experience less psychological and physiological strain in response to stressors than those with a weak sense of self-control (Bandura, Reese, and Adams, 1982; Bandura, Taylor, William, Mefford and Berchas, 1985; Holahan, Holahan and Belk, 1984).

The hypothesis that the patients who would use more approach strategies of coping would perceive less severe consequences of illness than those who would use avoidance strategies found support only in the sample of diabetic patients. In the cancer group, support was found only with respect to interpersonal consequences. Although the cancer patients, who used avoidance coping strategies, did score higher on the measures of physiological and psychological consequences, the differences were not statistically significant, indicating that coping strategies did not make much difference in the perceived severity of physiological and psychological consequences among cancer patients. It was also evident that both the patient groups resorted to avoidance coping strategies more than to approach strategies. It may be due to the chronicity of illness. Depression is the most frequently reported feeling in the case of chronic illnesses. It is characterized by dejected mood, loss of desire to do things, general tiredness, and inability to concentrate. The depressed person thinks that nothing can be done to change the undesirable life conditions. The feeling of depression generally sets in at a stage when the patient has tried many unsuccessful treatments, and is faced with new problems of adjustment in day-to-day living. Dalal (1999) considers emotional reaction of depression beneficial in the sense that it is preparatory to the later adjustment that must be made as a consequences of illness.

Studies focusing on the effects of various coping modes report inconsistent results. Some studies indicate that approach coping decreases emotional distress, whereas avoidance coping increases emotional distress (Felton and Revenson, 1984; Mitchell and Hudson, 1983). Other studies suggest an opposite pattern (Baum, Fleming and Singer, 1983; Marrero, 1982). It appears that the effectiveness of coping modes can be evaluated with reference to the nature and consequences of stress. There is some evidence to suggest that avoidance or rejection coping mode is effective when outcome measures are immediate or short-term, whereas approach mode of coping is more effective when outcome measures are long-term (Mullen and Suls, 1982).

The hypothesis that patients who would use approach strategies of coping would consider self and doctor as more effective agents of illness control than supernatural factors found support only in the case of diabetic patients. Lazarus (1983) has pointed out that effectiveness of coping strategies depends on mainly the controllability of situation. The findings of the present study support this conclusion. Diabetic patients, who adopted approach strategies of coping, believed in the controllability of illness by self and doctor more than patients who used aoidance strategies of coping. Lazarus and Folkman (1984) suggested that people tend to use avoidance coping when they believe they can do nothing to change the stress condition. Approach coping is used when people believe that their resources on the demands of the situation are changeable.

The findings also indicated that patients used both the approach and aoidance strategies of coping at the same time. This finding seems to go with studies, which indicate that no single method is uniformly applied or is effective with all stressful situations (Ilfeld, 1980; Menaghan, 1982; Pearlin and Schooler, 1978). Two important patterns of coping have been identified. First, individuals tend to be consistent in the way they cope with a particular type of stressor, i.e., when faced with some problem, people tend to use the same method they used in the past (Stone and Neale, 1984). Second, people seldom use just one method to cope with a stressor; instead their efforts typically involve a combination of strategies including the avoidance methods (Holahan and Moos, 1985). Katernadahl (1999) has reported that subjects with panic attacks display less healthy attitudes and behaviours and use negative coping strategies quite frequently. Several background and personal factors, such as their age, gender, social class, philosophical or religious commitments, emotional maturity and self-esteem (Moos and Schaefer, 1986) and personality traits of optimism, locus of control, neuroticism, and extraversion (McCrae and Costa, 1986; Parkes, 1986; Scheier, Weintraub and Carver, 1986) have also been found to be linked with coping strategies.

Suls (1982) has indicated that sometimes people in a patient's social network may undermine effective coping by providing bad examples or poor advice. Physical aspects of a person's environment may also affect how well he or she copes with the health problems. A dull, confining and depressing hospital environment is likely to generate avoidance coping strategies (Moos, 1982). In an adult education programme. Barlow, Williams, and Wright (1999) found that self-management programme for arthritis increased patients' self-efficacy, cognitive symptom management, communication with doctors, exercise and relaxation. In addition, a significant decrease was found in terms of pain and visits to the health professionals.

The present investigation demonstrates that approach coping is more adaptive form of coping than avoidance. Other studies with cancer and tuberculosis patients (e.g., Calden, Dupertuis, Hokanson and Lewis, 1960; Rogenstine, van Kammen, Fox, Docherty, Rosenblatt, Boyd and Bunney, 1979) also offer a similar conclusion. It may be concluded that while illness controllability beliefs are important in the experience of illness consequences, patient's own strategies of coping with disease are equally important.

REFERENCES

Awasthi, P., Mishra, R.C. and Shahi, U.P. (2006), Health beliefs and behaviour of cervix patients. *Psychology and Developing Societies.* 18 (1), 37-58.

Bandura, A., Taylor, C.B., Williams, S.L., Mefford, I.N. and Barchas, J.D. (1985), Catecholamine secretion as a function of perceived coping self-efficacy. *Journal of Consulting and Clinical Psychology,* 53, 406-414.

Bandura, A., Reese, L. and Adams, N.E. (1982), Microanalysis of action and fear arousal as a function of differential levels of perceived self-efficacy. *Journal of Personality and Social Psychology,* 43, 5-21.

Barlow, J.H., William, B. and Wright, C. (1999), Instilling the strength to fight the pain and get on with life: Learning to become an arthritis self-manager through an adult education programme. *Health Education Research,* 14, 533-544.

Baum, A., Fleming, R. and Singer, J.E. (1983), Coping with victimizations by technology disaster. *Journal of Social Issues,* 39, 117-138.

Baumann, L.J. and Leventhal, H. (1985). I can tell when my blood pressure is up, can't I? *Health Psychology,* 4, 203-218.

Calden, G., Dupertuis, C.W., Hokanson, J.E. and Lewis, W.C. (1960). Psychosomatic factors in the rate of recovery from tuberculosis. *Psychosomatic Medicine.* 22, 345-355.

Chandrasekhar, C.B., Isaac, M.K., Kapur, R.L. and Parthsarathi, R. (1981), Management of priority mental disorders in the community. *Indian Journal of Psychiatry,* 23, 174-178.

Cohen, S. and Herbert, T.B. (1996), Health psychology: Psychological factors and physical disease from the perspective of human psychoneuroimmunology. *Annual Review of Psychology,* 47, 113-42.

Dalal, A.K. (1999), Health beliefs and coping with chronic illness. In G. Mishra (Ed.), *Psychological Perspectives on Stress and Health* (pp. 100-125), New Delhi: Concept.

Echebarria, A. and Paez, D. (1989), Social representations and memory: The case of AIDS. *European Journal of Social Psychology,* 19, 543-552.

Edwards, C.R.W., Baird, J.D., Frier, B.M., Shepherd, J. and Toft, A.D. (1995). Endocrine and metabolic diseases including diabetes mellitus. In C.R.W. Edwards, I.A.D. Bouchier, C. Haslett and E. Chilvers (eds.), *Davidson's Principles and Practice of Medicine* (17th ed., pp. 724-728). Churchill Lingstone: Great Britain.

Felton, B. and Revenson, T. (1984), Coping with chronic illness: A study of illness controllability and the influence of coping strategies on psychological adjustment. *Journal of Consulting and Clinical Psychology,* 52, 343-353.

Furnham, A. (1988). *Lay theories: Everyday Understanding of Problems in the Social Sciences.* Oxford: Pergamon.

Gilbert, D.T. (1990), How mental system believes? *American Psychologist,* 46, 107-109.

Helman, G.G. (1990), *Culture, Health and Illness.* London: Wright.

Herzlich, C. (1986), Representations sociales de la Sante et al de la maiadie er leur dynamique dans le champs social. In W. Doise *et al.* (Eds.), L'Etude *des Representations Sociales.* Lausanne: Delachaux and Niestle.

Herzlich, C. (1993), *Health and Illness: A Social Psychological Analysis.* New York: Academic Press.

Holahan, C.K., Holahan, C.J. and Belk, S.S. (1984), Adjustment in aging: The roles of life stress, hassles and self-efficacy. *Health Psychology,* 3, 315-328.

Holahan, C.J. and Moos, R.H. (1985), Life stress and health: Personality, coping and family support in stress resistence. *Journal of Personality and Social Psychology,* 49, 739-747.

Ilfeld, F.W. (1980), Coping Styles of Chicago Adults: Description. *Journal of Human Stress,* 6, 2-10.

Ingledew, D.K., Hardy, L., Cooper, C.L. and Jemal, H. (1996), Health behviours reported as coping strategies: A factor analytical study. *British Journal of Health Psychology.* 1, 263-281.

Jodelet, D. (1990a), *Folies et Representations Sociales.* Paris: Presses Universitaires de France.

Katernadahl, D.A. (1999), Illness attitudes and coping processes in subjects with panic attacks. *Journal of Nervous and Mental Disease,* 187(9), 561-565.

Kelley, H.H. and Michela, J.L. (1980), Attribution theory and research. *Annual Review of Psychology,* 31, 451-501.

King, H. (1999), WHO and the International Diabetes Fedration: Regional partners. *Bulletin of the World Health Organization,* 77, 12.

Lambart, H. (1997), Illness, inauspiciousness and modes of healing in Rajasthan. *Contributions to Indian Society.* 31, 253-271.

Lazarus, R.S. (1983), The costs and benefits of denial. In S. Bresnitz (Ed.), *Denial of Stress.* New York: International Universities Press.

Lazarus, R.S. and Folkman, S. (1984). *Stress, Appraisal and Coping.* New York: Springer.

Leventhal, H. and Cameron, L. (1987), Behavioural theories and the problem of compliance. *Patient Education and Counselling,* 10, 117-138.

Leventhal, H., Meyer, D. and Nerenz, D. (1980). The commonsense representation of illness danger. In S. Rachman (Ed.), *Contributions to Medical Psychology* (pp. 7-30). Oxford, England: Pergamon Press.

Leventhal, H., Prohaska, T.R. and Hirschman, R.S. (1985), Preventive health behaviour across the life span. In J.C. Rosen and L.J. Solomon (Eds.). *Prevention in Health Psychology,* Vol. 18. Hanover: University Press of New England.

Leventhal, H., Safer, M.A. and Panagis, D. (1983), The impact of communications on the self-regulation of health beliefs, decisions and behaiour. *Health Education Quarterly,* 10, 3-29.

Mages, N.L. and Mendelsohn, G.A. (1979), Effects of cancer on patients lives: A personological approach. In G.C. Stone, F. Cohen, and N.E. Adler (Eds.), *Health Psychology: A Handbook.* San Francisco: Jossey-Bass.

Marrero, D. (1982), *Adjustment to Misfortune: The Process of Coping with Diabetes Mellitus in Children and their Parents.* Unpublished doctoral dissertation, University of California, Irvine.

McCrae, R.R. and Costa, P.T., Jr. (1986), Personality, coping, and coping effectiveness in an adult sample. *Journal of Personality,* 54, 385-405.

Menaghan, E. (1982), Measuring coping effectiveness: A panel analysis of marital problems and coping efforts. *Journal of Health and Social Behaviour,* 23, 220-234.

Mishra, R.C. (2001), *Health cognition and practices among the Kharwars of Naugrah Region of Varanasi.* Presented at the National Seminar on Tribal Health and Family Welfare, New Delhi.

Mitchell, R.E. and Hudson, C.A. (1983), Coping with domestic violence: Social support and psychological health among battered women. *American Journal of Community Psychology*, 2, 629-654.

Moos, R.H. (1982), Coping with acute health crises. In T. Millon, C. Green and R. Meagher (Eds.), *Handbook of Clinical Health Psychology*. New York: Plenum.

Moos-Moris, R., Petrie, K.J. and Weinman, J. (1996). Functioning in chronic fatigue syndrome: Do illness perception play a regulatory role? *British Journal of Health Psychology*, 1, 15-25.

Moos, R.H. and Schaefer, J.A. (1986). Life transitions and crisis: A conceptual overview. In R.H. Moos (Ed.). *Coping with life crisis: An integrated approach*. New York: Plenum.

Moscovici, S. (1990), Preface. In D. Jodelet (Ed.), *Folies et Representations Sociales*. Paris: Presses Universitaires de France.

Mullen, B. and Suls, J. (1982), The effectiveness of attention and rejection of coping styles. *Journal of Psychosomatic Research*, 26, 43-49.

Parkes, K.R. (1986), Coping in stressful episodes: The role of individual differences, environmental factors, and situational characteristics. *Journal of Personality and Social Psychology*, 51, 1277-1292.

Pearlin, L.I. and Schooler, C. (1978), The structure of coping in a middle aged community sample. *Journal of Health and Social Behaviour*, 19, 2-21.

Poon-King, Henry, M.V. and Rampersad, I. (1968), Prevalence and natural history of diabetes in Trinidad, *Lancet*, 1, 155.

Prohaska, T., Leventhal, E.A., Leventhal, H. and Keller, M.L. (1985). Health practices and illness cognition in young, middle aged and elderly adults. *Journal of Gerontology*, 40, 569-578.

Radley, A. (1994), *Making sense of illness*. London: Sage.

Rao, D.N. and Ganesh, B. (1998). Estimate of cancer incidence in India in 1991. *Indian Journal of Cancer*, 35, 10-18.

Redd, W.H., Silberfarb, P.M., Andersen, B.L. and Andrykowski, M.A. (1991), Physiologic and psycho-behavioural research in oncology. *Cancer*, 67, 813-822.

Rogenstine, C.N., Van-Kammen, D.R., Fox, B.H., Docherty, J.P., Rosenblatt, J.E., Boyd, S.C. and Bunney, W.E. (1979). Psychological factors in the prognosis of malignant melanoma: A prospective study. *Psychosomatic Medicine*, 41, 147-164.

———Divergent strategies of optimists and pessimists. *Journal of Personality and Social Psychology*, 51, 1257-1264.

Shah, S.N. (1998), High prevalence of type 2 diabetes in population of North Eastern India. *The International Journal of Diabetes in Developing Countries*, 18, 97-107.

Shah, S.N. (2001), Containing the global epidemic of Diabetes. *Asian Journal of Diabetology*, 3, 11.

Singh, A.K. (1987), The myth of the healthy tribal. *Social Change*, 16, 125-135.

Stone, A.A. and Neale, J.M. (1984), New measure of daily coping: Development and preliminary results. *Journal of Personality and Social Psychology*, 46, 892-906.

Suls, J. (1982), Social support, interpersonal relations and health: Benefits and liabilities. In G.S. Sanders and J. Suls (Eds.). *Social Psychology of Health and Illness.* Hillsdale, NJ: Erlbaum.

Turk, D.C., Rudy, T.E. and Salovey, P. (1985), Implicit models of illness. *Journal of Behavioural Medicine,* 9, 453-474.

Weiner, B., Perry, R.P. and Magnusson, J. (1988), An attributional analysis of reactions to stigmas. *Journal of Personality and Social Psychology*, 55, 738-748.

Williams, C.J. (1990), *Cancer Biology and Management: An Introduction.* New York: Wiley.

15

Psychosocial Mediators of Health

Anubhuti Dubey

The Indian literature is full of pharses like '*Tan Swastha to Man Swastha*", "*Tandoorusti Hazar Niyamat Hai*" and so many others. These phrases indicate the cultural value posed on the health and well-being of the individual. There were Sanskrit shlokas and poems clearly stated about what to eat in which season and what to avoid, what to do and what not to do. But due to technological advancement, stress to compete with world, westernization etc. the cultural beliefs of people are changing and it has given rise to many diseases, particularly life style diseases. The studies have proved that Indians are genetically prone to heart diseases. The top ten causes of illness and death are accidents, suicide and diseases like, cancer, diabetes, stroke and other diseases affected by quality and style of life. These are largely the result of psychological factors, including behavioural pathogens, lack of behavioural immunogens, psychosocial stress and poor coping strategies. The biopsychosocial model of health and illness refute that biological, social and psychological factors interact in an interdependent or systemic way of maintaining health or causing illness. Biological factors include the genetic structures and processes. For example, weight is influenced by inheritance (Allison, Heshka, Neale Lykken and Heymsfield, 1994). Psychological factors can include cognitions, motivations, emotions and attitude. Evidences support the view that under episode of stress more food intake was revealed by some people (Arnow, Kenardy and Agras, 1992). Social factors include the models around us, the support network we have. The emphasis of the article is only on the psychosocial mediators in health and illness. Mediators shape a person's responses to stress. They are the internal and external resources the person can bring to assess and interpret the magnitude stress, to assess his or her own capacities for addressing the stress, and to formulate a coping strategy to overcome the stress. Many key mediators such as attitude towards exercise, motivation to change sedentary life style, change in maladaptive coping strategies, strengthening social network, inculcating positive thinking, etc. are modifiable through psychosocial intervention.

Psychosocial Factors

The physical body degenerates naturally. This process can be enhanced by the way we live and treat our body. For example, smoking, higher level of fat intake, inadequate sleep, less physical activities and overall a sedentary life style allow ourselves to become physically unfit and continually cause distress to body. Besides this biological degeneration our thoughts and feelings are important factors in making us ill and delaying the process of recovery. Past researches in health and illness had accumulated the evidences that sedentary life styles, cognitive appraisal, our attitude towards health will determine our health status, as well as, whether we follow the advice of health care professionals. The health habits—the usual health related behaviours, which become the part of everyday patterns or life style—often contains many risks for illness and injuries. Although some risk factors are inherited through genes but many are behavioural. For example, smoking, chewing tobacco, eating saturated fats and sedentary life style are risk for heart diseases and certain types of cancers.

Behavioural Pathogens

Health is the most valuable asset of human being. The individual behaviours play a significant role in health and illness. The life style of an individual is a sum total of his or her habits and behaviour. There may be some habits which are health damaging and some are health promoting. The health damaging habits or behavioural pathogens are significant risk factors for chronic diseases and ultimately leads to poor quality of life and death.

The research evidences had proved that certain habits are damaging to health, like smoking, alcoholism, overeating, overwork, etc. Indulgence on these substances over a period of time leads to risk of cancer, cardiovascular diseases and other chronic diseases. In a study Dubey (2003) found that all the 15 male cancer patients had oral cancer and all of them had a habit of chewing tobacco as old as 15 to 25 years. At the time of study they were receiving chemotherapy or radiotherapy or a combination of both. Several studies had shown that this social/cultural habit of *"paan"* chewing is detrimental to dental health and one of the major causes of oral cavity cancer. It can be argued that *paan* leaves have some medicinal value but in Indian subcontinent it has been used with tobacco and betel nut, which make it lethal, when used continuously. Most of the chewables used in Indian subcontinent in the form of *"Gutkha"* are harmful in some way or the other and most of them are carcinogenic. In a survey conducted by Dubey (2006), the 200 undergraduate students of the university were asked about their habit of chewing gutkha and its effects on health. About 40 per cent students were using as many as ten pouches a day. About 80 per cent students had awareness of its bad effects on health, as it may cause oral and neck cancer, besides tooth decay and discolouring of teeth. When they were asked if they knew its bad effects on health why not give up this bad habit. Nearly 90 per cent said that they started it for fun and now it is difficult to leave because of peer pressure. It was also asked that have they ever tried to quit the habit. Only 10 per cent had given an affirmative reply.

Chewing tobacco or smokeless tobacco is more dangerous because absorption through the gums is the most efficient route of nicotine administration. Smokeless tobacco also impairs the sense of taste and smell, causing user to add salt and sugar to food, which may contribute to high blood pressure and obesity.

Like tobacco, cigarette smoking and other such substances had served an antecedent cues and consequences. The smokers generally say that smoking play a central role in emotional regulation. The experiences of unpleasant emotions like, anxiety, anger, boredom and depression may solemnize through smoking. The consequent relaxing effect then reinforces them to take another cigarette. Besides this peer and adult models and peer pressure also encourages for smoking and for other such products. These substances produce psychological and physical dependence. Psychological dependence means a state of emotional and mental preoccupation with the effects of the substance and a persistent carving for it. The worst part of it that psychological dependence mentally paralyzes the user to use the substance. The physical dependence means that the user body becomes totally dependent on the substance especially drugs and the prolonged use of it make the body so used to function under the effect of the drug that the body only functions normally with the presence of drug. WHO (1998) found that about 1.1 billion people worldwide smoke cigarettes. The biopsychosocial factors influence people's beginning and continuing to smoke. The smokers and users of other substances also appear to be less health conscious and are more likely to engage in unhealthy behaviours (Istvan and Matarazzo, 1984).The smokers not only affect the health of oneself but also of those very close to them. Those with regular close contact with smokers (spouses, family members, coworkers and friends) are at risk for a variety of health problems (Marshell, 1986). Prenatal and neonates of smokers are vulnerable to develop cognitive deficits and physical ailments. A study suggests that parental cigarette smoking may actually lower cognitive performance among adolescents (Bauman, Flewelling and LaPrelle, 1991). Smokers are at the obvious risk of developing heart disease and lung cancer and also smoking increases the risk of chronic bronchitis, peptic ulcers, respiratory problems and fire accidents. Similarly, an excessive intake of alcohol for a long period of time may damage heart, liver and brain. At the psychological level it may cause lowered alertness, slowed reaction time, impaired motor functioning, short term memory loss, slurring words, etc.

Besides the substance abuse two other important behavioural pathogens are related to eating patterns and work patterns. Both overeating and undereating, and eating unhealthy food all create danger to important vital organs of body. Nutritional food and good eating habits are fundamental building block for good health. The present urban modern diet incorporates high saturated fat, and cholesterol, low complex carbohydrates, high sodium and high alcohol, which leads to obesity, coronary heart disease, hypertension and some types of cancer. Products like coffee, tea, soft drinks, and chocolates all contain caffeine in some amount or other. Caffeine or caffeine intoxication is a syndrome, which may caused by chronic caffeine use. Caffeine intoxication brought on by excessive caffeine use and its symptoms include chronic insomnia, irritability, anxiety, muscle twitches and headaches. Caffeine addiction characterized as the effects of caffeine begins to wear off, users may feel let down, mentally and physically depressed, exhausted and weak. To overcome these effects people normally take another cup of coffee or tea. Habitual practice leads to tolerance and psychological dependence. The relationship between caffeine consumption and heart and circulatory disorders are not very clear. However, coffee is considered as gastric irritant, which contribute in developing ulcers and digestive problems.

Obesity has become a major health problem of affluent and urbanities worldwide. Obesity is associated with high blood pressure, diabetes, heart disease, kidney problems, stroke and psychological problems. Approximately 50 per cent of Indian urban population is overweight. Obesity is basically the resultant of more calories intake than expended by metabolism or exercise. The opposite of overeating would be not eating at all, simply for the reasons of beauty. Extreme stress to one's physical status leads many youngsters not to eat at all this can cause eating disorders. Anorexia, an eating disorder endangers the health of the individual.

Earlier in Indian social and cultural life people follow the Ayurvedic prescriptions of food choices. The rich tradition of Ayurveda advocates the vegetarian food with full of fresh seasonal fruits and vegetables and avoiding food which has opposite effects, e.g. cold drink, ice cream should not be taken with milk coffee within a short interval. But westernization, party life in urban areas and easy availability of packaged junk food had washed out all these beliefs.

Behavioural Immunogens

The basic aim of preventive medicine and health psychologists is to modify the health behaviours of individuals, which are stated earlier as behaviour pathogens. Health behaviours are influenced by multiple factors. Behavioural immunogens is characterized by the health promoting behaviours like exercise, healthy diet, and proper sleep, relaxation and positive psychosocial environmental cues (Matarazzo and Leckliter, 1988). The poor health habits cannot be changed so easily because it involves change in attitudes, strong motivation to change, adherence to change desirable health practice and also maintaining adherence over-extended period of time. Behaviour modification incorporates multimodal approach.

Physical Activity and Fitness

The benefits of regular physical activity are paramount. Regular physical activity improves more than 50 different physiological, metabolic and psychological aspects of human life (Gates, 1992). Exercise improves the body shapes and muscles tone, which are great morale boosters. It also gives the individual a self-discipline in life. Physical fitness has both physiological and psychological benefits.

The physiological benefits of regular exercise or physical activity incorporates improved cardio respiratory efficiency, improved skeletal mass, weight control and overall health and life span. The risk of chronic diseases like hypertension, osteoarthritis and diabetes can be reduced through daily exercise. Regular vigorous physical activity was found to be associated with 2-5mm Hg average decrease in diastolic blood pressure. Hypertension is a strong predictor of CHD risk; therefore, this modest decrease in blood pressure has a large effect (Alpret, Field, Goldstein and Perry, 1990). Osteoarthritis, the most prevalent joint condition in women was also found to be improved through exercise. Supervised fitness walking and weight loss programme can improve physical capacity and knee joint osteoarthritis symptoms (Kover, Allegrante, MacKenzie, *et al.*, 1992; Felson, Zhang, Anthony, *et al.*, 1992).

Physical fitness appears to be related to the aspects of quality of life, like longevity, work performance, ageing, and social relationships. A classic study conducted at the Institute for Aerobic Research in Texas found that exercise does increase longevity. Participants who changed from a sedentary life style to one that included a brisk 30 to 60 minutes walk each day experienced significant increases in their life expectancies (Blair, Kohl, Paffenbarger *et al.*, 1989). Regular moderate exercise may make people less susceptible to disease but it may depend upon whether they perceive exercise as pleasurable or stressful activity. Dubey and Jaiswal (2002) conducted a study on those who regularly walk 4-5 km. in the morning and those who did not do it or other physical activity. The health status of morning walkers was better on the physical, mental, social and emotional health dimensions. However, on spiritual and environmental health there were no significant difference found. It was also found that morning walkers had positive health habits and they significantly less frequently struck with seasonal and acute illnesses as compared to their counterparts.

Physical exercise has its potential physiological benefits, which are easily noticeable. The psychological benefits are different to quantify. However, the psychological aspects are generally mentioned as reasons to continue to exercise such as motivation, attitude and appraisal. Physical fitness improves appearance and energy level. Feeling good about personal appearance and enhance energy level for work performance can provide tremendous boost to self-esteem. Improved strength, flexibility and energy for recreational activities all help in enhancing self-confidence and esteem. With advancing age biological degeneration is natural. The key issues is that decline in physiological functioning differ in active individual and those who lead a sedentary life. Evidences suggest that the active 60 year old person may be as physically fit as the inactive 30-40 year old.

Exercise interventions have promising effects with the chronically ill patients. It appears to decrease anxiety, nausea from chemotherapy and decrease pain for cancer patients (Carvey and Burish, 1988), and found useful for essential hypertension (Wittrock, Blanchard and McCoy, 1988) and with myocardial infraction patients and improve quality of life (Blumenthal and Emary, 1988). Exercise alone cannot bring physical fitness; it should be accompanied with healthy diet and food habits. Healthy eating is influenced by cultural factors, social pressure, family traditions, social events that involve eating and busy work schedule. Each culture has both healthy and unhealthy eating habits and also the patterns of what we eat, when we eat and how much we eat. Most of us take the eating activity as for granted. The first step towards changing the health status is to recognize the fact that the food we eat is for more reasons than just for survival. Proper nutrition and healthy eating can increase resistance to stress as well as disease and promote well-being.

The busy life, cut throat competition and enormous stress curtails the sleeping hours. One of the most effective ways of combating with stress is sleeping well and taking a good night's rest. A good night sleep restores the body's equilibrium. The sleeping hygiene should be maintained to get a good sleep. Some sleeping rules are—do not get heavy meals before going to bed, do not take stimulants like alcohol, tea or coffee before going to bed, exercise moderately daily etc. Taking a warm bath before going to bed would also work effectively. A good sleep relaxes the body. Relaxation puts the person in a state where he may be able to think about the problems with calm and cool mental piece of mind and may visualize all the possible aspects of solving it.

Positive Mental State

To be physically fit and active healthy diet along with proper sleep and moderate work out is prescribed. But above all the positive mental state is essential. *Eustress* in lieu of negative stress will enhance the positive mental state. Now the issue is that what characterizes the positive mental state. Jahoda (1958, 1963) introduced the notion of positive mental state and had given the criteria of mental health into six main categories —

- (i) Attitude towards self (self-awareness, correctness of the self-concept, sense of self-identity).
- (ii) Growth, development and self-actualization (self-fulfilment, growth, motivation).
- (iii) Integration (balance of psychic forces, a unifying outlook on life, resistance to stressful condition).
- (iv) Autonomy (inner-control of behaviour).
- (v) Perception of reality (perception free from need distortion, empathy).
- (vi) Environmental Mastery (adequacy in interpersonal relations, adaptation, adjustment, problem solving).

Positive mental state can be achieved by thinking positively. Focus on the positive aspects and not wallow oneself in self-pity. Positive thinking, a constructive thinking, incorporates to be optimistic but with a sense of realism, thinking about future and plan realistically about future, try to find some control, hope, self-efficacy, hardiness etc. All of these are personality characteristics, which construct a psycho-immune system within the individual. This psycho-immune system give resistance to the individual to fight against any kind of stressor, whether a short-term stressor (e.g. facing a examination, struck in traffic, going for an interview or suffering with viral fever etc.) or a long-term stressor (e.g. chronic disease of oneself or spouse, bereavement, death of spouse, etc.). Broad personality traits such as those included in Big Five model of personality (Costa and McCrae, 1985) may be important predictors of health behaviour patterns (Booth-Kewley and Vickers Jr., 1994). The big five personality factors are—neuroticism, extraversion, and openness to experience, agreeableness and conscientiousness. Neuroticism includes the disposition to experience relatively strong negative emotions and vulnerability to stress, has been associated with the presence of harmful health behaviours and absence of positive health behaviours. Extraversion is the tendency to be outgoing and sociable and to experience positive emotions, has been linked to negative behaviours like substance use (Labouvie and McGee, 1986) and to the positive health behaviours like exercise compliance (Blumenthal, Sanders, Wallace, Williams and Needles, 1982). Agreeableness is the tendency to be tolerant and accepting rather than cynical and hostile may be related to better exercise habits, self care and less substance use and better dietary control. Conscientiousness is the tendency to be goal oriented, methodical and reliable and openness to experience was linked with less substance use. Low level of conscientiousness in childhood and poor mental in adulthood are related to dying at earlier ages from diseases such as heart disease and cancer (Friedman *et al.*, 1995). Similarly, high levels of anxiety, depression, anger hostility, pessimism appears to be associated with developing heart diseases and other chronic illnesses (Everson *et al.*, 1996). Negative emotions like depression and stress are related to impaired immune systems (Dunn, 1995; Leonard, 1995), whereas positive emotions appear to enhance immune functioning (Stone *et al.*, 1994). In considering well-being among survivors of life-threatening illnesses such as breast cancer, initial optimism and marital status predicted follow-up adjustment. There is substantial continuity of subjective well-being across many years among survivors of breast cancer, rooted partly in personality and social connection (Carver *et al.*, 2005).

Optimistic individuals are those who tend to have positive expectancies for the future, whereas pessimistic are those who tend to hold more negative expectations for the future (Scheier and Bridges, 1995). Optimistic persons adjust more favourably to important life transitions than do persons who are more pessimistic in outlook

(Aspinwell and Taylor, 1992). Optimism not only results in more effective coping responses (Taylor and Brown, 1988) but also produces more effective coping responses (Dubey, 2003) and leads to more satisfaction with life (Dubey and Agarwal, 2004). Optimism and future orientation also speed up recovery in surgical patients (Upadhaya, 2002). Optimism was found to be linked with more positive appraisals of stressors, as well as, greater use of problem solving strategies and greater use utilization of social support. However, pessimism has been shown to be related to avoidant forms of coping such as denial, distancing and disengagement from the stressful situations. Optimism was found to mitigate distress by promoting more active and less avoidant forms of coping in men at risk for AIDS (Taylor *et al.*, 1992). Pessimism places patients of breast cancer at risk for adverse outcomes in several respects, such as disruption of social and recreational activities rather than solely with regard to emotional distress (Carver, Lehman and Antoni, 2003).

Research evidences to date suggested that dispositional optimism is beneficial for physical and psychological well being. Although being optimistic has psychological benefits of reducing anxiety and carry out everyday activities without being continuously in thought with it (Perloff, 1983), but there are some potential costs of over optimism especially in case of preventive health behaviour. Optimistic see a pink future in everything, they may fail to engage in preventive behaviour or take appropriate precautions (Perloff, 1983). Optimistic outlook can be maintained by being vigilant. Trying to be optimistic all the time about all things can wear you out. This is not really positive thinking. It is another form of denial. Positive thinking is a habit, like cursing, so it takes practice to develop. Self-discipline is also involved in positive thinking. Self-discipline is not self-denial. Rather, it's a reordering of priorities where one desire must be set aside or sacrificed for the sake of another more worthy desire. In that sense, self-discipline is a path to greater fulfilment.

It is the contention of Scheier and Carver that sometimes attributions determine expectancies, which in turn influences emotional and physical health (Tennen *et al.*, 1986). Thompson (1985) speculated that finding positive meaning in the face of adversity may itself be due to dispositional optimism. Cancer patients experience positive as well as adverse consequences from cancer diagnosis and treatment. Benefit finding related positively to trait optimism and to positive reframing and religious activity as coping reactions. Benefit finding related inversely to emotional distress (Urcuyo, Boyers, Carver, and Antoni, 2005).

Future orientation means plans, aspirations, expectations and fears about the events likely to happen in near or distant future was also found to mediating in health and illness. Future orientation has both cognitive and motivational value. The significant role of future orientation was found in encouraging preventive health behaviour, health education and experiences of chronic illness. Rothspan and Read (1996) studied the present and future time perspective in college students. They emphasized that safer sex behaviours might reduce the exposure to HIV would positively correlate with future orientation. Their findings suggest that high future oriented students were less likely to be sexually experienced and had fewer sexual partners. High future oriented students were more likely to use alternate methods of reducing exposure to HIV. Future orientation predicts lower scores in surgical patients. Optimistic personal control and detached future predict better recovery from surgery (Upadhya, 2002). Future orientation also predicted 12 per cent variance in overall life satisfaction in chronically ill patients (Dubey and Agarwal, 2004).

Another important psychosocial mediator of health is perceived control. Perceived control is the feeling of being control of making decisions and take effective actions to avoid undesirable outcomes and produce desirable ones. Perceived control had explained 21.2 per cent variance in using active coping strategies and optimism accounted for 3.5 per cent variance followed by future orientation which explained 3 per cent variance. The perceived control would emerge as an important predictor of the use of active coping strategies, when there is a crisis in life (Dubey, 2003). Perceived control also predicted 2.7 per cent variance in quality of life when the participants were afflicted with a chronic disease (Dubey, 2003) and also predicted 12.3 per cent variance in the present satisfaction with life and 41.6 per cent variance in future satisfaction with life in chronically ill patients (Dubey and Agarwal, 2004). Health locus of control (Wallston, Wallston and DeVellis, 1978) also predicts a wide range of health behaviours. Internal health locus of control is positively associated with exercise behaviour (Normen, Bennett, Smith and

Murphy, 1997) and health promoting dietary behaviour (Steptoe and Wardle, 2001). Basically internal locus of control reflects the motivation and intention to engage in health promoting activities. Internal locus of control individual believe that other than chance or luck their own behaviour are stronger determinants of their health, therefore, they are more likely to involve in health protective behaviour. However, in the objectively uncontrollable situations, perceived control is not adaptive. In rheumatoid arthritis patients with severe disease greater level of control over disease were associated with poorer psychosocial adjustment and overall well-being (Affleck, Tennen, Pfeiffer and Fifield, 1987). These findings suggest that perception of control may only be adaptive when some degree of control is possible.

The internal dispositions work subtly to shape one. Factors like, heredity traits, physical health status and elements of mental and emotional health mould the individual. Problems in any element may cause deterioration in overall psychosocial health.

The external factors are characterized as the factors in our life on which we do not have any direct control, like who raised us or how we are raised and the physical environment in which we live. The impact of families on the health of individual is profound. Children reared in happy nurturing democratic families are more likely to become well adjusted adults. The children raised in dysfunctional families are often confused and psychologically bruised. Dysfunctional families do have a negative impact on the psychosocial health of child because of the persistent stressors, uncertainties and threats of physical and emotional abuse and negative behaviours. Several studies over the years had been emphasizing the fact that good family relations provide happiness and well-being (Diener, 1984). Social support provides the person under stress a perceived help, caring and comfort. The absence of supportive network has been linked to loneliness and negative health outcomes (Berkman, 1985; Lynch, 1977). Disabling chronic health problems increased the value to be placed on relationship (Weinberg and Williams, 1978). Dubey (2003) studied the role of family environment in predicting the use of active coping strategies in a group of participants afflicted with chronic health problems like, diabetes, cancer and heart diseases. She found that cohesive and caring relationship in family and system maintenance (e.g. organization and control) in family emerged as significant predictors of active coping strategies. These two variables together predicted 13.1 per cent variance. Social resources can elevate coping efforts by enhancing self-efficacy and by providing information and guidance (Thoits, 1986). Dubey and Sweta Singh (2005) found that the children (aged between 8 to 12 years) with asthma and diabetes who perceived their relationship with parents and siblings as caring and not overprotective and conflicting were well adjusted in home, school and social avenues, and reported more future oriented outlook even afflicted with a chronic disease. Supportive family, positive interactions and good communication has been found to be associated with low levels of stress, high levels of stress-coping behaviour, good psychological health, active adaptation to acute and chronic illness and high levels of adherence to treatment (Wamboldt and Wamboldt, 2000). Supportive relationship with family leads the female cancer to see more positive future, better perception of control and optimism and more use of active coping strategies (Dubey and Sharma, 2005). Increases in social support and greater use of positive reinterpretation and growth contributed to the superior adjustment that optimists experienced (Brissette, Scheier, and Carver, 2002).

Family can act as models of positive coping behaviour. Social models such as film stars; popular personalities also influence the health habits of people by observation and imitation. Whether people will exercise is also influenced by the factor such as modelling, reinforcement and encouragement made by peers and family. Rossow (1992) found that the strongest predictor of eldest child's teeth cleaning behaviour was mother's cleaning behaviour.

Coping Strategies

Coping is defined as the efforts made by the individual (action-oriented and emotion-oriented), to manage, master, tolerate, or minimize the environmental and internal demands and conflicts, which tax or exceed a person's resources. The relationship between coping and health can be viewed in two ways—(i) Coping has a direct relationship to health (how an individual copes with a stressful situation or condition and how it has a direct impact on his or her health). (ii) Coping has an indirect relationship to health (what is the relation of coping to health behaviours or mood, because it was thought that behaviours or mood in turn affect health). Here, the contention is that coping affects health through its impact on the mediating variables such as health habits. Coping may have adaptive or maladaptive effects on an individual's overall health status. The indirect effect of coping on health status was demonstrated by Conger (1956) that people drink in response to stress as a method of reducing tension. Drinking is normatively considered a maladaptive response because it neither helps resolve the underlying problems nor does it effectively regulate distress. In fact, alcohol use generally increases distress, and alcohol abuse has devastating effects on health of the drinker as well as on the health of the family relations. Maladaptive health behaviours such as smoking and high risk sexual behaviour (Chesney, 1988) and decreases in exercise (Ogden and Mitandabari, 1997) have also been interpreted as coping responses to stress. Alcohol, high-risk sexual behaviour, and recreational drug use in particular are considered behavioural forms of escape-avoidant coping (Lazarus and Folkman, 1984) that can be directly harmful to health.

Bulk of the studies have examined the impact of the use of particular kind of coping strategies which people use to cope with a disease such as cancer, myocardial infarction, rheumatoid arthritis, asthma, or HIV/AIDS, and a disease-related outcome such as recurrence, recovery, disease progression, or mortality. Maladaptive coping (e.g., catastrophizing) and decreased self-perceived ability to decrease symptoms may adversely affect health outcome and may modify the effect of GI disease type and neuroticism on health outcome Overt denial and behavioural disengagement predict greater distress in breast cancer patients whereas humor and acceptance were prospective predictors of less distress (Carver *et al.,* 1993), avoidance emotion focused coping was related to poor psychological adjustment in diabetic patients (White, Richter and Fry, 1992), active problem focused coping was related to high self-esteem, life satisfaction and compliance with medical advice in coronary artery heart disease patients (O'Brien, 1992). However, Kothari and Agarwal (1999) reported that religion was the most preferred coping pattern by rural and urban patients waiting for abdominal surgery, heart surgery and cancer surgery.

Studies have also supported the view that different personalities have affinities for different coping strategies which they carry with them into stressful episodes but which they can change according to situational demands. Amirkhan, Risinger and Swickert (1995) showed that person bound factors exerted an influence on the choice of a coping strategy equal to, if not greater than that of situational characteristics. Certainly situational considerations are essential to the precise prediction of coping but the knowledge of personality alone permits estimation of responses with a reasonable degree of accuracy. Patients cognitive and behavioural coping responses to the diagnosis may account for individual differences in psychological adaptation (Pearlin and Schooler, 1978). In addition to its association with disease directly, dispositional optimism has been related to other routes to biological endpoints, including the use of more active and problem-focused coping strategies (Carver, Scheier, and Weintraub, 1989; Taylor *et al.*, 1992), greater psychological well-being, and better health habits (e.g., Park, Moore, Turner, and Adler, 1997). Dubey (2003) found that personal control, optimism, and future orientation together explained 27.7 per cent variance in active coping strategies in chronically ill patients group.

While stress of any kind undoubtedly has an effect, it would be a mistake to think that all of the effects of stress are negative. Many of loss events, although painful, were accompanied by a sense of maturation and personal growth. There is a growing literature on the positive aspects of stress, sometimes called "post-traumatic growth" (Tedeschi, Park, and Calhoun, 1998) or "the perceived benefits of stress" (Aldwin and Sutton, 1998). While coping may moderate the effects of stress, being able to perceive (and act upon) a "silver lining" may result in long-term effects which can be positive. These positive changes may include material gain, changes in perspective, stronger social bonds, increased coping skills, mastery and self-esteem (Aldwin and Stokols, 1988), increased self-knowledge.

Affleck, Tennen, Croog, and Levine (1987) found that men who perceived benefits from having a myocardial infarction had better survival at a five-year follow-up. Presumably these men had made improvements in their diet and health behaviour habits, which may have aided in their survival. Stein, Folkman, Trabasso, and Richards (1997) showed that caregivers of AIDS patients who expressed positive appraisals of their experience were less likely to be depressed and showed more positive outcomes 12 months after bereavement. Individuals coping with the chronic illnesses such as cancer, diabetes and heart disease, found that perceiving benefits like closeness in relationship, better understanding of people and life, recognizing own potentials all were associated with greater long-term outcomes (Dubey, 2003). It has been shown that only unresolved life events are emotionally distressing, and successfully resolved life events do not contribute to individual's burden of stress. There is evidence that received social support has salutary effects primarily among people coping with events like illness, while social support is associated with poor outcome (greater anxiety) among people coping with interpersonal events.

Intervention

Intervention programme can be launched at two levels: (i) to promote health and prevents diseases and (ii) to better the quality of life of that already disease. To achieve the first aspect of promoting healthy behaviour and changing risk factors for disease promotion programmes can be organized at school settings, work places and health care settings. Media can also play a significant role in health promotion and disease prevention. Health promotion campaigns may be utilized to facilitate an overall healthy life style and increased physical activity. Psychological processes that affect the development of health habits include the operant conditioning, classical conditioning, cognitions and emotional patterns. The consequences of behaviour, reinforcement and punishment, causes the change in health habits (Sarafino, 2001). Classical conditioning affects health habits by establishing cues that serve as antecedent to the behaviour. Cognitions play one of the most important roles in the performance of health related behaviours. 'Health Belief Model' is the most influential theory, which proposes a series of cognitive activities that leads the people to practice healthful behaviours and taking preventive actions (Becker and Rosenstock, 1984). Correct knowledge about the relevant health issues also enhances the chances of change in health behaviour. In case of quitting smoking and drinking and promoting exercise the most effective approaches were those which incorporate behavioural and cognitive methods (Sallis and Owen, 1999; Fiore, Jorenby and Baker, 1997; Monti *et al.*, 1993).

Psychological interventions in chronic illness have focus on specific small patient groups. These interventions include stress management, cognitive restructuring, relaxation, coping skills training, social support interventions, self-knowledge and self management enhancing programmes. The psychological interventions have successful in reducing stress and increasing quality of life. Dubey and Sharma (2005) proposed a cognitive behavioural intervention programme for women carcinoma cervix cancer patients. This programme includes a base line assessment of optimism, future orientation, personal control, coping strategies and family relations, and then counselling for ten sessions started for one month and thereafter second assessment of all the above mentioned variables were taken. The results clearly showed the positive impact of intervention. The separate counselling session was conducted for the care givers also. The patients, their doctors and care givers all said to be benefited by the counselling. The doctors said that now the patients are more responsive to the treatment regimen. Baum (2000) shown that intervention with breast cancer and melanoma patients have effects on the immune system and enhanced survival.

Although intervention are effective but collaborative interventions between psychologists and health care professionals are required, which will increase the relevance of intervention.

Conclusions

Many factors contribute in the health status of an individual. The factors like, the attitudes, beliefs, social support, one's readiness to change are all the factors which are controllable, whereas, access to health care, genetic predispositions are uncontrollable factors. Both of these sets of factors are potential reinforcing and enabling factors that may influence one's health decisions. Although cultural factors influences health in many ways but our knowledge about this influence is not well researched and need to be expanded. Implementing positive behaviours (e.g., exercise; controlling intake of food, tobacco, and alcohol; and active relaxation or stress-reduction techniques) have all been shown to have positive effects on overall well-being, no matter at what age they are begun. Although these are physical behaviours, they often rely on and benefit from strong psychosocial mediators, particularly optimism, future orientation, perceived control and appraisal and social relationships one have.

REFERENCES

Affleck, G., Tennen, H., Croog, S., Levine, S. (1987). Causal attribution, perceived benefits, and morbidity after a heart attack: An 8-year study. *Journal of Consulting and Clinical Psychology, 55*, 29-35.

Affleck, G., Tennen, H., Pfeiffer, C. and Fifield, C. (1987). Appraisal of control and predictability in adapting to a chronic disease. *Journal of Personality and Social Psychology,* 53, 273-279.

Aldwin, C., and Stokols, D. (1988). The effects of environmental change on individuals and groups: Some neglected issues in stress research. *Journal of Environmental Psychology, 8,* 57-75.

Aldwin, C. M., and Sutton, K. (1998). A developmental perspective on post-traumatic growth. In R. G. Tedeschi, C. L. Park, and L. G. Calhoun (Eds.), *Post traumatic growth: Positive change in the aftermath of crisis* (pp. 43-63). Mahwah, NJ: Lawrence Erlbaum Associates.

Allison, D.B., Heshka, S., Neale, M.C., Lykken, D.T., and Heymsfield, S.B., (1994). A genetic analysis of relative weight among 4,020 twin pairs, with an emphasis on sex effects. *Health Psychology*, 13, 362-365.

Alpret, B., Field, T., Goldstein, S. and Perry, S. (1990). Aerobics enhances cardiovascular fitness and agility in preschoolers. *Health Psychology,* 9, 48-56.

Amirkhan, J.H., Risinger, R.T. and Swickert, R.J. (1995). Extraversion: A "Hidden" Personality factor in coping? *Journal of Personality,* 63:2.

Arnow, B., Kenardy, J. and Agras, W.S., (1992). Binge eating among the obese. *Journal of Behavioural Medicine,* 15, 155-170.

Aspinwell, L.G. and Taylor, S.E. (1992). Modelling cognitive adaptation: A longitudinal investigation of the impact of individual differences and coping on college adjustment and performance. *Journal of Personality and Social Psychology,* 63, 989-1003.

Baum, A. (2000). Behavioural and psychological interventions to modify path physiology and disease course. In B.D. Smedley and S.L. Syme (eds.) *Promoting health: Intervention Strategies from Social and Behavioural Research* (pp. 451-488). Washington DC: National Academy Press.

Bauman, K.E. Flewelling, R.K. and LaPrelle, J. (1991). Parental cigarette smoking and cognitive performance of children. *Health Psychology*, 10, 282-288.

Becker, M.H., and Rosenstock, I.M. (1984). Complience with medical advice. In S.J. Steptoe and A. Mathews (eds.). *Health Care and Human Behaviour* (pp. 175-208). London: Academic.

Berkman, L.F. (1985). The relationship of social networks and social support to morbidity and mortality. In S. Cohen and S.L. Syme (Eds.) *Social support and health.* (pp.241-262). Orlando, FL: Academic Press.

Blair, S.N., Kohl, H.W. III, Paffenbarger, R.S. *et al.*, (1989). Physical fitness and all causes mortality: A prospective study of healthy men and women. *JAMA,* 262, No. 7, 2395-2401.

Blumenthal, J.A. and Emary, C.F. (1988). Rehabilitation of patients following myocardial infraction. *Journal of Consulting and Clinical Psychology*, 56, 374-381.

Blumenthal, J.A., Sanders, W., Wallace, A.G., Williams, R.B., and Needles, T.L. (1982). Physiological and psychological variables predict compliance to prescribed exercise therapy in patients recovering from myocardial infraction. *Psychosomatic Medicine*, 44, 519-527.

Booth-Kewley, S. and Vickers Jr., R.R. (1994). Association between major domains of personality and health behaviour. *Journal of Personality*, 62:3.

Brissette, I., Scheier, M. F., and Carver, C. S. (2002). The role of optimism and social network development, coping, and psychological adjustment during a life transition. *Journal of Personality and Social Psychology*, *82*, 102-111.

Carver, C. S., Lehman, J. M., and Antoni, M. H. (2003). Dispositional pessimism predicts illness-related disruption of social and recreational activities among breast cancer patients. *Journal of Personality and Social Psychology*, *84*, 813-821.

Carver, C.S., Pozo, C., Harris, S.D., Noriega, V., Scheier, M.F., Robinson, D.S., Ketham, A.S., Moffet, F.L. and Clark, K.C. (1993). How coping mediates the effect of optimism on distress: A study of women with early stage breast cancer. *Journal of Personality and Social Psychology*, 65, 375-390.

Carver, C. S., Scheier, M. F., and Weintraub, J. K. (1989). Assessing coping strategies: A theoretically based approach. *Journal of Personality and Social Psychology*, *56*, 267-283.

Carver, C. S., Smith, R. G., Antoni, M. H., Petronis, V. M., Weiss, S., and Derhagopian, R. P. (2005). Optimistic personality and psychosocial well-being during treatment predict psychosocial well-being among long-term survivors of breast cancer. *Health Psychology*, *24*, 508-516.

Carver, M.P. and Burish, T.G. (1988). Etiology and treatment of the psychological side effects associated with cancer chemotherapy: A critical review and discussion. *Psychological Bulletin*, 104, 307-325.

Chesney, M. A. (1988). *Women, Work-related Stress and Smoking*. Wenner-Gren Center Foundation and MacArthur Foundation Women, Work and Health Symposium, Stockholm, Sweden.

Conger, J. J. (1956). Alcoholism: Theory, problem and challenge. II. Reinforcement theory and the dynamics of alcoholism. *Quarterly Journal of Studies on Alcohol*, *13*: 296-305.

Costa, P.T., Jr. and McCrae, R.R. (1985). *The NEO Personality Inventory Manual*. Odessa, FL: Psychological Assessment Resources.

Douglas, A., Drossman, MD, Jane Leserman, Zhiming Li, Francis Keefe, Yuming J.B. Hu, and Timothy, C. Toomey, (2000) Effects of Coping on Health Outcome Among Women with Gastrointestinal Disorders, *Psychosomatic Medicine*, 62:309-317.

Dubey, A. (2006). *Habit of Eating Gutkha and Paan in University Students: Cognitions and Beliefs*. Department of Psychology, D.D.U.Gorakhpur University, Gorakhpur.

Dubey, A. (2003). *Role of some Psychological Variables in Chronic Illness.* Doctoral Dissertation. Department of Psychology, D.D.U.Gorakhpur University, Gorakhpur.

Dubey, A. and Agarwal, A. (2004). Feeling well in spite of chronic illness. *Psychological Studies,* Vol. 49, No.1, 63-68.

Dubey, A. and Jaiswal, D. (2002). A comparative study of health status and health habits in morning walkers and non-morning walkers. M.A. Dissertation. Department of Psychology, D.D.U.Gorakhpur University, Gorakhpur.

Dubey, A. and Sharma, L. (2005).Cognitive Behavioural Intervention: A Study on cancer patients. Paper presented at International Seminar on Stress, M.G. Kashi Vidyapeeth, Varanasi. Feb. 21-22.

Dubey, A. and Singh, S. (2005). Future orientation, family environment and adjustment in chronically ill children and their siblings. M. A. Dissertation. Department of Psychology, D.D.U.Gorakhpur University, Gorakhpur.

Dunn, A.J. (1995). Psychoneuroimmunology: Introduction and general perspectives. In B. Leonard and K.Miller (eds.) *Stress, the immune system and psychiatry* (pp. 1-16). New York: Weily.

Everson, S.A., Goldberg, D.E., Kaplan, G.A., Cohen, R.D., Pukkala, E., Tuomileht, O.J. and Salonen, J.T. (1996). Hopelessness and risk of mortality and incidence of myocardial infraction and cancer. *Psychosomatic Medicine,* 58, 113-121.

Felson, D.T., Zhang, Y., Anthony, J.M. *et al.* (1992). Weight loss reduces the symptomatic osteoarthritis in women: The Framingham study. *Annals of Internal Medicine,* 116, 197-206.

Fiore, M.C., Jorenby, D.E. and Baker, T.B. (1997). Smoking cessation: Principles and practice based upon the AHCPR guidelines, 1996. *Annals of Behavioural Medicine,* 19, 213-219.

Freidman, H.S., Tucker, J.S., Schwartz, J.E., Tomlinson-Keasey, C., Wingard, D.L. and Criqui, M.H. (1995). Psychosocial and behavioural predictors of longevity: The ageing and death of the 'Termites'. *American Psychologists,* 50, 69-78.

Gates, R. (1992). Fitness is changing the world: For women. *IDEA Today,* July-August, 58.

Holahan, C.J. and Moos, R.H. (1987). Personal and contextual determinants of coping strategies. *Journal of Personality and Social Psychology,* 52, 946-955.

Istvan, J. and Matarazzo, J.D. (1984).Tobacco, alcohol and caffeine use: A review of their interrelationships. *Psychological Bulletin,* 95, 301-326.

Jahoda, M. (1958). *Current Concept of Positive Mental Health.* Basic Books: New York.

Jahoda, M. (1963). Mental Health. In A. Deutsch and H. Fishman (Eds.) *The Encyclopedia of Mental Health*, Franklin Watts, Inc. New York.

Kothari, S. and Agarwal, M. (1999). Coping patterns among patients undergoing major surgery. *Psycho-Lingua*, 29 (1), 69-76.

Kover, P.A., Allegrante, J.P., MacKenzie, C.R. *et al.*, (1992). Supervised fitness walking in patients with osteoarthritis of knee: A randomized, controlled trial. *Annals of Internal Medicine*, 116, 529-534.

Labouvie, E. and McGee, C.R. (1986). Relation of personality to alcohol and drug use in adolescence. *Journal of Consulting and Clinical Psychology*, 54, 289-293.

Lazarus, R. S., and Folkman, S. (1984). *Stress, Appraisal, and Coping*. New York: Springer.

Leorard, B.E. (1995). Tress and the immune system: Immunological aspects of depressive illness. In B. Leonard and K.Miller (eds.) *Stress, the Immune System and Psychiatry* (pp. 113-136). New York: Weily.

Matarazzo, J.D. and Leckliter, I.N. 1988). Behavioural health: The role of good and bad habits in health and illness. In S. Maes, C.D. Spielberger, P.B. Defares and I.G. Sarason (eds.) *Topics in Health Psychology* (pp. 3-18). New York: John Wielly and Sons.

Marshell, E. (1986). Involuntary smokers face health risks. *Science*, 234, 1066-1067.

Monti, P.M., Rohsenow, D.J., Rubonis, A.V., Naiura, R.S., Colby, S.M., Goddard, P. and Abrams, D.B. (1993). Cue exposure with coping skills treatment for male alcoholics: A preliminary investigation. *Journal of Consulting and Clinical Psychology*. 61, 1011-1019.

Normen, P., Bennett, P., Smith, C., and Murphy, S. (1997). Health locus of control and leisure time exercise. *Personality and Individual Differences*, 23, 769-774.

O'Brien, M.T. (1992). Multiple sclerosis: The relationship among self esteem, social support and coping behaviour. *Applied Nursing Research*, 6 (2), 54-63.

Ogden, J. and Mitandabari, T. (1997). Examination stress and changes in mood and health related behaviours. *Psychology and Health*, *12*: 288-299.

Park, C. L., Moore, P. J., Turner, R. A., and Adler, N. E. (1997). The roles of constructive thinking and optimism in psychological and behavioural adjustment during pregnancy. *Journal of Personality and Social Psychology*, *73*, 584-592.

Pearlin, L.I. and Schooler, C.C. (1978). The structure of coping. *Journal of Health and Social Behaviour*, 19, 2-1.

Perloff, L.S. (1983). Perceptions of vulnerability to victimization. *Journal of Social Issues*, 39: 41-61.

Lazarus, R.S. and Folkman, S. (1984). *Stress, Appraisal and Coping*. Springer: New York.

Lynch, J.J. (1977). *The Broken Heart: The Medical Consequences of Loneliness.* New York: Basic Books.

Rossow, I. (1992). Intrafamily influences on health behaviour: A study of interdental cleaning behaviour. *Journal of Clinical Peridontology,* 19, 774-778.

Sallis, J.F. and Owen, N. (1999). *Physical Activity and Behavioural Medicine.* Thousand Oaks, CA: Sage.

Sarafino, E.P. (2001). *Behaviour Modification: Principles of Behaviour Change* (2nd edn.) Mountain View, CA: Matfield.

Scheier, M.F. and Bridges, M.W. (!995). Person variables and health: Personality perdispositionsand acute psychological states as shared determinants for disease. *Psychosomatic Medicine,* 57: 255-268.

Steptoe, A., and Wardle, J. (2001). Locus of control and health behaviour revisited: A multivariate analysis of young adults from 18 countries. *British Journal of Psychology,* 92, 659-672.

Stone, A.A., Neale, J.M., Cox, D.S., Napoli, A., Valdimarsdottir, H., and Kennedy-Moore, E. (1994). Daily events are associated with a secretory immune response to an oral antigen in men. *Health Psychology,* 13, 440-446.

Taylor, S. E., Kemeny, M. E., Aspinwall, L. G., Schneider, S. C., Rodriguez, R., and Herbert, M. (1992). Optimism, coping, psychological distress, and high-risk sexual behaviours among men at risk for AIDS. *Journal of Personality and Social Psychology, 63,* 460-473.

Tedeschi, R. G., Park, C. L., and Calhoun, L. C. (1998). Post-traumatic growth: Conceptual issues. *Posttraumatic growth: Positive change in the aftermath of crisis* (pp.1-22).Mahwah, NJ: Lawrence Erlbaum Associates.

Tennen, H., Affleck, G. and Gershman, K. (1986). Self blame among parents of infants with perinatal complications: The role of self-protective motives. *Journal of Personality and Social Psychology,* 50, 690-695.

Thompson, S. (1985). Finding positive meaning in a stressful event and coping. *Basic and Applied Social Psychology,* 6, 274-295.

Thoits, P.A. (1986). Social support as coping assistance. *Journal of Consulting and Clinical Psychology,* 54, 416-423.

Upadhaya, S. (2002). Influence of optimism, future orientation and detachment on health in derivational environment. Unpublished doctoral dissertation. Department of Psychology, D.D.U. Gorakhpur University, Gorakhpur.

Urcuyo, K. R., Boyers, A. E., Carver, C. S., and Antoni, M. H. (2005). Finding benefit in breast cancer: Relations with personality, coping, and concurrent well-being. *Psychology and Health, 20,* 175-192.

Wallston, K.A., Wallston, B.S. and DeVellis, R. (1978). Development of Multidimensional Health Locus of Control (MHLC) Scales. *Health Education Monographs,* 6, 160-170.

Wamboldt, M. and Wamboldt, F. (2000). Role of family in the onset and outcome of childhood disorders: Selected research findings. *Journal of American Academy of Child and Adolescent Psychiatry,* 39, 1212-1219.

White, N.E., Richter, J.M., and Fry, C. (1992). Coping, social support and adaptation to chronic illness. *Western Journal of Nursing Research,* 14, (2), 211-224.

Weinberg, N. and Williams, J. (1978). How the physically disabled perceive their disabilities. *Journal of Rehabilitation,* 44, 31-33.

Wittrock, D.A., Blanchard, E.B. and McCoy, G.C. (1988). Three studies on the relation of process to outcome in the treatment of essential hypertension with relaxation and thermal biofeedback. *Behaviour Research and Therapy,* 26, 53-66.

World Health Organization (WHO) (1998). *Tobacco Epidemic: Health Dimensions.* Retrieved (28 February 2000) from http:http://www.rediffmail.com/cgi-bin/red.cgi?red=http%3A%2F%2Fwww%2Ewho%2Eorg and isImage=0 and BlockImage=0.

16

Health Cognition and Practices

Ramesh Chandra Mishra

This chapter deals with health behaviour of Kharwar women living in Naugarh region of Varanasi (now part of Chandauli district in UP). During the last 3-4 decades much has been said and written about tribal people of India, including the problems of their education and health. Tribals constitute one of the weaker sections of the Indian society. Census report indicates that tribal people, who represent about 15 per cent of the total Indian population, are distributed in approximately 427 tribal communities. Tribes refer to those communities that are put under a special schedule in the Constitution of India. However, generally speaking a tribe refers to a group of people characterized by a common and distinct name, a group sentiment and a common and specific territory. It is generally endogamous and has common institutional agencies for maintaining order in the community. It follows its own beliefs, rituals and taboos along with other social, economic, political and cultural traditions. As such, tribes exist as distinct cultural groups (Mishra, Sinha and Berry, 1996). Such tribes have been found to live in each state of India, but their population varies considerably across different regions. For example, the tribals are so numerous in Bihar (now Jharkhand) that it is considered as the "homeland" of tribes. The tribal people are regarded as the earliest inhabitants of the country, and as such they are called Adivasi (original inhabitants) in official language.

For a long time tribal people have remained away from the main stream society. They preferred to live in forest and hilly areas with subsistence level economic activities based on hunting, gathering and rudimentary agriculture. After the independence of the country from the British rule, special attention was given to tribal population. A policy for their integration with groups of the mainstream society was evolved. Over the interim period, several programmes have been framed and implemented to ensure the overall development of tribal people. Education and health are two most important areas in which a variety of intervention efforts, both from the government and voluntary organizations, are still going on. The level of success achieved in these domains of development varies considerably across regions. An overall picture suggests that the success has been less than optimal everywhere.

Psychologists who have worked with the problems of health and education of tribal people maintain that the main barriers of their development in these domains result from the cultural features of the groups. The kind of changes inended through various programmes have often been inconsistent with those that have been in practice in tribal communities over generations. Their traditional knowledge and skills have been good enough to sustain them in their environment. However, a number of changes have taken place (some forcibly and others voluntarily) in their life due to developmental activities of the government and other influences resulting from their contact with other cultural groups. Education, urbanization and wage employment have played significant role in this context. The life of tribal people, who have access to these elements of acculturation, is very different from those who are still bound to their traditional culture. It is the latter that is primarily regarded as the target of all change programmes including those of health.

Health represents an important area of human life in which the principles of psychology seem to have direct applications. Broadly speaking, health is a state of physical, mental, social and spiritual well-being of individuals; it is not merely the absence of disease and infirmity (WHO, 1998). While there is a notion of health held by medical practitioners, research suggests that the meaning of health and disease is constructed differently across cultures (Helman, 1990; Radley, 1996). People hold different viewpoints about health and illness, and they nurture different types of beliefs and practices with regard to the maintenance of health and treatment of diseases (Singh, Tripathi, Verma and Mishra, 1999). Health Psychology has been developed to understand the behavioural problems associated with health. Promotion and maintenance of health, prevention and treatment of illness, identification of etiological and diagnostic correlates of health, illness and related dysfunction, and improvement of health care system and health policy information represent the major concerns of health psychology (Matarazzo, 1980, 815).

Research demonstrates that psychosocial factors are involved at all stages of health and illness, ranging from those behaviours that keep people healthy to those that produce long-term and debilitating diseases. Yet we do not have a clear understanding of how people in different societies and cultures explain the causes of ill-health. We also do not know about the types of treatment they believe in, who they turn to when they become ill, what system(s) of medicine they use, and how their beliefs and practices related to biological and psychological changes help them cope with the problems of health or diseases. These issues have been highlighted in recent works on health and illness (Furnham, 1998). It has been argued that programmes aimed at the prevention of diseases and promotion of health and well-being need to incorporate an understanding of the cultural values, traditions, beliefs and patterns of family interactions.

Everyone accepts the importance of health, but none is free from ailments. Sinha (1990) has stated that psychological well-being or good health is desirable but difficult to define. Singh, Tripathi, Verma and Mishra (1999) carried out a study with the practitioners of Allopathic, Ayurvedic, Homeopathic and Unani medicinal systems. They found that a majority of the practitioners described meaning of health in terms of physical fitness and well-being of individuals. Much of the evidence suggests that the professional practice of health is based on assumptions in which cultural factors are largely ignored (Beardsley and Pederson, 1997; Capewell, 1994; Lewis, Fernandez and Kleinman, 1994; McName and Gergen, 1992; Misra, 1999; Tanakamatsumi and Draguns, 1997). Antonovsky's (1979) analysis of health and disease concepts suggests that health is influenced by specific social and cultural contexts. Culture influences health behaviour through the generation of specific knowledge, beliefs, customs and habits (Helman, 1985). Mechanic (1986) has also emphasized the importance of viewing health within a given cultural context.

Viewed in this perspective, the portrayal of an accurate picture of an individual's health and well-being appears to be a challenging task. Health research needs to focus on local cultural contexts and community conceptions as well as on beliefs, attitudes and behaviour of individuals. These aspects require thorough understanding in order to bring any change in health behaviour and health status of individuals.

In the present study an attempt was made to understand the health cognition and practices of the Kharwar cultural group living in Naugarh region of eastern U.P. The purpose was to grasp people's viewpoint on several issues pertaining to their health.

Method

Sample and Setting

The study was conducted with 100 females between 25-60 years of age. The sample was drawn from the Kharwar group residing in hilly regions of Naugarh Block of Chandauli district (earlier part of Varanasi) in eastern U.P.

The Kharwar represent a settled agricultural community with an elaborate village life. They consider themselves as Rajput and engage in many Rajput cultural practices, such as worshipping weapons during *Dashehra* (an important Hindu festival). Their houses have mud walls and tiled roofs with enough space to store agricultural produce. They have a community Panchayat, a village *Pradhan* (the headman) and a *Baiga* (the priest). Baiga occupies a prominent place in their life. Prior to cultivation of land and harvest, he propitiates the local deities. He also determines the auspicious days for initiating a number of activities.

As there are no irrigation facilities in the region, the Kharwars of Naugarh grow only rainy season crops. These are often damaged by wild animals roaming around. Hence, guarding crops against wild animals is a round-the-clock activity. The agricultural yield can feed them hardly for 3-4 months. For the rest of the year, they have to depend solely on forest resources.

There is great scarcity of drinking water in the whole region. During summers, the villagers have to depend on *chuan* (seepage water), which appears to be a major cause of diarrhoea among people. No medical facilities are available to people in the whole region.

Even today one has to walk or ride a bicycle for about 10-20 kms. to find a doctor. Most of the delivery deaths are reported in transit between the village and the hospital. Some Kharwars have a good knowledge of herbs, roots and seeds that have got medicinal values, but people do not like these now-a-days. They prefer tablets and capsules that are handy and easy to use. The health status of the community is distressingly poor. There are very few primary schools to cater to the needs of primary education of children. For the last few years couple of NGOs have started programmes of primary education and health care in some villages, but the facilities to serve to the health needs of people are very meagre. On the whole, the Kharwar life is full of many difficulties and constraints. Due to pressures of economy the new generation is moving out in search of wages. Consequently a number of changes can be noticed in some families, while the majority continues to live a traditional life.

Field observations of people's health behaviour indicated that for the first few days they observe the progress of the disease. A common belief is that poison accumulated in one's body due to several reasons comes out in the form of a disease. If the illness does not go away, people consult the local *baiga* (the priest), who tells what type of *puja* (worship) is to be performed, and which god is to be propitiated. Then traditional healers are consulted. Doctors are consulted at the last stage when the patient is completely taken over by the disease. A number of changes in these practices are taking place now-a-days. The new generation seems to favour allopathic system of medicine more than the older generation.

Tools

In order to explore the health cognition and practices of the Kharwar, a questionnaire was prepared. It probed into the meaning of health, major health problems, control for diseases, responsibility for diseases, ways of maintaining good health, and prevention from illness. A local female research assistant interviewed women individually. The responses were content-analyzed by two indepedent judges. The degree of agreement ranged between 85-100 per cent on various components of health behaviour.

Results

Meaning of Health and Knowledge of Diseases

Analysis with respect to the meaning of health revealed that the participants generally described health as a disease-free state, characterized by body strength. They named fourteen diseases; the nine most commonly mentioned health problems are given in Table 16.1.

Table 16.1: Major health problems reported by women

(In percentages)

Health Problems	*Young*	*Old*	*Difference*	*Critical Ratio*
Diarrhoea	100	98	2	1.00
Fever	84	90	6	0.89
Conjunctivitis	86	44	42	4.40**
Arthritis	24	50	26	2.69**
Cough/Cold	48	54	6	0.60
Unwanted pregnancy	74	40	34	3.43**
Headaches	52	26	26	3.86**
Skin diseases	16	48	32	3.75**
Child mortality	58	34	24	2.40*

** $p < .01$ * $p < .05$

The distribution of reported health problems according to age (i.e., below 30 years and above 50 years) revealed that both young and old women were fully aware of these problems, and that the problems were well represented in their cognition. Diarrhoea and fever appeared to be the most important problems of health. Significant differences in the cognition of health problems according to age can be observed on conjunctivitis, headaches, unwanted pregnancy, child mortality (young>old), arthritis and skin diseases (old>young).

Attribution of Causality to Health Problems

Women were asked to tell the causes that they considered responsible for the causation of various health problems. They could mention multiple causes. The analysis revealed that these causes could be grouped into three broad categories, namely environmental (weather, food, water), personal (own behaviour, carelessness, habits), and supernatural (evil eye, evil spirits, local deities). These causes of illness were found to co-exist in the psyche of women.

With respect to the attribution of environmental causes (Table 16.2), significant difference between the young and old women was evident only on child mortality (young>old). With respect to personal causes (Table 16.3), the overall pattern revealed that younger women mentioned these causes more frequently than older women did. Differences between the two groups were significant on fever, conjunctivitis, arthritis, cold-cough, headaches, skin diseases and unwanted pregnancy.

Table 16.2: Percentage of women attributing environmental causes to various health problems

Health Problems	*Young*	*Old*	*Difference*	*Critical Ratio*
Diarrhoea	76	64	12	1.31
Fever	74	78	4	0.47
Conjunctivitis	96	80	16	1.82
Arthritis	68	66	2	0.21
Cough/Cold	86	78	8	1.04
Unwanted pregnancy	36	40	4	0.41
Headaches	40	40	0	0.00
Skin diseases	28	44	16	1.66
Child mortality	58	30	28	2.82**

** $p < .01$

Table 16.3: Percentage of women attributing personal causes to various health problems

Health Problems	*Young*	*Old*	*Difference*	*Critical Ratio*
Diarrhoea	52	36	16	1.61
Fever	70	46	24	2.63**
Conjunctivitis	80	56	26	3.11**
Arthritis	76	48	28	2.88**
Cough/Cold	72	48	24	2.45*
Unwanted pregnancy	64	34	30	3.00**
Headaches	74	66	8	0.87
Skin diseases	62	30	32	3.21**
Child mortality	32	20	12	1.37

** $p < .01$ * $p < .05$

The analysis of supernatural causes (Table 16.4) revealed that these were quite strongly held by young and old women. Except for unwanted pregnancy and child mortality older women attributed supernatural causes to health problems more frequently than the younger women did. Difference between the percentage of young and old women for the attribution of these causes was significant on conjunctivitis, arthritis, headaches, skin diseases, unwanted pregnancy and child mortality.

Table 16.4: Percentage of women attributing supernatural causes to various health problems

Health Problems	*Young*	*Old*	*Difference*	*Critical Ratio*
Diarrhoea	48	64	16	1.61
Fever	62	74	12	1.29
Conjunctivitis	74	96	22	3.08**
Arthritis	60	92	32	3.75**
Cough/Cold	68	76	8	0.89
Unwanted pregnancy	70	48	22	2.23*
Headaches	56	86	30	3.31**
Skin diseases	14	42	28	3.12**
Child mortality	86	66	20	2.34*

** $p < .01$ * $p < .05$

Attribution of Control for Disease

Table 16.5 presents the locus of control for health problems reported by women. Doctor was not regarded as an important agent of disease control. The lowest level of control was attributed to self. The local *vaidya* and healer were considered as main control agents. The old women tended to consult a healer significantly more often than younger women did. The younger women tended to consult a healer significantly more often than the older women did.

Table 16.5: Percentage of women reporting various control agents for health problems

Control Agents	*Young*	*Old*	*Difference*	*Critical Ratio*
Doctor	26	24	2	0.23
Healer	14	44	30	5.88**
Vaidya	60	40	20	2.00*
Family	20	28	8	0.94
Self	12	14	2	0.30

** $p < .01$ * $p < .05$

Maintenance of Health

Analysis of the factors reported as responsible for good health revealed that a majority of the respondents indicated food/water, cleanliness and personal habits as major factors in health maintenance (Table 16.6). Doctor was also considered as an important factor. While younger and older women did not differ significantly with respect to the perceived importance of other factors, younger women mentioned doctor as a factor more often than the older women did.

Table 16.6: Percentage of women reporting different factors in good health

Factors in good health	*Young*	*Old*	*Difference*	*Critical Ratio*
Food/water	100	100	00	0.00
Cleanliness	100	96	4	0.51
Good habits	76	68	8	1.48
Doctor	84	52	32	3.43**
Others	6	7	1	0.33

** $p < .01$

Prevention of Illness

With respect to illness prevention, the findings (Table 16.7) revealed that both the age groups considered food, water and cleanliness as the most important factors in illness prevention. Medical check up and satisfaction of spirits were mentioned as other factors. Significant difference between young and old women was observed on satisfaction of spirits.

Table 16.7: Percentage of women reporting different ways of illness prevention

Illness Prevention	*Young*	*Old*	*Difference*	*Critical Ratio*
Food/Water	100	100	00	0.00
Cleanliness	100	100	0	0.00
Medical checks	34	22	12	1.34
Satisfying spirits	52	84	32	3.43**
Others	4	2	2	0.66

** $p < .01$

Discussion

The findings of the study indicated that problems of health, their prevention and treatment find representation in the cognition of Kharwar women more or less in a similar manner as is held by people in general. Studies carried out with Kharwar people reveal that they have been in contact with people of other groups for a long time (Dubey, 1993; Mishra, 1997). As a part of developmental programme the modern medical facilities were also brought to them. The NGOs working in this area have primarily focused on the health of women and children. These interventions seem to have considerably changed their ideas about various aspects of health. Their presently held notion of health matches fairly well with the one generally held by people inducted in the modern medical tradition.

In asking women about their health problems the general expectation was that they would mention some culture-specific problems. The findings did not fulfil this expectation. There was nothing culture-specific in what they reported. This finding may be interpreted in two possible ways. In the first place, we may say that the health problems are experienced in the same manner almost everywhere, and people also describe these problems using a terminology that is largely commonly shared. The second possibility is that the Kharwar women had different names for these diseases, but when it came to the level of communicating to the researcher, they translated the symptoms of the diseases into a language that was supposed to be known to the researcher.

On the other hand, differences noted with respect to the report of diseases indicate that the cognition of health problems including their causation and control do vary across individuals. For example, headaches, problems of eye, unwanted pregnancies, and child mortality were of greater concern for younger women, whereas arthritis and skin diseases were of greater concern for relatively older women.

Analysis of facors related to illness causation revealed that personal factors were considered more important by younger than older women. On the other hand, the relative importance of supernatural factors varied considerably across younger and older women according to health problems. This suggests that people may weigh differently the importance of a particular factor in the context of a given health problem. A more interesting observation is the co-existence of personal, environmental and supernatural factors as explanations for the same health problems. This suggests that Kharwar women believe in multiple effects on health, all operating at the same time. Such a state often characterizes the psyche of culturally changing individuals and communities. In a study with culturally changing tribal groups of Bihar (Mishra, Sinha and Berry, 1996) co-existence of attitudes was found as the most dominant strategy for dealing with inroads from other cultures. In the specific context of health, Mishra (1997) has previously noted multiple attribution of causality (e.g., food, water, habits, evil spirits) to physical health problems (e.g., diarrhoea, conjunctivities, eye defects) by members of the Kharwar community. These findings indicate that culturally rooted belief systems are not easily altered in the course of developmental changes taking place among groups or individuals.

Some studies (e.g., Dalal, 1999) indicate that people of traditional societies often hold external factors (e.g., fate, God) responsible for health problems more than internal (personal) or environmental factors. The findings of the present study do not offer any strong support to this notion. Kharwar women did believe in supernatural causes of illness, but they also admitted the importance of personal and environmental factors in disease causation. The belief that health problems do have an outside locus is very much there, but the role of an individual's own behaviour in its causation is not altogether denied.

The findings also indicated that women in general did not consider doctor as an important agent of disease control. The traditional systems of health care (e.g., consulting a *vaidya* or healer) were more often used than consulting a doctor. It might have happened because a doctor was neither easily available, nor was it financially affordable by people of the community. The older women turned to a healer more frequently than to *vaidya,* whereas younger women consulted a *vaidya* more often than a healer. Older women also recognized family as an agent of control of health problems slightly more frequently than younger women did.

A preference on the part of women to switch to the modern medicinal system for health care was also evident. Studies indicate that in the process of social and cultural change, traditional institutions of the society often undergo change. Sometimes these institutions tend to co-exist with other new institutions, but often the new institutions tend to replace the old ones. An individual's level of acculturation plays a significant role in this process. Mass media is most important in this respect. In the case of Kharwar, the traditional health care systems are not completely destroyed. There is a need to strengthen the traditional systems of medicine among the tribal communities, because these can provide people with a viable and readily available option for health care in their immediate surroudning without dependence on others. Its utility is recognized and pleaded for in some recent work (e.g., Joshi, 2000).

The findings of the present study indicate that Kharwar women have a clear understanding of health problems. They hold clear ideas about the causation of disease, maintenance of health and prevention of illness. People concerned with health problems of Kharwar women of Naugarh region can make use of these findings to organize delivery of health services in a fruitful manner.

REFERENCES

Antonovsky, A. (1979), *Health, Stress and Coping.* San Francisco: Josey Bass.

Beardsley, L. and Pederson, P. (1997), Health and culture centred intervention. In J.W. Berry, M.H. Segall and C. Kagitcibasi (Eds.), *Handbook of Cross-cultural Psychology, Vol. 3, Social Behaviour and applications.* Boston: Allyn and Bacon.

Capewell, S. (1994), Are health and illness defined by society or by doctor? *Proceedings of Royal College of Physicians,* 24, 181-186.

Dalal, A.K. (1999), Health beliefs and coping with chronic illness. In G. Misra (Ed.), *Psychological Perspectives on Stress and Health.* New Delhi: Concept.

Dubey, V.K. (1993), *The Agony of Life.* Varanasi: National Council of Development Communication.

Furnham, A. (1988), *Lay Theories: Everyday Understanding of Problems in the Social Sciences.* Oxford: Pergamon.

Helman, C. (1985), Psyche, soma and society: The social construction of psychosomatic disorders. *Culture, Medicine and Psychiatry,* 9, 1-26.

Helman, C. (1990), *Culture, Health and Illness.* London: Wright.

Joshi, P.C. (2000), Relevance and utility of traditional medical systems (TMS) in the context of a Himalayan tribe. *Psychology and Developing Societies,* 12, 5-29.

Lewis-Fernandez, R. and Kleinman, A. (1994), Culture, personality and psychopathology. *Journal of Abnormal Psychology*, 103, 67-71.

Matarazzo, J.D. (1980), Behavioural health and behavioural medicine: Frontiers for a new health psychology. *American Psychologist*, 35, 807-817.

McName, S. and Gergen, K.J. (1992), *Therapy as Social Construction*. London: Sage.

Mechanic, D. (1986), Health and illness behaviour. In J.M. Last (Ed.), *Public Health and Preventive Medicine*. East Norwik, CT: Appleton-Century Crofts.

Mishra, R.C. (1997), Family support and health care in a cultural changing village community in northern India. *Social Science International*, 13, 10-18.

Mishra, R.C., Sinha, D. and Berry, J.W. (1996), *Ecology, Acculturation and Psychological Adaptation: A study of Adivasis in Bihar*. New Delhi: Sage.

Misra, G. (1999), *Psychological Perspectives on Stress and Health*. New Delhi: Concept.

Radley, A. (1994), *Making Sense of Illness: The Social Psychology of Health and Disease*. London: Sage.

Singh, T., Tripathi, K.N., Verma, S. and Mishra, R.C. (1999). The notion of health in theory and practice. In G. Misra (Ed.), *Psychological Perspectives on Stress and Health*. New Delhi: Concept.

Sinha, D. (1990), Concept of psychological well-being: Western and Indian perspectives. *NIMHANS Journal*, 8, 1-11.

Tanakamatsumi, J. and Draguns, J. (1997), Culture and psychopathology. In J.W. Berry, M.H. Segall and C. Kagitcibasi (Eds.), *Handbook of Cross-cultural Psychology, Vol. 3, Social Behaviour and Applications*. Boston: Allyn and Bacon.

World Health Organization (1988), *Charter for Action to Achieve Health for All* (Ottawa Charter). Geneva: WHO.

17

Language Related Impairments in Children

Nishi Tripathi and *Bhoomika R. Kar*

Learning disabilities affect one in seven people according to the National Institute of Health. It is believed that in the U.S. 1-5 per cent children in a classroom are learning disabled and up to 10 per cent mildly disabled (Karanth, 2003). Learning disabilities as reported in the western countries are common in India as well but with a different context. In specific learning disability is observed in 7-8 per cent of the general population in the age range of 0-18 years (Suresh and Sebastian, 2003). Included therein are reading, spelling and writing disabilities. The most common difficulty with language is reading, writing and spelling.

Reading Impairments

Reading disability was explained as a deficit in functional coordination resulting in a failure of the integration of information in a degree of speed and accuracy required for reading. Reading involves visual and semantic decoding, temporal processing, phonological processing, orthographic, syntactic and contextual analysis and comprehension. An inefficient synchrony of these underlying mechanisms results in reading disability. In children with learning disability a phonological deficit impairs decoding thus preventing the reader from using his/her intelligence and vocabulary to get the word's meaning (Shaywitz, 1996). A recent National Institute of Health study showed that 67 per cent of young students identified as being at risk for reading difficulties were able to achieve average or above average reading ability when they received help early (CCLD, 2003).

Reading Disability is supposed to be a failure in learning to optimize the coordination of sub-processes involved in reading with the consequence of errors in integrating reading related information represented in working memory (Lachman, 2002). Word reading is related to this dominant interaction between the simultaneous (top-down) and successive (bottom-up) processes. Simultaneous processing is dominant in visual coding whereas successive processing plays a major role in phonological coding (Das, Naglieri and Kirby, 1994). Visual information can trigger hypothesis on the semantic level (bottom-up) and activated semantic information can influence the speed and quality of the creation of a visual representation (top-down). In reading the bottom up information from visual analyses plays an important role in the decoding process.

Writing Impairments

Writing related problems include errors in spelling, punctuation, capitalization, and handwriting. It is believed that at least three factors may account for students' difficulties in writing (Graham and Harries, 1990). First, their problems in producing text may interfere with other important writing processes such as generating ideas. Second, their lack of knowledge about writing or their ability to access what they do know may impact on their ability to operate and deploy the cognitive process considered central to effective writing. Third, the cognitive moves or writing strategies employed by learning disabled children may be immature or ineffective. This also calls for an evaluation of the cognitive profile of children with a specific learning disability.

Many children with poor writing skills also have poor co-ordination and visual perceptual skills. Another aspect of writing involves written expression. In informal assessment, subjective judgment is used to assess the age levels in writing expressions. The ability to spell is essential because it allows the child to read correctly what is written.

Language Impairment and Learning Disability

The connection between language impairment and learning disability has witnessed a renewed interest in the recent past. Even as early as in the pioneering work of Orton (1937) learning disability (LD), in particular reading disability, was reported to be associated with spoken language deficits. Myklebust (1954), a pioneer in the field, observed that children with reading difficulties often had spoken language deficits. Subsequently, however, this early recognition that learning disability was closely associated with langauge learning deficits was overshadowed and neglected when the emphasis in learning disability shifted to the sensory-motor aspects of learning such as the visual, auditory and motor processing skills.

The Langauge and Learning Disability Connection

Since 1970s there has been a renewed interest in the language and learning disability connection. With the emergence of the new discipline of psycho-linguistics in the 1970s and the study of the acquisition of language in children received a tremendous boost and took centre stage in this newly developing field. The perception of learning disability as a disorder that affected children in their school age had begun to change in the last couple of decades of the twentieth century. Children identified as having learning disability in the 1950s and 1960s had grown into adulthood with some persisting difficulties. It increasingly appeared that learning disability was a life span disorder and not merely restricted to school age. The recognition that learning disability manifests well into adolescence and adulthood with changing manifestations, despite early intervention coupled with the realization that language acquisition too is a process that spans several years led to a shift from visually based theories of reading disabilities to language-based theories.

The renewed acknowledgement of this connection was a consequence of several factors. A substantial number of children with learning disability were seen to have associated speech disorders such as fluency and articulation disorders. Children with communication disorders such as 'Specific Language Impairment' and other such developmental language disorders in their preschool years are documented to have later developed signs of learning disability (Bashir, Wiig and Abrams, 1987). Higher incidence of communication disorders both in children with learning disability and among their family members has also been reported (Catts, 1989; Scarborough, 1990).

Metalinguistics

A second major factor that led to the recognition of the importance of language in learning disability is the identification and acknowledgement of the role of metalinguistic skills in learning to read. Broadly defined metalinguistic skill refers to learning to treat language as a focus of cognitive reflection, that is, "thinking about language to use langauge to think" (van Kleeck, 1994). The role of metalinguistic skills in reading acquisition was first documented with reference to phonological awareness and early reading acquisition in children learning to read English. Subsequently, however this area of study has broadened to include other aspects of metalinguistic skills and the latter is now seen as providing a link for moving children from social to increasingly instructional uses of language.

Phonological Awareness

A child's phoneme or phonological awareness is generally examined by getting him or her to perform a set of tasks such as rhyming, phoneme deletion, counting, segmentation and oddity tasks. In the simplest of these tasks a child is required to state whether a given pair of words rhyme or not. In tasks such as phoneme counting the child is required to listen to given words and count the number of phonemes in a word whereas the segmentation task requires that the word be broken down in to the smallest units possible, as illustrated. In the deletion task the subject is required to delete a particular phoneme (first, last or middle) and to say the remaining part of the word.

Consequently phoneme awareness is seen as an essential step in the acquisition of reading. However it was also observed that with increased exposure to reading there was an increase in phonological awareness thus supporting not just a causal, but also perhaps a reciprocal role for phonological awareness in reading acquisition.

Similar results have been obtained in experimental investigations on readers of the Indian alphasyllabaries. In a series of studies on phonological awareness in children and adults (literate and non-literate) whose primary language and script was one of the Indian languages/scripts such as Kannada or Hindi, Prakash and Rekha (1992), Prakash, Rekha, Nigam and Karanth (1993), Prakash (2003) and Prema and Karanth (2003), established that phonological awareness is neither as evident nor as crucial to successful reading in these writing systems. On tasks such as rhyme recognition, syllable deletion, phoneme deletion and phoneme oddity the different sub-groups of their population—children learning to read alphasyllabaries and adult monoliterates in alphasyllabaries (those who had learnt to read only an alphasyllabary like Kannada or Hindi), performed well in rhyme-recognition and syllable deletion tasks, but with a few exceptions they rarely performed well on the phoneme segmentation tasks. In contrast the biliterate adults (those who knew how to read Kannada and English or Hindi and English) with exposure to the alphabetic script of English were able to carry out the phoneme segmentation and oddity tasks successfully. As compared to Kannada monolinguals the bilingual—biliterates who had exposure to the alphabetic script performed significantly better in tasks such as phoneme stripping and phoneme deletion. These results would support the theoretical position that phonological awareness is more a concomitant of, rather than a requisite for successful reading in alphabetic scripts as suggested by Morais, Bertelson, Cary and Alegria (1986).

Study 1

The present study examined the prevalence of language, reading and writing problems in children from 2nd to 8th standard and to identify children with learning disability using NIMHANS index of SLD (Kapur, *et al.,* 2002). Coloured progressive matrices/Standard Progressive Matrices (CPM/SPM) (Raven, 1998; Raven, 2000) was used to assess the intellectual functions of children with dyslexia in the age range of 7-11 years and SPM for the children above the age of 11 years children with learning disability were further assessed on reading and writing tests, developed by the investigators to examine the types of reading and writing errors in both English and Hindi langauge. The profiles of children with language, reading and writing difficulties would aid in understanding the underlying cognitive processes affected, thus give an insight into the remedial strategies which work on the underlying cognitive processes first and then on the specific language, reading and writing skills.

Forty-three children from 2nd to 8th standard perceived as learning related problems perceived by the teachers were taken for assessment on the NIMHANS index of SLD to identify children with specific learning disability. Out of these 43 children 14 had left school at the time of assessment. Hence, 29 children were assessed on NIMHANS index of SLD. Out of these 29 children, 18 children (8-12 years of age: mean: 10.7; SD: 1.67) were identified as learning disabled. Out of these 18 children 15 were boys and 3 were girls. Their academic performance ranged between 2 to 50 per cent (mean: 25.5; SD: 19.4) performance in the previous exam conducted). These children showed specific difficulties in language, reading and writing tests (see Figure 17.1).

The results presented in Table 17.1 indicate that high prevalence rates of language and writing problems were found in upper standards from 4th to 8th standards and reading problems were round in a decreasing order in upper standards. Eighteen Children who performed at 2 grades below the grade, in which they were studying on reading writing and mathematics tests, were identified as learning disabled (Tripathi and Kar, 2003).

Table 17.1: Frequency distribution of problems related to English language, reading and writing across 2nd to 8th standard as perceived by the teachers

Standard	*Language Problems Frequency %*	*Reading Problems Frequency %*	*Writing Problems Frequency %*
2nd	69	82.3	88.6
3rd	90	55	92
4th	64	62.2	88.6
5th	42.8	67	71.4
6th	77.8	53	84.4
7th	74.2	41.7	82.2
8th	65	68.7	70.2

Study 2

The second part of the study examined the types of errors in language, reading and writing in children with learning disability. These 18 children with learning disability (8-12 years of age: mean: 10.7; SD: 1.67) were further assessed on language, reading and writing tests. Out of these 18 children, 8 children had both reading and writing disability and 10 children had reading difficulties only. Academic performance of these children was also recorded on the basis of previous class marks. While doing the assessments with reading writing tests in English language it was realized that the poor performance is more because of the difficulties related to second langauge acquisition. Hence, reading and writing tests were also developed and administered for Hindi language for children from 2nd to 8th standard. These tests included passages to read and write and test of reading comprehension. Reading and writing Tests on English and Hindi langauge was developed to assess children with learning disability on language, reading, and writing problems with respect to the class in which he/she is studying.

English Reading Tests on English language consist of reading and comprehension based on that paragraph. Writing tests consist of copying a paragraph and also writing the answers of the questions based on that paragraph. A list of fifteen words was developed from the respective class textbook to examine the children on the spellings. The children were given a distinction on these words. Children with learning disability were assessed on reading and writing tests on English language and while doing the assessments with reading and writing tests in English language it was realized that the poor performance is more because of the dificulties related to second language acquisition. Reading Tests on Hindi language consist of reading and comprehension based on that paragraph. Writing tests consist of copying a paragraph and also writing the answers of the questions based on that paragraph.

These children were formally assessed on language, reading, and writing tests and those children who performed at 2nd standard below the standard in which they were studying on language, reading and writing tests, were identified as language impaired. Figure 17.1 presents the errors committed while reading in English and Hindi language on grade appropriate reading tests in terms of the frequency of errors.

The results presented in Figure 17.1 indicate that the most common reading errors in English language is inability to use phonetic cues, ignoring punctuation, reading word by word, guessing at words, adding and spelling out words and the most common reading errors in Hindi language is inability to use phonetic cues, guessing at words, reading word-by-word, adding and spelling out words, and ignoring punctuation.

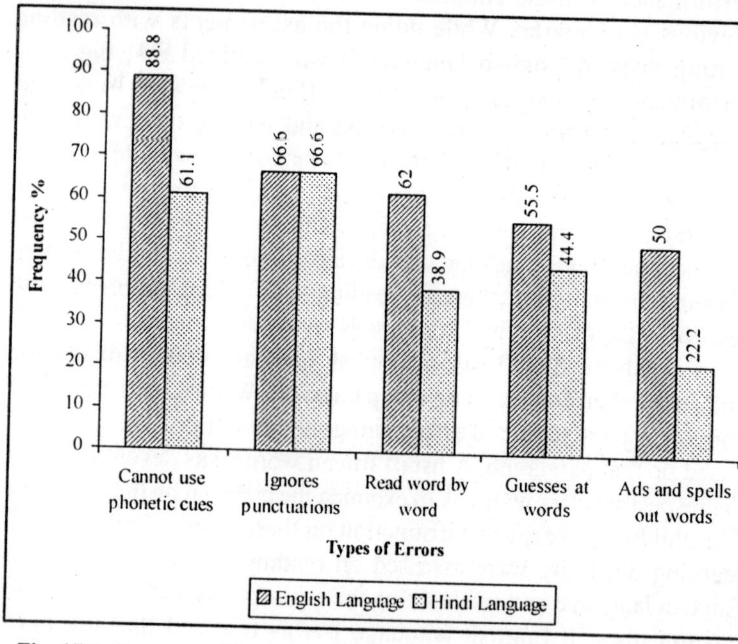

Fig. 17.1: Frequency Distribution of Types of Reading Errors in English and Hindi Languge

Table 17.2: Frequency Distribution of Types of Writing Errors in English and Hindi Language

Types of Writing Errors in English and Hindi Language			
English language	*Frequency %*	*Hindi Language*	*Frequency %*
Adds letters	55.5	Omits matra	27.2
Missed out a letter	55.5	Missed out a letter	22.2
Wrong capitals	44.4	Substitutes letters	16.7
No space between words	22.2	Adds letters	16.7
Substitute letters	22.2	Omits a sentence	16.7

Result of Table 17.2 depicts that the most common writing errors in English language is adding letters, missed out a letter, wrong capitals, no space between words, and substituting letters and the most common writing errors in Hindi language is omitting matra, missed out a letter, substituting letters, additing letters and omitting a sentence. On the whole the findings of the Figure 17.1 and Table 17.1 suggested that children with learning disability showed more reading and writing errors in English language in comparison to Hindi language.

Discussion

Results indicate that high prevalence of reading and writing problems persist across all standards in children with learning disability. The frequency distribution percentage of language, writing and reading indicate that high prevalence of language related problems was observed in English language in comparison to Hindi language (Table 17.1). We found that children having difficulty with English language also had difficulty with Hindi language, though to a lesser extent which nullifies the second language learning effect on reading. This highlights the need to reconsider the overestimated effect of second language acquisition on reading and writing ability. It appears that reading disability pertains to a specific difficulty in language processing irrespective of the fact whether it is their first or second language. English, being the second language could be the reason for consistent high prevalence of problems related to language. Such difficulties related to second language acquisition extent to further difficulties in learning to read. However this can be understood from a different angle also. When children learn to read and write they would have already mastered the language. So, it is natural for them to relate written symbols and language structure they have mastered (Prakash, 2003). It is also reported that phonemic awareness is not so crucial in learning to read Indian languages such as Hindi, Kannada and Oriya (Karanth and Prakash, 1996). Such reports explain the dependence on phonological strategy used for learning English language.

The reading and writing tests findings of accuracy of the children with learning disability indicated that reading comprehension was poor for both Hindi (hit rate: 26.6%) and English (hit rate: 14.4%) language but better for Hindi langauge. Children with learning disability were found poor on reading comprehension in English langauge, which is partially dependent on rapid decoding skills, sometimes called as bottom-up processing skills as well as on top-down higher level processing. Poor reading comprehension could be because the child takes time to decode the words phonologically and does not retain the entire sentence as each word is processed at a time and not as a logical sequence of words. Episodic context and easier search for related words in one's first language could be one reason, which helps the child comprehend the text better in Hindi language despite of the reading difficulties.

The performance of children with learning disability showed phonetics, reading speed, writing errors, and poor concentration as the most prevalent problems related to both English and Hindi language. Reading tests of English and Hindi language showed that the common reading errors in English language is inability to use phonetic cues, ignoring punctuation, reading word by word, guessing at words, adding and spelling out words and the most the most common reading errors in Hindi language is inability to use phonetic cues, guessing at words, reading word-by-word, spelling out words, adding words and ignoring punctuation (Figure 17.1). The inability to engage in phonological coding has been suggested the major cause of reading disability (Torgesen, Wagner and Rashotte, 1994). Children with learning disability showed difficulty in word recognition resulting in an error like joining letters and reading. Inability to use phonetic cues affects their ability to join letters and pronounce a word. Prakash and Rekha (1992) documented that children studying in Kannada medium schools showed a spurt in performance on phoneme awareness tasks such as phoneme stripping and phoneme oddity after having been introduced to English in fourth grade. They concluded that the difference in phonemic awareness was due to the orthographic nature of the two scripts with phonemic awareness increasing when introduced to the alphabetic script of English. It is accepted that impairment of temporal processing mechanisms results in deficits in phoneme discrimination abilities that affect reading ability (Barth, Steinbuchel, Wittman, Kappert and Leyendecker, 1999). Reading word by word is suggestive of difficulty with working memory and temporal processing. Children have frequently guessed at words, which could be due to deficit in working memory. With some exceptions, Torgesen recognized that the majority of reading disabled children had shorter memory spans than those who are not reading disabled (Torgesen, 1995; Torgesen and Houck, 1980). Das and Mishra (1991) reported weak correlations between memory span and naming time as well as between these two variables and speech rate, which is a measure of phonological coding and articulation. This, coupled with the results of such studies as those by Bowey, Cain and Ryan (1992) that observed rather weak connections between working memory and reading disability, suggests that many poor readers have average or even good memory spans and it may be uneconomical for remedial programmes to focus mainly on memory enhancement. Their performance was replete with spelling punctuation, capitalization errors. Their writing was short, poorly organized and impoverished in terms of ideation.

On tests of Writing in English and Hindi language, 50% of the children with reading disability showed writing difficulties also, with higher frequency of errors in writing English than Hindi. The most common writing errors in English language is adding letters, missed out a letter, wrong capitals, no space between words, and substituting letters and the most common writing errors in Hindi language is omitting matra, missed out a letter, substituting letters, adding letters and omitting a sentence. On the whole the findings suggested that children with learning disability showed more errors in English language in comparison to Hindi language. Phonological processing seems to be the most affected component of reading process in Hindi language also. Errors in reading Hindi language such as inability to use phonetic cues, guessing at words, reading word by word, spell out words appear to be similar to those in reading English language along with errors related to the use of matras, which is specific to Hindi language. Differences in phonological awareness, depending on whether one has learnt an alphabetic or syllabic orthography, along with the ideographic have been documented (Share, 1995). It was also demonstrated that performance on phonological awareness tasks improved significantly in children after being exposed to alphabetic and syllabic scripts (Leong, 1997). However, the frequency of such errors in Hindi language is lesser as compared to those in English language, which could be due to the first language advantage.

Errors in writing pertained to difficulties in visuospatial analysis, spontaneous writing and inability to use phonetic cues. It has been reported that errors in writing include omissions, case confusion, mis-sequencing of letters, reversals, and substitutions (Berninger and Alsdorf, 1989). Hammill and McNutt (1981) observed that writing skills are among the best correlates of reading. According to them, writing skill include competence in writing, spelling, punctuation, capitalization and distinguishing one letter from another. Phonological processing appears to be the most affected process involved in reading. According to them writing skills include competence in writing, punctuation, spelling, capitalization and distinguishing one letter from another. These aspects of writing skills are related to the processes through which the child learns to read.

Error of guessing at words is closely linked to the difficulty in decoding the words phonologically. Due to the importance of phonological processing in word decoding, successive processes are naturally expected to be more important at this level. Similarly, Share (1995) suggested a "domain-general temporal processing dysfunction" in reading disabled children to account for inconsistencies in phonological processing literature. Working memory is directly related to phonological processing and syntactic awareness. The time taken for phonological decoding fades the memory for the earlier part of the sentence, which indicates the link between working memory and reading ability. The inability to engage in phonological coding has been suggested as the major cause of reading disability (Torgesen, Wagner and Rashotte, 1994).

Highest prevalence of language and writing related problems could be interrelated. Problems related to language pertain to the difficulties in second language acquisition, phonological awareness particularly with respect to English language. Such difficulties in language acquisition and dependence on phonological awareness relates to the problems observed in reading. Difficulties in learning to read relate to problems in writing. Problems related to reading seem to show a pattern of progressive decrease in higher standards, i.e. after 2nd standard whereas high frequency of reading problems were reported in 8th standards which could be a reflection of an intraction between language processing and visual processing.

It has been reported that orthographic processing is not as impaired in learning disabled as phonological processing in English language (Siegel, 1999). However, we have observed that orthographic processing is also affected along with phonological processing in Hindi language. The level at which correspondences between phonology and orthography are maximal could differ from one language to another. However, it is generally agreed that the relationships between varieties of phonological awareness and the ability to read words holds for various European languages such as German, Spanish, English and French despite some variation in the phonological input provided by different languages (Goswami, 1999). The specific deficits in phonological coding and visuospatial analysis observed on reading writing tests needs to be understood in terms of the status of cognitive processes mediating the interaction between language processing and visual processing.

Our preliminary observations on the nature of language, reading and writing errors showed that phonological decoding and visuospatial analysis is primarily affected in learning disability in both English and Hindi language, however, orthographic processing seems to be equally affected in Hindi language. There is a need to explore the mechanisms underlying the specific skills and cognitive components involved in reading particularly in Hindi language. Out of the 18 children identified as learning disabled 8 of them had severe writing difficulty and 10 children had both reading and writing disability. This figure is particularly alarming as these 18 children are continuing with their regular school education being promoted by the school authorities despite the specific learning disability without any realization of professional help required for them.

Implications

These findings hold enormous significance for the education of children in India, both in English and in Hindi language. For years there has been a standoff between the east and the west on the issue of learning disability. Easterners, including Indians, dismissed the issue of reading difficulties in children as the consequence of the vagaries of writing systems like English and French; while the westerners attributed the seemingly lower incidence of the developmental dyslexias in eastern countries to the lack of awareness and sensitivity among teachers who had to cope with large number of students in less than ideal conditions. We are now finding learning difficiency in Indian children, not only in English medium schools but also in the Hindi medium schools, laying to rest the claim, that learning difficiency was entirely due to the bizarre nature of opaque alphabetic scripts like English (Gupta, 2002, Suresh and Sebastian, 2003).

Increasingly with more research into language impairments and metalinguistic skills in particular, the nature of the language and script are gaining importance as possible contributory factors for our educational practices, particularly those concerning the teaching of reading as also those that concern the reading disabled need to be carefully thought out, planned and implemented. For education in English as the medium of instruction, the extensive research on and recognition of the importance of phonemic awareness, has now led to a series of assessment and remediation protocols and procedures; which with some modifications could perhaps be implemented for Indian children having difficulty in learning to read English. However, it needs to be acknowledged that for most of these children, English would still be a second language and the amount of input that the family can provide for language scaffolding needs to be considered. If our findings are substantiated further by empirical research, it is likely that we could guide parents into making informed choices on the medium of instruction, particularly for children with learning/reading difficulty rather than be influenced solely by perceived "Social status" of a given language.

We need, to recognize and capitalize on some of the inherent merits of our transparent alpha syllabic scripts and the tradition of rote learning, at least in the initial stages; as well as acknowledge the need to emphasize meaningful reading given the transparency of our writing systems once the child masters the syllabary. It is important that we recognize the differences in the environmental/social factors that operate in their context as against ours before we implement their recommendations in our conditions (as in the case of the "phonics" method of teaching).

Acknowledgements

The participation of the children and cooperation extended by the school authorities is deeply acknowledged.

REFERENCES

Barth, K., Steinbuchel, N.V., Wittman, M., Kappert, H. and Leyendecker, C. (1999), Temporal processing and its correlation to phonological awareness and to reading and writing efficiency. In Evelin Witruk and Thomas Lachmann (Eds.), *Abstracts of the international conference on basic mechanisms of language and language disorders,* 26-30. Leipziger Universitatsverlag.

Bashir, A.S., Wiig, E.H. and Abrams, J.C. (1987), Language disorders in childhood and adolescence: Implications for learning and socialization. *Pediatric Annals,* 16, 145-156.

Berninger, V.W. and Alsdorf, B. (1989), Are there errors in error analysis? Journal of *Psychoeducational Assessment,* 7, 209-222.

Bowey, J., Cain, M. and Ryan, S. (1992), A reading-level design study of phonological skills underlying fourth grade children's word reading difficulties. *Child Development,* 63, 999-1011.

Catts, H.W. (1989), Defining dyslexia as a developmental language disorder. *Annals of Dyslexia,* 39, 50-64.

Coordinated Campaign for Learning Disabilities (CCLD), (2003), LD—In Depth: Early Warning Signs of Learning Disabilities.

Das, J.P. and Mishra, R. (1991), The relationship between memory span, naming time, speech rate and reading competence. *Journal of Experimental Education,* 59, 129-139.

Das, J.P., Naglieri, J.A. and Kirby, J.R. (1994), *Assessment of Cognitive Processes,* Boston: Allyn and Bacon.

Goswami, U. (1999), The relationship between phonological awareness and orthographic representation in different orthographies. In M. Harris and G. Hatano (Eds.), *Leaning to read and write: A cross-linguistic perspective.* New York: Cambridge University Press.

Graham, S. and Harris, K.R. (1990), "Cognitive Strategy Instruction in Written Language for Learning Disabled Students." Unpublished manuscript.

Gupta, A. (2002), Developmental dyslexia in a bilingual child. *Journal of Personality and Clinical Studies,* 18, 19-26.

Harris, M. and Hatano, G. (1999), *Leaning to read and write: A cross-linguistic perspective.* New York: Cambridge University Press.

Hammill, D.D. and McNutt, G. (1981), Correlates of reading: The consensus of thirty years of correlational research. Austin, TX: Pro-Ed.

Kapur, M., John, A., Rozario, J. and Oommen, A. (2002), *NIMHANS index of specific learning disabilities.* In U. Hirisave, A. Oommen, and M. Kapur, Psychological assessment of children in the clinical setting. Bangalore: National Institute of Mental Health and Neurosciences (pp. 88-140).

Karanth, P. (2003), Introduction. In P. Karanth and Joe Rozario (Eds.) *Learning Disabilities in India: Willing the mind to learn.* New Delhi: Sage Publications, 17-29.

Karanth, P. and Prakash, P. (1996), A developmental investigation of onset, progress and stages of literacy acquisition—Its implications for instructional process. Unpublished project report, NCERT, New Delhi.

Lachman, T. (2002), Reading disability as deficit in functional coordination. In E. Witruk, A.D. Friederici and T. Lachman (Eds.), *Basic Functions of Language, Reading and Reading Disability,* 165-198. Netherlands: Kluver Academic Publishers.

Leong, C.K. (1997), Paradigmatic analysis of Chinese word reading: research findings and classroom practices. In C.K. Leong and R.M. Joshi (Eds.). *Cross-language studies of learning to read and spell-phonological and orthographic processing* Dordrecht: Kluwer.

Morais, J., Bertelson, P., Cary, L. and Alegria, J. (1986), Literacy Training and Speech Segmentation. *Cognition,* 24, 45-64.

Myklebust, H. (1954), *Auditory Disorders in Children: A manual for differential diagnosis.* New York: Grune and Stratton.

Orton, S. (1937), Reading, writing and speech problems in children. New York: Norton. As cited in A.G. Kamh, and H.W. Catts, (Eds.), 1989, *Reading disabilities: A developmental language perspective.* Allyn and Bacon: MA.

Prakash, P. (2003), Early Reading Acquisition. In P. Karanth and J. Rozario (eds.), *Learning disabilities in India: Willing the mind to learn.* New Delhi: Sage Publications, (pp. 63-75).

Prakash, P. and Rekha, B. (1992), Phonological awareness and reading acquisition in Kannada. In A.K. Srivastava (Ed.), *Researches in Child and adolescent psychology.* New Delhi: NCERT, Scarborough, 1990.

Prakash, P., Rekha, D., Nigam, R. and Karanth, P. (1993), Phonological Awareness, Orthography and Literacy. In R. Scholes (Ed). *Literacy and Language Analysis.* Lawrence Erlbaum Associates: New Jersey.

Prema, K.S. and Karanth, P. (2003), Assessment of Learning Disability: Language Based Tests. In P. Karanth and J. Rozario (Eds), *Learning Disability in India: Willing the mind to learn.* New Delhi: Sage.

Raven, J.C. (1998). *Coloured Progressive Matrices.* London: H.K. Lewis and Co. Ltd.

Raven, J.C. (2000). *Standard Progressive Matrices.* London: H.K. Lewis and Co. Ltd.

Scarborough, H.S. (1990). Very early language deficits in dyslexic children. *Child Development,* 61, 1728-1743.

Share, D.L. and Stanovich, K.E. (1995). Cognitive processes in early reading development: Accommodating individual differences into a model of acquisition. Issues in *Education,* 1, 1-57.

Shaywitz, S.E. (1996). Learning disability. Scientific American. November, 98-104.

Siegel, L.S. (1999). The Cognitive Components of Learning Disability. In Evelin Witruk and Thomas Lachmann (Eds.), *Abstracts of the International Conference on Basic Mechanisms of Language and Language Disorders,* September 26-30. Leipziger Universitatsverlag.

Suresh P.A. and Sebastian, S. (2003). Epidemiological and neurological aspects of learning disabilities. In P. Karanth and J. Rozario (eds.) *Learning Disabilities in India: Whilling the Mind to Learn.* New Delhi: Sage Publications, (pp. 30-43).

Torgesen, J. and Houck, G. (1980). Processing deficiencies in learning disabled children who perform poorly on the digit span task. *Journal of Educational Psychology,* 72, 141-160.

Torgesen, J.K., Wagner, R.K. and Rashotte C.A. (1994). Longitudinal studies of phonological processing and reading. *Journal of Learning Disabilities,* 27: 276-86.

Torgesen, J. (1995). Instructions for reading disabled children: Questions about knowledge and practice. *Issues in Education: Contributions from Educational Psychology,* 1, 91-96.

Tripathi, N. and Kar, B.R. (2003). Teachers' Perception of Learning Related Problems in Children in school setting in Allahabad City. (Accepted)

Van, K.A. (1994). Metalinguistic Development. In E. Wallach and K.G. Butler (Eds.), *Language Learning Disabilities in School-Age Children and Adolescents.* Second edition, Merrill/MacMillan: New York.

18

Understanding Community Health Intervention

Shikha Dixit

In recent years health psychology has become a broad based and expanded area of research. Traditionally, health psychology followed the positivistic paradigm in order to understand the behaviours and attitudes of individuals in health and illness conditions. The focus has been on the study of cognitions and behaviours of individuals facing different types of illnesses. In essence, the individual and his reactions to states of body that are understood in biomedical terms have been the mainstay of health psychology. Such an individuation has led to the neglect of group-based social and cultural notions in understanding health and illness. However, it is now well accepted that social and cultural dimensions cannot be separated from the individual cognitions. Human behaviour in the context of health and illness has to be understood as rooted in social, cultural and historical background. The mechanistic model of man is insufficient to understand health and illness behaviours in a dialectic relationship with the social and cultural factors. As noted by Joffe (2002):

> …'health' is a highly social, emotive and symbolic entity. Consequently, theories and methods appropriate to the specific qualities of this entity must be used in health psychology. Social, emotive and symbolic facets are best captured by an approach concerned with the meanings people make in non-artificial response situations. In order to pursue these concerns, English-language health related psychological work has often

> turned to an approach that originated in France: social representations theory (SRT). (p. 560)

The social and cultural aspects of health can be understood through an analysis of collective community level representations. Understanding health and illness at the community level is important for formulation of community health care systems. For effective community level intervention it is imperative to understand shared beliefs and cognitions regarding health related phenomena. Such beliefs and cognitions form the basis of health related lay knowledge at the group or community level. The main objective of the present paper is to explore health intervention issues at the community level. The present paper is an attempt to understand the impediments that might surface in community development and intervention. The paper proposes that many such impediments might be rooted in shared cultural codes or social representations pertaining to health related aspects. It is proposed that in order to understand and study the ever-expanding issues in health psychology, a culturally sensitive approach is required. The paper explores Moscovici's social representations approach in this regard. Social representations are closely linked to cultural practices and identities of communities. Understanding of social representations can lead to addressing of some pertinent issues in intervention among communities. The present paper discusses some of the issues that can be addressed through a study of social representations of health among any community and links these issues to intervention and community development context.

Health Intervention, Culture and Community

It is important to note that an intervention and community development programme on health and illness cannot isolate the biomedical conditions of the community from the social and cultural context. As noted by Morant (1998), health "is a social and cultural notion which relates to the collective practices and identities of communities, and its social construction reveals much about a society's fundamental beliefs concerning what is meant to be human" (p. 633). This conceptualisation of health is the basis of the arguments developed in the present paper. Since this paper seeks to understand the deeper nuances and issues of community intervention, it is important to understand what we mean by a community. As noted by Howarth, Foster and Dorrer (2004), "By 'community', it is necessary to explain, we mean the socially constructed spaces within which people develop common codes for understanding, confronting, and identifying with one another. These codes, or representations, permeate social relationships, cultural practices and power relations" (p. 230).

The above notions of health and community are well suited to understand the issues of community intervention in urban, rural, tribal and other settings as well. The social and cultural roots of health related beliefs among any community should be understood in-depth, so that an effective intervention can be planned. In this context the following points are important:

1. Shared codes of health related meanings and practices should be explored for understanding the complex linkages of health representations to social relationships, cultural practices and power structure.
2. Urban communities are in a state of constant flux and change. Even rural and tribal cultures cannot be conceived of as static, primitive and lacking dynamism. It is, therefore, important to understand the dynamic forces that influence conceptualisations of health and illness in communities. Sahu (1991) notes that culture of a community has a direct influence on its health culture. Since most cultures are generally in some state of transition and change because of dynamism in social institutions, their health culture cannot be understood as static.
3. The health cultures of most communities might be anchored in traditional and folk beliefs regarding treatment patterns and medicine and yet be influenced by modern medical practice. Folk concepts of etiology of illness may co-exist with other incompatible modern representations.
4. Social scientists who emphasize the socio-cultural context of health and treat it as a historically situated construct, distinguish the social representations of health from the biomedical model. The biomedical model is more concerned with disease and illness rather than health. As mentioned by

Weitz (2001), the biomedical model views illness as a deviation from the normal state; as having universal and specific meaning; as caused by unique biological factors; as being similar to breakdown of a machine and as amenable to unambiguous biological definition and something that can be cured through scientific medical procedures. Thus, the biomedical model is inadequate to understand the cultural and lay conceptualisation of health and illness. According to Farr (1993), before formulating a health intervention campaign there is a need to explore the lay conceptions of the community.

At this juncture it is important to note that individuals in groups are not passive processors of information but constantly thinking autonomous entities, producing social representations through communication and interaction. In this process the contemporary version of common sense or lay knowledge is formulated (Moscovici, 1981).

The Social Representations Approach

An exploration of the above stated aspects of health culture of communities might provide a baseline from where health interventions can take-off. In order to understand the health culture and representations of health, shared or social representations need to be explored before designing any intervention. The social representations approach offers a useful paradigm for understanding shared codes and addressing many intervention related issues. The present paper posits that community interventions pertaining to health and illness issues should be informed through social representations of phenomena of interest. According to Moscovoci (1981) social representations originate through the processes of inter-individual interaction in everyday life. He has conceptualised social representations as ideas, concepts, statements and explanations that refer to the contemporary view of common sense. This common sense social knowledge can be equated with the myths and belief systems of traditional societies. The dynamic nature of social reality requires reconstitution of everyday common knowledge.

The following features noted by Augoustinos and Walker (1995) form the basis of any definition of social representations: Social representations are consensual universes of thought that are created through interactive processes in a collectivity. Social representations are like theories that create the repertoire of common knowledge. This commonsense is basic to construction of meaning and social reality and is structured around both, images and concepts. Social representations are different from Durkheim's collective representations. Collective representations are static, hegemonic and relevant to traditional and primitive societies. Social representations are plastic and dynamic and are characteristic of a society where the social, political and scientific patterns are in a state of change. The two main features of Moscovici's theory are: A distinction between consensual and reified universes and the conceptualisation of the processes that generate social representations.

At this juncture it should be noted that the present paper does not aim to provide a detailed review of the social representations approach. From this point onwards the paper seeks to discuss those aspects of social representations approach that are relevant for understanding the health related issues in the context of community intervention. Further, the paper will also discuss a study in the Indian context among the Bondo tribe of Orissa (Mishra, 2006; Sharma, Dixit, and Mishra, 2007) in order to explicate the discussion.

Social Representations: Insights for Community Intervention

The following section provides a discussion on certain aspects of the social representations framework relevant to community development and intervention. Some of these aspects have been discussed by Howarth, Foster and Dorrer (2004) in the context of research done on mental illness and women's representations of healthy eating. Howarth *et al.* (2004) have discussed the role of competing knowledge systems, maintenance of stigma through the operation of social representations and the influence of identity on social representations in the context of community-based health research. The points discussed below in this section explore the inputs and insights that a study of social representations of health can provide for the purpose of intervention.

Expert and Lay Knowledge Systems

The social representations approach makes a distinction between two knowledge worlds. The consensual world is the world of everyday knowledge whereas the reified universe is the world of expert scientific knowledge. Commonsense knowledge forms the basis of social representations. Common people construct and use representations to make sense of reality. In the area of health, the reified world of bio-medical knowledge might get interpreted, simplified and transformed into the consensual universe pertaining to common beliefs about health and illness conditions and related questions. Reified complex ideas that originate in medical science and scientific discourse might provide inputs to the collective knowledge base of images and concepts. Such knowledge may be simplified but culturally meaningful. This knowledge in turn composes the lay knowledge of common people.

It is proposed that for designing an effective intervention programme lay social representations should be studied and considered. This step is important to understand the hierarchy and heterogeneity of knowledge regarding a particular issue in a community. The view of the health service providers may be dominated by the expert and reified bio-medical norms. Such a view may hold the indigenous forms of illness representations and treatment patterns as detrimental to intervention. Such locally embedded knowledge might be treated as irrelevant and inferior. This would create a schism between the health administrators and the laypeople. Such differences might lead to the failure of even a well-designed intervention. Howarth *et al.* (2004) have discussed the problem of competing knowledge systems of the professional and the client. The impact of such competition can be disastrous for community development. For example, in a rural or tribal setting the problem could become compounded as the tribal people or villagers, especially in very remote areas, may not consider the biomedical view of the doctors and health professional as an expert view. For them the view of the local healers could denote expertise. Due to the impact of media and other sources the notions of modern medicine could be known to people and perhaps acceptable in some cases but the local and the professional knowledge systems may be in a constant conflict. These may lead to decision dilemmas among the locals. It is, therefore, mandatory to understand both the local or lay social representations as well as the professional social representations in order to address the issues of knowledge related power and ensure active and successful participation in intervention, both at the lay and the expert level.

Regarding differences in knowledge systems, Howarth *et al.* (2004) have noted that community psychology approach does not favour one form of knowledge over other. As noted by Howarth *et al.*, social representations approach does not view the differences between expert and lay knowledge 'as deficiencies' or 'biased thought'. In this way both community psychology and social representations approach offer similar perspectives. Implications of the differences between lay and expert knowledge systems in the area of eating disorders have been discussed by Howarth *et al.* They have noted that lay representations are often neglected in health promotion programmes. Generally, these programmes focus on healthy eating as the best life style strategy. Since healthy eating is a matter of individual choice in mainstream professional practice, eating disorders carry an implication of less responsible eating behaviour. The individual at risk is blamed for making a wrong choice. Victims are not required to express their own representations and as a result they feel restricted, which in turn blocks their active participation in a health promotion programmes. In this connection Howarth *et al.* have noted that, "If health promotions are to be effective then the socially and dialogically constituted nature of competing knowledge systems needs to be recognized" (p. 234).

Relationship between Cognition and Culture

An understanding of the sense-making processes regarding health and illness conditions in terms of local cultural realities is paramount to intervention and policy decisions. Illness can be understood as a social construction. Biological entities such as bacteria and viruses exist and result in illness but people may construct the meaning of illness in terms of entities other than biological. Culture provides a normative standard for decision-making and ways of behaving and is an important basis for defining and maintaining health as well as making treatment choices (McElroy and Jezewski, 2001). Jezewski

(1990) defined culture "as a shared system of learned and shared codes or standards for perceiving, interpreting and interacting with others and with the environment" (as cited in McElroy and Jezewski, 2001, p.191). The idea that perception and interpretation involve a shared system of codes, brings us to the question of how the cognitive processes of perception, interpretation and sense-making are linked to shared codes. The focus of mainsteam health psychology has been to understand the health related behaviours of the individual. The individual is studied as an information processor operating in a detached manner and devoid of all social and historical contexts. Illness cognitions and individual perceptions have been the mainstay of such an approach. However, such an approach separates the individual from the social context. Social representations approach provides a framework for understanding health related cognitions as embedded within the local cultural reality. This implies that meaning assignment to any aspect of health and illness is a process that is socially and culturally informed. The processes of anchoring and objectification, as conceptualised in the social representations approach, provide ways in which this meaning assignment takes place. As noted by Joffe (2002), "These processes ensure that the core values and norms of the society get stamped on to new events and drive the mutations that occur as knowledge circulates in a society" (p. 564). The process of anchoring utilizes known and familiar reference points and categories to understand the new and the unfamiliar. Anchoring involves categorizing and naming the unfamiliar. An unfamiliar idea turns into realty through the process of objectification. Objectification refers to the process through which an ambiguous and abstract idea acquires an iconic quality. Anchoring is a social equivalent of the basic cognitive activity of categorization whereas objectification is closer to the process of symbolization (Joffe, 2002).

The processes of anchoring and objectification are important in understanding the meaning given to health related phenomena at the collective level of the community. Such meanings are not purely cognitive but are complex manifestations of the interplay among political, cultural and emotional aspects. Thus any intervention programme can realistically meet the needs of a community if the first step involves the effort to understand the ways in which a community understands the unfamiliar aspects of illness *via* familiar culturally shared categories.

Multiple Representations and Cognitive Polyphasia

Bhasin (2003) has demonstrated that among tribals of Rajasthan the traditional as well as the biomedical practices coexist. For a harmonious balance between the two systems it is imperative to understand the associated social representations. This can provide insights as to how the traditional system can be used by health adminintrators for the benefit of the community. As noted by Bhasin (2003):

> Although certain illnesses such as evil eye are thought to be cured only by indigenous healers, this does not preclude the use of biomedicine to treat the symptoms. Gonzales (1966) reports that in Guatemalan, the symptoms are treated with biomedicine, while the cause of illness is dealt with through a folk specialist. Traditional theories of illness etiology are often multifactorial and multilevel (i.e. immediate and ultimate levels of causation) which permits the use of different treatment resources for different causal factors and levels (Cosminsky, 1977). (p. 81)

The above cited work is not within the social representations framework but it demonstrates that in a tribal community, traditional and contemporary biomedical meanings of illness causation and treatment might co-exist. This might be true not only in the case of a tribal community but also a rural, semi-rural or urban community. Such a situation creates a scenario where multiple meanings and interpretations of the same phenomenon need to be explored for any intervention. An assumption regarding homogeneous meanings on the part of health care providers might render an intervention system ineffective. Multiple meanings may not always have a harmonious existence. The first step to any intervention should be to check for incompatible meanings existing simultaneously. As noted by Wagner, Duveen, Verma and Themel (2000):

> Issues of community and health are tightly linked to local cultures and to the system of traditional representations about health and illness. These systems, however, are rarely static

> but in constant flux through economic and technological developments...In this process the novel often plays the role of an icon of modernity in situations that evoke the idea of progress, while the traditional prevails in more static social structures such as the family. This co-existence of rarely compatible representations is called cognitive polyphasia. (p. 301)

The above discussion clearly portrays the need for an exploration of social representations of health related phenomena in order to understand cognitive polyphasia. Since cognitive polyphasia is a reflection of the pattern of change and dynamism within a community (Wagner *et al.*, 2000), it can be effectively utilized by health planners for assessment of health culture of a community. In a study conducted to investigate the social representations of madness in North India by Wagner, Duveen, Themel and Verma (1999) it was demonstrated that the representational systems of traditional and modern thinking were situated social representations. The two different representational systems were expressed in different contexts. The modern system was linked to public life whereas the traditional to family context. The study also demonstrated that social representations are flexible and dynamic. Thus, the interaction of traditional and modern representational systems provides and understanding of forces and contexts of change in health related cultural beliefs. Cognitive polyphasia and situated nature of social representations might provide important inputs to health planners. The situated representational systems and cognitive polyphasia could be understood through a study of anchoring and objectification of the phenomenon of interest.

Social Representations of Health and Identity

Social groups and communities utilize social representations to define and maintain their group identity. Howarth *et al.* (2004) have discussed the identity function of social representations in the context of health and illness. As noted by Howarth *et al.*, identity is an important aspect of the social representations framework. An understanding of identity provides us with cues as to how and why people use health representations to obtain different goals. Social representations form the basis of communication processes as well as understanding the differences with other communities. One important function of social representations is to position us with reference to common identities of our groups. Such positioning may serve various identity functions. The social representations approach offers a framework through which it is possible to understand people's collective reactions to others' negative representations of their groups. The process of making sense of health and illness related phenomena within everyday context provides a possibility for 'critique and transformation' (Howarth *et al.*, 2004, p. 237) of social representations of health. People may resist dominant representations and negotiate those alternative social representations that foster and facilitate positive group identities (Duveen, 2001).

The dominant representations rooted in biomedical discourse might sometimes stigmatize health practices of communities who face health challenges. If the health care professionals and administrators hold the dominant representations then they might face resistance from target communities. Because of the dichotomy of traditional *versus* scientific, such a situation is likely to arise in rural and tribal contexts. It is, therefore, important that interventions takes into account the impact of health related meanings and practices on group identity. In recent years social science scholars are not interested in the biological underpinnings of the disease *per se* but with sense-making of the states of health and illness and the conflicts and decision dilemmas that people face during illness (Radley, 2004). Therefore, an understanding of the sense-making processes regarding health and illness conditions in terms of local cultural realities is paramount to intervention and policy decisions.

A Case in Point

This section of the paper will briefly discuss a study of social representations of health and illness done on Bondo tribe of Orissa. The study reported here was part of a larger study on conceptualisation of health and illness among Bondos (Mishra, 2006). The study in question was one section of a doctoral dissertation and the author of this paper was one of the supervisors. The fieldwork and data-collection was solely done by the concerned research scholar. Some aspects of the larger study were also developed as a conference paper (Sharma, Dixit, and Mishra, 2007). The present paper draws attention on some general findings of the larger study and the above-mentioned conference paper and attempts to interpret them in the context of community intervention. Using Moscovici's approach to social representations the study demonstrated that lay conceptualisations of health and illness among Bondos were dynamic and closely associated to their socio-economic conditions and environment. Data was collected from three groups of Bondos: Upper Bondos who are most isolated; middle Bondos who are in the process of transition; and lower Bondos who are living among non-tribals. The Upper Bondos live in the hills and do not have much contact with outsiders. The middle Bondos live at a lower height and have some interaction with outsiders as accessibility to their habitations is better than that of upper Bondos. They are relatively less isolated and some of these people have acquired formal education in the local school. The lower Bondos are settled in the plains and are assimilated with the general population of the plains. In general, the lower Bondos are closer to modern influence. The Bondos in the hills are very close to their tribal identity and have strong beliefs in their traditional customs and cultural norms. They can be regarded as a closed community.

The important findings of the study are discussed very briefly in the following section. The findings reported here are not exhaustive. Only some of the findings are noted here in order to showcase those aspects of social representations of health and illness in the Bondo community that provide credence to the theoretical arguments presented in this paper. The following findings are important in the context of the present paper:

1. For Bondos the social representations of health were anchored in several cultural concepts of good life. Accordingly, health was conceptualised as ability to work and the absence of illness. The meaning of illness was anchored as no desire to work, a state of unhappiness, lack of appetite, facial expressions of looking ill, disturbance of sleep and feeling of weakness. It may be noted that the idea of disease among the Bondos was not same as among the medical experts. Certain diseases, for example, fever, body-ache, cold and cough were understood as normal state of affairs among upper Bondos. Perception of health was influenced by specific beliefs that were related to consequences of ill health.

2. On the basis of the analysis, certain categories of meaning pertaining to the concept of illness emerged. Absence of illness was not understood as an absence of disease. The concept of illness was closely related to effects of evil eye and evil spirit. The belief regarding influence and intrusion of external elements (evil eye and evil spirit) on the human body was common among the upper Bondos and the middle Bondos. The lower Bondos believe less in evil eye but maintain the belief in the intrusion of the evil spirit. Thus, the concept of health was closely associated with absence of influence of external factors on body.
3. The Bondos, especially the upper Bondos have labour intensive life style. They thus require to be physically fit for everyday functioning and daily activities. Ill health interferes with the effective performance of social roles. No difference in response was observed between men and women regarding the notion of the ability to work. But a notable difference was observed when data was compared between men and women of the plains and the hills. Physical labour does not have equal dimensions in these two contexts. A strong linkage between work and the concept of health prevails among women respondents in Bondo hills as compared to the plains. According to men in the hills, ill health made them so weak that they could not drink the local liquor and indulge in other leisure activities. On the other hand, according to women in the hills, illness resulted in loss of strength and in turn negatively influenced their work in the agricultural fields and prevented them from carrying out other chores such as collecting wood from forest, fetching water from the stream and collecting fruits. The differences in responses of men and women can be ascribed to their social roles. Women in this community are expected to manage the family as well as the economic activities. Women are older than their husbands and after marriage the woman has to take care of the young husband. Even when the husband becomes an adult the woman continues to take all responsibility.
4. Women in the plains gave more importance to domestic work. The reason for such change in priority of work in the plains

can be traced to the influence of the mainstream society, which limits the role of women to domestic chores. Women respondents in the plains felt that illness hampers their domestic work.

5. Men of the hills and men of the plains maintained different perceptions on nature of work. Men from the highland stated that they did not work in the fields as much as the womenfolk and that they spent their time in drinking and gossiping. On the contrary, men of the plains stated that they worked in the field and earned for the family. Women in the plains assisted men in some specific tasks such as sowing and harvesting. Differences in work roles were reflected in the conceptualisation of health and illness.
6. The study revealed that the need for livelihood induces the Bondos to maintain their physical strength and health, which is indispensable for the struggle for existence. The conceptualisation of health was thus associated with physical capability and functional fitness. A person who could perform daily chores important for livelihood was defined as healthy. Meaning of health was thus contextual, which emerged from practical experience and socio-cultural factors.
7. The belief in evil eye was common among the Bondos of the hills. Evil eye was considered as a major cause of illness. An envious or jealous person casts it. Illnesses such as giddiness and body-ache were ascribed to the effect of evil eye. Lower Bondos who believe in evil spirits and *biru* (a ritualistic healing practice) did not identify evil eye as the major cause of illness. But evil eye was perceived to be the cause of financial loss, breaking of marriage and sudden death or accidents. Interaction with the mainstream society, and influence of non-tribes could be the reasons for the change in health related beliefs pertaining to evil eye. It can be inferred that the belief in evil eye might serve as a regulatory force in social life of Bondos.
8. Health was perceived as an endogenous concept whereas illness as an exogenous concept among Bondos of the hills. Health was conceptualised as a natural internal state of a person whereas illness was seen as a consequence of the possession

by an evil spirit or casting of evil eye. A conflict between self and evil spirit emerged as a perceived cause of illness. This was demonstrated by beliefs such as: When ill and weak people cross the village boundary and the hills, the evil spirits possess them and lead them to death. Bondos in the plains believed that children fall ill when they eat in front of strangers. In general, Bondos attributed illness condition to external forces.

9. The Bondos also identified violation of social norms as a cause of illness. Such beliefs were common among Bondos from the hills. They believed that violation of norms and rules invites the wrath of supernatural powers. It is interesting to note that social violations such as criminal offence and adultery were not considered as violations causing ill health. The illness causing violations were generally related to ritualistic practices in different contexts. For example, eating paddy or *suan* (a type of grain) before offering it to the Gods, eating medicine during the *bent parab* (hunting festival) or eating mangoes before *chaita parab* (a certain festival).

Overall, the findings stated above are in line with the major ideas presented in the previous sections of this paper. These findings clearly demonstrate the linkages between culture of a community and conceptualisation of health and illness. Health culture to a large extent grows out of the traditions and cultural practices in a community. It is, therefore, important to study the social representations in a community in order to develop effective intervention practices. In order to understand the health related cognitions of people, it is important to understand the cultural embedding of such cognitions.

While the upper Bondos demonstrated beliefs in evil eye, evil spirit and magic, the social representations of health among the lower Bondos were more in line with the representations among the non-tribals and medical experts. The social representations of upper and middle Bondos were more identity protective. Lower Bondos demonstrated an existence of cognitive polyphasia. Belief in evil spirits and ritualistic healing existed together with belief in biomedical practice, and this could be due to the state of transition. Any intervention therefore needs to take into account the fine balance between the opposing belief systems. Although social representations of health are a source of dynamism in the community leading to more openness and change, they also result in identity related resilience that leads to maintenance of traditional beliefs. Social representations not only present the outcome of the complex processes of change, they themselves have a bearing on the diversity and social change. In some contexts they may play 'identity protective' and 'system justifying' role (Joffe and Bettega, 2003).

The social representations of health and illness emerged as consensual categories of meanings that were utilized by different Bondo groups to make sense of conditions of health and illness. These categories reflected the dynamic and changing nature of representations. The health culture of the Bondo community is in a state of transition due to interaction with mainstream society. The dynamism in the Bondo community can be understood using the social representations framework. Durkheim's notion of collective representations is not applicable because of its emphasis on static representations. Social representations might also orient action and therefore form a basis for understanding health choices and treatment preferences as well as other health related behaviours.

Social representations theory postulates that common knowledge originates in the world of science. However, it may not always be possible to locate social representations in the scientific or expert domain. This is especially true of tribal and rural groups who do not have access to common scientific discourse. The results of the study suggested that anchoring and objectification of health beliefs arise from consensual universe. The consensual universe for Bondos is mainly the universe of their traditional practices. However, the consensual universe interacts with the reified universe in the case of lower Bondos and results in cognitive polyphasia. Overall, the representations of health and illness among Bondos can be located in the culture, tradition, history and forces of transition. The processes of anchoring and objectification as conceived in the theory of social representations are of great significance in the present context since these processes enable the researcher to locate the social representations of health and illness in the tribal culture.

The above discussion provides evidence for the theoretical aspects of social representations theory presented in this paper in the context of community development and intervention. The content of anchoring and objectification, cognitive polyphasia, identity protective function of social representations, impact of interaction with mainstream society on social change and an identification of forces of resilience and change in social representations are all important in understanding the issues of community development and designing of intervention programmes.

Conclusion

Culture provides a normative standard for decisions and ways of behaving and is an important basis for defining and maintaining health as well as making treatment choices. Thus to develop an effective system of health delivery among communities, there is a need to examine the confluence of professional, popular and folk cultures. The paper demonstrated the importance of studying social representations for insights regarding community development and intervention. Approaching community level intervention from a purely expert or scientific perspective may lead to rejection of the programme by the target community. The identity protective functions of social representations might even become more rigid if the intervention is perceived as a threat to common beliefs and cultural practices. It should be added at this point that in addition to studying the social representations of the target community for whom the health delivery system has to be developed, the social representations of the various stakeholders such as health administrators, financial institutions, health professionals and grassroots workers should also be explored. Such an exploration will lead to understanding the schism between professional and locals and provide directions for design of effective health programmes.

REFERENCES

Augoustinos, M., and Walker, I. (1995). *Social Cognition: An integrated introduction*. Sage: London.

Bhasin, V. (2003). Sickness and therapy among tribals of Rajasthan. *Studies of Tribes and Tribals, 1* (1): 77-83.

Duveen, G.M. (2001). Representations, identities, resistance. In K. Deaux and G. Philogene (Eds.), *Representations of the Social: Bridging Theoretical Traditions* (pp. 257-270). Oxford: Blackwell.

Farr, R.M. (1993). Theory and method in the study of social representations. In D. Canter and G. Breakwell (Eds.), *Empirical Approaches to Social Representations* (pp. 15-88). Oxford: Clarendon Press.

Howarth, C., Foster, J., and Dorrer, N. (2004). Exploring the potential of the theory of social representations in community-based health research and vice versa? *Journal of Health Psychology, 9* (2), 229-243.

Joffe, H. (2002). Social representations and health psychology. *Social Science Information, 41* (4), 559-580.

Joffe, H., and Bettega, N. (2003). Social representations of AIDS among Zambian Adolescents. *Journal of Health Psychology, 8* (5), 616-631.

McElroy, A. and Jezewski, M.A. (2001). Cultural variation in the experience of health and illness. In G. L. Albrecht, R. Fitzpatrick, and S. C. Scrimshaw (Eds.), *The handbook of social studies in health and medicine* (pp. 191-209). Sage: London.

Mishra, M. (2006). *Conceptualization of health and illness among the Bondos in Orissa.* Doctoral dissertation submitted to Indian Institute of Technology Kanpur, Kanpur, India.

Morant, N. (1998) Representations, communities and health. *Social Science Information, 37* (4), 633-637.

Moscovici, S. (1981). On social representations. In J. P. Forgas (Ed.), *Social Cognition: Perspectives on Everyday Understanding* (pp. 181-209). Academic Press: London.

Radley, A. (2004). *Making sense of illness: The social psychology of health and disease.* Sage Publications: London.

Sahu, S.K. (1991). *Health Culture in Transition.* Khama Publishers: New Delhi.

Sharma, A.K., Dixit, S., and Mishra, A. (2007). *Social representations of health and illness among the Bondos: Sources of resilience and change in the community.* Paper presented in National Seminar on Population and Health Status in Orissa. Organized by P.G. Department of Population Studies, F.M. University, Balasore.

Wagner, W., Duveen, G., Themel, M. and Verma, J. (1999). The modernization of Tradition: Thinking about madness in Patna, India. *Culture and Psychology, 5* (4), 413-445.

Wagner, W., Duveen, G., Verma, J., and Themel, M. (2000). "I have some faith and at the same time I don't believe"—Cognitive Polyphasia and Cultural Change. *Journal of Community and Applied Social Psychology, 10*, 301-314.

Weitz, R. (2001). *The sociology of health, illness and health care: A critical approach.* Wadsworth/Thomson Learning: Belmont, CA. USA.

19

Developmental Impact of Physical Condition and Family Type on Familial Relations

Shradha Joshi and *Aradhana Shukla*

Orthopaedic disabilities are also known as locomotor disabilities or physical disabilities and health impairments. The term Orthopaedic is related to a physical deformity or disability of the skeletal system and associated with motor function (Dutch, Smith and Luckasson 1992). A child with a physical disability has a problem with the structure or functioning of the body. A child with health impairment has a limitation on the body's physical well-being that requires on going medical attention. Berdine and Blackhurst (1985) defined Orthopaedic children as those whose physical or health problem results in an impairment of normal interaction with society to the extent that specialized services and programmers are required. Hallahan and Kauffman (1991) defined such children with disabilities as those whose non-sensory physical limitations or health problem interfere school attendance or learning to such an extent that special services, training, equipment, materials, or facilities are required.

The individuals with Disabilities Act (Idea-1977) USA, provides a definition of Orthopaedic disabilities as an impairment, which adversely affects a child's educational performance. This term includes impairments caused by cogenital anomaly (e.g. clubfoot, absence of a limb etc., impairments caused by disease (e.g. poliomyelitis, bone tuberculosis, etc.) and impairments from other causes (e.g. cerebral palsy, amputations, and burns which causes contracture).

The PWA Act 1996 refers to Orthopaedic disability as locomotor disability and defines it as disability of bones, joints or muscles leading to substantial restriction of the movement of the limbs or any form of cerebral palsy.

Orthopaedic disabilities can broadly be categorized into four sets each including a number of impairments. They are:

1. **Neurological impairement**
   (i) Cerebral palsy
   (ii) Epilepsy
   (iii) Spina Bifida
2. **Masculoskeletal Condition**
   (i) Osteogenesis imperfeeta
   (ii) Tuberculosis of Bones and Joints
3. **Congenital Malformations**
   (i) Common Malformations
   (ii) Malformation due to teratogens

Causes of Orthopaedic disability are as follows:

- Poor nutrition during pregnancy. Babies born prematurely or severely underweight may often have cerebral palsy and other disabilities.
- Genetic factors.
- Infectious disease such as diarrhoea can lead to dehydration, high fever and sometimes brain damage resulting in fits or cerebral palsy.
- Poor sanitation and crowded living conditions together with poor food make disease such as tuberculosis and the other severe disabilities.
- Lack of immunization against diseases such as polio, rubella etc.
- Birth defects and mental retardation on account of inappropriate medicines during pregnancy.
- Accidents resulting in loss of limbs, blindness and other disabilities.
- Leprosy infection.
- Disability caused by poisons in food, water, air or work place. Pesticides particularly can cause serious damage, e.g. fluoride poisoning mainly from drinking water can cause bone damage.
- Ageing.

Concept of Family Environment

Three terms have been used in respect to the type and quality of environment prevailing in home. These are authoritarian, democratic and permissive; these terms have been used in relation to both home and school environments and defined in behavioural terms by different authors. Platt *et al.* (1962) state that authoritarian control is employed by parents. This continuum stems from parents who are restrictive and coercive, permitting the child little freedom or limit the range of activity, to the parents who are lax and ineffectual and unable to control the child. Between those two extremes are the parents who allow the child freedom but who is capable of asserting when and where desired. According to Shah (1982), Authoritarian parents rely too heavily on one's means to enforce obedience. For this purpose they use many repressive restraints. They hold a strong concentration that child must obey and that it is the responsibility of parents to mark children to obey their parents. Authoritarian parents take advantage of child's weakness to secure complaints even subservience.

Maslow (1941) in contrast stated that "A good home is said to be one in which the child is given fullest opportunity for self-expression within the limits of parental affection and supervision". Malm (1952) characterized, "A home with affection; democracy, lack of conflict; comradeship; good personal adjustment, security and appropriateness of attitude: Douvan and Adelison (1966), defined a democratic family as one, "in which the child is allowed a fair degree of autonomy; is included in important discussion massing and is controlled primarily by reasoning and verbal discipline." On the other hand an authoritarian family is that in which rules are made and implemented without consulting the children, autonomy is limited and discipline is predominant by physical punishment.

According to Cronbach (1977) "home differs in many respects warmth encouragement of independence, pressure for achievement and so on. Warm parents express their own love and encourage the child to express his feeling and family members react to each other on emotional level. Other extreme is hostile rejection. The parents dislike children and are continuously critical and punitive. In some homes the child has little influence and freedom while other homes are often caused by democratic practices. Here, policies are worked out between parent and child or explained carefully." Danesh (1978) pointed out, "authoritarian families are power oriented, tend to have dichotomous conceptions, have emotional and intellectual rigidity. In contrast democratic homes bow to the whims of the child."

Keeping these views in consideration this study was planned in four-way factorial design and aimed to ascertain the pattern of familial culture of Orthopaedically disabled and non-disabled young participants as affected by their age, types of physical condition, types of residential setting and family.The hypotheses were as follows:

- Variation in age would cause variation in familial culture.
- Variation in physical condition would cause variation in familial culture.
- Variation in residential type would cause variation in familial culture.
- Variation in family type would cause variation in familial culture.

Method

Sample

One hundred and sixty participants ranging between 10-16 years served as participants and they were arranged according to the requirements of 2*2*2*2 factorial design with 2 levels of age (10-12 and 13-15 yrs), 2 levels of physical condition (Orthopaedically disabled and non-disabled), 2 residential settings (urban and rural) and types of family (joint and nuclear), i.e. 10 participants were placed in each cell.

Measure

In this measure only one tool was employed and it is mentioned below:

Family Environment Scale (FES). It was constructed and standardized by Vohra. It is a scale having 98 items which can be answered in Yes/No form. It consists of seven areas which are considered as most important dimension in order to access the environment of any family. The dimensions are Competitive Framework, Cohesion, Expression, Independence, Moral Orientation, Organization and Recreational Orientation.

Data collection was done individually and best attempts were made to avoid the external distractions.

Table 19.1: Experimental Design used in the Study

	A							
	A1 B				A2 B			
	B1 C		B2 C		B1 C		B2 C	
	C1	C2	C1	C2	C1	C2	C1	C2
D1	10	10	10	10	10	10	10	10
D								
D2	10	10	10	10	10	10	10	10

Legends
A = Levels of Chronological Age
A1 = 10-12 years
A2 = 13-15 years
B = Levels of Physical Condition
B1 = Orthopaedically Disabled
B2 = Non-Disabled
C = Types of Residential Setting
C1 = Urban
C2 = Rural
D = Types of Family
D1 = Joint
D2 = Nuclear

Result

Obtained results were analyzed by four way analysis of variance and interpreted in terms of chronological age, physical condition, residential settings and family type as the effectors of familial culture. Findings are given in Table 19.2.

A close perusal of Table 19.2 (i) reveals that the main effects of chronological age was insignificant (F, 1,144 = 1.17 $P > .05$). Mean values of older (X = 124.89) and younger (X = 133.48) children revealed nominal difference. The next main effect of physical condition was significant (F, 1,144 = 5.42 $P < 0.01$) and it revealed that the disabled children felt more distortion (X = 120.01) as compared to their non-disabled (X = 131.01) counterparts. The third main effect of residential settings revealed its significance (F, 1,144 = 5.46 P < 0.01). It was that urban participants felt less distractions (X = 143.66) rather than rural participants (X = 131.43). The last main effect of family type was also significant (F, 1,144 = 6.19 P < 0.01) and it was noticed that children of joint family (X = 117.03) experienced more familial distortion than nuclear family (X = 133.98).

Table 19.2: Summary table of ANOVA showing the impact of chronological age, level of physical conditions, residential setting and types family type on familial culture.

Source of variations	*SS*	*Df*	*MS*	*F*
A	1.26	1	1.26	1.17
B	5.85	1	5.85	5.42
C	5.81	1	5.89	5.46
D	6.68	1	6.68	6.19
AB	6.37	1	6.37	5.90
AC	7.03	1	7.03	6.51
AD	8.08	1	8.08	7.48
BC	5.60	1	5.60	5.19
BD	6.63	1	6.63	6.14
CD	6.24	1	6.24	5.78
ABC	7.76	1	7.76	7.19
ABD	7.28	1	7.28	6.74
ACD	7.81	1	7.81	8.44
ABCD	8.81	1	8.81	8.16
ABCD	7.73	1	7.73	7.16
Error (within)	155.52	144	1.08	
		159		

The two-way interaction of chronological age* physical condition was also significant (F, 1,144 = 5.90 P < 0.01). Similarly, chronological age * residential setting interaction was also significant (F, 1,144 =6.51 P < 0.01). Likewise, chronological age* family type interaction was significant (F, 1,144 = 7.48 P < 0.01). All these interactions showed significant influence on familial culture. The physical condition* residential setting interaction was also significant (F, 1,144 = 5.19 P < 0.01). The physical condition* family type interaction was also significant (F, 1,144 = 6.14 P < 0.01) and revealed its influence of familial condition. The residential setting* family type interaction was significant (F, 1,144 = 5.78 P < 0.01) and it was found that both the variables yielded their significant impact on familial culture.

The chronological age * physical condition * residential setting interaction was significant (F, 1,144 = 7.19 P < 0.01) and it was shown in Figure 19.1. Figure reveals that all the variables displayed their influence on familial culture. The chronological age * physical condition * family type interaction was significant (F, 1,144 = 6.79 P < 0.01) and it is appeared in Figure 19.2. In this way context chronological age * residential setting * family type interaction was also significant (F, 1,144 = 8.44 P < 0.01) and it is appeared in Figure 19.3. The physical condition * residential setting * family type interaction showed its impact in significant manner (F, 1,144 = 8.16 P> 0.01) and it is appeared in Figure 19.4.

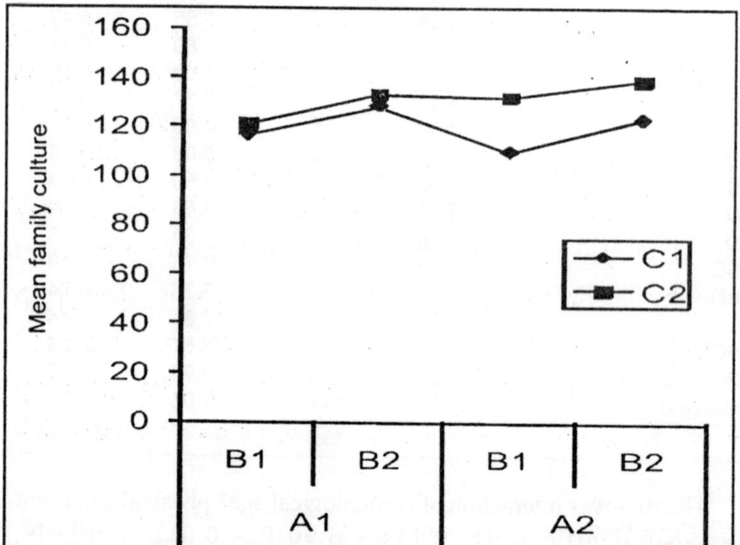

Legends

A	=	*Types of Chronological Age*			
A1	=	10-12 years	A2	=	13-15 years
B	=	*Types of Physical Condition*			
B1	=	Orthopaedically Disabled	B2	=	Non-Disabled
C	=	*Types of Residential Setting*			
C1	=	Urban	C2	=	Rural

Fig. 19.1: Mean values showing the Impact of types of chronological age, types of physical condition and types of residential setting on familial culture

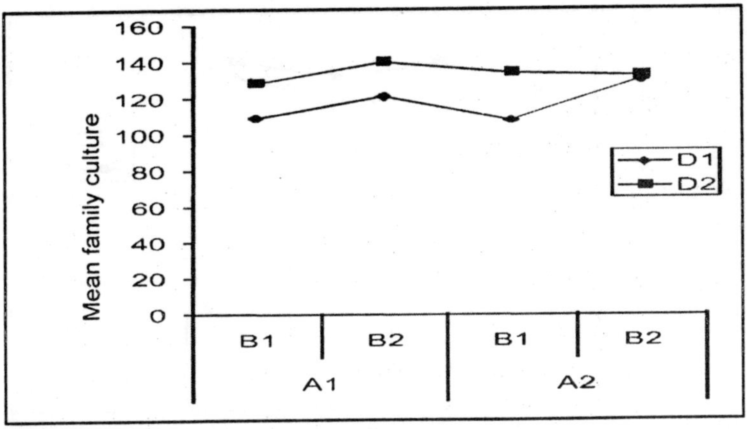

Legends

A = *Types of Chronological Age*
A1 = 10-12 years A2 = 13-15 years
B = *Types of Physical Condition*
B1 = Orthopaedically Disabled B2 = Non-Disabled
D = *Types of Family*
D1 = Joint D2 = Nuclear

Fig. 19.2: Mean values showing the impact of types of chronological age, types of physical condition and types of family on familial culture

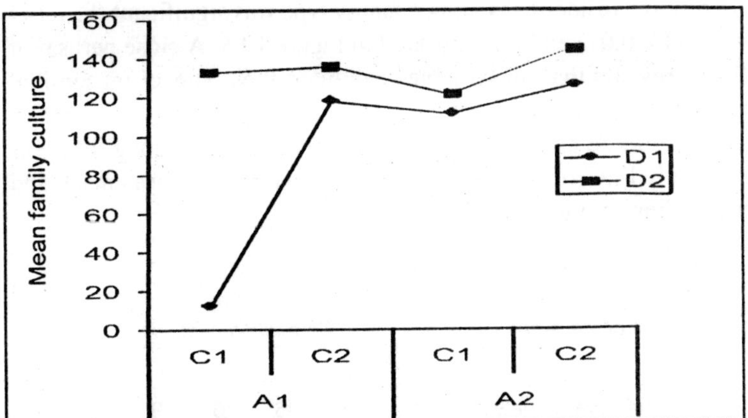

Legends

A = *Types of Chronological Age*: A1 = 10-12 years, A2 = 13-15 years
C = *Types of Residential Setting*: C1 = Urban, C2 = Rural
D = *Types of Family*: D1 = Joint, D2 = Nuclear

Fig. 19.3: Mean values showing the impact of types of chronological age, types of residential setting and types of family on familial culture

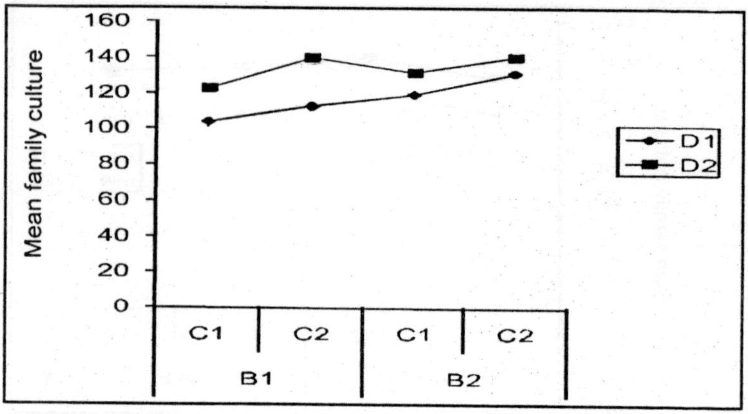

Legends

B = *Types of Physical Condition*
B1 = Orthopaedically Disabled   B2 = Non-Disabled
C = *Types of Residential Setting:* C1 = Urban, C2 = Rural
D = *Types of Family:* D1 = Joint, D2 = Nuclear

Fig. 19.4: Mean values showing the impact of types of physical condition types of residential setting and types of family on familial culture

The four-way interaction of chronological age * physical condition * residential setting * family type was significant (F, 1,144 = 7.16 P> 0.01) and it is appeared in Figure 19.5. A close perusal of figure reveals that all variables exhibited their impact on familial culture.

In order to ascertain the pattern of relationship among the areas of Family Environment Scale a correlational analysis was made and the findings are given in Table 19.3.

Table 19.3: Correlational analysis of data

S.N.	*Name of the areas*	*Correlation coefficients*						
		1	*2*	*3*	*4*	*5*	*6*	*7*
1	Competitive framework	—	.56	.48	.76	.49	.59	.61
2	Cohesion		—	.59	.49	.61	.74	.59
3	Expression			—	.51	.58	.46	.61
4	Independence				—	.59	.61	.68
5	Moral orientation					—	.64	.71
6	Organization						—	.76
7	Residential orientation							—

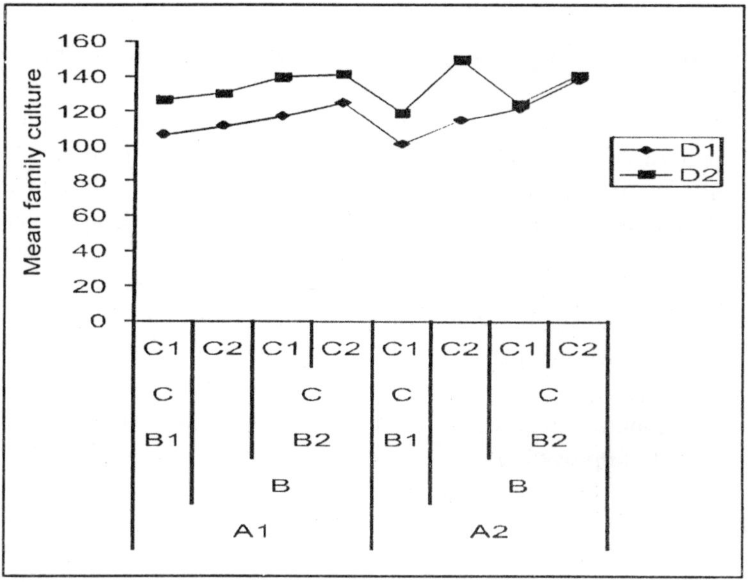

Legends

A = *Types of Chronological Age*
A1 = 10-12 years A2 = 13-15 years
B = *Types of Physical Condition*
B1 = Orthopaedically Disabled B2 = Non-Disabled
C = *Types of Residential Setting*
C1 = Urban C2 = Rural
D = *Types of Family*
D1 = Joint D2 = Nuclear

Fig. 19.5: Mean values showing the impact of types of chronological age, types of physical condition, types of residential setting and types of family on familial culture

A close perusal of the table indicates that all the dimensions are closely related to each other and it was shared by all variables.

Discussion

Obtained data were analyzed by analysis of variances and interpreted in terms of age, disability, residential setting and family types of age, as affecters of familial culture. Prior to the conception of this work some hypotheses were formulated and the findings will be discussed accordingly.

Variation in Age would cause Variation in Familial Culture

The first and foremost concern was related with the development pattern of familial culture. It was hypothesized that increase in age would cause difference in familial culture. Although the developmental pattern was not significant yet we got age related change. Older participant's produced positive oriented towards their familial culture as compaired to their younger counterparts.

Different authors have also defined the home or family according to their own thoughts. Murdock (1949) states that, 'the family is a social group characterized by common residence, economic co-operation and reproduction, it included both sexes, who maintain a socially approved sexual relationship and one of more children, own or adopted of the sexual co-habituating pain.' The international dictionary of education mentions that "family is a primary social group of parents, offspring's and possibly others members of household."

Chauhan (2004) stated that child rearing consist of practices embedded in cultural patterns and beliefs. Child rearing most often viewed in the context of the personality development of an individual. To a large extent these practices determine the behaviour and the expectations surrounding a child's birth and infancy. They also influence childhood, adolescence and also the way these children parents in future. Theorists like Bronfenbrenner and Super and Harkness have forwarded their thought regarding personality development in a cultural context.

Tripathi (2004) investigated the self-perception of physically disabled girls and their mother's perception of their disabled daughters. Fifty-four disabled girls and their mothers were interviewed. The age range of disabled girls was 14 to 19 years and their mother age range was 35 to 56 years. The data was quantitatively and qualitatively perceive themselves negatively and their mothers also did not perceive them positively.

Mendiratta (2004) stated that culture provides context wherein child's development takes place. The beliefs, values, practices that parents have for child's development are rooted within this context. Socialization of child thus cannot be viewed in isolation. There are various factors like, parenting style, personality traits, family type, socialization situation provide to the child, parents' understanding about soc ally context that influence adults perspective regarding self and the child which in turn influences the adult child interaction. This adult child interaction influences the adult child development. The present paper attempts to understand the linkages between the parental beliefs and child development within the cultural context.

On the basis of this discussion it is surely fair to say that variation in age causes variation in financial experiences.

Variation in Residential Type would cause Variation in Familial Culture

Villages are heterogeneous in terms of location, life style and their relationship with urban centres (Muthayya, 1988). When we talk about rural development it represents a process of change from existing level to a planned new level where quality of life is better. In this way rural development seems to be a continuous process which remains positive and purposive (Reddy, 1982; Singh and Ray, 1980). The main objective of rural development is to improve the psycho-social conditions and lifestyle of the peonle of villages. However, this fact seems to have been overlooked in the process of developmental planning (Sinha, 1984). On this context it is also important to note that the way people interpret the developmental programme determines their acceptance and adoption. The interpretation of programmes depends on peoples past experiences, their general attitudes towards life and the values of the social system. (Muthayya, 1980) the existing level of socio-economic development also plays an important role. Socially disadvantaged, for instance, perceive their problems in a different framework. According to them the village problems include poverty, unemployment, and lack of roads. They perceive lesser accessibility to the facilities and lesser degree of satisfaction (Aneesuddin and Naidu, 1984; Muthayya, 1980).

Variation in Family Type would cause Variation in Familial Culture

Last but not least was the hypothesis in which impact of family on familial culture was measured. Here, it was assumed that perception of family set would vary with variation in family type, i.e. joint and nuclear families. Our hypothesis was confirmed and we found that the participants residing in joint or nuclear families did produce variation in the experience of familial set-up.

In affirmation of the salience of family as a context of development, numerous studies have investigated the role of family variables on various aspects of development in early years. Misra and Tewari (1984) determine the influence of digital variables and proximal variables on the cognitive development of school. Using regression analysis the researchers observed higher contribution of proximal have variables compared to that of distal variables. Studies with older children have explored the links between their perceptions and recollections of child rearing practices and some aspects of social and moral development (Sethi and Gupta, 1984; Sahoo and Nanda, 1990).

Studies on familial influences on children with special needs cover a wide range of topics from parent's and sibling's knowledge about familial set-up and circumstances prevailing there variables pertaining to familial influences assume greater significances for the care and development of the children with special needs, since parental knowledge and understanding about the disability affects their behaviour in terms of acceptance, help seeking, future aspirations, and support given to the child. Several of there links have been empirically substantiated (Kapur, 1992).

The review of studies pertaining to the relation between familial variables and developmental outcomes shows that rarely here the family been treated as a unit and the intra familial interaction pattern studied properly.

The family unit as a whole is likely to change its modes and areas of functioning as consequences of social change, as indicated by Kumar's conception of the changed manifestations in modern families of the traditional norms of continuity between the adults and child's world (Kumar, 1993). Any change in the family structure needs to be understood in terms of what caused the change and for how long the change has persisted, for example, a family may follow a joint structure due to emotional cohesiveness or due to emotional compulsion on the other hand a family may be rendered nuclear by one individual's derive to achieve independent success leaving the other members in another nuclear structure. The two units, however, will not be isomorphic as context for child's socialization. There is a need to articulate and contextualize the transitions that a primary group such as family experiences (Anand Lakshmy, 1993) in order to understand their salience in child development.

REFERENCES

Anand Lakshmy, S. (1993), Psychosocial experiences of childhood in India; implications for mental health. In M. Kapur; S. Kelaur; R.Tarter and R.Wilson (Eds.), *Child mental health: Proceedings of the Indo-US symposium*. Banglore, NIMHANS.

Bajaj, B. and Raut, P. (2004),Trait-Anger and Anger Expression Among Parent and Child, *14th Annual Conference of National Academy of Psychology on Psychology and Development in Department of Humanities and Social Sciences,* Indian Institute of Technology, Kharagpur.

Biswas, A. and Aggrawal, J.C. (1971), *Encyclopaedic Dictionary and Directory of Education,* Vol. I, Academic Pub., New Delhi.

Bloom, M. (1968), *Stability and change in human characteristics*. John-Willy and Sons, New York.

Chapman, J.W. (1988), Learning disabled children's self concept. *Review of Educational Research,* 58(3), 347-371.

Chauhan, G.S. (2004), "A Cross-Cultural view of child rearing practices and construction of personality and behaviour", 14th Annual Conference of National Academy of Psychology on Psychology and Development in Department of Humanities and Social Sciences, Indian Institute of Technology, Kharagpur.

Cooley, E.J. and Ayers, R.R. (1988), Self Concept and Success failure attributions of non-handicapped students with learning and disabilities. *Journal of Learning Disabilities*, 21(3), 174-178.

Cronbachl, I. (1977), *Educational Psychology*, (IIIrd Ed.), Harcourt Brace Jovanovich, New York.

Danesh, H.B. (1978), The Authoritarian family and its Adolescence. *Canadian Psychiatric Association Journal*, 23(7), pp. 479-485.

Douvan, E. and Adelison, J (1966), *The Adolescence experience,* Willey, New York, pp. 95-98.

Good, C.V. (1973), *Dictionary of Education*, (IIIrd Ed.), McGraw Hill Co., New York.

Grolniek, W.S. and Ryan, R.M. (1990), Self-perception motivation and adjustment in children with learning disabilities: A multiple group comparison study. *Journal of Learning Disabilities,* 23, 3, 177-184.

Harter, S. (1985), Competence as a Dimension of Self-Evaluation: Towards a Comprehensive Model of Self Worth in Leahy, R.L. (ed). *The Development of Self.* Orlando: Academic Press, Inc.

Hussain, A. (2006), Self-concept of Physically challenged adolescents. *Journal of the Indian Academy of Applied Psychology,* Vol. 32. No.1. pp. 43-46.

Kapur, M. (1992), Siblings relationship in families with mentally handicapped children. Unpublished Masters dissertation, Lady Irwin College, University of Delhi, Delhi.

King, G.A.; Sted, I.Z., Gilpin, K.M. and Cathers, T. (1993), Self-Evaluation and Self-Concept of Adolescents with Physical Disabilities, *American Journal of Occupational Therapy*, 47(2) 132, 140.

Kumar, K. (1993), Study of childhood and family. In T.S. Saraswathi and B. Kaur (Eds). *Human Development and Studies in India: An Agenda for Research and Policy,* Sage.

Mahapatra, P. Rani, Moltra, C., J. and Alam, P. (2004), "Impact of disability on social adjustment: An Empirical study on Orthopedically challenged", 14th Annual Conference of National Academy of Psychology on Psychology and Development in Department of Humanities and Social Sciences, Indian Institute of Technology, Kharagpur.

Malm, M. and Jamison, O.G. (1952), *Adolescence,* McGraw Hill, New York, pp. 282-283.

Maslow, A.H. (1941), The Dynamic of Psychological Security and Insecurity, *Character and Personality,* 10, pp. 331-334.

Mendiratta, A. (2004), "Parental beliefs, Child Development within cultural context", 14th Annual Conference of National Academy of Psychology on Psychology and Development in Department of Humanities and Social Sciences, Indian Institute of Technology, Kharagpur.

Misra, G. and Tiwari, B.K. (1984), Environmental correlates of cognitive development. *Indian Journal of Applied Psychology*, 24(1), 41-52.

Mishra, U. (2001), The Experience of Social Change in Rural India: A Qualitative Analysis of Panchayati Raj in selected villages. Unpublished Ph.D. Works, C.C.S Meerut University. Meerut.

Murdock, G.P. (1949), *Social Structure,* McMillan Co., New York.

Muthayya, B.C., Aneesuddin, M. and Naidu, K.K. (1984), The rural disadvantaged: a psychosocial study in Bihar and Orissa. *Journal of Rural Development,* 3 (3), 175-248.

Muthayya, B.C. (1988), Dynamics of Rural Development in J. Pandey (Ed). *Psychology in India: The State of the Art.* Vol.2 (pp.225-278). New Delhi: Sage.

Platt *et al.* (1962), Comparison of Child Rearing Attitude of Mothers and Fathers of Emotionally Disturbed Adolescents, *Child Development*, 33, 117-122.

Reddy, G.R. (1982), Panchayati Raj and Rural Development in Andhra Pradesh, India. In Norman T. Uphaff (Ed), *Rural Development ana Social Organization in Asia*, (Vol. 1), New Delhi: Macmillan.

Sahoo, F.M. and Nanda, U. (1990), Socialization parameters of learned helplessness. *Psychological Studies*, 35 (1), 52-61.

Sethi, A.S and Gupta, (1984), Moral judgment level and perceived maternal child rearing attitudes of boys and girls. *Journal of Psychological Researches*. 28(2), 102-106.

Singh, S. and Ray, J.J (1980), Modernization and Development among Indian Farmers. A modern profile of some old theories, *Economic Development and Cultural Change*, 28 (2), 509-522.

Shah, (1982), *Personality Development in Children*, Multi-Tech. Pub. Co., Bombay.

Stott, L.H. (1974), *The Psychology of Human Development*, Holt, Rinehart and Winston, New York, p. 208

Tripathi, N. (2004), "Perception of disability: Disabled girls and their mothers". 14th Annual Conference of National Academy of Psychology on Psychology and Development in Department of Humanities and Social Sciences, Indian Institute of Technology, Kharagpur.

Wolman, B.B. (1977), *International Encyclopaedia Psychoanalysis and Neurology*, Van Nostrand Reinhold Co., New York.

SECTION-V

CONCLUSION

20

Improving Quality of Life in Impoverished Society

Aradhana Shukla

Towards new horizons of tribal development culture, cultural processes and products/forms will be best understood and crystallized if they are contrasted with "nature", natural processes and products. Nature consists of physical objects such as earth, mountains, deserts, rivers, oceans, and stars and planets, biological entities, such as, flora and fauna, and a variety of elements. These objects, entities and elements are active, reactive and interactive according to the laws and principles of nature and give rise to variant climates, biomes, infinite kind of flora and fauna ranging from one celled amoeba to the structurally far more complex Homo sapiens. Human beings also like any other living animal that are born grow and survive in accordance with the natural laws and principles. However, human being are also unique because they are born with genetically determined in-built and instate potentials to grow in such a way that they acquire capacities to transcend the constraints of natural lawas and processes. One of these potentials is concerned with cultural processes and provides latent capacity for acting upon natural objects, modifying or transforming and refining them with a view to making survival easier, more comfortable and pleasurable headonically as well as mentally.

It must be kept in mind that in human beings natural and cultural processes as well functions are like antonyms. Natural processes are spontaneous exhibiting the principle of least resistance and are impulse guided. On the other hand, cultural processes are deliberate, requiring best effort and guided by imagination and constructive thoughts. Wherever, there is interaction between man and nature, man endeavours to quell the natural processes and subjugate them to cultural processes, eating, mating, seeking safety and living like amidst fellow human beings are natural in activities for survival. In social interaction, to be selfish and guided by one's heads and feelings is illustrative of natural processes while being sensitive to the needs and feelings of others, showing tolerance and compassion, indulging in and encouraging prosocial and proactive behaviour and having positive thinking, etc., exemplify cultural processes.

It is fashionable today in mainstream psychology, in both theoretical as well as empirical work, and other social scientific disciplines, to talk about culture. Culture has quickly become one of the most important and pressing issues facing psychologist and laypersons alike use the words culture, race, and ethnicity interchangeably, as if they are all the same terms denoting the same concepts. In addition, people often use the word culture to describe people of different nationalities. Do these terms all refers to the same concept? While there is clearly some overlap among them, there are also important differences among these words and concepts. A recognition of these differences is important for a clear and fuller understanding of cross-cultural research and its impact on psychological knowledge.

Before embarking on the task of learning about cultural influences on behaviour, it is important and useful to tackle the question of what the word culture means. Differences observed across studies and theories in various psychological disciplines are often related to differences in the usage of culture not only as a theoretical or explanatory concept but as an empirical construct in research. A researcher's definition, whether explicit or implicit, ultimately has an impact on how he or she views culture as influencing people's lives; my own views are no exception.

Common Usage of the Word Culture

We use the word culture in many different ways in everyday language and discourse. As mentioned earlier, sometimes we use the word culture to mean race, nationality, or ethnicity. For example, we often refer to people of African-American ancestry as coming from

African-American culture, or Chinese people as coming from Chinese culture. But we also use the word culture to reflect trends in music and art, food and clothing, rituals, traditions, and heritage. In short, we use the word culture to refer to many different things about people—physical and biological characteristics, behaviours, music, dance, and other activities.

Kroeber and Kluckholn (1952) and later Berry, Poortinga, Segall, and Dasen (1992) have described six general categories in which culture is discussed:

- Descriptive uses highlight the different types of activities or behaviours associated with a culture.
- Historical definitions refer to the heritage and tradition associated with a group of people.
- Normative uses describe the rules and norms that are associated with a culture.
- Psychological descriptions emphasize learning, problem solving, and other behavioural approaches associated with culture.
- Structural definitions emphasize the societal or organizational elements of a culture.
- Genetic descriptions refer to the origins of a culture.

These categories make it clear that we use the concept and terms culture to describe and explain a broad range of activities, behaviours, events, and structures in our lives.

Used in the ways just described, culture has become increasingly fashionable in the United States in the past few years; we speak of cultural diversity, cultural pluralities, and multiculturalism in many areas of life, including school and the workplace. It is also important to recognize, however, that the word culture may have different meanings or emphases in other cultures. If we refer to culture in Japan, for instance, a Japanese person may think first of flowers arranging or a tea ceremony rather than the aspects of culture we normally associate with the word. Likewise, while learning about culture in this book, it is important to remember that this view of culture is only one view, and other cultures may have other views. We should not forget that our studies of culture and the ways in which we understand cultural influences on behaviour conceptually (this book included) all stem from a particular view of culture—one that is rooted in American thinking and science and cultivated in other countries like, India.

Because we use culture to refer to so many different things about life, it is no wonder that it generates so much confusion and ambiguity. We can get a better understanding of the complex nature of culture if we look at all the aspects of life referred to by the word culture.

How do Culture Change?

Hofstede (1980) defined culture as the 'collective programming of the mind', with that programming being operationalized in terms of value dimensions. Hofstede argued that these cultural values originated from both external and internal factors operating within each society. The internal factors were labelled 'ecological' and included aspects of nation's geography, economy, hygiene, demography, gene pool, history, technology, urbanization and material resources. The external influences included forces of nature, such as climate changes or environmental disasters, and forces of man, such as trade, scientific discovery and the internationalization of the media.

Hofsted (1980) maintains that societal norms and cultural values do change in response to change in these internal and external factors. In order to anticipate future developments in the 'collective programming of the mind' and hence, in social behaviour, it is important to examine the structure of these change factors and their change over time.

Cultural activities and behaviours of individual members in all communities and countries are characterized by the same kind of individual differences as observed in the assessment of other psychological processes. These individual differences are jointly determined by (i) genetic make up or heredity which determine, the strength of cultural potentials, (ii) psychic factors, such as one's upbringing familial interaction, socialization, schooling and unique develop mental experiences, which provide opportunities for acceleration or retardation of the manifest actions of cultural potentials, and (iii) environmental factors, which provide resources and directions for cultural operations leading to varied forms of cultural products of all communities and countries of the world, the processes and psychological force and countries of the world, the processes and psychological forces the underlie them are the same. They can be better understood if treated as dependent variables like any basic psychological process.

The validity of cross-cultural and cultural psychology has been further challenged by some newly emerged trends on international scenario. Herman and Kempen (1998) have brought out some irrepressible, challenge to the theory of cultural dichotomies as determinants of behaviour and human personality in their thought provoking article entitled "Moving Cultures". These authors pointed out that in an increasingly interconnected global society, the conceptualization of independent coherent and stable cultures becomes totally irrelevant. They have cogently argued that cultural differences in the form of dichotomous distinctions do not meet the challenge of globalization and its implications for a psychology of culture and self. First, the pervasive influence of cultural contacts and connections owing to globalization is all aspects of educational, social, political and economic life. On this terrestrial sphere, the emergence of collateral mixtures and hybridization have become an order of the day. Such a trend has undermined the idea of cultures as internally homogenous and externally distinctive phenomena. Second, it is a crucial fact that even apparently or phenotypically opposite cultures have become integral components of one world civilization. In modern times cultures conceptualized as mutually distinguishable behavioural contexts are not more tenable. Finally, it is important to note that the increasing. Complexity of cultural aspects of life has rendered the idea of cultural distinction and dichotomisation utterly misleading.

Dichotomisation or categorization of culture entails the tacit assumption that culture is a product that provides context or medium for personality and behavioural development. It is under this assumption that people talk of western and oriental cultures, like American, English, French, Arab, German, Chinese, Japanese, and Indian cultures. Quite often cultures are differentiated from one another on religious of grounds, such as Christian, Muslim, Hindu and Jewish. On the basis of habitats also cultures are categorized as rural and urban. Some of the ways in which culture has been categorized in cross-cultural comparison studies are based on nationality, geographical locations and developmental level of tribal and non-tribal, native born and immigrant citizens of a country, etc. It is worth noting that criterial ambiguity in categorization leads to innumerable ways of categorizing cultures and creation of taxonomic chaos.

This point can be illustrated by taking the case of Indian culture. If one endeavours to differentiate the distinguishing features of Indian culture item consists of as many basic cultures as there are officially recognized by languages or dialects. That was the reason that in mid-1950 states were reconstituted. The states of Uttar Pradesh, Bihar, Jharkhand, Bengal, Assam, Maharashtra, etc., are believed to have different cultures. Then there are tribal and non-tribal cultures, rural and non-rural cultures. Caste and class, religions, vocations, joint and nuclear families, etc., and they are also employed for categorization of cultures. As a matter of fact, if one delves deep into the lifestyles, belief systems, social interactional pattern, one may easily finds two neighbouring families belonging to the same class and caste having drastically opposed cultural patterns and practices, cognitive styles and personality characteristics. Likewise it is also easy to find four brothers having identical genetic roots, upbringing and socialization ethos but different belief systems, ethical values, cognitive styles and biases. On the basis of such incisive, observations it is reasonable to conclude that neither the conceptualization of culture as context of psychological development nor the theory of cultural determinism is a valid way of studying culture.

Some conclusions are evident from what has been said already. Psychology will only fulfil its claim to be cross-culturally valid if studied properly. A clearer delineation is required between those who seek to characterize cultures, and those who wish to understand the psychology of individuals. However, other aspects of the path ahead are less clear. The aspects of human experience that have been most excessively studied are those that are of prime interest to those living in affluent urban societies. We have more theories of self-concept, social identity, negotiation and interpersonal attraction than of poverty, community, social networks, arranged marriage or relationship, harmony. We have numerous (Western) theories of leadership developed in contacts where hierarchy is less evident, but only a few from contexts where hierarchy is more salient (for example, Sinha, 1980). We have theories of acculturation, but thus have been tested largely in relation to those movements of peoples, that are towards Western cultures. Our field needs to be exploring concepts and theories that are derived from less represented cultural traditions, such as the examination of "Interpersonal relatedness" by Cheung *et al.* (2001). These imbalances may be rectified in time.

An issue that is more directly related to future paths for cross-cultural psychology has to do with the emergent conceptual frame-works discussed above. Increasingly, culture and cultural difference is being thought of in terms of values and value difference. Does this provide us with a sufficiently broad base upon which to rest cross-cultural studies? There is rather extensive evidence that members of individualist cultures seek to maintain consistency between their values and self-concepts and their behaviour conversely members of collectivist culture have been shown to have greater concern to behave in ways that are appropriate to the requirements of differing situational circumstances (Smith and Bond, 1998). Thus, while values may provide a good basis for predicting individual behaviour in Western cultures it is likely that role requirements will give a more reliable, basis in non-western cultures for instance. Miller's (1984) studies underlined the greater propensity of Indians than Americans to account for others behaviour in terms of role requirements.

Compared to the effort made to conceptualize cultural variations in values, attention to roles and the ways in which they are defined in different cultures has been minimal. Approaches that are relevant to a role centred approaches to cultural difference are most typically presented in a manner that does not highlight the actual concepts of role. An example would be Kagitcibasi's (1996) conceptualization of differing types of family relationships. She delineates a typology of types of family relationships ranging from an enmeshed network of roles involved in extended family relationships to the roles comprising the nuclear family.

Thinking in terms of roles rather than values also leads one to differing conceptualizations. For instance, Diener and Diener (1995) have given considerable attention to cultural variations in life satisfaction. Life satisfaction is a decontextualized concept which one might expect to be related to one's values and the degree to which they find fulfilment. Conversely, thinking in terms of roles led (Kwan *et al.*, 1997) to formulate the concepts of relationship harmony. If one's satisfactions in life are dependent upon the adequacy of specific role relationships, then this concept should have increasing predictive validity in cultures where roles rather than values are the primary guides to one's actions. Kwan *et al.* (1997) found that their relationship harmony measure accounted for variance additional to that exclaimed by the Diener life satisfaction measure both Hong Kong and in the U.S.A.

Thus in the case of Thui's study of Guamis, a concept arising from a closer focus on relationships within collectivist cultures proved to have a more general validity. If one way forward is to focus more upon role relationships, the consequences may prove beneficial not just to an understanding of collectivist cultures it may also help Western researchers to become aware of overlooked phenomena within their own cultures.

The Constellation of Individual Modernity

Effective participation in modern society is hypothesized to require a core syndrome of cognitions and motivations. To assess this core, sociologists like Khal (1968) and Inkeles and Smith (1974) have developed comprehensive batteries of standardized questions and administered these questionnaires to adult samples in a variety of developing countries. Other researchers have focused on single countries, comparing the responses of people from groups at different presumed stages in the modernization process, such as city dwellers *versus* inhabitants (e.g. Armer and Youtz, 1971; Guthrie, 1977; Schnaiberg, 1970).

These instruments, whether they use questions which are imposed-etic or derived-etic, show a high degree of agreement in their outcomes. This overlap suggests that a common denominator of psychological characteristics is emerging across these many studies, as may be seen in Table 20.1.

Table 20.1: The profile of a modern person

Yang (1988) has synthesized the results from both the cross-cultural and intracultural studies and produced the following profile of the modern person:
A sense of personal efficacy (anti-fatalism).
Low social integration with relatives.
Egalitarian attitude towards others.
An openness to innovation and change.
A belief in sex equality.
High achievement motivation.
Independence or self-reliance.
Active participation in social organizations.
Tolerance of, and respect for, others.
Cognitive and behavioural flexibility.
Strong future orientation.
Empathetic capacity.
A high need for information.
The propensity to take risks in life.
Secularization in religious belief.
A preference for urban life.
An individualistic orientation towards others.
Psychological differentiation.
A non-local orientation.

Is individualism another name for modernity? Alert readers will note some conceptual similarity between modernity and individualism as psychological profiles. Yang (1988) contends that about two-thirds of the above overlap with the profile of individualism. If individualism and collectivism are conceptualized as opposite ends of a continuum, then increasing modernization would lead to a gradual individualization of psychological process.

One could take the economic index of gross national product per capital as a rough approximation of societal modernization. If this step is taken, then Hofstede's (1980) research shows a strong correlation between modernity (as measured by wealth) and cultural individualism of + 0.82. Bond's (1988b) work demonstrates a similar link between wealth and psychological individualism. Furthermore, Hofstede's (1980) longitudinal research across a four-year span indicate that individualism was the only one of his four dimensions to increase on average across his entire sample of 40 countries during that period.

These lines of work thus suggests that economic development, which is generally increasing, goes hand with a change in certain broad patterns of behaviour. These patterns are central to the contrast between collectivism and individualism which has informed and unified our presentation in this text. Should we then conclude that the content of this text may become a historical artifact, doomed to obsolescence?

Last But Not Least

These and other innovations are only beginning to emerge, to be conceptualized and integrated into the psychological literature. Were such ideas slow in coming? We think not. Their emergence had to await the diffusion of 'western' psychology to different cultural milieux and the nurturing of local psychologists who are capable of challenging the biases of the discipline in its own terminology, using its established procedures.

We have now reached this stage. The development of cross-cultural social psychology is one of its manifestations. Its consequences will be an intellectual by synergy that will enable us to transcend the limitations imposed by our different cultural origins. We may then be able to claim that we have a more truly universal understanding of humanity's social behaviour.

And the end of all exploring will be to arrive where we started
And know the place for the first time.

—T.S.Eliot, *The Four Quarters*

REFERENCES

Armer, M. and Youtz, R. (1971). Formal education and individual modernity in an African Society, *American Journal of Sociology*, 76, 604-26.

Berry, J.W., Poortinga, Y.H., Segall, M.H. and Dasen, P.R. (1992), *Cross-Cultural Psychology: Reseach and Application*. New York: (Cambridge University Press.

Cheung, F.M. and Leungk (1998). Indigenous personality measures: Chinese examples. *Journal of Cross-cultural Psychology*, 29(1), 233-248.

Diener, E. and Diener, M. (1995, April), Cross-cultural correlates of life satisfaction and self-esteem. *Journal of Personality and Social Psychology,* 68(4), 653-663.

Guthric, G.M. (1977), A socio-psychological analysis of modernization in the Philippines, *Journal of Cross-Cultural Psychology,* 8, 177-206.

Hofstede, G. (1980), *Cultures consequences: International Differences in Work-Related Values,* Beverly Hills, CA: Sage.

Inkeles, A. and Smith, D.H. (1974), Becoming Modern: *Individual change in six developing countries,* Cambridge, M.A.: Harward University Press.

Kroeber, A.L. and Kluckholn, C. (1952), Culture: *A Critical Review of Concepts and Definitions.* (Vol. 47, No. 1). Cambridge MA: Feabody, Museum.

Miller, J.G. (1984), Culture and the Development of Everybody Social Experiences, *Journal of Personality and Social Psychology,* 46, 961-978.

Scnaiberg, A. (1970), Measuring modernism: Theoretical and Empirical Explorations, *American Journal of Sociology,* 76, 399-425.

Sinha, D. (1980), *Socialization of Indian Child,* Agra, National.

Smith, P.B. and Bond, M.H. (1999), *Social Psychology: Across Cultures (2nd ed.),* Boston, MA: Allyn and Bacon, Inc.

Young, K.S. (1988), Will Societal Modernization Eventually Eliminate Cross-Cultural Psychological Differences?, in M.H. Bond (Ed.), *The Cross-Cultural Challenges to Social Psychology,* Newbury Parg, C.A.: Sage.

Index